TCP\IP
Application Layer Protocols for Embedded Systems

Acknowledgments

Thanks to my wife Jill and children, Megan, Elise and Marc for their support and patience during this project.

Thanks also to my parents, Maury and Celeta for the gift of a TRS-80 in 1979 that began a wonderful career.

Finally, thanks for extremely valuable and helpful reviews from Thomas Herbert and Dan Klein.

1 Introduction to Internetworking

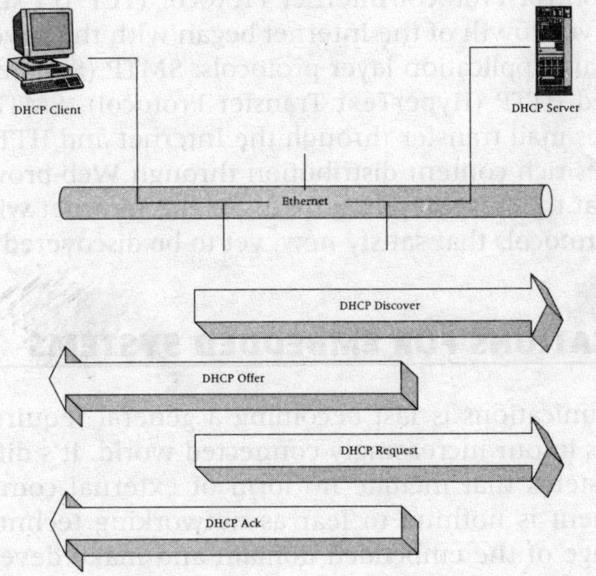

This chapter will provide an introduction to internetworking using the Internet protocols and cover some of the basic principles that will be necessary for application layer protocol development. This chapter provides a foundation of networking principles and terminology.

INTRODUCTION

While we wonder about the practicality of embedded systems in refrigerators that have the capability to communicate over the Internet, there are many examples of useful embedded systems in which communication technologies create very useful products. Embedded systems are now transmitting electric meter readings over low-bandwidth wireless links to alleviate the need to read them visually. Embedded systems with Global Positioning System (GPS) technology and wireless links are used to pinpoint the exact location, speed, oil pressure and other parameters of fleets of trucks anywhere in the country. These example applications are not only useful but also financially viable.

This book is devoted to application layer protocols because they are the most important areas of development since the inception of the Transmission Control Protocol/Internet Protocol (TCP/IP) suite of protocols. The explosive growth of the Internet began with the development of two very important application layer protocols: SMTP (Simple Mail Transfer Protocol) and HTTP (HyperText Transfer Protocol). SMTP is the protocol that provides mail transfer through the Internet and HTTP is the protocol that provides rich content distribution through Web browsers. It's almost certain that the next step of growth for the Internet will be new application layer protocols that satisfy new, yet to be discovered needs.

COMMUNICATIONS FOR EMBEDDED SYSTEMS

Communications is fast becoming a general requirement for embedded systems in our increasingly connected world. It's difficult to find embedded systems that include no form of external communication. This requirement is nothing to fear as networking technologies can meet the challenge of the embedded domain and make developing these systems much simpler.

A networked application is nothing more than a program that has the capability to communicate over a network with another networked application. With the TCP/IP protocol suite and the standard Berkeley Sockets API (Application Program Interface), creating networked applications is simple, as we'll see in the client and server example later in this chapter.

Embedded systems commonly utilize one of two interfaces for connectivity, Ethernet or Serial link. An Ethernet connection requires the availability of a local network by which the device may connect (commonly using an RJ-45 connector). Connecting via a serial link opens many other avenues since communication can take place through another device acting as a gateway or through a modem (wireless or landline). We'll revisit these options and their tradeoffs in Chapter 2.

NETWORK ARCHITECTURE

Networked applications typically follow what is known as the client-server model. In this model, a server extends some service to one or more connecting clients. An example of this model is the Web server and client. The Web server provides a service through the distribution of information. The browser, or Web client, renders the collected information to the user. The client and the server communicate with each other using what is known as a protocol. In this case, the protocol is HTTP. HTTP, and protocols in general, provide a common language that a client and server "speak" to have a common basis for communication.

It is also interesting to note that these protocols are independent of operating system and platform architecture. The Web server here could be running on a Sun SPARCstation using the Solaris operating system (UNIX variant) where the client could be a Windows 2000 desktop. Although the operating systems and the physical architectures differ, the client and server can still communicate. The Web server and client could even be written in different languages, and since they agree on a standard set of protocols (TCP/IP and HTTP in this case), the semantics of their communication is guaranteed.

Protocol Layering

Modern computer networks are known as packet-switched networks. When a user requests a large document from an HTTP server, the protocols split the document into smaller pieces that are ultimately defined as packets. These packets include not only the information they are intended to transfer (known as the payload), but also information to tell the network where the information is going and where it fits into the collection of packets that make up the larger stream (the header).

The process of generating these packets is through the layers of the protocol stack (see Figure 1.1). The top-most layer is called the application layer. The HTTP protocol fits into this layer. Under the application layer is the transport layer that most commonly contains the TCP and UDP (User Datagram Protocol) protocols. Next is the network layer which is contains the IP protocol, and finally the data link layer which provides access to a variety of physical interfaces such as Ethernet or Serial links.

At each layer of the protocol stack, a packet is created that encapsulates the information passed down from the previous layer. For example, the Web client will pass down an HTTP request message to the transport layer.

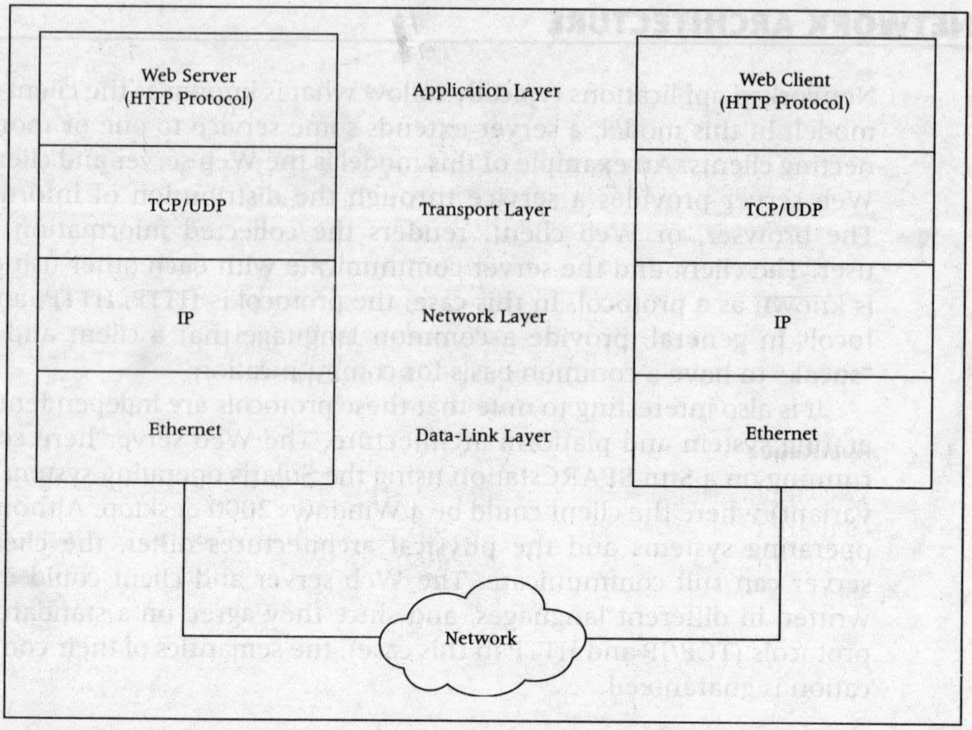

FIGURE 1.1 The layers of a protocol stack.

The TCP protocol will then encapsulate that message by a transport layer Protocol Data Unit (PDU). This PDU continues down through the stack, with each succeeding layer adding its own headers to form the PDU for that layer. Once the packet reaches the data link layer, it's on its way to its destination. When the packet arrives at the destination, the process continues, but in reverse. Each layer of the protocol stack analyzes and removes the headers and passes the resulting PDU up through the stack to its intended recipient (see Figure 1.2). Each layer is important in its own way; we'll talk more about each later on in this chapter.

Protocol Layers

Now that we've discussed some of the preliminaries of protocol architecture, let's peer into each layer to better understand why they're there and what they do.

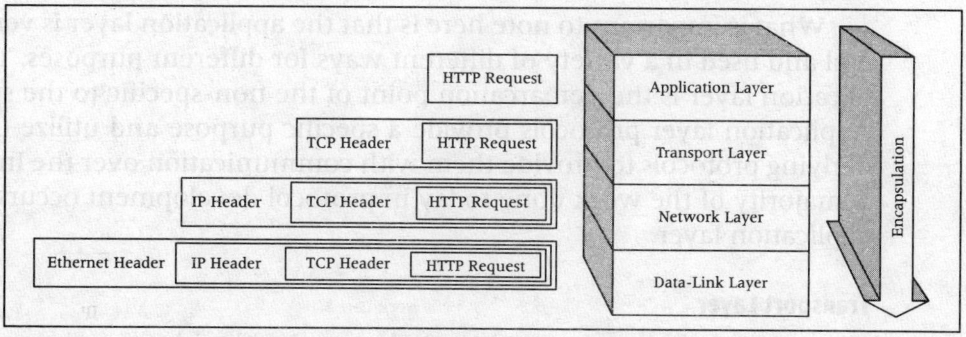

FIGURE 1.2 PDU construction through the protocol stack.

Application Layer

The application layer is associated with the largest number of protocols that are most closely identified by their applications. For example, HTTP is commonly associated with the Web browser application, but HTTP has found applications in many other environments. In previous sections, we've discussed the HTTP protocol for browsing the Web, but many others exist (see Table 1.1 for a brief list).

TABLE 1.1 Examples of application layer protocols.

ABBREVIATION	PROTOCOL NAME	DESCRIPTION
FTP	File Transfer Protocol	Used to move files between hosts on the Internet
SMTP	Simple Mail Transfer Protocol	Used to transfer electronic mail throughout the Internet
NTP	Network Time Protocol	Allows Internet hosts to synchronize their clocks from tuned sources on the Internet
NNTP	Network News Transfer Protocol	Used to propagate Usenet News through the Internet
HTTP	HyperText Transfer Protocol	Used for media-rich content distribution on the Internet
TELNET	Remote Login Protocol	General bi-directional, byte-oriented communications facility
SOAP	Simple Object Access Protocol	Used to distribute services on the Internet in a platform-independent manner

What is important to note here is that the application layer is very general and used in a variety of different ways for different purposes. The application layer is the demarcation point of the non-specific to the specific. Application layer protocols provide a specific purpose and utilize the underlying protocols to provide them with communication over the Internet. A majority of the work done today in protocol development occurs in the application layer.

Transport Layer

The transport layer is most commonly associated with two protocols, TCP (Transmission Control Protocol) and UDP (User Datagram Protocol). Each is useful, but they differ in some very significant ways.

TCP is a connection-oriented protocol in which communication is viewed as a full-duplex, reliable stream between two parties. Since nodes on the Internet can sometimes lose packets, TCP takes care of making sure that the receiving party receives all data in the order that it was sent by the sender. In this way, it is known to be reliable, but connections can be lost in TCP. TCP guarantees only that the data received is in the order in which it was sent. Additionally, both endpoints of a TCP connection may send and receive data simultaneously; thus, it operates in a full-duplex fashion. TCP also takes care of breaking down the data received from the host application into individual packets that can be transmitted over the particular link. This size is known as the Maximum Segment Size (MSS) which is negotiated between the two protocol stacks during TCP synchronization.

UDP is a connectionless protocol that can be viewed as providing simple message passing. UDP provides no guarantee that packets will arrive. Packets may even arrive out of order. Even with this flaw, UDP is used often by application layer protocols where data integrity can easily be provided by application layer timeout and packet retransmission.

Ports

From Figure 1.2, we can see that when a packet is received it is passed up through the protocol stack until ultimately we have an application layer PDU (Protocol Data Unit), but how do we know where the packet should actually go? The transport layer includes the concept of a *port* that is used as an endpoint on a particular host. This allows a particular service to create an address for itself at the host. Take for example an HTTP server. HTTP commonly lives at port 80. When we send an e-mail, the packets arrive at port 25. Ports allow a host to provide multiple services. Ports in the range 0 to 1023 are called *well-known* ports and are reserved for known services.

Ports in the range 1024 to 49151 are called *registered ports* and can be used for known servers or can be allocated dynamically. Finally, the remaining ports (49152 to 65535) are *dynamic* ports (or *ephemeral* ports). These ports can be assigned to client services. Since from a user perspective, all communication occurs through ports, clients typically create a dynamic port to allow them to communicate with the server.

Network Layer

The Internet Protocol (IP) is associated with the network layer. This protocol is responsible for creating packets that are addressed to the destination host. The destination and the source are identified by IP addresses (all discussion in this text will assume IPv4 addressing). An IP address is a four octet (byte) structure that uniquely identifies nodes connected to the Internet. IP addresses were historically segmented into five classes that further define the distribution of nodes on a network (see Figure 1.3).

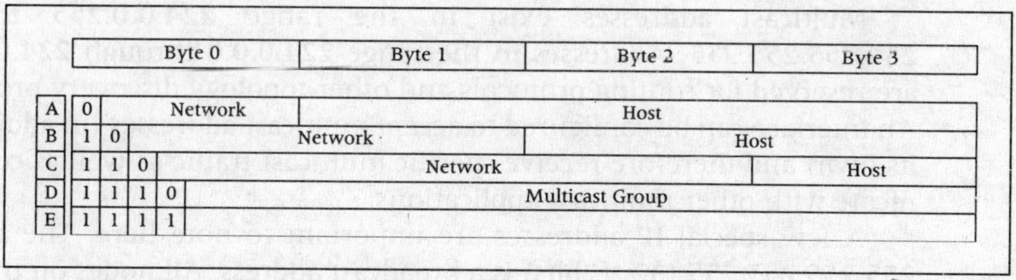

FIGURE 1.3 Classes of Internet addresses.

Addresses were segmented into classes to provide a hierarchy for management. Let's say a new company required an internal subnetwork that was connected to the Internet. If the company had fewer than 254 computers, a class C address block (see Figure 1.3) would provide them with what they need (eight bits for the host address). If the company had more than 254 computers, but fewer than 65000 then they could use a class B address block (16 bits for the host address). Finally, a class A address would provide a company with the ability to network 24^{2} - 2 computers.

So let's look at an example of an address class and the IP addresses that result. Let's say you are assigned a class C address block. In a class C address, there are 24 bits for the network and eight bits for the host (as shown in Figure 1.3). An example of a range in this class is 205.15.192.1 through 205.15.192.254. This is an IP address in dotted-decimal notation and is a very common representation (the hexadecimal equivalent is

0xCD0FC001 through 0xCD0FC0FE). Since this is a class C address, the network portion is represented by "205.15.192" and the final byte represents the actual hosts within the network.

From Figure 1.3, we can see that for classes A, B, and C, the address is split by the network and host. "Host" represents the maximum number of hosts and "network" represents the maximum number of networks (of hosts). Class A provides a small number of networks each with a large number of hosts where class C provides a large number of networks each with a small number of hosts.

Note that the class system is historical, and IP addresses are now considered classless. This means that allocations of IP addresses to an organization are based upon an IP address and a netmask. The netmask determines the network portion of the address. For example, consider an IP address of 192.168.1.1 and a netmask of 26. The 26 represents the number of left-most contiguous bits (in this case 0xFFFFFFC0), or six bits for the host portion of the address.

Multicast addresses exist in the range 224.0.0.255 through 239.255.255.255. Addresses in the range 224.0.0.0 through 224.0.0.255 are reserved for routing protocols and other topology discovery protocols. An interface can be configured to accept multicast addresses (in addition to its own) and therefore receive specific multicast traffic as well as communicate with other multicast applications.

A few special IP addresses are important to note here. The address 255.255.255.255 (32 '1' bits) is a broadcast address. All nodes on the local network will receive packets sent to this address. Address 127.0.0.1 is the *loopback* address and is used for network testing (packets loop back through a special piece of software called a *loopback device*).

One final comment on IP addresses before we continue our discussion of the network layer: three blocks of network addresses are used for internal purposes. The first is class A (10.0.0.0 to 10.255.255.255), the second is class B (172.16.0.0 to 172.31.255.255) and the final is class C (192.168.0.0 to 192.168.255.255). These addresses are called "non-routable" in that they can be used solely for internal purposes and will never be routed over the Internet. In many cases, organizations use these addresses and perform Network Address Translation (NAT) or IP Masquerading to convert the non-routable addresses to routable addresses at the default gateway.

The network layer provides the means to get our packet (which contains our intended destination IP address) through the network and to its destination. Since TCP takes care of getting the packet data to the appropriate application on a host (from a receive perspective), IP takes care of getting our packet to the actual host through the network.

The network layer includes other protocols that are related to IP, such as the Internet Control Message Protocol (or ICMP). ICMP is used to handle error messages that are received from the network and to notify other hosts of errors that it encounters. The most popular use of ICMP is the echo request/reply. These echoes are commonly known as *ping* packets.

Data Link Layer

Finally, the data link layer provides the interface between the host computer and the network. There are many types of data link layer interfaces, such as Ethernet, or serial interfaces such as are used with modems. Talking to an Ethernet network requires a device driver that takes care of communicating with the actual hardware (known as a MAC driver). Ethernet devices are block devices that accept completed Ethernet PDUs including data link headers and Cyclic Redundancy Check, (CRC). Serial interfaces also use a device driver for access to the serial device, and another protocol layer to provide PDU encapsulation for transmission over the serial link. The most popular protocols here are the Point to Point Protocol (PPP) and the Serial Line Interface Protocol (SLIP). Both of these protocols provide point-to-point links between exactly two devices.

The data link layer must respond to asynchronous events from the physical layer (incoming packets) as well as managing outgoing packets from upper layer protocols. For this reason, the data link layer is commonly split from the rest of the stack as a separate task, or as an interrupt-driven entity that queues incoming and outgoing data.

BASIC NETWORK CONFIGURATION

Now that we've covered some of the basics of the TCP/IP stack, let's look at what's required for basic network configuration.

The Manual Solution

Host configuration for network communication through a protocol stack requires the application of a small set of parameters (although in more complex networks the configuration parameters can be quite involved).

The first parameter needed in configuration is the IP address of our device. IP address selection is based upon the particular network to which our device is connected. Therefore, we can either request an address from the managing authority of the network or perform the configuration dynamically (more on this later in this chapter).

Along with the IP address, we need to set a netmask, introduced earlier in this chapter. The *netmask,* as can probably be inferred by the name, is a mask that is used to identify the network portion of an IP address. Going back to our IP address example, our class C address used 24 bits for the network and eight bits for the host. Our netmask would then be 255.255.255.0 (since masking our address of 205.15.192.16 with 255.255.255.0 yields 205.15.192.0—our network). The netmask is commonly identified with the IP address in the form 205.15.192.16/24.

With the IP address, we have a name that allows us to converse with others on the network (really, it allows others to converse back to us). However, what about talking to others? The capability to communicate with other nodes requires a bit more complexity. As we've discussed, our node can be on a local network that is made up of a collection of hosts. However, this network can also be connected to the Internet that provides many other hosts to which we can communicate. So the question is, how do we talk to hosts on our local network compared to others on the Internet? The solution to this problem is called "routing," and for our example is very simple.

Let's say that 205.15.192.28 is the address of a host to whom we want to communicate. You'll notice that this address is very similar to our own IP address (205.15.192.16). If we apply our netmask (255.255.255.0) to both addresses, we find that the network is the same. This means that our host and the host to whom we want to speak are on the same local network. The routing decision then is to send our packets through the interface that is configured with our IP address. However, what happens if the networks differ? This brings us to our next parameter, the default gateway.

The default gateway is the IP address that represents the destination for all packets that don't match our local network. It's called a gateway because it serves as the gateway to another network. So that's pretty simple. The routing decision is either local (based upon a netmask match) or global (based upon a netmask mismatch). Not all configurations are this simple, but most embedded system products with a single physical interface can utilize this basic structure.

The final element in our configuration is another IP address for a Domain Name System (DNS) server. The DNS server provides a lookup service to resolve fully qualified domain names (such as http://www.mynetwork.com) to an IP address. This is required because we route packets based upon IP addresses, not names.

The basic elements of manual IP address configuration are listed in Table 1.2.

TABLE 1.2 Basic network configuration parameters

PARAMETER	*DESCRIPTION*	*EXAMPLE*
IP address	IPv4 address of our device	192.168.1.1
Netmask	Network mask of our address	255.255.0.0
Default gateway	Host to direct packets whose destination address does not match the local network	192.168.1.254
DNS server address	Resolver address for a server used to map a fully qualified domain name to an IP address	18.76.100.1

The Automatic Solution

Rather than statically configure each device (which can be an administrative nightmare given a high number of devices), nodes can be dynamically configured. Dynamic configuration is very popular because it means the IP addresses can be recycled and allocated on an as-needed basis. The Dynamic Host Configuration Protocol (DHCP) is used to perform this task. A DHCP client communicates with a DHCP server on the local network to notify it of its presence and then to receive data for configuration.

Since communication can't officially take place when a client hasn't configured its network interface (classic chicken and egg problem), the DHCP client broadcasts packets to reach the server (see Figure 1.4). When the client broadcasts a discover packet (request for configuration) the server will respond with an offer (a proposed configuration). The client can then accept the configuration via the DHCP request for which the DHCP server will acknowledge the completed negotiation. At this point, the client performs configuration with the provided data and the process is complete.

For anyone who's had to track down a host on an Ethernet network that has erroneously used an already allocated IP address, DHCP is a welcome addition to the TCP/IP stack.

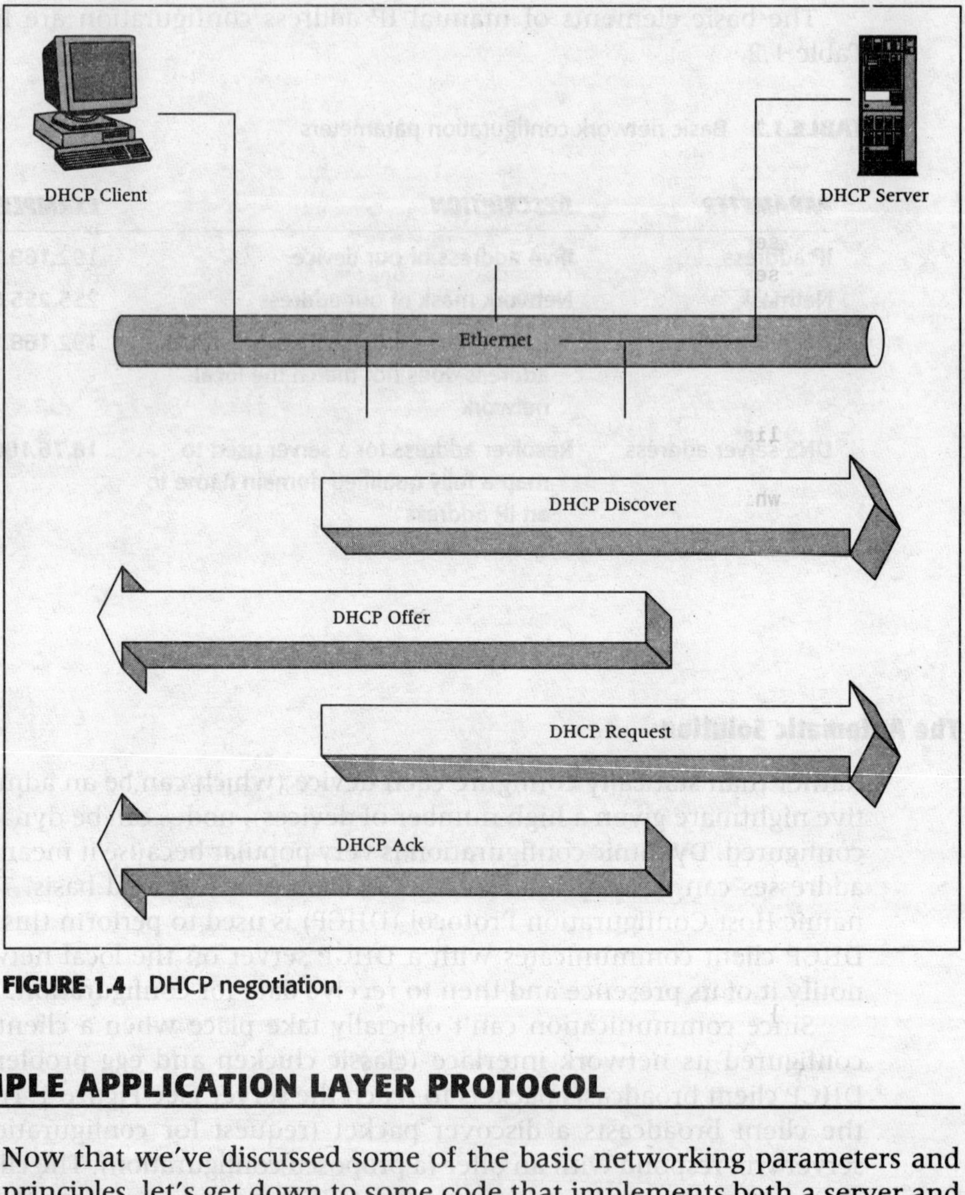

FIGURE 1.4 DHCP negotiation.

A SIMPLE APPLICATION LAYER PROTOCOL

Now that we've discussed some of the basic networking parameters and principles, let's get down to some code that implements both a server and a client in the C language. First, let's look at the server (see Listing 1.1).

LISTING 1.1 Simple daytime (TCP) server.

```
int main ( void )
{
  int serverFd, connectionFd;
```

```
    struct sockaddr_in servaddr;
    char timebuffer[MAX_BUFFER+1];
    time_t currentTime;

    serverFd = socket(AF_INET, SOCK_STREAM, 0);

    memset(&servaddr, 0, sizeof(servaddr));
    servaddr.sin_family = AF_INET;
    servaddr.sin_addr.s_addr = htonl(INADDR_ANY);
    servaddr.sin_port = htons(DAYTIME_SERVER_PORT);

    bind(serverFd, (struct sockaddr *)&servaddr, sizeof(servaddr));

    listen(serverFd, 5);

    while ( 1 ) {

      connectionFd = accept(serverFd,
                             (struct sockaddr *)NULL, NULL);

      if (connectionFd >= 0) {

        currentTime = time(NULL);
        snprintf(timebuffer,
                  MAX_BUFFER, "%s\n", ctime(&currentTime));

        write(connectionFd, timebuffer, strlen(timebuffer));
        close(connectionFd);

      }

    }

}
```

The daytime server was a classic server example and was historically used for test purposes. Although most UNIX implementations still include a daytime server, it is commonly disabled, as it is unnecessary and viewed as a security risk.

The daytime server performs the simple task of emitting the current date and time as a string to a connected client. Upon writing the time data to the socket, the server closes its side of the socket and then awaits another connection.

A socket is the communications pipe between two applications. The socket can connect to applications running on the same host, or halfway around the world through the Internet. The socket is the basic primitive of the Sockets API (otherwise known as the BSD Sockets API). Appendix A provides a primer to those who wish to brush up on the BSD Sockets API. To see some of the Sockets API calls in action, refer back to our simple daytime server in Listing 1.1.

The first call that we make is to the `socket` primitive to allocate a socket descriptor. Note that we use the `SOCK_STREAM` constant in our call. This specifies that we want a TCP socket (as opposed to a UDP socket, or another available from the protocol stack). We'll make use of the returned socket descriptor (`serverFd`) in most of the subsequent calls. In the next call, `bind` specifies a port address (`DAYTIME_SERVER_PORT`) to be used for our server and also defines who can connect to our server (`INADDR_ANY`). `INADDR_ANY` is called an unspecified address because it acts as a wildcard to allow sockets from any IP address to connect. Once we've successfully identified ourselves, we can enable incoming connections via the `listen` call. This call tells the TCP/IP stack that connections are allowable on the port defined for our socket. Finally, the `accept` call informs the protocol stack that we are ready to accept connections on our new server socket.

When a client does connect to our server, the `accept` call will return with a new socket descriptor. This new socket will be used for communication with the client. The reason that a new socket is created for communication is to allow the server to continue to accept new connections while existing clients remained connected. For multi-threaded servers or cases when clients can remain connected for a long time, this is very important. In this simple implementation, we'll allow only one connection at a time.

Once we have our new socket, we gather the current time (using the UNIX system `time` call) and then write the ASCII version of the time into our temporary character buffer. We then use the `write` call to emit our character string to the connected client and finally shut down the connection with the `close` call. The server then loops back to the `accept` call to await another client connection.

So, that looks very simple. Don't worry about some of the other parameters used here, as we go into detail of the Sockets API in Appendix A.

We've looked at a simple server implementation, so what does the client look like? This is shown in Listing 1.2.

LISTING 1.2 Simple daytime (TCP) client.

```
int main ( int argc, char *argv[] )
{
```

```
int connectionFd, in;
struct sockaddr_in servaddr;
char timebuffer[MAX_BUFFER+1];

if (argc != 2) {
  return(0);
}

connectionFd = socket(AF_INET, SOCK_STREAM, 0);

memset(&servaddr, 0, sizeof(servaddr));
servaddr.sin_family = AF_INET;
servaddr.sin_port = htons(DAYTIME_SERVER_PORT);

inet_pton(AF_INET, argv[1], &servaddr.sin_addr);

connect(connectionFd,
          (struct sockaddr_in *)&servaddr, sizeof(servaddr));

while ( (in = read(connectionFd, timebuffer, MAX_BUFFER)) > 0) {
  timebuffer[in] = 0;
  printf("\n%s", timebuffer);
}

close(connectionFd);

return(0);
}
```

As before, we first create a socket (of the TCP variety using `SOCK_STREAM`). We also specify the port that we're interested in, but in this case it's not to bind to our socket but instead as the target for our socket connection. The port number (`DAYTIME_SERVER_PORT`) provides the target at the host, but now we also have to define what particular host we're interested in. This is done through the *inet_pton* call. This call takes a target address (in character string format) and converts it to an address the sockets layer can use. The term sockets layer is used to define the layer above the Transport layer which is commonly the BSD Sockets API. The call formally converts the presentation address (such as "192.168.1.1") to the network address (0xC0A80101). Note that we're getting our string address from the command line in the client application (argv[1]).

So at this point, we've defined our socket as well as specified the host and port number to which we want to connect. The next call, *connect*, actually creates the connection to our server. We'll then read from the socket and display the data that's returned. Since we know that character data will be returned (it's part of the protocol), we null-terminate our string and then display it using the `printf` call. The `read` call will return the number of characters that were read. Two special cases here are '–1' and '0'. A '–1' return specifies that an error occurred and the actual error condition can be identified using the `errno` variable (in UNIX systems). A '0' return specifies that the socket has been closed at the server. In either case, we'll simply exit.

Another important point to note here is that it's not actually necessary for the application to be sitting on the `read` call when the data arrives. The TCP/IP stack will take care of buffering the data so that when the client application finally gets around to calling `read`, the buffered data will be returned. This is important in systems in which blocking semantics are not provided (more on this in Chapter 2).

One item to note here is the difference between data buffering for TCP and UDP. While TCP will buffer data and then notify the peer when no additional data can be buffered, UDP will simply drop incoming packets once the internal buffers are full. This relates back to the fundamental issue of reliability between TCP and UDP. Both protocols will buffer data, though, even if the user application is not sitting on the read call.

An example of the `dayserv` server output is presented in Listing 1.3. Note that in this example, we've built and run the applications on a Linux desktop. Since the BSD API is a standard, it's much easier to develop our application layer protocols on an operating system such as Linux prior to porting to the embedded device. For this reason, the examples in this book will be shown running on Linux. The examples can also be run on a Windows desktop using the Cygwin. The Cygwin package provides a standard UNIX development environment on Windows and can be downloaded from the Red Hat Web site (http://www.redhat.com).

LISTING 1.3 Sample emission of the daytime client interfacing with the server.

```
[root@plato daytime]# make
gcc  -Wall -c dayserv.c
gcc  dayserv.o -o dayserv
gcc  -Wall -c daycli.c
gcc  daycli.o -o daycli
[root@plato daytime]# ./dayserv &
[1] 845
[root@plato daytime]# ./daycli plato
```

```
Mon Sep  3 22:08:00 2001

[root@plato daytime]#
```

As an alternative to developing a client for applications in which the protocol is completely ASCII based (only text passed through the socket), a standard *telnet* client can be used. In this case, telnet creates a socket based upon the passed parameters and permits transmission and receipt of text data. An example of using telnet in this way is provided in Listing 1.4.

LISTING 1.4 Using telnet as a text-based client for the daytime server.

```
[root@plato daytime]# telnet plato 13
Trying 192.168.2.151…
Connected to plato.mtjones.com.
Escape character is '^]'
Mon Sep  3 22:09:28 2001

Connection closed by foreign host.
[root@plato daytime]#
```

In looking at the source for the server and client, it's probably clear now that some symmetry exists with the Sockets API calls (see Figure 1.5). For a *client* `connect`, there was a prior *server* `bind/accept`. For every successful `read`, there was a prior `write`. These relationships are important and can help solidify the understanding of the Sockets API.

PROTOCOL SUITE OVERVIEW

Now we'll put together a list of the most common protocols that may be encountered and where they fit within the architectural layers we've discussed. Some of them have already been covered in some length (HTTP, TCP, UDP, IP) but others will be new (see Figure 1.6 for the sample protocol diagram).

Most visibly different are the contents of the network layer. As we mentioned before, the network layer's primarily component is the Internet Protocol, but numerous other protocols are here in support of IP.

Address Resolution Protocol (ARP) is used to provide a mapping of IP addresses to their corresponding hardware address (such as a MAC address for Ethernet). When communicating over Ethernet, the hardware address is used as the destination address within the Ethernet frame. In order to

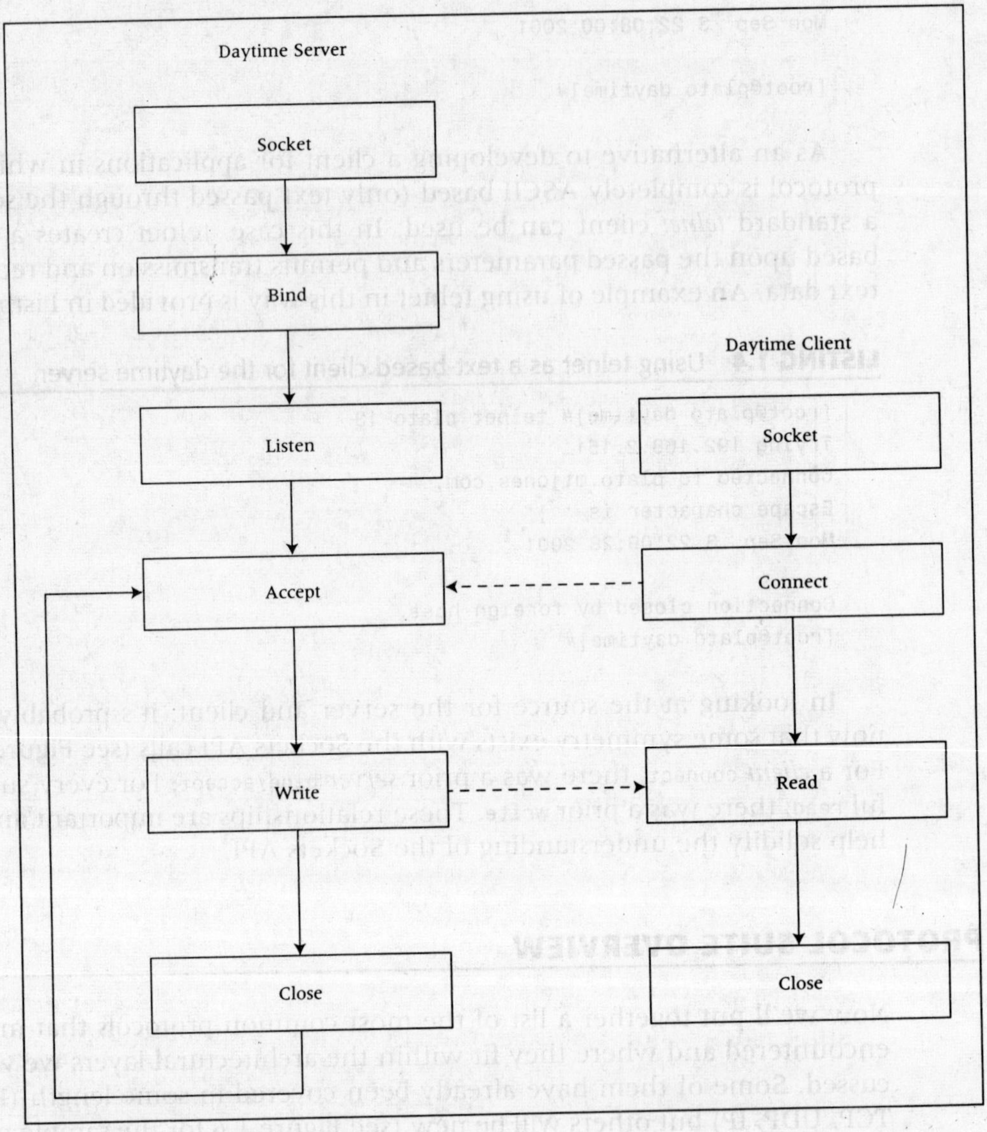

FIGURE 1.5 Sockets API call symmetry.

determine the mapping of IP address to hardware address, ARP uses broadcast packets to ask which host holds a particular IP address. If a host is on the network that has that IP address, a packet is sent as a response that includes the hardware address and the IP address. An ARP table is used to cache these entries so that the interrogation process need not clutter the network. Additionally, devices on a network can monitor ARP traffic. Even

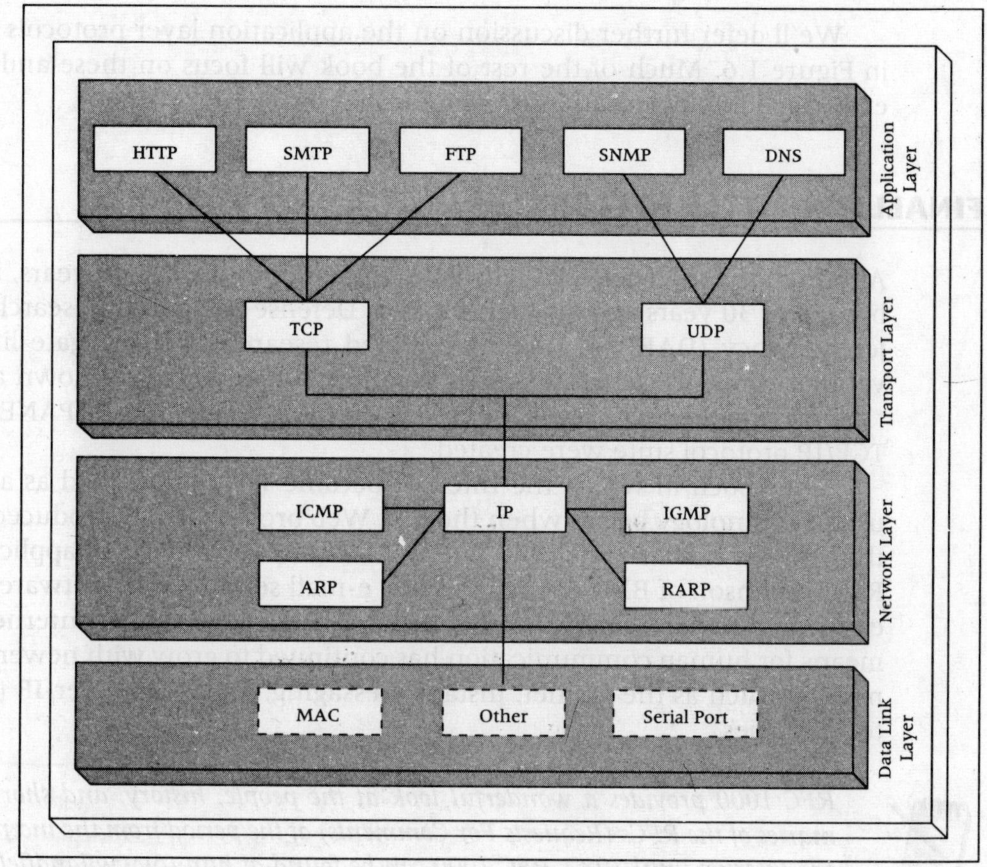

FIGURE 1.6 Sample protocols in their respective layers.

when an ARP request or reply isn't targeted to a particular device, it can still cache the information in the event it needs the data later.

RARP is the reverse of ARP (Reverse Address Resolution Protocol). Given a hardware address, the IP address associated with that physical address is returned.

ICMP is the Internet Control Message Protocol. ICMP messages are commonly protocol stack-to-protocol stack messages and are invisible to the application layer. ICMP is used for ping (echo request and reply) as well as to notify the protocol stack of errors (an example is "host unreachable").

IGMP is the Internet Group Management Protocol. This protocol is used to permit a host to participate in multicast communication that extends beyond the connected LAN.

We'll defer further discussion on the application layer protocols listed in Figure 1.6. Much of the rest of the book will focus on these and their embedded implementations in detail.

FINALLY, A LITTLE HISTORY...

Although the Internet is largely a phenomenon of the last 10 years, it was born over 30 years ago through the U.S. Defense Advanced Research Projects Agency (DARPA). DARPA initiated research to investigate linking various kinds of packet networks together, which became known as the "Internetting Project." Over the course of this research, the ARPANET and TCP/IP protocol suite were created.

The epoch in which the Internet became widely regarded as a truly useful technology began when the first Web browser was introduced, and the browser has remained the Internet's most popular type of application. Ray Tomlinson of BBN created the first e-mail send/receive software as an easy coordination mechanism for ARPANET developers. The Internet as a means for human communication has continued to grow with newer technologies such as the Usenet, instant messaging, and Voice-over-IP (VoIP) technologies.

RFC 1000 provides a wonderful look at the people, history, and short summaries of the RFCs (Requests For Comments) of the period from the inception of the Internet until 1987. RFC 1000 can be found at http://www.landfield.com/rfcs/rfc1000.html.

Network Protocol Evolution

The TCP/IP suite of protocols was not the first set of protocols to be used over the networks that became the Internet. In 1970, the Network Working Group (NWG) under Steve Crocker created the Network Control Protocol.[1] With the NCP came standardization of the ARPANET network interface. This allowed others to connect to the growing network and build new protocols and applications using the new interface. Within a year, 15 universities and private corporations could communicate with each other over the ARPANET.

1 Leiner, Barry et al., "A Brief History of the Internet," *Internet Society*, http://www.isoc.org/internet/history/brief.shtml

An interesting archeological side-note can be found in RFC 78. This document discusses network connectivity testing done between the RAND Corporation and the University of California at Santa Barbara in November 1970.

The host-to-host asymmetric protocol known as the NCP was later built upon by Robert Kahn and Vinton Cerf and became the standard TCP/IP networking protocol.

The BSD SocketS API

The Socket model for network programming was invented on the BSD (Berkeley Systems Distribution) operating system in the late 1970s. BSD was Berkeley's name for their UNIX implementation since the name UNIX was owned at the time by Bell Labs (AT&T). AT&T's version of UNIX was weak in terms of interprocess communication (or IPC) and the Computer Systems Research Group at Berkeley set about to fix this and succeeded. The result was the Sockets model and API. This abstraction fueled further growth in protocol development and is to this day the standard for application layer protocol development.

The Protocol Standards Process

In the beginning were the Network Working Group and a set of committed individuals including Jon Postel, who managed protocols through the standardization process. In 1968, staff members and graduate students from the first four proposed ARPANET sites (UCLA, UCSB, SRI, and the University of Utah) met to discuss the forthcoming network. Though the first meetings were broad and grand (the first Interface Message Processor or IMP had not yet been created) the framework laid out by these early pioneers set the stage for things to come.

The protocols and operational aspects of the network were initially documented in a series of documents called Internet Experimental Notes. These documents were the precursor to the publication process that exists now, the Requests for Comment (RFCs).

The Network Working Group (NWG) became the Internet Engineering Task Force (IETF). The original meetings of the NWG that encompassed a handful of engineers and scientists have become the international IETF meetings where attendance is counted in the thousands.

The RFC process is a cooperative one whereby candidate documents (Internet Drafts) are opened for review by anyone who has the time and energy to do so. If accepted, the Internet draft (draft specification) moves to the RFC track, and in time may be ultimately adopted as an Internet standard.

Draft specifications may also document conventions or processes. These documents become known as BCPs or Best Current Practices. A very interesting BCP (BCP 9, RFC 2026) documents the standards process and is entitled *The Internet Standards Process – Revision 3.*

SUMMARY

In this chapter we've looked at the Internet network architecture and a brief overview of the protocols that are used to make it work. We looked at the basic networking parameters that are used to give a protocol stack an identity on a network and discussed the options for their configuration (manual or automatic through the Dynamic Host Configuration Protocol). We then presented a sample stream server and client using the BSD Sockets API and provided a brief discussion of the API calls used within them. Finally, we looked back at the early beginnings of the Internet and the people who brought it to life.

RESOURCES

Leiner, Barry et al., "A Brief History of the Internet," *Internet Society.* http:// www.isoc.org/internet/history/brief.shtml

2 TCP/IP and Embedded Systems

In Chapter 1 we discussed some of the basics of TCP/IP networking and presented a brief overview of application layer protocols. In Chapter 2, we'll look at the intersection of TCP/IP and embedded systems. This intersection yields interesting problems and characteristics that are not present in traditional desktop systems design.

INTRODUCTION

What is an "Embedded" System?

An important semantic point to close before we really get into this chapter is the definition of an embedded system. As the saying goes, there are as many definitions as there are embedded system developers, but a good common one exists:

An embedded system is a specialized computer system that provides a dedicated function such as control, monitoring, or other services within a larger system.

Note that from this definition, a desktop personal computer does not qualify. Nor do any other general-purpose devices such as Personal Digital Assistants (PDA). The embedded computer in the microwave fits this definition, as does the computer within our car's radio. Even cellular phones still fit this definition, although that definition is changing with the higher integration possible today (cell phone/PDA integration).

It's important to note that an embedded system in no way implies a real-time system. A real-time system responds to unpredictable external stimuli in a timely and predictable way. All of the protocols discussed in this text have very soft requirements with respect to timing and therefore embedded aspects will be the secondary focus.

One other interesting distinction of most embedded systems is that the software that is developed for them is built (compiled and linked) on another computer. When we build software on a standard desktop PC, we compile the source and run it on the same machine. In an embedded system, we commonly "cross-compile" our code on one system (the host) and then execute on our embedded system (the target). The host and target commonly differ by architecture, so the cross-compiler generates code that is not executable on the host.

Characteristics of Embedded Systems

Let's now look at some of the characteristics of embedded systems regarding their capability of connecting to the Internet.

RTOS or no RTOS

One of the classic arguments in embedded systems software design is whether to use an operating system/kernel (or Real Time Operating System, or RTOS). The operating system (OS) provides a basic layer of services to simplify the job of the embedded application developer. From the other end of the spectrum, the OS can create resource constraints that drive the cost of the end device higher. It's very hard these days not to justify the use of an operating system or kernel, especially when the device must communicate using Internet protocols.

A TCP/IP stack (and accompanying upper layer socket interface and lower layer device driver) puts additional constraints upon the embedded system design. For example, the TCP/IP stack must have a relatively accurate time source for timer management (to handle the various timeouts and timing activities that take place in the stack). The stack must also have a resource management system for packets. This could be a standard dynamic memory management system (Malloc/Free) or a custom system that pre-allocates packet buffers for speed.

It is possible to use a TCP/IP stack with no kernel as long as you provide the services that it needs (timer, memory manager, etc.). In systems with minimal requirements, this can yield a very small and fast implementation.

When possible, the best arrangement is an OS that is pre-configured with a network stack. For example, all embedded Linux distributions automatically include a standard TCP/IP stack. Commercial RTOS vendors such as QNX Software and Wind River Systems optionally include networking stacks. Other than simplicity for development (you concentrate on your application instead of the OS/stack), there are other benefits to this model. The largest benefit is that of available software. Consider an embedded Linux distribution. Since the Linux distribution on the desktop and in the embedded device are virtually the same, networking protocols and applications can be quickly and easily ported. This means that the mass of code available for standard desktop systems can be easily tailored for the embedded environment saving time and effort.

Blocking or Non-Blocking Calls

The standard socket layer defines blocking semantics such that a call to read from a socket with no data available will cause the call to block until data is available. The write call behaves in a similar manner. If the number of octets being written is greater than the available space in the buffer, the write call blocks until sufficient space in the write buffer is available. If an OS is not available, these blocking semantics are also not available. The socket layer can work in a non-blocking manner, though in many cases this can be inefficient. Some commercial stacks provide a callback mechanism such that when some type of event occurs for a given socket, a user-defined application is called. This type of architecture can be extremely efficient.

Single or Multi-threaded Designs

With an RTOS, the stack may be defined as a single task or be split among the protocol layers. In most cases, this distinction exists between the stack and the data link layer. The Media Access Control (MAC) or serial port (for PPP/SLIP) is commonly split from the TCP/IP stack software due to their asynchronous nature. Recall from Chapter 1 that this split is due to the asynchrony of the layer's processing requirements.

Memory Management Issues

Embedded systems are commonly designed for minimal cost. With cost reduction comes reduction in the available resources such as Flash/non-volatile memory and RAM. Having a minimal amount of RAM means that extreme care must be taken regarding the method that the TCP/IP stack uses for the allocation of packets.

The method for allocation of packets can typically be configured in embedded stacks, particularly those that are OS/kernel agnostic. The two primary methods are dynamic allocation or pre-allocation.

The dynamic allocation of packets means that whenever a packet is needed, it is dynamically allocated from the heap subsystem. The heap is nothing more than a large block of memory that can be broken down into smaller pieces depending upon application needs. The heap is also used for generalized resource management, so it's a common base for systemwide memory management. The general problem with dynamic memory management is garbage collection. When a packet is returned to the heap, it must fold the packet back in to join blocks whenever possible for large allocable segments. If the returned blocks were simply left in their original size, you'd ultimately end up with the inability to allocate blocks over the largest available block size and an inefficient search algorithm to find the block closest to your requested size.

Pre-allocation is the allocation of packets (commonly of a fixed size) and then immediate queuing for quick allocation and release. With fixed-size packets, there is no garbage collection, which makes the method both simple and efficient. Pre-allocation can be based upon a dynamic memory management model (for initial allocation of packets) or can simply be defined as blocks of memory reserved for the application.

IP-BASED NETWORK INTERFACES FOR EMBEDDED SYSTEMS

Many embedded systems include some form of communications link. Having an IP-based link means that many types of communication can be multiplexed over the single link. Whether the link is used as a central part of the design or simply as a link for debugging, a communication link offers many advantages for deeply embedded designs.

Communication Links

In this section, we'll look at some of the available IP-based communication possibilities for embedded systems. These are serial links, wireless links (dependent upon a serial link), and finally Ethernet.

Serial Links

By far, the most common communications link on embedded devices is the serial port (RS-232). The advantage of the serial port is that it requires no significant configuration. The user simply configures the peer's communication parameters (speed, parity, data bits, stop bits) and communication is possible. Note that in most cases, the parameters for low-bandwidth links are set at 9600 baud with no parity, 8 data bits and 1 stop bit. This is a good default setting when trying to communicate with a device in which you don't know the parameters.

The drivers needed for serial ports are also very simple. They commonly include an input and output buffer in which incoming and outgoing characters are routed. An interrupt is commonly provided by the UART chip (Universal Asynchronous Receiver Transmitter) to notify the processor of the presence of an input character, or when a new character can be transmitted. When no additional characters are waiting to be transmitted from the output buffer, the transmit interrupt is disabled (and then re-enabled once new characters are provided by the application). Incoming characters are also interrupt driven. The newly received character is moved from the UART registers to the input buffer for application use. In short, the driver is easily developed and understood.

Newer UARTs (such as the Texas Instruments 16C754) include four serial ports on chip, and internal buffer capabilities. This allows the chip to work on larger buffers of incoming and outgoing characters rather than interrupt the processor for each byte, which results in better I/O efficiency.

On top of the serial device driver are the data link layer protocols that provide end-to-end connectivity to a peer on the remote end of the link. The two main protocols here are SLIP (Serial Line Interface Protocol) and PPP (Point-to-Point Protocol). Either SLIP or PPP is mandatory for operating TCP/IP over a serial link.

In the discussions that follow, we'll use the term "remote" to refer to the embedded device at a remote location.

SLIP

SLIP is an older point-to-point protocol used primarily on dedicated or dial-up POTS (Plain Old Telephone System) lines. SLIP encapsulates IP datagrams within a SLIP frame for transmission to the peer. The primary problem with SLIP is that it does not support any kind of error detection and correction or compression. SLIP also does not support the dynamic allocation of IP addresses for the client—the client must be statically configured before the session begins). Compressed SLIP (or CSLIP) provides compression of IP headers to make better use of low-bandwidth links. SLIP and CSLIP also do not permit more than one upper layer protocol to share the link.

PPP

PPP is a much more recent protocol and is the standard for communicating over POTS. PPP uses frame encapsulation as does SLIP, but it supports dynamic IP address assignment (from server to client) and includes support for compression to make better use of POTS lines. PPP also supports variable sized frames (unlike SLIP's static datagram size) and includes the capability to negotiate features during PPP session negotiation.

PPP also supports multiple forms of authentication such as the Password Authentication Protocol (PAP) and the Challenge Handshake Authentication Protocol (CHAP). Additionally, PPP can carry multiple upper layer protocols simultaneously.

Wireless Links

Wireless links, other than 802.11-like standards, are really nothing more than a variation on serial links. A wireless modem is typically connected to the embedded computer via serial port and all configurations and communication takes place over this port. Two types of wireless links in the U.S. are Circuit Switched Cellular (CSC) and Cellular Digital Packet Data (CDPD). Both of these technologies are based upon the older cellular infrastructure, although newer wireless offerings are coming (such as Global System for Mobile communications or GSM).

Wireless Technologies

The CSC modem provides connectivity in a connection-based manner. The embedded application "dials-in" through the modem to a gateway using PPP. This requires that the application be programmed with a preset user name and password in order to bridge to the Internet. Carriers charge based-upon connect time which means that even if the application transfers no data, the account is charged. The user name and password must be registered to an account with an ISP to which the CSC modem will connect.

The CDPD mode provides connectivity in a different manner. It operates in a fashion similar to Ethernet. Once the modem connects via SLIP, we're on the network and can receive and send packets. There is no need for the modem to disconnect and therefore the CDPD modem can simplify the embedded application. Carriers typically charge users based upon the number of bytes transferred, although most also offer a plan to communicate at a flat rate.

CDPD can be an easier communications asset because of the simplicity of its operation. With CDPD, the embedded system is always available. This is a big advantage over CSC. CDPD can also be more cost efficient due to a lack of airtime charges that are present with CSC.

Both cellular technologies are slow in comparison to common data rates. A link with 14.4 Kbps is common on either of these links. Therefore, these links may not be useful for large data transfers.

A larger disadvantage is the coverage for the technologies. Both CDPD and CSC are available in metropolitan areas, but inaccessible in remote areas. This makes them difficult to use in certain applications such as trucking when the vehicle spends most of its time in remote areas (such as on interstate highways).

A local wireless option for higher speed data communication can involve the use of spread spectrum modems. These modems can be expensive, but can operate at distances of up to twenty miles line-of-sight (LOS) with proper antennas. Moderate bandwidths can also be achieved. As do the other wireless options, spread spectrum utilizes point-to-point protocols for IP connectivity (SLIP or PPP). Since the peer from the embedded system (commonly known as the base station is not part of any commercial infrastructure, there is no cost for operating this type of link.

Satellite handsets (such as those available from Inmarsat) provide the ability for global communication. The data rates are still slow with these satellite links, but they can be used anywhere on the planet. If the embedded application truly needs global coverage, satellite links are a good choice. It's important to understand that the handset is bulky and has greater power requirements than may be available in many applications.

A final option is the use of ORBCOMM satellites. A Subscriber Communicator (SC) provides the ability to transmit and receive small amounts of data through the ORBCOMM satellite network (in the form of an e-mail). The satellites operate in a low Earth orbit, and based upon their orbits can typically transfer data between the remote asset and the end user in less than six minutes (store-and-forward architecture). The remote asset talks directly to the ORBCOMM satellite through the SC to a passing satellite. The satellite downlinks received data to a series of Earth-based ground stations that ultimately direct the data to the intended user.

While ORBCOMM is cheaper than Inmarsat and requires less power and space, the amount of data that can be transferred is limited. Additionally, since the SC communicates through a satellite and a series of ground terminals, ORBCOMM communications are not real-time.

Ethernet

Ethernet is a great interface for high-speed communications. It is a local interface and thus requires direct connection between the remote target and peer for communication. While not useful in truly remote environments (such as mobile embedded systems), Ethernet has a place in non-mobile embedded systems in a variety of environments. For example, in factory-control applications, Ethernet can easily be distributed in an assortment of topologies.

Ethernet operates over what is known as CSMA/CD (Carrier Sense, Multiple Access/Collision Detect). Ethernet is a shared bus among a number of users (Multiple Access). Before a packet is written onto the wire, the host must listen for any other hosts that are currently sending a packet (Carrier Sense). If the host senses the carrier (no hosts are writing), a packet is sent. While the packet is sent, the host listens for other hosts writing (Collision Detect). This activity is provided by the MAC device that is commonly a single chip. IP packets are passed to the MAC device driver where they are managed by the chip. MAC frames are received by the MAC device and are passed up the TCP/IP stack, usually by interrupt.

Ethernet is now quite common as a wireless protocol. While the 802.3 spec refers to wire-based Ethernet, the 802.11 spec refers to a wireless Ethernet. Wireless Ethernet is most commonly deployed in office and home environments to build LANs without wires.

Comparison of Link Features

A comparison of the features and their relative merits is provided in Table 2.1.

Note that the reference to operating cost is the cost of operating the communications link within its environment. For example, spread spectrum is a point-to-point medium that requires no infrastructure other than what is provided by the system designer. Therefore, no other costs are identified and the operating cost is zero. The Inmarsat handset places calls through one of four Inmarsat spacecraft. Since the number of channels available on each spacecraft is limited, the cost of the link is very expensive.

TABLE 2.1 Communication link comparisons.

Architecture	*Bandwidth*	*Operating Cost*	*Proximity*
Direct-Serial	Direct-Connect - high	0	Connected
Ethernet	Direct-Connect – very high	0	Connected
Wireless Ethernet	Wireless - high	0	200 feet
CDPD	Wireless - low	Low	Metropolitan
CSC	Wireless - low	Moderate	Metropolitan
Spread spectrum	Wireless - high	0	20 miles LOS
Inmarsat	Wireless - low	High	Global
ORBCOMM	Wireless – very low	Moderate	Global

Link Selection

There is no single correct link; the right link matches the needs for the system as determined by the designer. Ultimately, the decision comes down to a handful of parameters. These include geographical distribution, reliability of the link, and cost.

Geographical Distribution

Geographical distribution refers to the location of the end system. Will it be in a very remote area, or within a metropolitan area? Can it be tied to local infrastructure (such as POTS dial-up)? Are a number of remote devices collected into clusters? The cluster problem can be solved in a number of ways, but the sharing of more expensive links is attractive in some implementations. In this method, the remote systems communicate via a local communications mechanism (cheaper RF LAN), with one system providing the link back to the remote management system.

Is the system mobile? Truly mobile systems such as freight trucks require an independent communication mechanism so that they are readily available. For mobile assets that return to a common location one or more times per day, a local communications mechanism (spread spectrum) can be used to interrogate assets as they arrive at the hub using low-power short-range links.

One final interesting method that is now in use by a number of gas and electricity utilities is bringing the hub to the device. Some electricity meters are equipped with low-power RF communications devices that can communicate over a short distance (< 100 feet). A vehicle with the appropriate transceiver then drives through the neighborhoods and each meter is read along the way.

Link Reliability

How important is the data being collected or generated at the remote embedded system? In some cases, logged data can simply be emitted through a direct-connect interface. This requires someone to travel to the remote system for data gathering. If the data is very important, it's better to collect data routinely rather than let it sit on the device. For a large number of remote devices, the direct-connect approach quickly becomes untenable.

If the data is truly important, the geography ultimately determines which communications assets can be used. Other solutions may be selected such as combinations of links. For example, an oil field may contain a number of drilling systems each with attached embedded systems for data collection and monitoring. Each of the embedded systems could provide a low-power RF communications link to a remote aggregation system (in the same area as the drilling equipment). If this site had access to a POTS line, a simple dial-up could deliver the collected and aggregated data to a remote management system. If a POTS line were not available, some other wider-area communications mechanism could be provided (such as ORBCOMM for low data rates, or CSC/CDPD for higher data rates).

Cost

While cost is always important, especially when dealing with a large number of assets that require connectivity, cost can be identified only after the issues of geography and reliability requirements are settled.

As discussed in the prior sections, in some cases the architecture of the communication system can utilize multiple links such as spread spectrum for remote areas and wide area modem for data aggregation to reduce overall system cost and operational cost.

Link Stability and Operation

It's very important to understand that wireless links can be very unstable. The available bandwidth can fluctuate greatly and connections can drop altogether. Application layer protocols designed to use in these environments must withstand long delays and loss of connections gracefully. Even non-wireless systems should be developed with these issues in mind; they will be more apparent (and easier to test) when operating within a wireless network.

Remote Communication Paradigms

When remote technologies are enabled with wireless links, a significant problem that arises is the capability to access the device remotely. Using a link that must be initiated by the remote system means that a host user cannot access the remote device at arbitrary times.

In this section, we'll look at some of the solutions for remote system availability. It's important to note that one wireless technology provides a solution to the problem of availability. The CSC modem, if so configured, can provide for dial-in access to the remote device. A remote user would then simply dial into the modem (through its cellular number). The device would then provide for PPP server setup so that an IP connection could be presented.

For CSC connections that provide no server capability, or certain other wireless options, different methods are necessary in order to schedule connectivity with the remote devices. These cases cover remote devices that initiate communication (connect to the network, such as in the case of POTS dial-up connected systems or CDPD-based systems).

Availability Notification

One of the simplest solutions is availability notification. When the remote device connects to the network, it notifies whomever may be interested that it is now available. The peer management system can then perform whatever actions are necessary (uploading new code, downloading stored data, etc.).

Notification upon availability is an acceptable architecture for systems that must connect asynchronously based upon some local event. For example, if the data storage resources on the embedded device are almost exhausted, the device could connect to push the data out to the peer management system. Alternatively, if some event occurred at the remote device such as an alarm condition, the device would connect to relay this information.

The issue is trying to synchronize the need of the remote device to connect to the management system with the need for the management system to connect to the device. If one party has control over setting up communication, some method is necessary to incorporate the needs of both sides.

Scheduled Availability

Another method is scheduled availability. In this mode, the remote device would connect to the network based upon a preset schedule (usually set by the peer management system). Many LEO (Low Earth Orbit) satellites use this method to search for a ground RF signal. Not doing this means that the satellite must periodically look for the signal; this is expensive from a power consumption perspective. Rather than do this, the ground system will set the next time to contact (and possibly a number of contacts after that) and the satellite will faithfully attempt to connect based upon the schedule.

A terrestrial embedded system can operate with a similar design. The peer management system can specify either that the embedded system connect to the network on an absolute time period (such as every day at 5:00 A.M.) or on a relative period (two hours after this contact).

The question then, is what happens if the peer management system fails to contact the device when its scheduled connect time is activated, or if the remote embedded device suffers a reboot and loses its connect schedule? In this case, the embedded system could enter a search mode whereby it connects at some preset period that is known to the peer management system.

Scheduled Availability with Notification

The best design is probably a combination of the two approaches. Whenever the remote embedded system is required to connect, the peer management system is immediately notified upon connection to the network. In this way, even if the schedule is lost or either of the two systems become confused, the peer will be notified so that it can reset the schedule with the remote system.

Time Synchronization

When coordinating the activities of two or more systems based upon time, the issue of time synchronization comes into play. Since the clocks that operate within embedded systems are never perfect (some drift will occur), eventually the times on clocks among the systems will vary. Once this occurs, systems are no longer coordinated and distributed system failure can occur.

The Network Time Protocol (or NTP as described in RFC 1305) provides the means to synchronize time and coordinate time distribution between networked hosts. NTP operates using a hierarchical master/slave configuration whereby servers synchronize time via national time standards. Slaves are updated via time stamps from the server that are sent while accounting for round-trip time delays that were measured in the network. Therefore, the server sends the client a new time that includes the predicted time of arrival of the message. The server and client exchanges take place over long intervals (5 minutes) to ensure valid round-trip time measurements and minimum offset errors.

INTERNET PROTOCOLS IN THE EMBEDDED DOMAIN

In this section, we'll investigate some of the issues of Internet protocols in the embedded domain.

Fragmentation

Fragmentation is the process of breaking down an IP datagram into smaller pieces as defined by the MTU (Maximum Transmit Unit) between the source and destination. The MTU can never be exceeded between two hosts along a route and therefore an IP datagram may be cut into smaller pieces. This not only takes time for the host performing the fragmentation, but also takes time at the destination where reassembly of the packet must occur. The best use of the available bandwidth takes place with optimal use of the MTU. For this reason, fragmentation should be avoided whenever possible. One solution to this problem is discussed in the next section, Path MTU Discovery. Fragmentation can also occur within intermediary routers for UDP datagrams.

Path MTU Discovery

Path MTU discovery (as defined in RFC 1191) is the process of determining the greatest MTU along the path from the source to the destination. Discovering this value is important because it means that communication can take place using the largest size packets without having to fragment the IP datagrams along the way. Fragmentation of datagrams leads to a decrease in overall performance and therefore it is valuable to avoid it.

Path MTU discovery is performed using a special bit in the IP header called DF (or Don't Fragment). This bit instructs any hops along the way not to fragment the packet (don't break it down into smaller packets). When a router receives the packet and is unable to forward it on without fragmenting it, an ICMP message is returned specifying that fragmentation was necessary and the IP datagram had the DF set. By sending varying sized IP datagrams between the source and destination, the source can identify the maximum size packet that can be delivered without fragmentation. This value is then used as the MTU for this particular connection.

One difficulty with path MTU discovery is that the Internet is a changing network. Routers and gateways disappear while new hops are added. For this reason, the MTU for a particular connection may change with time and yield a connection that must perform fragmentation. When this occurs, the connection could be torn down and then the discovery process started again for optimal use of the new path.

Slow Start Algorithm

The Slow Start Algorithm used within the TCP protocol (as defined by Stevens in RFC 2001) specifies that the rate at which new packets should be emitted onto the network is the rate by which acknowledgments are received by the other end. In TCP, data packets are acknowledged using an ACK (defined as a bit in the TCP header flags). Rather than emitting packets onto the network, based upon the size of the window advertised by the peer (how much data the peer will accept at a time), the sender looks at received ACKs as a gate for the capability to send more data. At start-up, the sender emits one packet and awaits an ACK. When the ACK is received, the amount of data that can be emitted is incremented by one packet. The new data window is called the congestion window and is an overlay of the receiver's window.

This algorithm is interesting because it defines flow control as being managed by both ends of the connection. The advertised window is defined by the receiver of the connection, while the congestion window is managed by the sender.

The Slow Start Algorithm is useful for remote embedded systems because wireless networks are commonly narrow pipes at the embedded system end and fat pipes at the wireless gateway (to the Internet). Due to this change in bandwidth, the algorithm can adaptively define the "real" window for transmission of data and thus reduce the chaos caused by recurring datagram drops and retransmits.

Compressed Datagrams

Jacobson observed that the datagram headers flowing between the peers of a network connection change very little. In fact, only half of the elements of an IP datagram header change over the life of the connection. Therefore, instead of transferring the entire 48 bytes of the IP datagram header, only the portions that change are transferred along with a unique ID to help identify the connection at the receiver. The receiver need only store the last datagram header to restore the full header once the minimal header is received.

Jacobson's algorithm can result in close to a 50% reduction in the headers that are transferred over a connection. Given a connection in which large amounts of data are transferred, a 20 byte per packet reduction can quickly add up to significant bandwidth savings.

Jacobson's algorithm is discussed in RFC 1144.

The Nagle Algorithm

The Nagle algorithm can be very important for effective use of available bandwidth, particularly in wireless networks. The basic result of the Nagle algorithm is to restrict the transmission of data through a connection until at least the maximum segment size (MSS) has been reached. The MSS is the largest chunk of data that a sender will transmit to the receiver. By restricting packets to full length, the ratio of packet data to header is reduced which means that the available bandwidth is better utilized.

However, what happens when the number of octets to be transmitted is less than the MSS? In this scenario, once 200 ms passes and an insufficient number of bytes is available, the packet is sent regardless of the number of octets (as part of an acknowledge packet to the peer).

There are times when the Nagle algorithm should be disabled. Take for example an application that is emitting real-time data to a remote console for display. In this case, from a rendering perspective, having the data available as soon as it's generated is desirable. It may not yield the best network performance, but given the user-interface constraints, we must move data quickly. Nagle can be disabled on a per-connection basis through a `setsockopt` call (discussed in Appendix B).

Nagle's algorithm and a greater definition of the problem it solves are covered in RFC 896.

TOOLS FOR DEBUGGING PROTOCOLS

In this section, we'll look at some readily available tools that are immensely helpful in debugging application layer protocols. Some tools provide the capability to "sniff" the network in order to look at the dialog between a client and a server. Others provide the capability to generate packets of varying types to test a particular application. We'll look at these next.

tcp dump

The `tcpdump` utility is a command-line utility for dumping network traffic. It is a standard UNIX utility that emits the packets received to the terminal or to a file.

`tcpdump` accepts a large number of options, but a few are most important when simply trying to look at packets generated for a given testing session. For example, if we wanted `tcpdump` to emit all packets sent by our host interface (192.168.1.1), we would say:

```
tcpdump src host 192.168.1.1
```

If we wanted to show packets sent or received by the interface, we could say:

```
tcpdump src host 192.168.1.1 and dst host 192.168.1.1
```

Note the use of the `and` operator to build a filter expression that includes two separate terms. This particular filter could be redefined using the simpler term:

```
tcpdump host 192.168.1.1
```

One final interesting filter that is instructive is the following:

```
tcpdump gateway 192.168.2.1
```

This expression searches packets for those that are routed through the gateway. The difference between packets that are directed to the gateway and those that are routed through the gateway is that in the latter case the packet's ultimate destination is not the gateway but some point beyond. Recall that a gateway is a host that acts as the bridge between the local network and a wider network (such as the Internet). In the case of a packet routed to the gateway, the Ethernet address will be that of the gateway, but the destination IP address in the IP datagram header will be that of the ultimate destination. This filter can also be defined (as defined in the `tcpdump` man page) as:

```
tcpdump ether host 08:00:18:ba:be:ca and not host 192.168.2.1
```

`tcpdump` is a very powerful utility with a variety of filter options and primitives.

Ethereal

`Ethereal` is a newer tool that provides graphical network sniffing. It is similar to `tcpdump`, but provides a point-and-click method for configuration. An advantage to `Ethereal` is that it performs parsing of packets down to their basic elements (very useful in protocol debugging). The capability to plug-in new parsers is provided, making it a necessary tool for protocol development.

ICMPush

The `ICMPush` tool provides the capability to send fully customizable ICMP packets from the command line. While not specifically targeted to application layer protocol debugging, `ICMPush` is a useful tool for TCP/IP stack testing and general network testing.

hping

The `hping` tool is a variation on `ICMPush`, but permits the construction of arbitrary TCP/IP packets to inject into a network. This tool is useful to validate a particular application layer protocol implementation by stressing it with erroneous and sometimes destructive packets.

Protocol Specific Tools

When developing application layer protocols, implementations of similar protocols can be helpful in validation. For example, when developing an SMTP server, a number of SMTP clients are necessary in order to provide a peer for communication with the server. In most cases, numerous implementations exist and can therefore readily used for verification.

Two Internet sites that are useful for finding protocol implementations are http://www.freshmeat.net and http://www.sourceforge.net. These sites provide a clearinghouse for open source software.

SUMMARY

In this chapter, we first investigated embedded systems and their characteristics. We looked at some of the decision points in an embedded system design that is to include networking protocols as well as issues that are created from TCP/IP stack inclusion. We then looked at some of the available communication options for remote embedded systems and the relative merits of each. Finally, we discussed some of TCP/IP characteristics that are important from an embedded system perspective and some of the available tools that are useful in the development and validation of application layer protocols.

RESOURCES

Wind River Systems. http://www.wrs.com

QNX Software Systems Limited. http://www.qnx.com

GNU/Linux. http://www.kernel.org

Inmarsat. http://www.inmarsat.com

ORBCOMM. http://www.orbcomm.com

Mills "Network Time Protocol (Version 3) Specification, Implementation and Analysis," RFC 1305, March 1992. http://www.landfield.org/rfcs/rfc1305.html

Mogul & Deering, "Path MTU Discovery," RFC 1191, November 1990. http://www.landfield.org/rfcs/rfc1191.html

Stevens, "TCP Slow Start, Congestion Avoidance, Fast Retransmit, and FastRecovery Algorithms", RFC 2001, January 1997. http://www.landfield.org/rfcs/rfc2001.html

Jacobson, "Compressing TCP/IP Headers for Low-Speed Serial Links", RFC 1144, February 1990. http://www.landfield.org/rfcs/rfc1144.html

Nagle, "Congestion Control in IP/TCP Networks," RFC 896, January 1994. http://www.landfield.org/rfcs/rfc896.html

tcpdump. http://www.tcpdump.org

Ethereal. http://www.ethereal.com

ICMPush. http://www.freshmeat.net/projects/icmpush/

hping. http://www.hping.org

3 Introduction to Application Layer Protocols

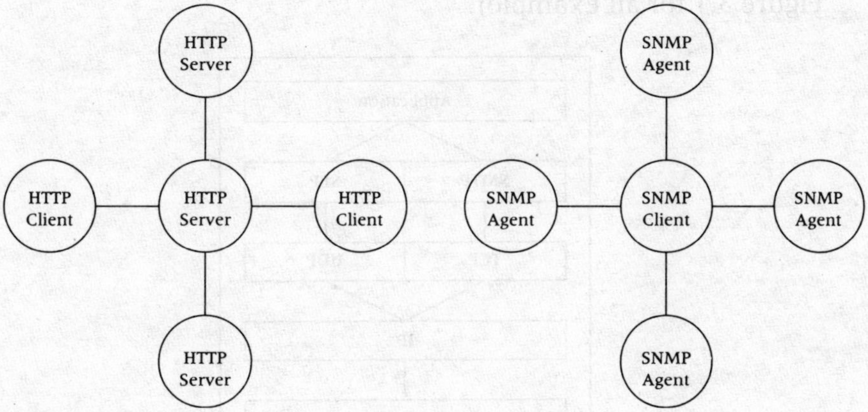

INTRODUCTION

In the previous chapters, we've covered the basics of networking as well as a brief introduction to embedded networking. In this chapter, we'll look at a variety of architectures and design characteristics of application layer protocols. The purpose of this is to understand the variety of ways that application layer protocols are designed, developed and used. As we'll soon discover, although the purposes for the protocols may differ, they share more similarities than differences. Finally, we'll look at some of the design characteristics of application layer protocols and how to decide which is right for a custom protocol design.

What is an Application Layer Protocol?

An application layer protocol, simply defined, is a protocol that exists at the application layer. From an API perspective, application layer protocols are built on the BSD Sockets API. Protocols at this layer are also commonly referred to as "applications," although in many cases this is not precisely true. For example, in an embedded system we may utilize an SMTP client to send e-mail from our device to an external host. If we visualize the protocol layering, our application then sits on SMTP that further sits on the TCP/IP stack. The SMTP client protocol provides us with a very simple API to communicate data through SMTP to an end user. Although these protocols may be integrated together in a single application, we honor the layering to aid in our understanding of the component relationships (see Figure 3.1 for an example).

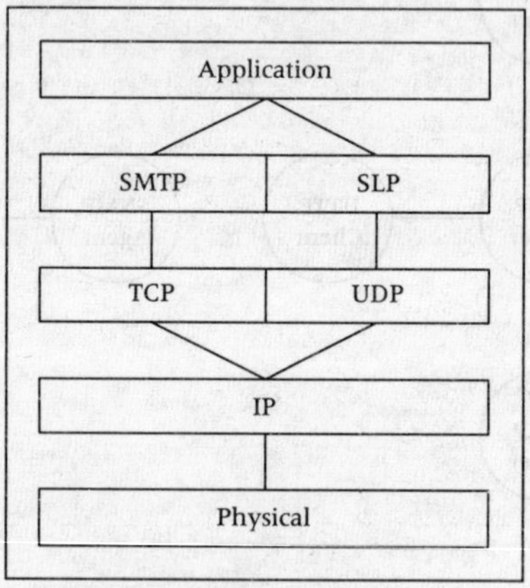

FIGURE 3.1 Application using application layer protocols.

While the TCP/IP suite provides the capability to move data between hosts on the Internet, the application layer protocols provide services that are meaningful to higher level applications (transporting e-mail, finding resources on a network, synchronizing time, etc.).

APPLICATION LAYER PROTOCOL ARCHITECTURES

Application layer protocols can be constructed in a variety of ways and use a number of different communication topologies. For example, HTTP is a traditional client-server protocol in which a browser (client) connects to a Web server and retrieves content. HTTP is also a stream-oriented protocol built on TCP. The server may provide content to a variety of clients distributed throughout the Internet.

The Simple Network Management Protocol (SNMP) is an interesting reverse architecture to HTTP. For example, the SNMP agent (server) provides the data that is collected by the client (network manager system), but the client in this case connects to many servers for monitoring. SNMP is also built on UDP since data can simply be requested again if a request or response packet is lost. In these two examples, a clear relationship exists between a client and a server (although their roles are reversed).

A final example is Service Location Protocol (SLP). In this protocol, a User Agent may request a particular service but instead of communicating directly to a server, the agent multicasts its request on the network to anyone who is listening. If a Service Agent hears the request and provides the service being requested, a reply is generated directly to the User Agent. This is a peer-to-peer architecture in which no central control exists; control is instead distributed throughout the network.

In the following sections, the organization of application layer protocols, including the varying means by which they communicate, will be discussed.

Standard Client/Server

The client/server architecture is by far the most common as the pattern fits the requirements of most application layer protocols. In this model, a server exists which serves as the repository for some type of data. Clients connect to the server to request and then receive data for processing or presentation. From our prior example of HTTP and SNMP, the topologies differ but the same relationships exist (see Figure 3.2).

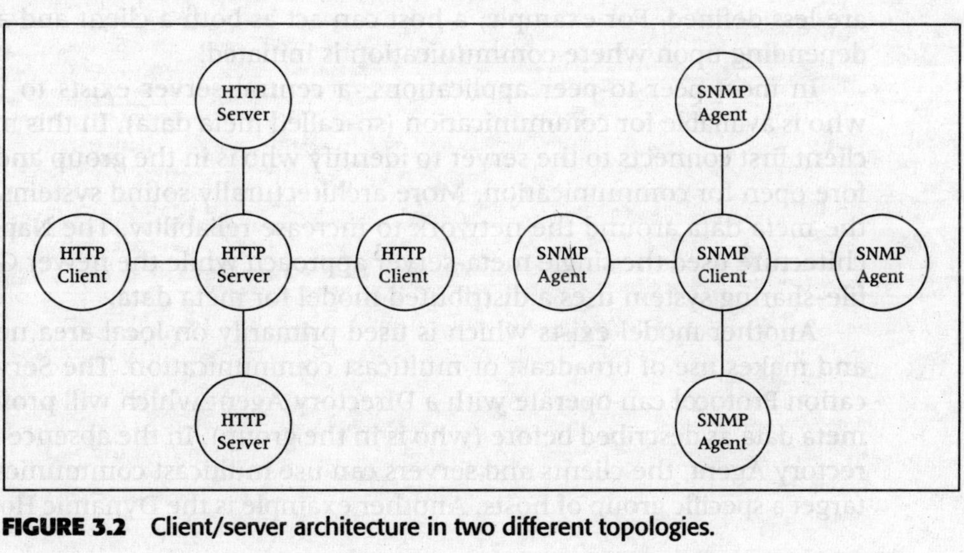

FIGURE 3.2 Client/server architecture in two different topologies.

In the HTTP example, there exists a one-to-many relationship to the server. In contrast, in the SNMP example there is a one-to-many relationship to the client. Each example represents the standard client/server model but serves a different purpose.

Another point to note on client/server, is that it is a request/response architecture. In both cases, a request is generated from the client and the server responds accordingly. This is also known as the "pull" model as data is conceptually pulled from the server to the client. The opposite approach is to have the server send data to the client when it's necessary to do so. This is called the "push" model as data is pushed to the client without a preceding request. The push model can be more efficient since data is transmitted only when necessary (such as when it changes) and the client need not periodically poll the server.

An example of an application layer protocol that provides both models is SNMP. Recall from Figure 3.2 that the client can request data from the servers (SNMP agents). SNMP agents also provide the capability to transmit what are known as *traps*. A trap is a message that is sent asynchronously from the server to the client upon detection of an anomalous condition that may need immediate attention. This type of communication is known as asynchronous because it is a "reply" with no associated request. Synchronous communication implies a request for every reply (see Figure 3.3).

Peer to Peer

In a peer-to-peer architecture, the roles of the entities that communicate are less defined. For example, a host can act as both a client and a server depending upon where communication is initiated.

In most peer-to-peer applications, a central server exists to identify who is available for communication (so-called meta data). In this model, a client first connects to the server to identify who is in the group and therefore open for communication. More architecturally sound systems spread the meta data around the network to increase reliability. The Napster architecture used the single meta-server approach while the newer Gnutella file-sharing system uses a distributed model for meta data.

Another model exists which is used primarily on local area networks and makes use of broadcast or multicast communication. The Service Location Protocol can operate with a Directory Agent which will provide the meta data as described before (who is in the group). In the absence of a Directory Agent, the clients and servers can use multicast communication to target a specific group of hosts. Another example is the Dynamic Host Con-

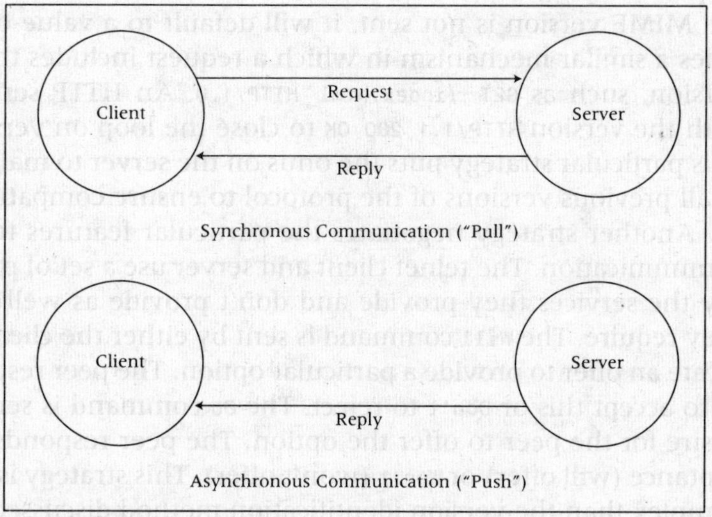

FIGURE 3.3 Synchronous vs. asynchronous communication.

figuration Protocol (DHCP). DHCP uses broadcast communication to identify the host on the local network that can provide configuration data.

SOLVING THE COMPATIBILITY PROBLEM

Before we begin to look at a few application layer protocols, let's consider a final design problem that must be considered. Once a protocol is utilized on the Internet, it's very unlikely that it will represent the final version. After a protocol is deployed, lessons are learned that can benefit the evolution of the protocol. These lessons are transformed into changes to the protocol design. However, what happens when an older client tries to communicate with a newer server (or vice versa)? This is the basic problem of version incompatibility.

The problem has been solved in a variety of ways for application layer-protocol designs. Two interesting solutions are version identification and capability negotiation.

In version identification, a node simply identifies its version as it begins communication with another node. A number of protocols use this method including SMTP and HTTP.

In SMTP, the field `MIME-Version: X.Y` is sent from the client to the server in the SMTP header, where `X.Y` represents the actual mime version. This informs the SMTP server how the message body should be interpreted. If the MIME version is not sent, it will default to a value of 1.0. HTTP provides a similar mechanism in which a request includes the HTTP protocol version, such as `GET /index.html HTTP/1.0`. An HTTP server will respond with the version `HTTP/1.1 200 OK` to close the loop on version consistency. This particular strategy puts the onus on the server to maintain knowledge of all previous versions of the protocol to ensure compatibility.

Another strategy negotiates the particular features to be used during communication. The telnet client and server use a set of primitives to identify the services they provide and don't provide as well as what services they require. The `Will` command is sent by either the client or server to indicate an offer to provide a particular option. The peer responds with either `Do` to accept this or `Don't` to reject. The `Do` command is sent to indicate the desire for the peer to offer the option. The peer responds with `Will` as acceptance (will offer) or `Won't` (won't offer). This strategy is somewhat more complex than the version identification method discussed earlier, but also has the disadvantage of requiring complexity in both the server and client.

OVERVIEW OF POPULAR EMBEDDED APPLICATION LAYER PROTOCOLS

We'll now look at some of the details of a number of application layer protocols that are useful in the embedded environment. Implementations for embedded systems will be discussed in later chapters for several of these.

HTTP—HyperText Transfer Protocol

The HyperText Transfer Protocol is fundamentally an ASCII-based data transfer protocol that provides the capability to move files of varying type between a server and a client. HTTP is most commonly associated with HTML documents (HyperText documents) as well as a rich variety of multimedia content (such as audio and video files).

HTTP is a traditional client/server protocol in which the client application (browser) connects to HTTP servers for content. HTTP transactions consist of a request message and a response message. The request can be quite elaborate, but the basic form is:

```
GET /filename HTTP/1.1
(* blank line *)
```

This request message specifies a file that the client would like to receive (`filename` that exists at the root subdirectory of the HTTP server content).

This is defined by the GET method. The HTTP/1.1 element specifies that the client can communicate via HTTP Version 1.1. The blank line after the request informs the server that the request is complete and the command is processed. If the specified file exists, a response could be generated as follows:

```
HTTP/1.1 200 OK
MIME-Version: 1.0
Content-Type: text/html
(* blank line *)
<HTML><BODY>Sample content</BODY></HTML>
```

The recipient of this message is the Web browser—it knows how to present the data to the user. HTTP can also perform the PUT method that moves content from the client to the server. HTTP is very flexible and is used in a variety of other ways than simply for Web data presentation.

Applications in the Embedded Domain

HTTP with HTML content is a very common configuration mechanism for complex embedded system products. Systems with complex configurations (such as Internet routers) commonly use HTTP as a configuration method, although a command line interface through a serial port is usually available to perform initial networking setup. HTTP with HTML is also used in less complex devices since the Web browser is so ubiquitous and readily available. For complex devices, Java is commonly used with HTML to provide data post-processing with user interaction on a client browser. Since the Java applets run in the browser environment, the HTTP server needs to support the GET method only for Java class files—it need not support a Java Virtual Machine internally.

SMTP—Simple Mail Transfer Protocol

The Simple Mail Transfer Protocol is another text-based protocol that permits e-mails to be transferred between hosts on the Internet. SMTP, like HTTP, permits the transfer of a variety of data including rich multimedia content. Binary data is transferred through MIME (Multipurpose Internet Mail Extensions). MIME provides encoding of binary content so that it can be transported through a strict ASCII protocol, commonly using the Base64 encoding method. All data transferred through SMTP is ASCII encoded so that it is compatible with older systems that use 7-bit ASCII for serial ports.

SMTP is a client/server protocol in which an e-mail client connects to the server to transfer e-mail messages. Clients construct e-mails and then connect to an SMTP server (or Mail Transfer Agent) to forward them towards their destination. This MTA may not be the final destination and therefore, multiple MTAs may be involved in the transfer.

Retrieving e-mails is performed through another ASCII-based protocol called POP or Post Office Protocol. POP allows e-mail clients to retrieve e-mails from servers whose purpose is to store them after receipt from another SMTP server.

Conversing with an SMTP server is an interactive process in which the client provides commands to the server and the server responds with status information regarding those commands. Let's look at a sample dialog between an SMTP client and server (see Listing 3.1). In this example, a client has connected to the SMTP server through port 25 (the reserved port for SMTP). Client dialog is shown in bold (with the 'C:' prefix).

LISTING 3.1 SMTP dialog between client and server.

```
S: 220 192.168.1.1 Sendmail 8.9.3/8.8.7; Sat 10 Feb 2001 16:19:14 -0700
C: HELO athome.com
S: 250 192.168.1.1 Hello IDENT:mtj@[192.168.1.2], pleased to meet you
C: MAIL FROM:me@athome.com
S: 250 me@athome.com...Sender ok
C: RCPT TO:you@overthere.com
S: 250 you@overthere.com... Recipient ok
C: DATA
S: 354 Enter mail, end with "." on a line by itself
C: Subject: Hi
C:
C: Hello There!
C: .
S: 250 RAAA03174 Message accepted for delivery
C: QUIT
S: 221 192.168.1.1 closing connection
```

From the example dialog, it's clear that this protocol is a simple command/response protocol using simple text.

Applications in the Embedded Domain

SMTP is a surprisingly useful protocol for embedded systems. As we'll see later in Chapter 6, it can be used as a command protocol in which commands are embodied by e-mail messages. SMTP handles its own reliability by attempting to deliver an e-mail repeatedly over as much as a few days until it arrives. SMTP also can provide notification for e-mails that are not delivered (via MTAs along the way).

SMTP is widely used as a notification mechanism for anomalous events. Servers can generate e-mails sent to administrators when attempted break-ins are detected or software behaves incorrectly.

For embedded systems that include inconsistent connection to the Internet (such as those that connect via wireless modems), e-mail is an easy way to perform notification of remote events that are deferred. The MTA (the first hop of the e-mail through the wireless network) provides delivery and the SMTP server for the peer provides storage for the e-mail until the administrator collects it through the e-mail client. The remote embedded system connects only long enough to push the e-mail to the gateway MTA and then can disconnect knowing that the e-mail will be delivered.

E-mail also provides for the delivery of multimedia content. Not only can HTML be used for data presentation, but also for more rich presentation such as images (such as are collected by remote cameras) as well as audio data.

SNMP—Simple Network Management Protocol

The Simple Network Management Protocol is a very simple protocol for collecting information from a variety of networked devices for managing and monitoring them. Data is universally structured in a hierarchical tree structure in which the endpoints of the tree represent data points and branches of the tree represent classes of data (or collections of a particular type).

SNMP is a traditional client/server protocol in which a network management system (the client in this model) sends commands to SNMP agents that are contained in the network assets. The agents act as the servers and return the data as requested by the network manager in a very structured format.

SNMP is a binary protocol in which both requests and responses are encoded within binary messages. Examples of SNMP running the `GetRequest` PDU and `GetResponse` PDU can be found in Chapter 8 in Figures 8.5 and 8.6.

SNMP traps (or asynchronous events) provide for immediate notification of issues to the network management system. This allows critical problems to be immediately noted to an administrator without waiting for a data collection cycle.

Since SNMP is a binary protocol, it can use network bandwidth much more efficiently than other text-based protocols.

Applications in the Embedded Domain

SNMP is a very popular protocol within the embedded domain. Network infrastructure assets such as routers, gateways, and switches all provide SNMP agents for their monitoring. SNMP provides a very simple way to collect a large amount of distributed data and presents it in a cohesive manner to a network administrator. Since the number of networked assets continues to grow, SNMP continues to solve the monitoring problem in a scalable way.

Despite SNMP's focus on data collection for networking equipment, it can be used quite effectively in the collection of other types of data. In Chapter 8 we'll look at the use of SNMP in the monitoring and control of a simulated remote antenna. SNMP requires simply that the data to be monitored be gathered within a MIB (Management Information Base) so that it integrates seamlessly into its hierarchical tree scheme.

SLP—Service Location Protocol

SLP is a lightweight binary protocol that provides for service advertisement and discovery of a variety of services. Services such as printers, or software such as a database can be advertised in a network to simplify their discovery by hosts that require their service.

SLP is divided into three elements: Directory Agent, Service Agent, and User Agent. The Directory Agent exists as the repository for service information. A Service Agent acts as an intermediary to the SLP and provides the means to advertise services provided by a node on the network. The User Agent is the user interface to the SLP and provides the means to find services within a network. In order to confine the advertisement and discovery process, SLP includes the concept of a scope that restricts the bounds of service usage.

SLP is interesting from a protocol perspective. Service and User agents can operate solely in a multicast environment where there is no Directory Agent. SLP can also operate with a Directory Agent when services are advertised and discovered through it. Without the Directory Agent, all Service Agents must interrogate incoming service requests from User Agents. That can result in a chatty and inefficient protocol.

SLP operates primarily over UDP, which means that the application layer must provide the reliability for lost packets. Simple retransmission, which is often the solution to this problem, is provided here. Although the protocol operates on a request/response basis, when operating in a multicast environment a request can result in more than one response. This is due to more than one Service Agent offering the requested service to the

User Agent. With a Directory Agent, the results can be encapsulated into a single response.

Applications in the Embedded Domain

SLP is a very useful protocol in the embedded domain. Consider consumer electronic devices that communicate over standard Ethernet networks. Configuration can be very problematic, especially with devices that may not have traditional user interfaces (such as a camera). After plugging the camera into the network, an SLP User Agent is used to find a computer for picture storage or a printer to generate printed copies of photos stored on the camera's internal disk. The camera manufacturer's post-processing software could also register as a service on a host computer and then permit connection with the camera for picture download and manipulation.

KEY DESIGN CHARACTERISTICS TO CONSIDER

Now let's look at some of the essential design decisions that must be considered when developing a new application layer protocol.

Synchronous/Asynchronous Relationship

Do the entities in the protocol communicate via request/response? Can more than one response be generated for a single request? Does the server generate data without a specific request? These questions relate to whether the protocol will be synchronous (strict request/response) or asynchronous (a request is not necessary for data to be sent from the server to client).

Synchronous protocols are developed primarily using stream protocols (such as TCP) while those that communicate asynchronously are usually developed with UDP datagrams. Examples are HTTP for synchronous (uses TCP) and SNMP for asynchronous (uses UDP). SNMP operates in a request/response fashion, but traps can be generated which are asynchronous.

One disadvantage of UDP for request/response is that a client and server can move out of sync with each other. Consider a client that emits a request message to a server. If the server does not respond right away, and the client times out, the client can then generate another request. However, if the first response then arrives, how does the client know that it's from the prior request and not the current? Protocols on UDP commonly use an ID in the messages that provide correlation between the request and the response. If the response ID does not match that of the request, then it's immediately known that a sync issue exists and the response can be discarded.

Reliability

Does the protocol require that the data be delivered in the order sent with guaranteed reliability (or definition of loss)? TCP provides for this type of reliability where UDP does not. In many cases, this kind of reliability is not necessary. Not receiving a response from a server can typically be remedied by reissuing the request. In applications in which audio data is transferred, dropping a packet simply means a slight garbling of the data at the peer. Having to retransmit in TCP mode would mean a break in audio until the stream was resynchronized. Therefore, in situations in which some loss can be tolerated, UDP is a good choice. When totally reliable transfer is needed, TCP is the choice.

Timing Sensitivity

Is the application sensitive to the delivery of its packets in bounded times? Does the application break down when the Internet is congested?

Some applications are very sensitive to timing. For example, consider a phone call over the Internet (Internet telephony). Some data loss is acceptable, but the delivery times of the packets must be bounded. Compare this to protocols that have no sensitivity to timing, such as FTP or HTTP. Protocols such as these use whatever bandwidth is available and therefore are known as *elastic*. Because these protocols are used for tasks in which timing is unimportant, the only effect this "elasticity" has is the session taking more or less time depending upon the available bandwidth.

As discussed in the reliability section, TCP is used primarily when in-order delivery of packets is needed. UDP provides for less reliability, but at a lesser computational cost than TCP. For example, UDP requires no connection setup time while TCP must perform this initial dialog between the client and server. TCP includes flow control while UDP simply emits packets in an open loop fashion. This open loop packet emission can create problems for the peer of the socket connection and must be dealt with by the sending application.

Another possibility is the Real Time Transport Protocol, or RTP. RTP is similar to UDP (lacks the flow control and reliability features of TCP) but includes hooks so that reliability can be added by the application. RTP is commonly used in applications which transfer audio or video data over the Internet.

Some timing-sensitive applications can be supported through buffering at the receive-end. Based upon congestion, the receiver will buffer incoming data and then play the stream. The data continues to arrive and is buffered, allowing the stream to be played without interruption. This method works for audio and video data with no feedback, such as music or any other prerecorded media. However, for applications such as Internet telephony or video conferencing, buffering doesn't provide as much of a solution because the buffering delay creates gaps. An example of this problem is a news broadcast in which a person is interviewed over a satellite link. The multi-second delays create gaps and interfere with our listen-and-then-speak protocol.

It should be noted that no protocol guarantees timed-delivery of packets over the Internet. The Internet is a shared resource and nothing exists to reserve or allocate bandwidth to a particular connection (other than within LANs where more control can be exerted). This attribute is commonly discussed under QoS (or Quality of Service) but is still unavailable at the WAN. Some current QoS protocol and architecture offerings are discussed in Chapter 13.

Communication Topology

Does the application communicate in a traditional client/server model or does it require communication to more than one node for a particular message? Do the parties involved in communication know of each other's existence?

Thus far we've discussed topologies in which two parties communicate, one being the client (the initiator of communication) and the other the server (the target). There are many other cases in which there does not exist a one-to-one relationship between the communicating entities. Consider for example the Dynamic Host Configuration Protocol. How does the client to be configured know to whom to send its configuration request message? The answer is that it doesn't and instead uses broadcast packets to reach every listening node. If a DHCP server is listening on the network, it responds directly to the requesting client and communication continues on a one-to-one basis.

Another example is multicast communication. The Service Location Protocol can operate in a mode in which User Agents (which represent applications that require a service) communicate with Service Agents (which represent the applications with services) in a multicast fashion. All nodes that have joined the multicast group can hear the requests and responses.

Therefore, when a User Agent sends a service request out and a Service Agent is listening on the network that provides the service, it will respond accordingly. Since the User Agent does not know where the Service Agents are or which one may provide the service, multicast communication provides the capability to reach a specific set of nodes that cooperate using SLP.

Multicast can be inefficient since all nodes must process a received message to know if it's useful to them, but it does offer an interesting paradigm to limit usage of bandwidth. Broadcast can provide similar functionality, but because all of the nodes have to process all the packets, the computational cost is increased.

Protocol Encoding

Is efficiency or simplicity the prime concern in the protocol? How important is it to observe the operation of the protocol by actually watching the dialog between client and server? Can a user simply communicate with the server through a telnet client?

SMTP and HTTP, along with other protocols we've discussed thus far, use text-based encoding. Other protocols, such as SNMP and SLP, use a less visible binary encoding. There are advantages and disadvantages to each solution to this problem. The capability to communicate with a server using a text-based protocol has its advantages. It's very easy to debug and one can begin to use the protocol without having to quickly develop the client side of the system. The disadvantage is that text-based protocols aren't as efficient as their binary counterparts. For example, the opcodes of SNMP (`GetRequest`, `SetRequest`) occupy a single octet. Within SMTP, the text commands can range from four characters to over ten. There are obvious savings there for binary encoding.

Security

Does the data that's passed through the protocol require some form of integrity checking to ensure each party knows who's at the other end of the link? Must the receiver know if the data was tampered with en route from the sender? Does the data need to be encrypted to prevent other "sniffing" entities between the sender and receiver from eavesdropping on the communication?

Numerous technologies exist to support these requirements. Public key cryptography provides for both the capability of communicating entities to know to whom they are communicating as well as encryption of data to avoid eavesdropping. In this model, a party distributes a public key and keeps a private key. The private key is used to encrypt and sign the data that is to be transmitted. The public key is used only for decryption. Therefore, when a node receives an encrypted data block, the public key can be used to decrypt and check the signature. If the public key works, then it can be assured that the data was sent only by a sender with access to the private key.

Note that a signature in this case is unique to the data being sent.

This type of functionality is commonly provided by the Secure Sockets Layer (SSL). SSL was developed by Netscape for use in e-commerce applications in which private information was transferred between a client and commerce server. At a minimum, the protocol requires a server certificate as part of the initial negotiation to prove to the client that it is the intended server (server authentication). Once both parties are convinced they are dealing with the intended parties, symmetric-key encryption is used to encrypt data transferred between the client and server for the remainder of the transaction. This provides for protection against tampering and eavesdropping.

SSL is provided as a Sockets API that mimics some of the standard BSD API calls. This makes use of the SSL much simpler because of its familiarity. Chapter 13 provides another look at SSL with a comparison to IPSec.

SOME FINAL DESIGN THOUGHTS

When designing a new application layer protocol, there are two basic methods to go about it. The first is to start from scratch. Although it's nice to begin without any design preconceptions, the second method is more popular. This method is to pick an existing protocol that most closely matches your design and then modify it to fit your special requirements. This is a very common method, evident by simply looking at the plethora of application layer protocols that exist. SMTP, HTTP, NNTP, and POP3 (all extremely popular and widely used protocols) have very similar architectures. It's probably not surprising that part of their success was starting with a successful base and then designing forward.

Three other very important points should be raised before we end our discussion of protocol design attributes. The first is simplicity. Anyone who has tried to solve a complex problem knows that the only way to accomplish it is by breaking the problem down into simpler problems that are more manageable. A simple protocol is easier to understand, maintain and extend. The next attribute is scalability. The Internet is an amazing example of a successful concept that grew beyond the wildest dreams of its developers. It's not surprising that part of this success is based upon the fact that the Internet protocols were so scalable that the Internet expanded from a handful of nodes to the millions of nodes that exist today. One can never tell how a protocol will be used, so therefore providing the ability to scale is important. The final attribute is extendibility. Since we can't predict the future, it's hard to know how protocols will be used once deployed. Therefore, the design must provide the capability to add new elements, either statically or dynamically, to extend for new unforeseen requirements.

SUMMARY

In this chapter, we investigated application layer protocols, their architectures, and issues that must be considered in their design. We reviewed a variety of popular application layer protocols in order to understand how they work as well as why they're important to us in the embedded domain. Finally, we investigated some of the primary considerations of protocol design as well as how a particular transport layer protocol is chosen.

4 Embedded SMTP Client

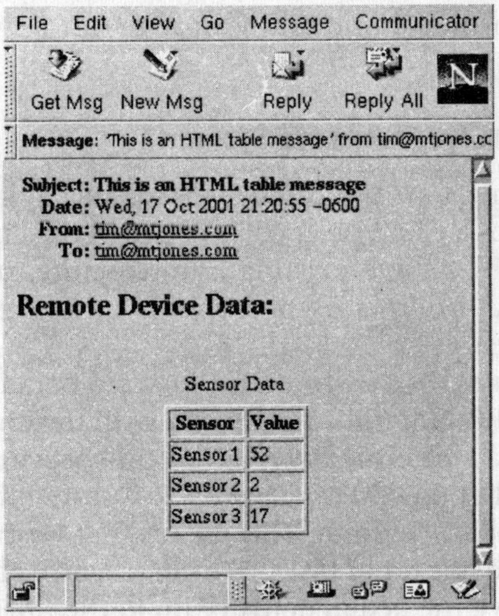

Now that we've covered the basics of networking including an introduction to application layer protocol design, we'll begin our detailed study of application layer protocols through the development of an SMTP client for embedded systems. Although the implementation is basic, it provides for delivery of e-mail through the SMTP client protocol using a very simple API.

INTRODUCTION

The Simple Mail Transfer Protocol is a text-based protocol that operates in the client/server topology. The client generates an e-mail that is represented by a mail header and body. The header defines addressing information and the body contains the actual payload to send to the recipient. The e-mail is transferred through what is known as an SMTP gateway that is commonly the client's mail server host. This gateway is the first hop of the mail prior to being transferred to the recipient. Since the recipient may not be available when the e-mail arrives, the mail is held at the recipient's mail server until it is collected. When a user connects to the mail server, the mail is collected through the user's e-mail client and it is then deleted from the mail server.

Although this is a very basic introduction to SMTP, all of the elements have been covered. In the following sections, we'll dig down into the details of the protocol and show how it can be used in the embedded environment.

Why Use an SMTP Client for Embedded Systems?

This is a good question and can be very easily explained. The primary reason that SMTP as a client protocol is useful in the embedded domain is that it is supported by a large existing infrastructure. It's also an interface for presentation that Internet users currently utilize and understand. In other words, it's there!

SMTP operates on the store-and-forward paradigm. When we send an e-mail, we rarely communicate directly with the end user's system, but instead through an intermediary. From our previous example, when we send our e-mail to the SMTP gateway, it is stored there and then migrated towards the end user system. This means that we can send our e-mail and then move on to our other tasks. We don't worry about when it will be delivered. We leave the actual delivery up to the SMTP infrastructure.

From an embedded systems perspective, especially those that operate over wireless modems that aren't always connected, this is an intriguing possibility. We have the ability to connect to the Internet via our wireless device, send our data through the e-mail transport, and then disconnect. The value here is cost savings since we connect only long enough to emit our data and then revert to the disconnected mode of operation.

The transient operation of wireless modems is not only a problem of cost but also of network availability. Wireless networks that operate using CDPD are predominantly available in metropolitan areas, but are rarely available in rural areas.

Let's take the example of a truck delivering goods across the U.S. For the majority of the time, this truck will not have access to the wireless network. When it is available, the embedded computer in the truck must take advantage of the opportunity and relay any information that is needed. Every 30 minutes, our truck could try to connect with the wireless network. If a connection is not possible, our device simply goes back to its dormant state and awaits the next connection period. If a connection is available, the device quickly formats the available data to transmit (such as position and possibly the temperature of goods being carried) and then emits this to the SMTP gateway. The truck can then disconnect and allow the store-and-forward paradigm to take care of the actual delivery.

Note that the peer-to-peer side of this argument is also interesting. The intended user of the data may be on a dial-up connection (again, a cost savings). Since the user isn't always online, trying to communicate directly with this user is not always possible. The store-and-forward method again solves this by providing the infrastructure to manage and buffer the data until the recipient can use it.

Other Uses

Using the Multipurpose Internet Mail Extensions (MIME), rich multimedia content can be delivered. E-mail can be used to transport audio data, video data or still images. Since each of these elements is represented as binary data; they simply become attachments within the e-mail message.

However, since SMTP is a text-based protocol, they must first be translated into text. This is typically performed through Base64 encoding that takes binary data and converts it into 7-bit printable-text (suitable for transmission through SMTP).

Consider a remote camera that monitors a site that has no human security. With this camera, we can take still images and then look for differences between images in a set. If a significant difference is found between two images (indicating that movement is detected in the field of view) then we begin to collect a series of images. These images are then buffered, and after our wireless modem has connected to the Internet, we emit them through an e-mail attachment.

Origin and Evolution

As we discussed in Chapter 1, e-mail was first created by Ray Tomlinson as a means to allow ARPANET developers to communicate over their network. Jon Postel, one of the great Internet pioneers, created SMTP and many other protocols. Jon's work defined the essential characteristics of good protocol design. His protocols were simple, scalable, and extendable. SMTP is a testament to this.

The SMTP protocol was introduced as RFC 821 in August of 1982. Extensions to SMTP, such as MIME, continue to this day.

PROTOCOL INTRODUCTION

SMTP has two basic players that communicate using the protocol. These are the Mail User Agent (MUA) and the Mail Transfer Agent (MTA). The MUA is the e-mail client. It is used to construct e-mails (per the SMTP and related RFCs) and send them to an MTA. The MTA is used to transfer the e-mail through the Internet to its destination. This could be to the final MTA or an intermediate MTA en route. See Figure 4.1 for a graphical view of the SMTP components.

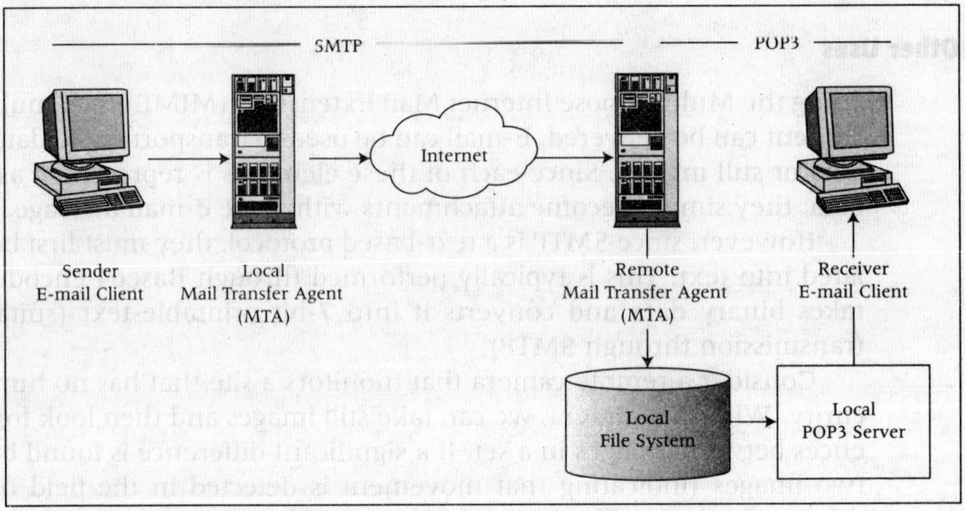

FIGURE 4.1 SMTP components and relationships.

The SMTP model of communication is based upon a full duplex stream socket in which text commands are sent from the client to the server and the server replies with responses that contain numeric status codes. The status codes determine the success or failure of a command. SMTP was designed as a lock-step protocol in which a command is issued and a response returned. Consider the following example:

```
RCPT TO:<user@remotehost.net>
250 OK
```

In this dialog, the client issues the RCPT TO command to the server with the e-mail address of the intended recipient. The text response of 250 indicates that the command was accepted and that the user named is a valid user on this host. If the user was not valid, the following dialog would be observed:

```
RCPT TO:<user@remotehost.net>
550 user@remotehost.net... User unknown
```

All SMTP commands and responses follow the same basic structure. One variation is the DATA command, which we'll discuss shortly.

E-mail from the Client Perspective

Let's now look at a real example of a dialog between an SMTP client and server. We'll first look at the entire dialog and then break down each step for detailed discussion. See Listing 4.1 for the complete example (server output is preceded by S: and client by C: in bold).

LISTING 4.1 SMTP dialog between a client and server.

```
S: 220 mtjones.com ESMTP Sendmail 9.8.3/9.9.7; Mon, 15 Oct 2001
   22:23:05
C: HELO mydomain.zz
S: 250 mtjones.com Hello IDENT:root@[192.168.2.151], pleased to meet
   you
C: MAIL FROM:<me@mydomain.zz>
S: 250 <me@mydomain.zz>... Sender ok
C: RCPT TO:<tim@mtjones.com>
S: 250 <tim@mtjones.com>... Recipient ok
C: DATA
S: 354 Enter mail, end with "." on a line by itself
C:
C: Content-type: text/html
C: Subject: Test email
C:
C: <HTML>
C: <BODY>
C: <CENTER>
C: <H1><FONT COLOR=blue>This is a test email</FONT></H1>
C: </CENTER>
C: </BODY>
C: </HTML>
C:
```

```
C: .
S: 250 WAA14066 Message accepted for delivery
C: QUIT
S: 221 mtjones.com closing connection
```

The dialog provided in Listing 4.1 results in an e-mail being sent to the specified recipient and is rendered in the e-mail client as shown by Figure 4.2.

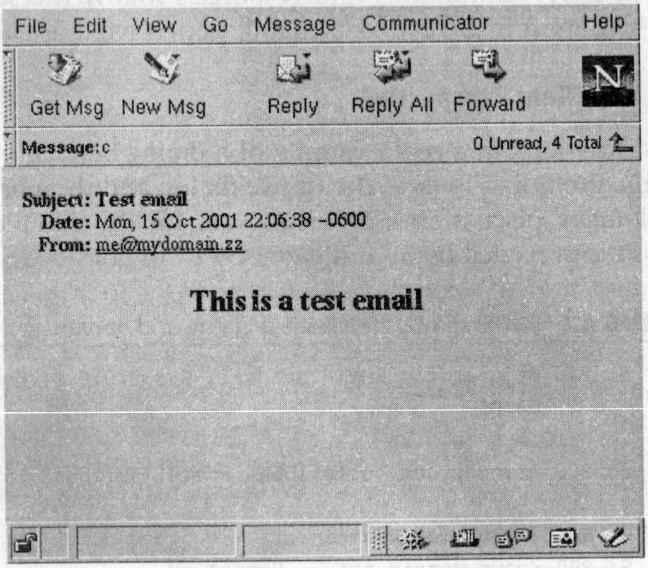

FIGURE 4.2 Resulting e-mail from dialog shown in Listing 4.1.

Let's now look at the dialog in detail to understand what's happening. In the first transaction of the dialog, we see a server introduction:

```
S: 220 mtjones.com ESMTP Sendmail 9.8.3/9.9.7; \\
   Mon, 15 Oct 2001 22:23:05
```

This salutation message introduces the SMTP server to the client. This line contains quite a bit of information such as our domain, the SMTP server software and version, and the local date and time. From the protocol design perspective, this is informative and can provide the client with some information to tailor its dialog depending upon the server in question. From another perspective, this information is dangerous because it allows others to see to whom they're speaking and to exploit any known security holes with the server protocol. For this reason, when possible, protocols should avoid emitting any information that can aid in the exploitation of the protocol.

Once we receive the salutation, we can move forward with our dialog. As in another type of communication, when people introduce themselves to us, we introduce ourselves back:

```
C: HELO mydomain.zz
S: 250 mtjones.com Hello IDENT:root@[192.168.2.151], \\
   pleased to meet you
```

The HELO command identifies the client (us) to the server. The server then responds with a numeric code (in this case it's a successful code) and provides a bit more information. Note in the IDENT section that it has resolved us to an IP address. Resolving in this way provides a bit more accountability of the e-mail transaction.

The next two transactions provide the sender and recipient of the e-mail. The first is the MAIL command that initiates the mail transaction:

```
C: MAIL FROM:<me@mydomain.zz>
S: 250 <me@mydomain.zz>... Sender ok
```

This command specifies from whom the e-mail is coming. Note that from the section on client-server introduction, you can't easily fool the server into thinking you're someone else. The 250 return code represents acceptance of a good command.

As a side-topic, check the "All Headers" option in your e-mail client for a particular e-mail.

The next transaction specifies to whom the e-mail should go:

```
C: RCPT TO:<tim@mtjones.com>
S: 250 <tim@mtjones.com>... Recipient ok
```

At this point, we could perform another RCPT TO command which would build up a distribution list for the message, rather than a single recipient.

After the sender and recipient are specified, the DATA command can be used to begin transfer of the mail data. The DATA command yields a 354 status code response from the server, and after this no other status is generated.

The server now awaits mail data with a final '.' on a line by itself as the end of mail data indication. Upon receiving this indicator, a status is provided indicating that the mail data was accepted:

```
C:
S: 250 WAA14066 Message accepted for delivery
C: QUIT
S: 221 mtjones.com closing connection
```

The server will now process the message and will append a time stamp to the message identifying when the message was received by the server. The client can then issue the QUIT command to end the TCP session with the server. The server responds with a successful status code and closes its side of the socket.

The client has now completed its side of the part of the e-mail process and may free any resources that are attached to the buffered e-mail at the client. As we'll see later, the client SMTP implementation uses no dynamic resources and simply uses the caller's buffer for transfer.

Before we end our discussion of the protocol commands, let's look at one final command that is interesting from a protocol design standpoint. The TURN command can be used in SMTP to reverse the roles of the client and server during a session. For example, when an MTA connects to another MTA to transfer a message, it typically performs the protocol as described above and then exits. The TURN command allows either MTA to switch their roles. In this way, during a single session, the MTAs can reverse roles and instead of a client transmitting a message, it becomes the server accepting messages. This isn't useful in our application, but it is interesting to study for the design of symmetrical protocols.

Related Protocols

While SMTP is the protocol that provides transport for e-mail messages through the Internet, other protocols are responsible for managing and buffering e-mail at the target system. The most popular is the Post Office Protocol, or POP. POP provides the means to collect messages from the mail server once received through SMTP and buffered for a valid user. POP is another text-based protocol that follows closely with SMTP. See Listing 4.2.

Note the similarities in this protocol. We see an initial salutation and then the synchronous command/response format as with SMTP. Instead of numeric error codes, the server simply responds with +OK for success and ERR for failure. The '.' comes back as the end-of-list indicator.

LISTING 4.2 POP3 dialog example.

```
S: +OK POP3 www.mtjones.com v9.18 server ready
C: user tim
S: +OK User name accepted, password please
C: pass XXX
S: +OK Mailbox open, 2 messages
C: list
S: +OK Mailbox scan listing follows
S: 1 480
S: 2 388
S: .
C: retr 1
S: +OK 480 octets
S: Return-Path: <me@mydomain.zz>
S: Received: from mydomain.zz (IDENT:root@[192.168.2.151])
S:        by mtjones.com (9.8.3/9.9.7) with SMTP id WAA14066
S:        for <tim@mtjones.com>; Mon, 15 Oct 2001 22:23:25 -0600
S: Date: Mon, 15 Oct 2001 22:23:25 -0600
S: From: me@mydomain.zz
S: Message-Id: <200110160423.WAA14066@mtjones.com>
S: Status:  O
S:
S:
S: Content-type: text/html
S: Subject: Test email
S:
S: <HTML>
S: <BODY>
S: <CENTER>
S: <H1><FONT COLOR=blue>This is a test email</FONT></H1>
S: </CENTER>
S: </BODY>
S: </HTML>
S: .
C: DELE 1
S: +OK Message deleted
```

Note that the message illustrated in the POP dialog is the same one sent from our prior example in Figure 4.2. IMAP (Internet Message Access Protocol) is similar to POP3 but solves some of its deficiencies. One solution is the capability to maintain the e-mail archive on the server instead of downloading all e-mails to the client. This allows users to switch among a variety of machines and still have access to their messages along with the archive.

Protocol Characteristics

SMTP is a very simple and easily defined protocol. The meat of the SMTP RFC is under 40 pages and can easily be read in less than an hour. The client implementation was originally written in about the same amount of time in a trial-and-error fashion. SMTP has scaled from the handful of participants in its early days to the millions of users that send e-mail each day. It is still one of the workhorse protocols of the Internet. SMTP has continued to evolve with extensions for MIME encoding that add the ability to transport rich multimedia content through SMTP. SMTP has covered the essential characteristics in a very concise way.

IMPLEMENTATION SUMMARY

The SMTP client implementation is extremely simple and shown in its entirety in Listing 4.4 (Listing 4.3 shows the basic SMTP structures). The first task, from `mailSend`, is to create a stream socket and try to connect to the mail server as defined in the `mailServer` variable.

In order to connect, we must first have the IP address of the server. The `mailServer` variable may contain a dotted-notation string IP address or a fully qualified domain name (FQDN), such as:

```
"192.168.1.1"          Dotted-notation IP Address
"mail.mine.com"        Fully Qualified Domain Name
```

We first assume that the string is a dotted-notation IP address and use the `inet_addr` function to convert the string to a 32-bit IP address. The `inet_addr` function will return a `-1` (or unsigned 0xffffffff) value to represent an error condition. The error condition essentially means that the string passed was not a valid string IP address. In this case, we assume that the address is a FQDN and use the `gethostbyname` function to translate the name into an IP address. This function communicates with the configured domain name server to resolve the address, the result of which is a 32-bit IP address. The construct described here is a useful pattern and allows resolution of domain names or IP addresses easily.

Once we have an IP address, we connect to the server using the `connect` call. We now have a socket connected between the mail server and us. All transactions over this socket, provided that we're connected to an SMTP server, will use the SMTP protocol.

Recall that SMTP is a command-response protocol in which a command is issued and the server responds with a numeric response code. Given this pattern, the dialog function was created to model the SMTP transactions. The dialog function takes three parameters: the socket, a command string, and a response code string. The command string is the command that we're issuing to the SMTP server and the response code string is the string-coded numeric string that we expect from the server for successful operation. In some cases, a command may not be issued and in others, a response is not expected. For example, our first dialog with the SMTP server is simply a salutation from the SMTP server once we connect. This string contains a numeric response `220` which tells our client that we're connected to a valid server. In other cases, we'll send a command but expect no response. When we're sending the body of our message, the SMTP server sends no response code. In fact, the SMTP server will not respond with anything until it receives the end-of-mail indication (a period on a line by itself). Therefore, the dialog function allows the three forms of communication.

Per Listing 4.1, our client issues the commands that are expected by the server and ends with the end-of-mail indicator and finally a `QUIT` command to close the connection

One other point to note is the use of the `do { } while(0);` construct within `sendMail`. At any point in our dialog, communication can break down which results in the closure of the connection and an error return to the user. This particular construct permits us to implement a basic `goto` structure without the ugly `goto` appearing in our code. The `break` statement causes execution to continue at the first statement outside of the loop. Since the `do-loop` provides at least one execution, the `while(0)` forces this loop to be executed only once. Whenever we encounter an error, we `break` which causes execution to leave the loop. If we finish the loop successfully, the same thing occurs. This could also be accomplished by a number of `if-then` constructs, but would result in highly indented (and ugly) code.

LISTING 4.3 Embedded SMTP client structures and prototypes.

```
/*
 * Embedded SMTP Client Header
 *
 * ./software/ch4/emsmtpc/smtpc.h
 *
```

```
 */

#define MAX_SUBJECT     80
#define MAX_SNDR 80
#define MAX_RCPT 80
#define MAX_CONTENT     80
#define MAX_SPECIAL     256

struct mailHeader {
  char subject[MAX_SUBJECT+1];
  char sender[MAX_SNDR+1];
  char recipient[MAX_RCPT+1];
  char specialHeaders[MAX_SPECIAL+1];
  char contentType[MAX_CONTENT+1];
  char *contents;
};

int sendMail(struct mailHeader *);
```

LISTING 4.4 Entire SMTP client code.

```
/*
 *  Embedded SMTP Client
 *
 *  ./software/ch4/emsmtpc/emsmtpc.c
 *
 */

#include <sys/types.h>
#include <sys/socket.h>
#include <netinet/in.h>
#include <netdb.h>
#include <string.h>
#include <stdio.h>
#include "emsmtpc.h"

char *hello_msg={"HELO my_embedded_board.com\n"};
char *mailServer={"mail.mtjones.com"};


/*
 *  strscan()
 *
 *  Extract the return code and check it against the passed
```

```
 *  reference code (str).
 *
 *  Returns 0 on success, -1 on error.
 *
 */

int strscan(char *line, char *str, int len)
{
  int i;
  for (i = 0 ; i < strlen(line) - len ; i++) {
    if (line[i] == str[0]) {
      if (!strncmp(line, str, 3)) return(0);
    }
  }
  return(-1);
}


/*
 *  dialog()
 *  Perform a dialog with the connected mail server.  If the
 *  command is present (non-NULL), send it through the socket
 *  to the server.  If the response is present, check it
 *  against the return code from the mail server.
 *
 *  Returns 0 on success, -1 on error.
 *
 */
int dialog(int sd, char *command, char *resp)
{
  int ret, len;
  char line[128];

  if (command != NULL) {
    len = strlen(command);
    if (write(sd, command, len) != len) return -1;
  }

  if (resp != NULL) {
    ret = read(sd, line, sizeof(line)-1); line[ret] = 0;
    if (strscan(line, resp, 3) == -1) return -1;
  }
```

```
  return 0;
}


/*
 *  sendMail()
 *
 *  Given a passed mailHeader structure, send the email to the
 *  mail server defined by the mailServer variable.
 *
 *  Returns 0 on success, -1 on error.
 *
 */

int sendMail(struct mailHeader *mail)
{
  int connfd, result, ret, goodMsg = 0;
  struct sockaddr_in servaddr;
  char mailRcpt[129];
  char line[256];

  connfd = socket(AF_INET, SOCK_STREAM, 0);

  bzero((void *)&servaddr, sizeof(servaddr));
  servaddr.sin_family = AF_INET;
  servaddr.sin_port = htons(25);

  servaddr.sin_addr.s_addr = inet_addr(mailServer);


  /* If the prior inet_addr results in a '-1' (or error), then
   * we assume that the gateway symbolic is not a dotted-
   * notation IP address.  It must therefore be fully-qualified
   * domain name and we use gethostbyname to resolve it.
   */
  if (servaddr.sin_addr.s_addr == 0xffffffff) {
    struct hostent *hptr =
          (struct hostent *)gethostbyname(mailServer);
    if (hptr == NULL) {
      /* Don't know what the mailServer represents... */
      return(-1);
    } else {
      struct in_addr **addrs;
      addrs = (struct in_addr **)hptr->h_addr_list;
```

```
      memcpy(&servaddr.sin_addr,
        *addrs, sizeof(struct in_addr));
      }
    }

    result = connect(
                connfd,
                (struct sockaddr *)&servaddr, sizeof(servaddr));

    do {

      /* Look for initial salutation */
      if ( dialog( connfd, NULL, "220" ) ) break;

      /* Send HELO and await response */
      if ( dialog( connfd, hello_msg, "250" ) ) break;

      /* Send MAIL FROM and await response */
      sprintf(line, "MAIL FROM:<%s>\n", mail->sender);
      if ( dialog( connfd, line, "250" ) ) break;

      /* Send RCPT TO and await response */
      sprintf(line, "RCPT TO:<%s>\n", mail->recipient);
      if ( dialog( connfd, line, "250" ) ) break;

      /* Send DATA and await response */
      if ( dialog( connfd, "DATA\n", "354" ) ) break;

      /* Send out the header first */
      sprintf(line, "From: %s\n", mail->sender);
      if ( dialog( connfd, line, NULL ) ) break;

      sprintf(line, "To: %s\n", mail->recipient);
      if ( dialog( connfd, line, NULL ) ) break;

      sprintf(line, "Subject: %s\n", mail->subject);
      if ( dialog( connfd, line, NULL ) ) break;

      if (mail->contentType[0] != 0) {
        sprintf(line, "Content-Type: %s\n", mail->contentType);
        if ( dialog( connfd, line, NULL ) ) break;
      }

      if (mail->specialHeaders[0] != 0) {
```

```
            if ( dialog( connfd, mail->specialHeaders, NULL ) ) break;
          }

          if ( dialog( connfd, mail->contents, NULL ) ) break;

          /* Send mail-end and await response */
          if ( dialog( connfd, "\n.\n", "250" ) ) break;

          if ( dialog( connfd, "QUIT\n", "221" ) ) break;

          goodMsg = 1;

        } while (0);

        close(connfd);

        return(goodMsg);
      }
```

SAMPLE TEST FUNCTIONS

Let's now look at a number of examples that use the `sendMail` function for a variety of different media formats.

Plain Text Mail

The first example is a vanilla text e-mail (see Listing 4.5). Note that the `mailHeader` structure (from Listing 4.3) does not actually include the body of the e-mail, but instead a pointer to it. This is to allow the user application to specify how much will be sent and avoid allocating a large buffer for each e-mail that is to be sent. This puts the requirement on the user application that once the `mailHeader` structure is defined, the pointer to the buffer containing the body is to be loaded. This process binds the header and body together for the entire e-mail.

We next define the header elements of our e-mail. The subject, sender, and recipient are loaded as normal strings (not CR terminated). The sender is what we identify, but may be a meaningless value. Note that the mail server automatically traces where the e-mail came from, so this information is stored with the e-mail when it's sent (look at all headers for more information). We next define the `content-type` that tells the mail client how to present the information. Since this is a plain text e-mail, we define our `content-type` as `plain/text`.

The next field is called `special-headers` and can contain include any string you want to hide in the e-mail. Simple prefix an "X-" to your header name and you can pass headers that will live with the e-mail, but are not commonly seen unless the client mailer intentionally views all header information. In the case of this e-mail, we demonstrate how to add a special header. Note that this particular element should have an `\n` appended to the end (the only e-mail header item that has this constraint).

Next, we add in our actual e-mail content. In this case, it's just a couple of simple sentences. Finally, we send the e-mail using the `sendMail` function.

LISTING 4.5 Example application sending plain text e-mail.

```
void text_example ( void )
{
  struct mailHeader mail;
  char   buffer[512];

  bzero((void *)&mail, sizeof(mail));
  bzero((void *)buffer, sizeof(buffer));
  mail.contents = buffer;

  strcpy(mail.subject, "This is text message");
  strcpy(mail.sender, "tim@mtjones.com");
  strcpy(mail.recipient, "root@mtjones.com");
  strcpy(mail.contentType, "text/plain");
  strcpy(mail.specialHeaders, "X-header: Boing\n");
  strcpy(mail.contents, "Here's a plain\ntext message\n");

  sendMail(&mail);
}
```

HTML Mail

The next example (see Listing 4.6) illustrates sending HTML data through the SMTP client. In the `mail.contents` is a very simple HTML document that will be interpreted and presented to the user. In order to inform the e-mail client that the data should be interpreted as HTML the `content-type` is set to `text/html`. Upon seeing this, the e-mail client will parse the message accordingly.

LISTING 4.6 Example application sending HTML e-mail.

```
void html_example ( void )
{
  struct mailHeader mail;
  char   buffer[512];

  bzero((void *)&mail, sizeof(mail));
  bzero((void *)buffer, sizeof(buffer));
  mail.contents = buffer;

  strcpy(mail.subject, "This is an HTML message");
  strcpy(mail.sender, "tim@mtjones.com");
  strcpy(mail.recipient, "mtj@mtjones.com");
  strcpy(mail.contentType, "text/html");
  strcpy(mail.contents,
          "<HTML>"
          "<BODY><H1><center>Example HTML Mail</center></H1>"
          "<BR><H2>This is sample text.</H2>"
          "</BODY></HTML>\n");

  sendMail(&mail);
}
```

HTML Mail with Dynamic Data

In our final example, see Listing 4.7, we'll demonstrate how to embed dynamic data within the HTML form. This is again very similar to our previous example in Listing 4.5 with the only difference being the block after our initial `mail.contents` copy. We assume that our dynamic data is contained with the sensor variables (these could be retrieved from an actual device) and then use the `sprintf` standard C library call to embed this integer data into the `mail.contents` string. This data is formatted into an HTML table with an appropriate caption.

One other item to note is the use of `<FONT>` within the text. Although statically performed here, the code could selectively color the sensor data based upon its fit within an acceptable range of values. In the example provided here, we color the first sample red. An example of what is generated by the `table_example` is provided in Figure 4.3.

LISTING 4.7 Example application sending HTML e-mail with dynamic data.

```
void table_example ( void )
{
```

```
struct mailHeader mail;
char   buffer[512];

bzero((void *)&mail, sizeof(mail));
bzero((void *)buffer, sizeof(buffer));
mail.contents = buffer;

strcpy(mail.subject, "This is an HTML table message");
strcpy(mail.sender, "tim@mtjones.com");
strcpy(mail.recipient, "tim@mtjones.com");
strcpy(mail.contentType, "text/html");
strcpy(mail.contents,
        "<HTML><BODY><H2>Remote Device Data:</H2><BR>"
        "<CENTER>"
        "<TABLE BORDER><CAPTION>Sensor Data</CAPTION>");

{
  int sensor1 = 52,
      sensor2 = 2,
      sensor3 = 17;

  sprintf(&mail.contents[strlen(mail.contents)],
        "<TR><TH>Sensor</TH><TH>Value</TH></TR>"
        "<TR><TD>Sensor 1</TD><TD><FONTcolor=red>%d</FONT>"
        "</TD></TR>"
        "<TR><TD>Sensor 2</TD><TD>%d</TD></TR>"
        "<TR><TD>Sensor 3</TD><TD>%d</TD></TR>"
        "</TABLE></CENTER>"
        "</BODY></HTML>",
        sensor1, sensor2, sensor3);
}

sendMail(&mail);
}
```

TESTING THE SMTP CLIENT

To verify the SMTP client, the `mailServer` variable must be set to a valid SMTP gateway. For test purposes, this can be set to whatever is set as your outgoing mail server on your e-mail client. Modify the sender and recipients in the example code (to avoid sending me unnecessary e-mail!). To verify that you have a valid SMTP gateway, you can easily check it by using a simple telnet session. For example:

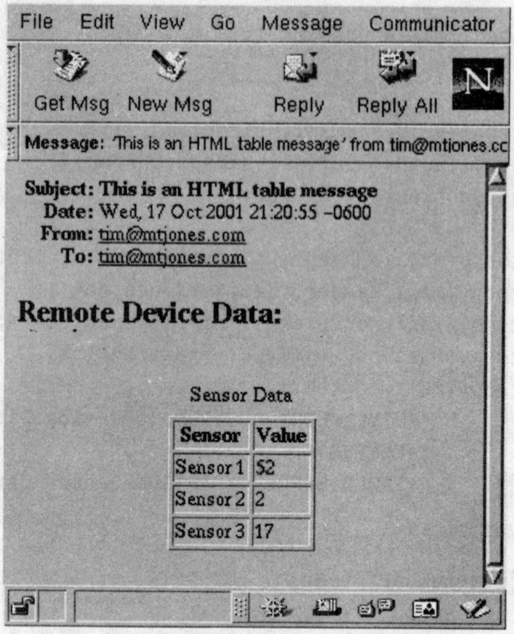

FIGURE 4.3 E-mail presentation from code in Listing 4.7.

```
telnet 192.168.1.1 25
```

This will create a TCP stream session to the specified host and port 25 (the SMTP reserved port number). You should immediately see the mail server salutation, which tells you that the server is taking connections:

```
220 192.168.1.1 ESMTP Sendmail 8.3.1/8.4.3; Mon, 15 Oct 2001 20:23:05
```

If this message is not seen, then a mail server does not exist on the host and you'll have to identify another server for your test.

ADDING EXTENSIONS

This chapter has presented a very simple SMTP client implementation, but this can be built upon to provide a number of other features. The capability to include attachments of MIME formats such as Base64 or Quoted-Printable is easily extended on this framework. With this, audio or video data could be transported. Software itself (as binary data) can also be transported through SMTP to provide software updates to devices in the field.

In the next chapter, we'll look at an SMTP server implementation and bring back our client to provide a command/response system over SMTP transport.

SUMMARY

In this chapter we looked at SMTP from the client perspective and how it can be used in embedded system designs. The actual protocol was detailed identifying the major commands that can be used. We looked at some of the related protocols (such as POP3) and viewed the scenario of an e-mail traveling between systems and ultimately being collected through POP3. Finally, we looked at a simple SMTP client implementation as well as ways that it can be used including presentation of HTML data.

RESOURCES

Postel, Jon, "Simple Mail Transfer Protocol", RFC 821, August 1982. http://www.landfield.org/rfcs/rfc821.html

5 Embedded SMTP Server

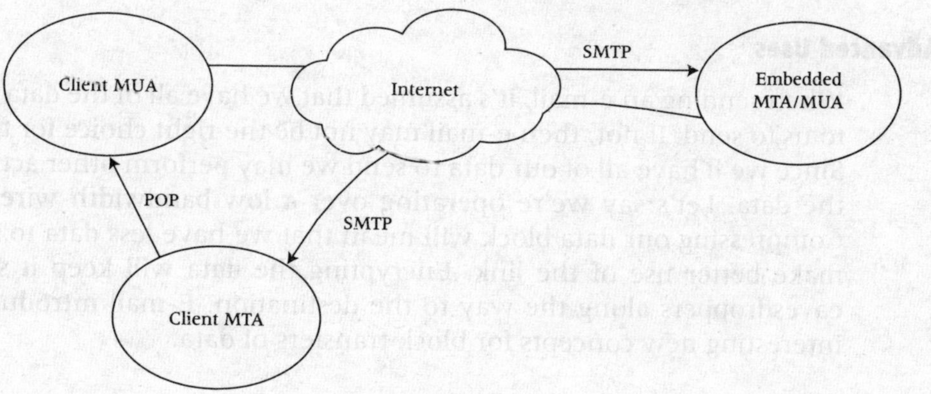

In this chapter, we'll continue our look into the Simple Mail Transfer Protocol. In Chapter 4 we investigated and implemented the client side of the protocol. Here, we'll implement the server side of SMTP and look at a variety of ways to make it useful in an embedded design.

INTRODUCTION

In Chapter 4, we discovered the uses of SMTP as a client protocol for transporting data (or commands) from a remote embedded system to a standard e-mail client. Now we'll look at the reverse scenario—the embedded system as the target of e-mail.

Why Use an SMTP Server for Embedded Systems?

It may not be immediately obvious why one would use SMTP as a means to communicate with an embedded system, but there are some interesting concepts from SMTP that are useful for a target embedded system. As a user interface, the e-mail client is a standard that is common on all workstations and desktop PCs. In other words, the interface is ubiquitous among computer users. Consider also that e-mail is now used not only to transport text messages between users on the Internet, but also to transport various types of binary data using MIME (Multipurpose Internet Mail Extensions) attachments. Therefore, e-mail can be used as a means to update firmware in remote devices or to even transport commands and responses through the Internet.

Advanced Uses

When sending an e-mail, it's assumed that we have all of the data available to us to send. If not, then e-mail may not be the right choice for transport. Since we'll have all of our data to send we may perform other activities on the data. Let's say we're operating over a low-bandwidth wireless link. Compressing our data block will mean that we have less data to send and make better use of the link. Encrypting the data will keep it safe from eavesdroppers along the way to the destination. E-mail introduces some interesting new concepts for block transfers of data.

Design Constraints

The use of SMTP in an embedded system creates some constraints that must be considered up front. Recall from Chapter 4 that when an e-mail is sent from a Mail User Agent (MUA or client), it is first transferred to an SMTP gateway that is known as a Mail Transfer Agent (MTA). While in some cases this is the final destination, in most cases it is the first hop through one or more additional MTAs to reach the final destination. When an e-mail is transferred between MTAs, the process is known as "relay." Although designs differ, if an MTA tries to communicate with the destination MTA and is unable to establish a connection, it will wait some amount of time and then try again. After some number of tries, the MTA will give up and notify the sender that the e-mail could not be sent to its destination.

From a communications perspective, this means that the device must be reachable when an e-mail is sent. Since the e-mailing activity is primarily asynchronous, we don't know when an e-mail will arrive; the recipient system must then be available all of the time. The device could be available on a scheduled basis (for example, between 8:00 P.M. and 10:00 P.M. every day), and in some designs this is a convenient design alternative. However, for others, availability is key.

Another approach is availability notification in which the device notifies a central server when it has connected and then synchronizes with external systems for communication. This can be useful for a variety of protocols, but SMTP is still best utilized with a dedicated connection since mail clients expect the server to be available when an e-mail is sent.

In summary, the various types of remote system availability include:

- Dedicated connection
- Scheduled availability
- Availability notification

PROTOCOL OVERVIEW

The Simple Mail Transfer Protocol is a very simple client/server protocol that allows a client to connect and send e-mail messages to or through a server. The client initiates communication and the server processes the received message. In this chapter, we'll be the e-mail processor. The implementation provided here will act as the target for SMTP communication and provide the ability to generate handlers (command processors) for e-mails that have a particular subject. In this implementation, the action to perform will be present in the subject line of the e-mail. Our parser will identify the subject and use this in subsequent code to perform a particular action.

Since we covered the details of the SMTP protocol in Chapter 4, refer to that chapter if a refresher is needed. From here forward, we'll look at the server side of SMTP and how it can be applied to embedded systems.

SERVER-SIDE SMTP DETAILS

In this section, we'll dig a little deeper into the SMTP commands with a focus on server-side details.

SMTP is provided by a simple text-based protocol in which commands are received at the server and a response generated back to the client. A command is a character string that is terminated by a `CR/LF` sequence. Some commands have no arguments in which case the command format will be `<CMD><CRLF>`. Commands with arguments commonly have a space between the command and each argument, such as `<CMD> <SP> <ARG>`. Other commands have slightly different formats, but have the same basic structure.

E-mail Structure

From the perspective of the server, an e-mail message is composed of a header, body, and an envelope (see Listing 5.1). The envelope is used by the MTA for delivery of the e-mail to its recipient. The envelope is defined using the SMTP commands `MAIL FROM` and `RCPT TO`. Note that in our examples, these are the only two commands used outside of salutation (`HELO`) and e-mail header and body. The `MAIL FROM` command is the important command for the MTA since it specifies where the e-mail is going. The `RCPT TO` command specifies from whom the e-mail is coming, but since this can be spoofed, the MTA does its own fact finding of this information.

The header of the e-mail is used by the MUA. From our example, `Subject` is the only header specified. Others include `Date`, `Message-Id`, `Reply-To` and others. Recall from Chapter 4 that user-defined headers are possible through the `X-` header mechanism. Custom headers should be defined using this mechanism. Note that headers are all lines after the `DATA` command until a blank line is found.

The body of the message is the actual contents of the e-mail being sent. This data is defined as the data after the `DATA` command and after a single blank line (following the headers).

In Listing 5.1 we see an example of the envelope/header/body structure of a sample e-mail. The lines prefixed with "ENV" represent the envelope of the e-mail that is used by the MTA. These are not commonly seen in an e-mail, as they are part of the SMTP dialog between an MUA and MTA. Lines prefixed with "HDR" represent the e-mail header and "BDY" represents the e-mail body.

LISTING 5.1 E-mail message structure.

```
ENV: MAIL FROM:<bong@mtjones.com>
ENV: RCPT TO:<bing@mtjones.com>
HDR: Sender: bong@mtjones.com
HDR: Message-ID: <3BD78F08.4B234473@mtjones.com>
HDR: Date: Wed, 24 Oct 2001 22:03:20 -0600
HDR: From: mtj <mtj@mtjones.com>
HDR: X-Mailer: Mozilla 4.61 [en] (X11; U; Linux 2.2.12-20 i686)
HDR: X-Accept-Language: en
HDR: MIME-Version: 1.0
HDR: To: bing@mtjones.com
HDR: Subject: UPDATE
BDY: Content-Type: multipart/mixed;
BDY:  boundary="------------92DE3BDD3EF72C21DB047FAE"
BDY:
```

```
BDY: This is a multi-part message in MIME format.
BDY: --------------92DE3BDD3EF72C21DB047FAE
BDY: Content-Type: text/plain; charset=us-ascii
BDY: Content-Transfer-Encoding: 7bit
BDY:
BDY: This is a test email.
BDY: --------------92DE3BDD3EF72C21DB047FAE
BDY: Content-Type: application/octet-stream;
BDY:  name="test.bin"
BDY: Content-Transfer-Encoding: base64
BDY: Content-Disposition: attachment;
BDY:  filename="test.bin"
BDY:
BDY: AAECAwQFBgc=
BDY: --------------92DE3BDD3EF72C21DB047FAE--
BDY:
BDY:
```

Note that all e-mails are constructed with 7-bit characters (high-bit is always zero). This means that SMTP cannot natively support binary data directly. In order to support binary data, a conversion into 7-bit characters must be performed. MIME provides the capability to perform these conversions.

WORKING WITH ATTACHMENTS

An attachment in an e-mail is nothing more than additional text that an MUA can parse and understand. The first clue that an attachment is present from the MUA is first `content-type` found. This will be of type `multipart/mixed`, which specifies that the e-mail is made up of a number of distinct elements of differing types. Along with this type is the boundary definition. The boundary is a string that is used to distinctly define the boundaries of the multiple parts of the e-mail. Consider the following in Listing 5.2:

LISTING 5.2 A raw e-mail showing attachments.

```
Sender: bong@mtjones.com
Message-ID: <3BD78F08.4B234473@mtjones.com>
Date: Wed, 24 Oct 2001 22:03:20 -0600
From: mtj <mtj@mtjones.com>
X-Mailer: Mozilla 4.61 [en] (X11; U; Linux 2.2.12-20 i686)
```

```
X-Accept-Language: en
MIME-Version: 1.0
To: bing@mtjones.com
Subject: UPDATE
Content-Type: multipart/mixed;
 boundary="------------92DE3BDD3EF72C21DB047FAE"

This is a multi-part message in MIME format.
--------------92DE3BDD3EF72C21DB047FAE
Content-Type: text/plain; charset=us-ascii
Content-Transfer-Encoding: 7bit

This is a test email.
--------------92DE3BDD3EF72C21DB047FAE
Content-Type: application/octet-stream;
 name="test.bin"
Content-Transfer-Encoding: base64
Content-Disposition: attachment;
 filename="test.bin"

AAECAwQFBgc=
--------------92DE3BDD3EF72C21DB047FAE--
```

The boundary delimiter is defined immediately after our `multipart` definition as a string. The boundary delimiter then appears in the e-mail to notify the MUA that a new section is to begin. This can include a new `content-type` and change of encoding. Note that in the first boundary is a `text/plain` section that simply contains some text to be sent with an attachment. A new-line (`CR/LF`) appears after the content information indicating that a user portion is provided. This is the simple text `string "This is a test e-mail."`

Another boundary delimiter is then provided of a different content section. This is our binary data attachment. Our original e-mail contained a simple text message and a binary file attached through the mail client. Our e-mail client encoded our binary attachment using Base64 encoding method and defined this in the header of this section (through the `Content-Transfer-Encoding` type). The `Content-Type` was defined as `application/octet-stream` since it was binary data that was unassociated with any particular application (as would be the case if our binary attachment was a JPG image or WAV audio file). This is also called "uninterpreted" data and an MUA would simply write it to a file. Our attachment is given a name and a file name in the section, which would be used by an MUA to associate a file name with the decoded attachment. Finally, after another blank line (to identify the beginning of the actual data) we see our binary data encoded as Base64 text (`AAECAwQFBgc=`). We'll look at this string in more detail including decoding in the next section.

Finally, another boundary delimiter is provided as the epilogue and is composed entirely of the end-of-e-mail indicator ('.' on a line by itself).

It should be clear from the example that this very simple delimiter method (for `multipart/mixed`) allows any number of attachments of varying `content-types`. Numerous other `content-types` exist. A sample of these can be seen in Table 5.1.

TABLE 5.1 MIME Content-Types.

Content-Type	Subtype	Use
multipart	mixed	Multiple E-mail bodies
text	plain	Plain text E-mail
application	octet	Application-specific Binary data
image	jpg	JPEG image
image	gif	Compuserve GIF image

In some cases, the MUA can determine the purpose of a file based upon the filename chosen within the e-mail body section. For example, if a section is of type `application/octet-stream` and the filename being transferred is `abc.class` then the MUA could process the file using an available JVM (Java Virtual Machine).

Base64 Decoding

Remember that e-mail can support only 7-bit data and therefore any data that cannot be represented in a 7-bit character must use another representation for SMTP transport. SMTP predominantly uses the Base64 encoding scheme to represent binary data. Base64 is an easy encoding/decoding method, but has the disadvantage of making the attachment 33% larger than the original binary version. This is because we take three octets and turn them into four (three 8-bit octets become four 6-bit octets).

Let's take our previous example and decode it from Base64 into simple binary text. Our Base64 encoded string was:

```
AAECAwQFBgc=
```

The '=' character at the end of the line is a pad and indicates that we've reached the end of the attachment data. Since we must have 24 bits for decoding (which become 32 bits in the original binary stream), the '=' indicates that no more data is to follow. When we reach this point, our decoding is complete.

We first convert this (for our decoding purposes) to hex values, based upon Figure 5.1.

This results in the working octet string:

```
0x00 0x00 0x04 0x02 0x00 0x30 0x10 0x05 0x01 0x20 0x1c
```

In Base64, each of the values in our working octet string is represented by a 6-bit quantity. If we now convert these values into 6-bit binary values, the following binary stream results:

0x00	A	0x10	Q	0x20	g	0x30	w	(pad)	=
0x01	B	0x11	R	0x21	h	0x31	x		
0x02	C	0x12	S	0x22	i	0x32	y		
0x03	D	0x13	T	0x23	j	0x33	z		
0x04	E	0x14	U	0x24	k	0x34	0		
0x05	F	0x15	V	0x25	l	0x35	1		
0x06	G	0x16	W	0x26	m	0x36	2		
0x07	H	0x17	X	0x27	n	0x37	3		
0x08	I	0x18	Y	0x28	o	0x38	4		
0x09	J	0x19	Z	0x29	p	0x39	5		
0x0a	K	0x1a	a	0x2a	q	0x3a	6		
0x0b	L	0x1b	b	0x2b	r	0x3b	7		
0x0c	M	0x1c	c	0x2c	s	0x3c	8		
0x0d	N	0x1d	d	0x2d	t	0x3d	9		
0x0e	O	0x1e	e	0x2e	u	0x3e	+		
0x0f	P	0x1f	f	0x2f	v	0x3f	/		

FIGURE 5.1 Base64 alphabet table.

```
000000 000000 000100 000010 000000 110000
010000 000101 000001 100000 011100
```

We now concatenate the 6-bit value stream together, and then parse 8-bit octets from the stream. This results in the following octet data:

```
00000000 00000001 00000010 00000011
00000100 00001010 00000110 00000111
```

Converting back to hex, we arrive at our original binary data:

```
00 01 02 03 04 05 06 07
```

As previously discussed, we've represented an eight octet binary stream as an 11 octet character string which, for larger attachments, can be wasteful of available bandwidth. Luckily, SMTP is an elastic protocol that will simply use whatever bandwidth is available without any ill effects. Base64 is a very simple encoding mechanism that provides us with the means to transport binary data through e-mail in a simple way.

Quoted-Printable Coding

The next most used coding scheme is called Quoted-Printable. This isn't implemented in the server (which will be presented later in this chapter), but the details are provided here for completeness.

Since Base64 is useful for predominantly binary data streams, what about data streams that utilize only small numbers of non-printable ASCII characters. Quoted-Printable is used for octet-streams that are primarily printable characters (only a small amount of non-printable binary data). For example, the binary string:

```
0x30 0x31 0x32 0x33 0x00 0x01 0x02 0x03
```

would be encoded in Quoted-Printable as:

```
0123=00=01=02=03
```

The '=' symbol informs the decoder that the two characters that follow represent a binary octet (hex-ASCII number). These two octets are collected from the stream and then turned into a single binary digit. Numerous other rules apply to the encoding and decoding, but this is the basic method used. As is probably visible from the example, this method is useful when the majority of data is already printable. Therefore, the MUA must determine which encoding method will result in the lesser transformation.

The encoding method is important because of the resulting size of the encoded files. A text file that's predominantly printable ASCII text will be smaller if encoded in Quoted-Printable than it would if encoded in Base64. Predominantly binary files are more efficiently encoded in Base64 than Quoted-Printable. Because the decision can be time consuming to determine which encoding method is best, mail clients commonly make this decision based upon the file extension (knowing generally which types of files have a particular binary/ASCII-printable mix).

CLOSING THE LOOP

The capability to send an embedded device an e-mail is useful in a number of domains, particularly for software updates. For the SMTP server to be useful, we need to be able to close the loop and generate a response e-mail for the received request. In this way, we can encode commands within our e-mails to the embedded device and allow the device to construct responses that are returned via SMTP. To do this, we bring back our SMTP client from Chapter 4 and integrate it into our server.

Note from Figure 5.2 that SMTP is involved in transferring e-mails between an MUA and MTA (as well as relay transfer between MTAs). But transfer of e-mail to an MUA occurs through the Post Office Protocol (see an example of this protocol in Chapter 4).

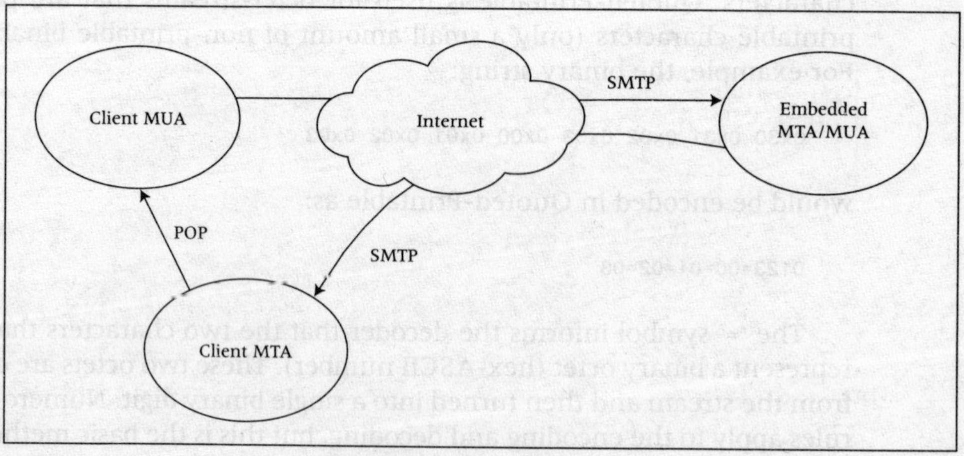

FIGURE 5.2 SMTP-based command/response system.

IMPLEMENTATION SUMMARY

The implementation of the SMTP server is very simple. A functional data flow of the SMTP server is shown in Figure 5.3.

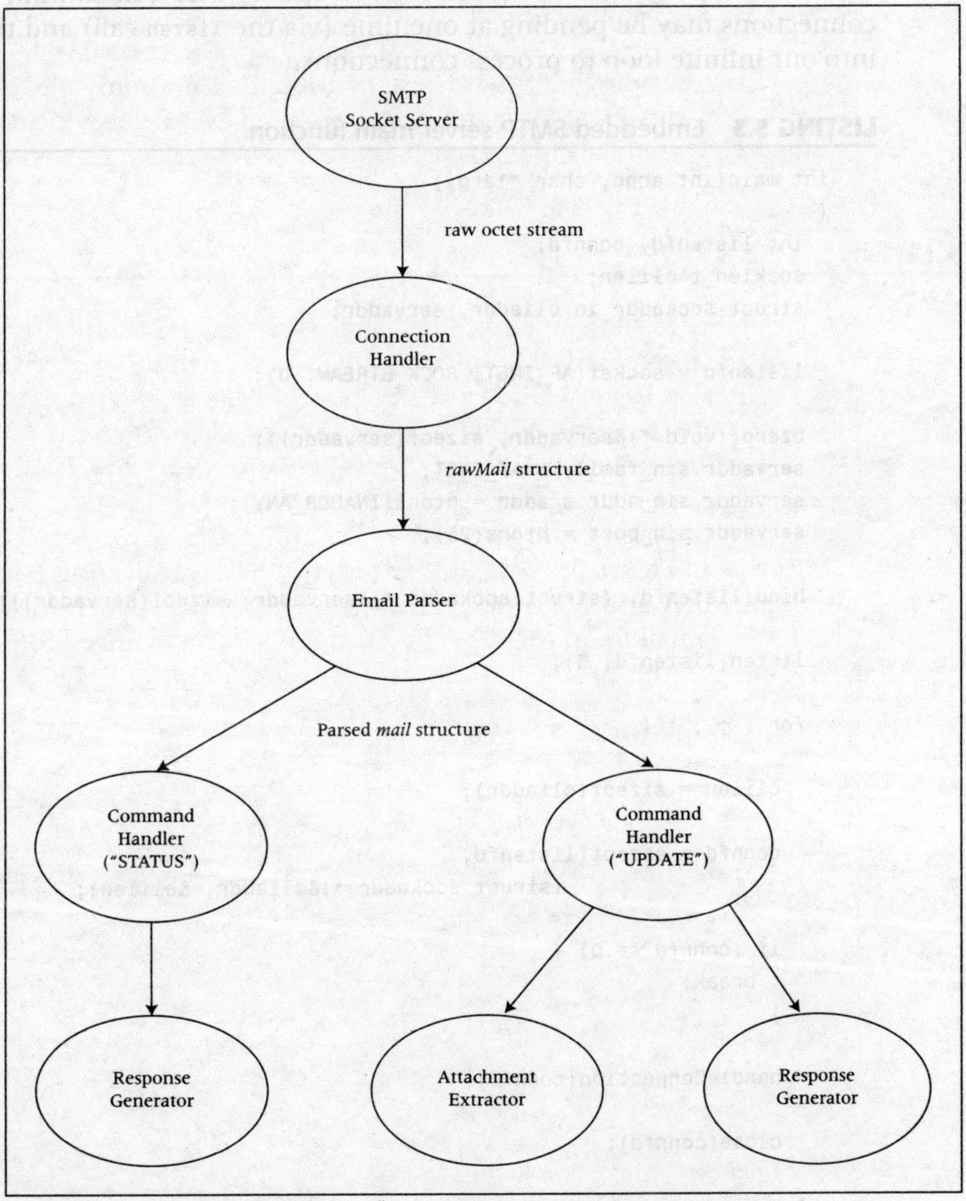

FIGURE 5.3 Functional data flow of the SMTP server implementation.

Main Function

Our main function is a simple TCP stream socket server that provides connectivity to at most one connection at a time (see Listing 5.3). At startup, we create the stream "listening" socket (server socket) and then bind it to the reserved port for SMTP (port 25). We specify that a maximum of five connections may be pending at one time (via the `listen` call) and then go into our infinite loop to process connections.

LISTING 5.3 Embedded SMTP server main function.

```
int main(int argc, char **argv)
{
  int listenfd, connfd;
  socklen_t clilen;
  struct sockaddr_in cliaddr, servaddr;

  listenfd = socket(AF_INET, SOCK_STREAM, 0);

  bzero((void *)&servaddr, sizeof(servaddr));
  servaddr.sin_family = AF_INET;
  servaddr.sin_addr.s_addr = htonl(INADDR_ANY);
  servaddr.sin_port = htons(25);

  bind(listenfd, (struct sockaddr *)&servaddr, sizeof(servaddr));

  listen(listenfd, 5);

  for ( ; ; ) {

    clilen = sizeof(cliaddr);

    connfd = accept(listenfd,
                    (struct sockaddr *)&cliaddr, &clilen);

    if (connfd <= 0) {
      break;
    }

    handleConnection(connfd);

    close(connfd);

  }
```

```
    close(listenfd);

}
```

Once a connection is accepted, the new client socket is passed to `handleConnection` to perform the activities of the SMTP server-side protocol. Once complete, the socket is closed and the next connection is awaited and processed.

This implementation is a single-threaded design handling one connection at a time. This does not mean that while a particular connection is being handled (via `handleConnection`) other connections will be refused. Based upon the Sockets API, simultaneous connections are simply queued, up to five through the `listen` call. This type of design is advantageous because it serializes the incoming mail. Since we handle one connection at a time, we don't need to worry about synchronization issues with e-mail handling.

Connection Handler

The connection handler, called from `main` with a connected socket, is the basic SMTP server protocol. We first initialize our mail structure that is the working copy of the e-mail that is to be received. This structure is passed on to later functions to perform whatever action was required. The format of the mail structure is shown in Listing 5.4.

LISTING 5.4 Working server e-mail structure.

```
#define MAX_MAIL        (8 * 1024)
#define MAX_ATTACHMENT  (7 * 1024)

typedef struct {
  unsigned char sender[80];
  unsigned char recipient[80];
  unsigned char subject[80];
  unsigned char filename[80];
  unsigned char rawMail[MAX_MAIL];
  unsigned char attachment[MAX_ATTACHMENT];
  int attachlen;
} parseMailType;
```

The `parseMailType` type contains a number of elements. The `rawMail` character array is the raw mail data that was received through the connection. It is called raw because it is the raw character list received through the connection without any parsing or other modification. All other fields are used in the parsing process. The fields `sender`, `recipient`, `subject`, `filename`, and `attachment` are all decoded from the `rawMail` array. Sizes for the character arrays may be updated based upon the actual use of the SMTP server. The size of `attachment` will always be smaller than the `rawMail` (since the decoding process will turn four octets of Base64 encoded text into three). If an e-mail arrives that exceeds the thresholds, an error will simply be returned and the e-mail will be ignored.

The connection handler is shown in Listing 5.5.

LISTING 5.5 SMTP protocol connection handler.

```
const char *salutation={"220 Embedded Mail Transport "
                         "(mtj@mtjones.com)\n"};
const char *conclose={"221 EMT closing connection.\n"};
const char *goahead={"250 OK\n"};
const char *gimmesome={"354 Gimme!\n"};
const char *closeit=
               {"221 Service closing transmission channel.\n"};

void handleConnection(int fd)
{
  int bufIdx = 0;
  int state = 0, len, i, stop=0;
  char buffer[81];

  memset((void *)&mail, 0, sizeof(mail));

  /* Indicate ready to go... */
  len = write(fd, salutation, strlen(salutation));

  /* Fix the nmap problem. */
  if (len <= 0) {
    return;
  }

  /* Wail for salutation response... */
  len = read(fd, buffer, 255);  buffer[len] = 0;

  if ((strncmp(buffer, "HELO", 4)) &&
      (strncmp(buffer, "EHLO", 4))) {
    closeConnection(fd);
```

```
    return;
  }

  write(fd, goahead, strlen(goahead));

  /* Wait for Mail From: */
  len = read(fd, buffer, 255);  buffer[len] = 0;
  if (strncmp(buffer, "MAIL FROM", 9))
    { closeConnection(fd); return; }
  grabAddress(buffer, mail.sender, 256);
  if (mail.sender[0] == 0)  { closeConnection(fd); return; }
  write(fd, goahead, strlen(goahead));

  /* Wait for Rcpt To: */
  len = read(fd, buffer, 255);  buffer[len] = 0;
  if (strncmp(buffer, "RCPT TO", 7))
    { closeConnection(fd); return; }
  grabAddress(buffer, mail.recipient, 256);
  if (mail.recipient[0] == 0)  { closeConnection(fd); return; }
  write(fd, goahead, strlen(goahead));

  /* Wait for DATA */
  len = read(fd, buffer, 255);  buffer[len] = 0;
  if (strncmp(buffer, "DATA", 4)) { closeConnection(fd); return; }
  write(fd, gimmesome, strlen(gimmesome));

  /* Loop to collect all of the email body */
  bufIdx = state = stop = 0;
  while (!stop) {

    if (bufIdx > MAX_MAIL - 80) { closeConnection(fd); return; }

    len = read(fd, &mail.rawMail[bufIdx], (MAX_MAIL-bufIdx));

    if ((len <= 0) || (bufIdx+len > MAX_MAIL)) {
      closeConnection(fd); return;
    }

    /* Search for the end in the current buffer */
    for (i = bufIdx ; i < bufIdx+len ; i++) {

      if      ((state == 0) && (mail.rawMail[i] == 0x0d)) state=1;
      else if ((state == 1) && (mail.rawMail[i] == 0x0a)) state=2;
      else if ((state == 2) && (mail.rawMail[i] == 0x0d)) state=1;
```

```
      else if ((state == 2) && (mail.rawMail[i] == '.'))  state=3;
      else if ((state == 3) && (mail.rawMail[i] == 0x0d)) state=4;
      else if ((state == 4) && (mail.rawMail[i] == 0x0a)) {
        stop = 1; break;
      }
      else state = 0;
    }

    bufIdx += len;

  }

  write(fd, goahead, strlen(goahead));

  state = 0;
  while (state++ < 10) {

    // Wait for QUIT
    len = read(fd, buffer, 80);  buffer[len] = 0;

    if (strncmp(buffer, "QUIT", 4)) {
      closeConnection(fd); return;
    } else break;

  }

  /* We now have an email in the mail structure, try now to parse
   * it.
   */
  parseMail(&mail, bufIdx);

  write(fd, closeit, strlen(closeit));

  return;
}
```

The connection handler provides the basic SMTP server implementation. We first emit the salutation (which notifies the client that it has reached a valid SMTP server and it's ready to receive the message). Next, we await the salutation response from the client. The server then proceeds through the next protocol elements, establishing from whom the e-mail is coming (via the `MAIL FROM` command) and to whom the e-mail is going (via the `RCPT TO` command). The `DATA` command is then awaited which indicates that we're going to receive the body of the e-mail. Receiving the body is the simplest part of the process. We simply buffer all characters received until we find a '.' on a line by itself. For performance, we read as much as is possible from the socket (up to the maximum available in the raw buffer) and then search that portion of the buffer for the lone '.'). The very simple state machine within the loop provides for this functionality. Once the end-of-e-mail indicator is found, we acknowledge receipt of the e-mail and then await the `QUIT` command from the client.

At this point in the server, we have our e-mail contained within the `rawMail` structure of `mail` as well as the `sender` and `recipient` fields parsed from the e-mail envelope. We now pass the `mail` structure (and the length of the `rawMail` portion, identified by `bufIdx`) to `parseMail` to perform further parsing and decoding.

Mail Parser

The purpose of the mail parser is to search for the subject string within the e-mail (from the header of the `e-mail contents`). The subject is interpreted as the command (or purpose) of the e-mail. Once the subject is found, the parser becomes a command decoder and performs an activity based upon the command found. See Listing 5.6 for the `parseMail` function.

LISTING 5.6 SMTP server e-mail parser.

```
int parseMail(parseMailType *mail, int len)
{
  int i = 0, index;

  int extractAttachment ( parseMailType *, int , int );

  /* First, grab the subject which is the location for the file */
  for (i = 0 ; i < len ; i++) {
    if (mail->rawMail[i] == 'S') {
      if (!strncmp(&mail->rawMail[i], "Subject:", 8)) {
        i+= 9;
        index = 0;
        while ((mail->rawMail[i] != 0x0d) &&
                (mail->rawMail[i] != 0x0a)) {
          mail->subject[index++] = mail->rawMail[i++];
        }
        mail->subject[index] = 0;
        break;
      }
```

```
      }
    }

    if (i == len) {
      return(-1);
    }

    /* This is our parser.  We look at the subject of the received
     * email and then determine how to deal with the email and its
     * contents.
     */
    if (!strncmp(mail->subject, "STATUS", 6)) {

      emitStatusResponse(mail);

    } else if (!strncmp(mail->subject, "UPDATE", 6)) {

      /* Extract the attachment from the email */
      extractAttachment(mail, i, len);

      /* At this point, the mail structure will have the attachment
       * stored in the attachment array.  The attachlen will contain
       * the length of the attachment, or -1 if an error occured.
       */

      emitUpdateResponse(mail);

    } else {
      /* Don't understand the command, silently ignore... */
    }

    return 0;
  }
```

Searching for the subject in the e-mail is a simple process of finding the string `Subject:` within the body of the e-mail. In order to optimize the search, we'll look for the character 'S,' and once we find this, we do a full compare for the `Subject:` string. The string following the subject is then copied to the `subject` field of our mail structure, excluding the trailing carriage return and line feed. If the subject is not found, we return a `-1` to indicate an error was encountered during the parse.

Now that we have the `subject` filled, we can review the commands that are available by the SMTP server. In our case, we support two different commands: STATUS and UPDATE.

STATUS is a simple command that requests status information from the device hosting the embedded SMTP server. This is provided by the function `emitStatusResponse` that can be found in Listing 5.7.

LISTING 5.7 Simple function to emit a status response.

```
int emitStatusResponse( parseMailType *mail )
{
  struct mailHeader response;
  char   buffer[512];

  memset(&response, 0, sizeof(struct mailHeader));

  /* Make the sender the new recipient */
  strcpy(response.recipient, mail->sender);

  /* Acknowledge receipt of the message */
  strcpy(response.subject, "Device Status");

  strcpy(response.contentType, "text/plain");

  response.contents = buffer;
  memset(response.contents, 0, sizeof(buffer));

  sprintf(response.contents,
          "Received status request from %s.\n\n", mail->sender);

  sendMail(&response);

  return(0);
}
```

This function should be reminiscent of our test functions from the SMTP test client. We grab the sender of the parsed e-mail and use it as the recipient of our e-mail to send. We give the new e-mail a subject and a content-type (simple `text/plain`) and then give a short string as the contents for test purposes. As we learned in Chapter 4, these functions can use HTML tags to provide a richer presentation of the status data. Finally, the mail is sent using the `sendMail` function.

The UPDATE command is a bit more complex because we're using it to receive a binary attachment in Base64 format. One application of this is to receive a software update that would be written into flash memory. From Listing 5.6, we see that the next step for the UPDATE command is to extract the attachment from the mail, which is not surprisingly called extractAttachment (see Listing 5.8).

LISTING 5.8 Function to extract a Base64-encoded attachment.

```
int extractAttachment ( parseMailType *mail, int i, int len )
{
  int  index, status;

  // Next, grab the filename
  for ( ; i < len ; i++) {
    if (mail->rawMail[i] == 'f') {
      if (!strncmp(&mail->rawMail[i], "filename=", 9)) {
        i+= 10;
        index = 0;
        while ((mail->rawMail[i] != 0x0d) &&
               (mail->rawMail[i] != 0x0a)) {
          if (mail->rawMail[i] == '"') i++;
          else mail->filename[index++] = mail->rawMail[i++];
        }
        mail->filename[index] = 0;
        break;
      }
    }
  }

  if (i == len) {
    printf("Couldn't find the filename...\n");
    return(-1);
  } else {
    printf("The filename was [%s]\n", mail->filename);
  }

  /* Finally, find the start of the Base64 encoded data and
   * decode...
   */
  for ( ; i < len ; i++) {
    /* We're looking for a CR/LF on a blank line after the
     * filename specification (since this is in the attachment
     * boundary).
```

```
    */
    if ((mail->rawMail[i] == 0x0d) &&
        (mail->rawMail[i+1] == 0x0a) &&
        (mail->rawMail[i+2] == 0x0d) &&
        (mail->rawMail[i+3] == 0x0a)) {
      i+=4;
      break;
    }
  }

  if (i == len) {
    printf("Couldn't find the Base64 MIME section...\n");
    return(-1);
  }

  /* At this point, i is the index to the start of the Base64
   * encoded section, start the decoding process...
   */
  mail->attachlen =
    b64decode(&mail->rawMail[i], mail->attachment);

  return(mail->attachlen ? 0 : -1);
}
```

The first task of extracting our attachment is searching for the string `filename=` which also places us in the content section where our encoded data can be found. This search, as before, looks for the first character and then performs a string compare when the character is found. Once found, we copy the `filename` into the `filename` field of our mail structure. If we were operating on an embedded system that provided a file system, we could use this to create the binary file (as is commonly done on standard MUAs). If the `filename` is not found, we return an error indication up the call list.

After the `filename` string within the attachment content section, we know (from Listing 5.2) that a blank line then separates us from the Base64-encoded data. We skip the next blank line and we will now be sitting on the first character of our encoded data within the `attachment` section. A call to `b64decode` then decodes the attachment found at our current position in `rawMail` into the `attachment` section of our mail structure. Since we've discussed the decoding of Base64 attachments in detail, the code for this can be reviewed on the CD-ROM. The `attachment` and `attachlen` fields within the mail structure can then be used by the application to process the decoded binary attachment.

The command handler function (from Listing 5.6) then emits a response to the sender of the e-mail through the emitUpdateResponse function (see Listing 5.9).

LISTING 5.9 Function to emit an update response for a received attachment.

```
int emitUpdateResponse( parseMailType  *mail )
{
  struct mailHeader response;
  char   buffer[512];

  memset(&response, 0, sizeof(struct mailHeader));

  /* Make the sender the new recipient */
  strcpy(response.recipient, mail->sender);

  /* Acknowledge receipt of the message */
  strcpy(response.subject, "Received Attachment");

  strcpy(response.contentType, "text/plain");

  response.contents = buffer;

  if (mail->attachlen) {
    sprintf(response.contents,
              "Received email attachment from %s.\n\n",
             mail->sender );
    sprintf(&response.contents[strlen(response.contents)],
              "File was %s of size %d\n", mail->filename,
               mail->attachlen);
  } else {
    sprintf(response.contents,
            "Error- Received no email attachment from %s.\n\n",
            mail->sender );
  }

  sendMail(&response);

  return(0);
}
```

This function is similar to Listing 5.7, except that a bit more data is included in the response. For example, if an error occurred in attachment processing or decoding, an e-mail with an error status is returned. Otherwise, we return a status e-mail that includes the name of the file received and its decoded length (actual binary length).

That's the conclusion of the SMTP server implementation. As we found with the SMTP client, the code to implement these protocols is both minimal and easy to understand.

TESTING THE SMTP SERVER

To test the SMTP server, it must first be situated on a target device. The easiest solution here is to run the baseline Linux version either on a Linux desktop or in a Cygwin shell on a Windows desktop.

Prior to execution, the e-mail client must be configured. The e-mail client must have the SMTP gateway (or outgoing mail server) set as the IP address or hostname of the device on which the SMTP server is running. Next, create a simple e-mail with the subject "STATUS" in the subject line addressed to any user (since all e-mail goes to the gateway and our server ignores this field). The SMTP server should respond with a device status e-mail back to the sender (given that the SMTP client gateway running on the device has also been updated, per Chapter 4).

EXTENDING THE SERVER

The SMTP server can be updated in a variety of ways. The most useful is support for your target-specific commands and e-mail responses. The `handler.c` file can be updated to support different commands via the `if-then` chain of string compares. Simply add a new check for your command name and perform whatever action is necessary (such as immediately sending a response or decoding an attachment).

An interesting modification to the SMTP server/client is an XML command handler. The Extensible Markup Language provides an easy way to encode data being transported between nodes. XML includes markup tags to delineate elements of structured data. Using XML is useful here because the parsing of the XML commands (in this case present in the e-mail body) becomes very simple and expressive. Open source XML parsers exist which are both tiny and fast. Responses would also be symmetrically emitted in XML. An example of this method is SOAP (Simple Object Access Protocol) and XML-RPC, which both use XML tags to implement a text-based remote procedure-call (RPC) protocol.

SUMMARY

In this chapter, we investigated the Simple Mail Transfer Protocol from a server perspective (target of transported e-mails). The uses of SMTP servers in embedded systems were discussed as well as some of the design constraints that the protocol places on an embedded system (such as system connectivity). The structure of e-mails was detailed along with the construction of attachments of various encoding types. With attachments, we looked into the various encoding methods that exist to transport binary data through SMTP (such as Base64 and Quoted-Printable) and detailed the encoding and decoding of Base64 attachments. Finally, we discussed the implementation of an embedded SMTP server that supports an attachment and Base64 binary attachment decoding.

RESOURCES

Stevens, Richard W., *TCP/IP Illustrated Volume 1—The Protocols*, Addison Wesley Longman, Inc., 1994.

Postel, Jonathan B., "Simple Mail Transfer Protocol," RFC 821, August 1992. http://www.landfield.com/rfcs/rfc821.html

Crocker, David H., "Standard for the Format of ARPA Internet Text Messages," RFC 822, August 13, 1982. http://www.landfield.com/rfcs/rfc822.html

Borenstein and Freed, "MIME (Multipurpose Internet Mail Extensions) Part One: Mechanisms for Specifying and Describing the Format of Internet Message Bodies," RFC 1521, September 1993. http://www.landfield.com/rfcs/rfc1521.html

Moore, K., "MIME (Multipurpose Internet Mail Extensions) Part Two: Message Header Extensions for Non-ASCII Text," K. Moore, RFC 1522, September 1993. http://www.landfield.com/rfcs/rfc1522.html

Freed and Borenstein, "Multipurpose Internet Mail Extensions," RFC 2046, November 1996. http://www.landfield.com/rfcs/rfc2046.html

6 Embedded POP3 Client

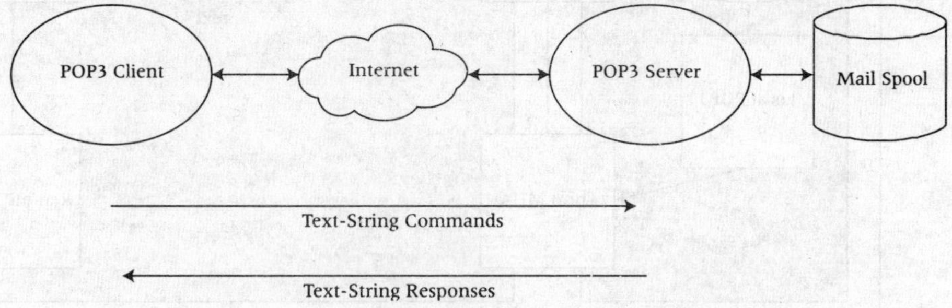

In this chapter, we'll finish our investigation of SMTP specific protocols with a discussion of the Post Office Protocol, Version 3 (or POP3). The POP3 protocol is a useful protocol for retrieving e-mail, and as we'll soon discover, POP3 can be very useful in the embedded environment.

INTRODUCTION

The POP3 protocol is yet another text-based protocol that closes the loop for mail systems. While SMTP is used to transfer e-mail from Mail User Agents (MUAs) to Mail Transfer Agents (MTAs), POP3 is the read side of the MUA.

When an SMTP server receives an e-mail message for a user, it stores the message away in some system-dependent way. It's interesting to note that there really is no specification for how this information is to be stored. The e-mail must remain intact so that its integrity is retained when finally received by the recipient. The POP3 protocol allows the user to retrieve the stored e-mails received via SMTP. In other words, SMTP is used as the e-mail outgoing protocol and POP3 is used as the e-mail incoming protocol. Figure 6.1 shows how e-mails are transferred using SMTP and POP3.

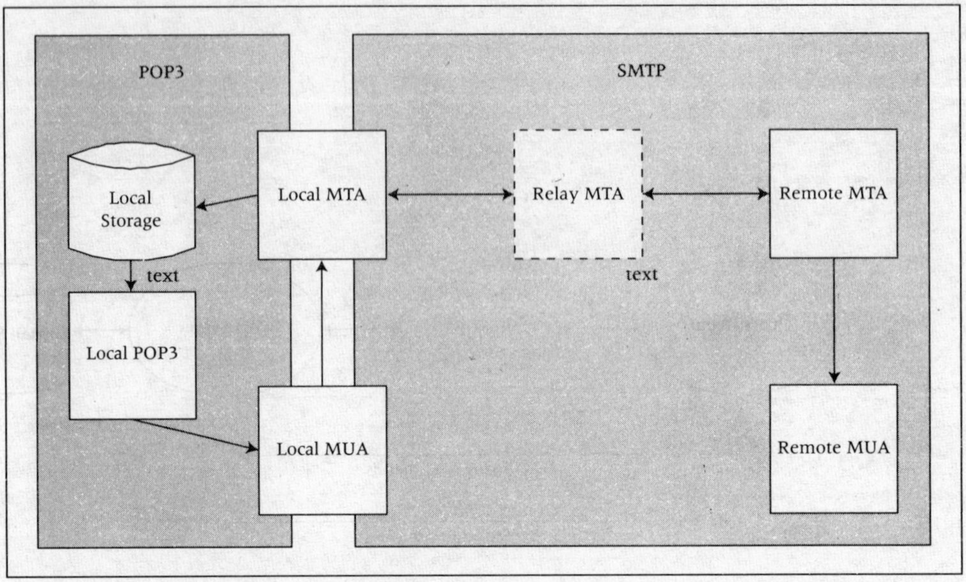

FIGURE 6.1 The POP3/SMTP e-mail transfer path.

Why POP3 for Embedded Systems?

POP3 is very interesting for embedded systems. Recall in Chapter 4 the discussion of a vehicle transport that contacts a central server in order to relay status information (such as position or payload temperature) and to receive information (road delays, change in itinerary). The SMTP server is an interesting model, but has the disadvantage that the server must be available when an e-mail is sent to it. If it's not available, the e-mail is returned to the user as undeliverable. This makes an SMTP server unusable in situations in which communication is not 100% available. In our truck example, we'll assume the use of wireless communications that is very dependent upon geography. Since we can't guarantee that the embedded system within the truck is always available, some other mechanism is required.

The first consideration is a new protocol that works around this deficiency. Given that protocols exist that can address this problem, these should be considered before reinventing the wheel.

POP3 is an interesting solution here because it addresses the issues of disrupted availability while allowing for the simple transport of e-mail. E-mail is desirable because, as discussed in Chapter 4, the user interface is ubiquitous and well understood even by novice computer users. Since POP3 is the protocol that collects e-mails from the mail server, our embedded system example changes from an SMTP server (where the e-mails are directed) to an MUA that simply collects the e-mails from the server. This is done once the wireless connection is made.

Advanced Uses

POP3 can be used to transport e-mails with rich content, including audio or video data. Since POP3 is a transport protocol related to SMTP, it offers some of the advantages that were discussed in the SMTP chapters.

Origin and Evolution

The original Post Office Protocol was released in October 1984 by J. K. Reynolds at the Information Sciences Institute as RFC 918. Four years later, POP3 was released (RFC 1081) and was revised over the next 8 years to RFC 1939 (Standard 53). As has SMTP, POP has remained a text-based protocol that is dialog based. POP3, like SMTP, may be done interactively through a telnet session and is very informative.

A competing protocol called IMAP (Internet Message Access Protocol - Version 4) was created in 1994 to provide for more complex mail operations. IMAP, for example, allows managing e-mail at the remote server rather than at the client. The advantage here is that e-mail can be viewed on any host from anywhere rather than being tied to a particular client host. IMAP also has its disadvantages, with speed and complexity as primary concerns.

Although IMAP is used in many organizations, the original POP3 is still widely used and continues to flourish.

PROTOCOL OVERVIEW

POP3 is a simple dialog-based protocol that operates in the text domain (that is, it's a human-readable protocol). POP3 is synchronous command/response based on which a command is issued and resulting response is generated from the POP3 server. Responses follow a very general pattern that makes the protocol quite simple from an implementation perspective. POP3 has a limited set of commands and the actual POP3 specification is about 15 pages of protocol discussion.

In this section, we'll look at the POP3 architecture and basic design of a POP3 API.

POP3 Architecture

While POP3 is a protocol between two actors, it is in general a client/server protocol (See Figure 6.2). The server commonly sits on a host with an SMTP server and has access to the stored e-mail files received for users managed within the particular domain. These e-mails are commonly stored linearly in a file by time of receipt. The POP3 server awaits connections on a well-known port (110) and upon receiving a socket connection, engages in a dialog with a client.

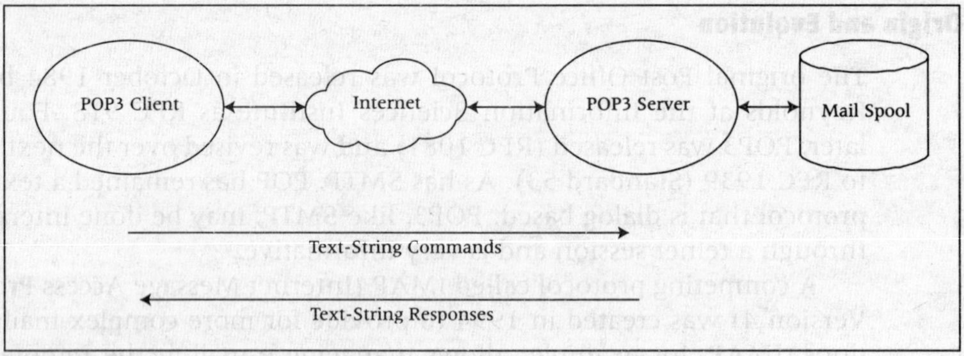

FIGURE 6.2 POP3 client and server.

The POP3 client is typically built in to an MUA. The client connects to the server to which it has been configured for incoming mail, and engages in a dialog to first authenticate itself to the server and then collect any e-mails that have been received.

The POP3 server is a state machine-based design that operates over a small number of states. The first state is the Authorization state which is used to identify users and authenticate them. The next state is the Transaction state which is used to collect and manage e-mails for the client at the server. Finally, the Update state is a special state from the server's perspective. When the client ends the POP3 dialog with the server, the connection ends from the client's perspective. However, at the server, cleanup is required to actually delete messages that were marked for deletion by the client.

The POP3 protocol, as discussed, can be performed interactively through telnet which can be instructive from a development perspective. A sample dialog is provided in Listing 6.1. User commands are shown in bold.

LISTING 6.1 Sample interactive dialog between a POP3 client and server.

```
[mtj@plato test]# telnet xyz123.com 110
Trying 192.168.1.6...
Connected to xyz123.com.
Escape character is '^]'.
S: +OK POP3 www.xyz123.com v8.59 server ready
C: USER me
S: +OK User name accepted, password please
C: PASS mypassword
S: +OK Mailbox open, 2 messages
C: STAT
S: +OK 2 732
C: LIST
S: +OK Mailbox scan listing follows
S: 1 356
S: 2 376
S: .
C: RETR 1
S: +OK 356 octets
S: Return-Path: <mtj>
S: Received: (from mtj@localhost)
S:  by xyz123.com (9.9.3/9.8.7) id LAA31307
S:  for me@xyz123.com; Wed, 7 Nov 2001 11:02:50 -0700
S: Date: Wed, 7 Nov 2001 11:02:50 -0700
S: From: "M. Tim Jones" <mtj@mtjones.com>
S: Message-Id: <200111071802.LAA31307@xyz123.com>
S: To: me@xyz123.com
S: Subject: Test1
S: Status:
S:
S:
S: This is a sample message.
S: .
C: DELE 1
S: +OK Message deleted
C: RETR 2
S: +OK 376 octets
S: Return-Path: <mtj>
```

```
S: Received: (from mtj@localhost)
S:  by xyz123.com (9.9.3/9.8.7) id LAA31312
S:  for me@xyz123.com; Wed, 7 Nov 2001 11:03:08 -0700
S: Date: Wed, 7 Nov 2001 11:03:08 -0700
S: From: "M. Tim Jones" <mtj@mtjones.com>
S: Message-Id: <200111071803.LAA31312@xyz123.com>
S: To: me@xyz123.com
S: Subject: Test2
S: Status:
S:
S:
S: This is another sample message.
S:
S: Last line.
S: .
C: DELE
S: -ERR Missing message number argument
C: DELE 2
S: +OK Message deleted
C: STAT
S: +OK 0 0
C: QUIT
S: +OK Sayonara
Connection closed by foreign host.
[mtj@plato test]#
```

Let's now walk through this dialog to understand how POP3 provides for e-mail transport.

First, we telnet to our POP3 server using the simple telnet command. Recall that telnet is a general byte-oriented communications facility. Characters entered through a telnet session are transferred to the peer, and vice versa. This gives us a general way of communicating with text-oriented protocols.

Since the POP3 server is at port 110, we specify this port on the command line (to avoid going to the default telnet port). The POP3 server immediately sends a salutation preceded by the status code (+OK) which informs the client that we're connected to a POP3 server and all is well.

```
S: +OK POP3 www.xyz123.com v9.59 server ready
```

Upon initial connection, we're in the Authorization state. We are unable to perform any commands until we move from the Authorization state to the Transaction state. This transition is performed when we authenticate ourselves to the server using the USER and PASS commands. These two commands identify our username and our password to the server. A status code and human-readable text is followed by each command.

```
C: USER tim
S: +OK User name accepted, password please
C: PASS mypassword
S: +OK Mailbox open, 2 messages
```

After the `PASS` command is accepted, and we've been authenticated by the server, it responds with a `+OK` status code and an indicator of how many messages are available at the server. We then perform a redundant `STAT` command, which tells the client how many messages are available, and the total size in octets of the messages (in this case 732 bytes).

```
C: STAT
S: +OK 2 732
```

The client can get more detailed information about the contents of incoming mail using the `LIST` command. This command provides a list of the available messages and the individual octet size of each. This is useful if we were to invalidate certain messages based upon size. Consider an embedded system with a limited amount of memory. If an e-mail found its way to our POP3 server that was 4 MB in size, we could immediately delete the message rather than try to download it and then realize that we can't deal with a message that big.

The `LIST` command results in a simple list of two value records, the mail index (`id` of the mail) and the size in octets. The end of the list is identified by a single '.' on a line by itself. Recall back to the SMTP discussions that this is identical to the end-of-mail indicator.

```
C: LIST
S: +OK Mailbox scan listing follows
S: 1 356
S: 2 376
S: .
```

Retrieving an e-mail is performed using the `RETR` command (retrieve). The client specifies the numeric `id` of the e-mail to be downloaded with the retrieve command. The POP3 server responds first with a status indicator (`+OK` in this case to inform the client that the command was successful) and then the message itself. Note that the status indicator is followed by the size of the e-mail to be downloaded. This is useful in dynamic systems in which the buffer to fill in is dynamically generated. The actual e-mail in its entirety comes next, followed by the end-of-e-mail indicator (CR/LF/'.'/CR/LF). Once this is received, the client knows that the POP3 server is back in command mode and awaiting instructions.

```
C: RETR 1
S: +OK 356 octets
S: Return-Path: <mtj>
S: Received: (from mtj@localhost)
S:           by xyz123.com (9.9.3/9.8.7) id LAA31307
S:           for me@xyz123.com; Wed, 7 Nov 2001 11:02:50 -0700
S: Date: Wed, 7 Nov 2001 11:02:50 -0700
S: From: "M. Tim Jones" <mtj@xyz123.com>
S: Message-Id: <200111071802.LAA31307@xyz123.com>
S: To: me@xyz123.com
S: Subject: Test1
S: Status:
S:
S:
S: This is a sample message.
S: .
```

The next command, DELE, is used to delete a message at the server. Note that this operation marks it for deletion but does not actually remove the message until we enter the Update state. If the message is deleted using the DELE command, but then the connection with the POP3 server is lost, we never reach the Update state and the message is not removed. Only if we transition from the Transaction state (in which we manipulate the mail at the server) to the Update state are messages removed from the server.

```
C: DELE 1
S: +OK Message deleted
```

The second DELE command that we perform in the sample dialog is not properly formed, contains no e-mail id, and is therefore noted with an error status, -ERR.

```
C: DELE
S: -ERR Missing message number argument
```

At the end of the dialog, we finally collect and remove the second e-mail at the server and perform a final STAT command. The server responds with the indication that 0 e-mails remain with a total of 0 octets.

```
C: STAT
S: +OK 0 0
```

We provide the QUIT command to end our session and tell the server to update based upon our actions. The server then goes to work to remove the e-mails marked for deletion (in this case, both of them) and the socket connection is closed with a final success indication.

```
C: QUIT
S: +OK Sayonara
```

This very simple dialog illustrates the simplicity of the POP3 protocol.

Basic Design

The POP3 client protocol implemented here uses a minimal number of commands to provide e-mail management. From our perspective, e-mail is simply a transport that is used to relay data or commands through SMTP between a user (client MUA) and an embedded system.

In order to provide the greatest flexibility for POP3 within an embedded system, this design is provided as an API. The API allows the embedded system designer to use POP3 in a manner consistent with the objectives. The POP3 API provides for e-mail collection from a POP3 server as well as parsing of the e-mail to simplify usage of the e-mail and its contents.

POP3 Client API

The POP3 API provides five functions to manage e-mail on a remote POP3 server. These functions are listed in Listing 6.2.

LISTING 6.2 POP3 client API.

```
int pop3cConnect ( char *pop3Server, char *user, char *pass );
int pop3cRetrieve ( mail_t *mail, int totalLen );
int pop3cParse ( mail_t *mail );
int pop3cDelete ( void );
int pop3cDisconnect ( void );
```

The API design was to match the behavior of the POP3 protocol while abstracting away the unnecessary details from the user perspective. Most of the functions deal with the mail_t type that is a structure that contains the necessary elements for a raw e-mail and its components. The mail_t structure is shown in Listing 6.3.

LISTING 6.3 `mail_t` **structure type.**

```
typedef struct {
  char *email;
  int  email_len;
  char subject[MAX_STRING+1];
  char sender[MAX_STRING+1];
  char recipient[MAX_STRING+1];
  char *bodyStart;
} mail_t;
```

The details of the structure will be outlined in the following summary of the POP3 API.

pop3cConnect Summary

The `pop3cConnect` function is used to connect to a POP3 server. The user must provide a server name which can be a simple IP address or a fully qualified domain name. The user must also provide a username and password that is registered on the POP3 server (the user must have an e-mail account on that system). This function will perform all of the required functions to connect to the POP3 server and move from the POP3 Authorization state to the POP3 Transaction state. The function returns the number of e-mails that are currently waiting at the server.

pop3cRetrieve Summary

The `pop3cRetrieve` function retrieves an e-mail from the POP3 server. The user passes in a `mail_t` pointer and the length of the e-mail buffer contained within the `mail_t` structure. The user must create both the `mail_t` structure and a buffer that is referenced by the structure. This is to allow the user to define maximum e-mail size that is to be received (since this will commonly be tied to the user application and can vary greatly). An example of this is provided in the implementation summary.

The `pop3cRetrieve` function grabs the first e-mail that is available and returns the length of the e-mail received. This e-mail will be captured within the `email` element of the `mail_t` structure and the length of the e-mail is also stored within the `email_len` field. On error, a `-1` is returned.

pop3cDelete Summary

The `pop3cDelete` function is used to mark an e-mail for deletion at the server. Although POP3 allows the user to specify which e-mail to delete, the API presented here has simplified this process. After connection, the `pop3cRetrieve` function will return the first e-mail that is available. If this function is called again, the same e-mail is returned. In order to retrieve any subsequent e-mails available at the server, the user must call the `pop3cDelete` function. This function not only deletes the current e-mail at the server, but then increments the e-mail `id` so that the next e-mail may be retrieved.

pop3cParse Summary

The `pop3cParse` function does not actually communicate with the POP3 server, but instead takes an e-mail structure collected from the server and parses out the necessary elements in order to deal with it. After `pop3cParse` is called, the remaining fields of the `mail_t` structure will be filled in upon successful parsing of the structure (see Listing 6.3). The subject field will contain the subject of the e-mail (as specified within the e-mail envelope). The sender and recipient fields will also be filled in (again, from the envelope). The field `bodyStart` will contain a pointer to the area in the `email` array where the actual body of the e-mail begins.

The parsing function could have used character pointers to point to the subject, sender and recipient, as was done with the `bodyStart` field. These elements within the e-mail structure could then have been null-terminated to identify the end of the field. The design decision here was to leave the actual e-mail intact in the event that user wanted to look for other elements (such as "X" headers or other header fields). Therefore, these fields were simply copied out for simplicity, but at the cost of greater memory usage.

pop3cDisconnect Summary

Finally, the `pop3cDisconnect` function closes out the connection with the POP3 server. Prior to closing the socket, the API emits the `QUIT` command to the POP3 server to force it into the Update state to remove any e-mails that were marked for deletion.

Each of the functions return either `-1` for failure, or some other value indicating success or detailed information about the return status (such as e-mail count or size).

Communication Structure (E-mail Structure)

E-mails that are transported through POP3 have the same restrictions as mentioned for SMTP in previous chapters. They must consist of 7-bit ASCII text and as such, attachments of binary data are encoded using a binary encoding method such as Base64 or Quoted-Printable (see Chapter 5 for more information on these methods).

Representation of e-mail in POP3 is limited to the RETR command. Once this command is performed, with an id representing the index of the e-mail to download, the e-mail is generated in its natural 7-bit text form. E-mails communicated via POP3 adhere to RFC 822. Let's look back an example from our prior dialogs (shown in Listing 6.4).

LISTING 6.4 E-mail transaction showing e-mail encoding.

```
C: RETR 1
S: +OK 356 octets
S: Return-Path: <mtj>
S: Received: (from mtj@localhost)
S:          by mtjones.com (8.9.3/8.8.7) id LAA31307
S:          for dan@4sonora.com; Wed, 7 Nov 2001 11:02:50 -0700
S: Date: Wed, 7 Nov 2001 11:02:50 -0700
S: From: "M. Tim Jones" <mtj@mtjones.com>
S: Message-Id: <200111071802.LAA31307@mtjones.com>
S: To: dan@4sonora.com
S: Subject: Test1
S: Status:
S:
S:
S: This is a sample message.
S: .
```

The e-mail in Listing 6.4 is shown bounded by the POP3 success indicator (+OK 356 octets\n) and the end-of-mail indicator (CRLF.CRLF). The e-mail is made up of two parts, the header and body. The header is starts at the beginning of the e-mail and ends after the first blank line after the header (in this case the blank line that follows the Status: line). The e-mail body is then a blank line and the text "This is a sample message." This is important because from a mailer perspective, the header is interpreted and commonly shown as a summary item. When the e-mail is displayed, only the body is shown.

From an embedded perspective, the e-mail is a large character array that can be interpreted in any way that's useful to the device. Headers can be "hidden" such as X- headers to convey more information, but limit its visibility to standard MUAs For example, standard mail clients will accept X-headers, but they will be ignored and hidden from the mail recipient. An X-header is a non-standard header that is typically provided for informational purposes only. A common X-header is "X-Mailer." This specifies the mailer software that was used to construct the particular message. Another, X-Priority is used by certain mailers to assign a priority to the message. Most mailers permit the construction of new X-headers to encode additional information for the receiver.

Characteristics

POP3 is derived from the SMTP text-based protocol and in many ways is symmetrical with SMTP. While the SMTP client provides for the transmission of e-mail, POP3 provides for the collection using a similar set of primitives. The text-based synchronous command/response protocol is also used in a variety of other protocols, including the Network News Transfer Protocol (NNTP) that is used to transport Usenet news among a distributed set of computers.

More recently-developed protocols such as HTTP still model this paradigm. Although less efficient than pure binary protocols, the capability to interface with the protocol via a simple telnet session makes testing easier and the protocol easier to understand.

IMPLEMENTATION SUMMARY

As discussed in the Basic Design section, the POP3 client is implemented as a very simple API that encompasses the possible tasks. Each of these functions will be covered in the following sections.

The API is "stateful," meaning that some information is retained across calls. For example, a successful `pop3cConnect` call must be performed before any of the other calls. This is because the `pop3cConnect` call creates the client socket and connects it to the named POP3 server. The `pop3cDisconnect` call is the last call to be made in a POP3 dialog to close down the session.

Support Functions

One important support function is the `dialog` function (see Listing 6.5). This function accepts an optional command to be sent to the POP3 server and then reads the response. Since POP3 responses included the status indicator (`+OK`, or `-ERR`), the function checks the status and returns a status report based upon this. The string passed in containing the command is also used to collect the POP3 server response.

LISTING 6.5 `dialog` **support function.**

```
static int dialog( int sock, char *command )
{
  int ret, len;
```

```
    if ( strlen(command) > 0 ) {
      len = strlen( command );
      if (write( sock, command, len ) != len) return -1;
    }

    ret = read( sock, command, MAX_LINE );
    if ( ret > 0 ) command[ret] = 0;
    else return -1;

    if (strncmp( command, "+OK", 3 )) return -1;

    return 0;
}
```

pop3cConnect

The pop3cConnect function must be called before any other API function. It provides for the initial connection to the POP3 server as well as authentication and transition from the POP3 Authorization state to the Transition state.

The code begins by creating a standard stream socket and defining the target of the socket as port 110 (the well-known port for POP3), and the address based upon the pop3Server argument passed in by the user. This may be an IP address or a fully qualified domain name; the function will figure out which. The pop3cConnect function can be found in Listing 6.6.

LISTING 6.6 pop3cConnect API function.

```
int pop3cConnect ( char *pop3Server, char *user, char *pass )
{
  int result;
  struct sockaddr_in servaddr;

  sock = socket( AF_INET, SOCK_STREAM, 0 );

  bzero( (void *)&servaddr, sizeof(servaddr) );
  servaddr.sin_family = AF_INET;
  servaddr.sin_port = htons( 110 );

  servaddr.sin_addr.s_addr = inet_addr( pop3Server );

  if ( servaddr.sin_addr.s_addr == 0xffffffff ) {
```

```
    struct hostent *hptr =
                  (struct hostent *)gethostbyname( pop3Server );
    if ( hptr == NULL ) {
      return -1;
    } else {
      struct in_addr **addrs;
      addrs = (struct in_addr **)hptr->h_addr_list;
      memcpy( &servaddr.sin_addr,
                *addrs, sizeof(struct in_addr) );
    }
  }

  do {

    result = connect( sock,
                   (struct sockaddr *)&servaddr,
                   sizeof(servaddr) );

    if ( result < 0 ) break;

    /* Look for the salutation */
    buffer[0] = 0;
    result = dialog( sock, buffer );
    if ( result < 0 ) break;
    result = -1;

    /* Send the USER login */
    sprintf( buffer, "USER %s\n", user );
    result = dialog( sock, buffer );
    if ( result < 0 ) break;
    result = -1;

    /* Send the PASS login */
    sprintf( buffer, "PASS %s\n", pass );
    result = dialog( sock, buffer );
    if ( result < 0 ) break;
    result = -1;

    /* Finally, get the number of emails waiting */
    strcpy( buffer, "STAT\n" );
    result = dialog( sock, buffer );
    if ( result < 0 ) break;

    sscanf( buffer, "+OK %d", &result );
```

```
      retIndex = 1;

    } while (0);

    if ( result < 0 ) {
      close( sock );
      sock = -1;
    }

    return result;
  }
```

The pop3cConnection function then attempts to connect to the remote POP3 server. Once connected, a single read is performed to gather the salutation that should be emitted right away. We check that the salutation has the success indicator (+OK), and if so, we move on with the protocol.

We then emit the POP3 USER command along with the username passed in by the user (see Listing 6.1 for a full listing of the initial dialog). After the USER command is sent, we await a status indicator from the POP3 server, and upon receiving +OK, we move forward. The PASS command follows the same pattern as the USER command.

Once the PASS command is completed and accepted, we may perform commands to the POP3 server. The last action we perform in pop3cConnect is a STAT command to identify how many messages are waiting. This information is also provided in the success indicator from the PASS command. The function completes by returning the result to inform the user whether we're connected to the POP3 server, or that an error resulted.

pop3cRetrieve

The pop3cRetrieve function is used to retrieve e-mails through a POP3 connection. See Listing 6.7 for the pop3cRetrieve function.

LISTING 6.7 pop3cRetrieve API function.

```
int pop3cRetrieve ( mail_t *mail, int totalLen )
{
  int result, i, bufIdx=0, state, stop, len;

  /* Send the Retrieve command */
  sprintf( buffer, "RETR %d\n", retIndex );
  result = dialog( sock, buffer );
```

```
if ( result < 0 ) return -1;

/* Skip the +OK response string and grab any data (end with
 * CRLF)
 */
len = strlen( buffer );
for ( i = 0 ; i < len-1 ; i++ ) {
  if ( (buffer[i] == 0x0d) && (buffer[i+1] == 0x0a) ) {
    len -= i-2;
    memmove( mail->email, &buffer[i+2], len );
    break;
  }
}

state = stop = 0;

while (!stop) {

  if (bufIdx+len > totalLen - 80) break;

  /* Search for the end-of-mail indicator in the current buffer */
  for ( i = bufIdx ; i < bufIdx+len ; i++ ) {
    if      ((state == 0) && (mail->email[i] == 0x0d)) state=1;
    else if ((state == 1) && (mail->email[i] == 0x0a)) state=2;
    else if ((state == 2) && (mail->email[i] == 0x0d)) state=1;
    else if ((state == 2) && (mail->email[i] ==  '.')) state=3;
    else if ((state == 3) && (mail->email[i] == 0x0d)) state=4;
    else if ((state == 4) && (mail->email[i] == 0x0a)) {
      stop = 1; break;
    } else state = 0;
  }

  bufIdx += (i-bufIdx);

  if (!stop) {

    len = read( sock, &mail->email[bufIdx], (totalLen-bufIdx) );

    if ( (len <= 0) || (bufIdx+len > totalLen) ) {
      break;
    }

  }
```

```
    }

    bufIdx -= 3;
    mail->email[bufIdx] = 0;
    mail->email_len = bufIdx;

    return bufIdx;
}
```

The pop3cRetrieve function uses the POP3 RETR command to retrieve a particular e-mail from the server. POP3 automatically provides a numeric id to all e-mails, which is used to then manage them (retrieve, delete).

Once the e-mail has been requested, the server responds with a status indicator. If the indicator is +OK, it's followed by the e-mail text. As shown in Listing 6.1, the e-mail follows the status indicator and is delimited by the end-of-e-mail indicator. This is the indication that the e-mail is complete and the client may continue.

An interesting side effect of TCP must also be handled here. When the server responds with the +OK status indicator, we should expect that we'd receive this as a segment and then read the e-mail through the socket. Instead, the status indicator and the beginning of the e-mail can be returned at the same time. This could be because the sending TCP/IP stack accumulated the data together to send out in a frame, or the receiving stack accumulated it within the receive socket buffer. Regardless of where this accumulation occurs, the application layer must be able to deal with this. In the pop3cRetreive function, after we get a successful response (as defined by the dialog function), we look for the CRLF sequence which represents the end of the status indicator. Any data after this is e-mail text that we must accumulate in the e-mail structure. This is why the memmove function is used to copy the text from the temporary buffer into the email field of the mail_t structure.

The loop that follows is used to find the end-of-mail indicator. This simple state machine looks at the new text within the e-mail buffer and once the indicator is found, we set the stop variable to exit the loop. If the indicator is not found, we continue to read data from the socket and accumulate it in the e-mail buffer.

Once complete, the number of characters read into the e-mail field is returned unless there is an error, in which -1 is returned.

pop3cParse

The pop3cParse function performs parsing of the mail structure into the more specific elements (from Listing 6.3) such as subject, sender, recipient, etc.

The parse function performs a number of activities to parse the elements shown in Listing 6.3. The pop3cParse function is shown in Listing 6.8.

LISTING 6.8 pop3cParse API function.

```
int pop3cParse ( mail_t *mail )
{
  int result;

  result = parseEntry( mail, "Subject:", mail->subject );
  if (result < 0) return result;

  result = parseEntry( mail, "From:", mail->sender );
  if (result < 0) return result;
  fixAddress( mail->sender );

  result = parseEntry( mail, "To:", mail->recipient );
  if (result < 0) return result;
  fixAddress( mail->recipient );

  result = findBody( mail );

  return result;
}
```

The parse function parses the subject, sender and recipient using a special internal function called parseEntry. This function searches the e-mail text for the search string as defined by the second parameter, and then stores the value associated with that in the variable reference by the third argument.

In Listing 6.1, it's apparent that each line of the header includes a character string name, such as "Subject: " and is followed by the value associated with that string, in this case "Test1". The parseEntry function, shown in Listing 6.9, uses a simple character compare and then string compares to minimize library calls.

LISTING 6.9 parseEntry internal function.

```
int parseEntry( mail_t *mail, const char *searchString, char *dest )
{
  int i, index, len;

  len = strlen(searchString);
```

```
/* Grab the subject */
for (i = 0 ; i < mail->email_len ; i++) {
  if (mail->email[i] == searchString[0]) {
    if (!strncmp(&mail->email[i], searchString, len )) {
      i += (len + 1);
      index = 0;
      while (!((mail->email[i] == 0x0d) &&
                   (mail->email[i+1] == 0x0a))) {
        if (mail->email[i] == 0) i++;
        else dest[index++] = mail->email[i++];
      }
      dest[index] = 0;
      break;
    }
  }
}

if (i == mail->email_len) {
  return -1;
}

return 0;
}
```

Upon locating the `searchString`, the characters that follow this string are simply copied into the `dest` string until the `CRLF` sequence is found. The function `fixAddress`, shown in Listing 6.10, is used to prune an e-mail address (primarily the `sender`) to remove the name phrase and return a pure e-mail address.

LISTING 6.10 `fixAddress` **internal function.**

```
int fixAddress ( char *address )
{
  int i, j, len;
  char string[MAX_STRING+1];

  len = strlen(address);
  for (i = 0 ; i < len ; i++) {
    if (address[i] == '<') break;
  }

  if (i++ == len) return 0;
```

```
    j = 0;
    for ( ; i < len ; i++) {
      if (address[i] == '>') break;
      string[j++] = address[i];
    }
    string[j] = 0;

    strcpy(address, string);

    return 0;
}
```

Finally, the function `findBody` is used to identify the start of the body of the e-mail. `findBody` is a very simple function that simply looks for the first blank line (`CRLFCRLF` sequence) after the e-mail header. Once found, the `bodyStart` field of the mail structure is loaded with this pointer. This function can be found in Listing 6.11.

LISTING 6.11 `findBody` **internal function.**

```
int findBody( mail_t *mail )
{
  int i, result=-1;

  for (i = 0 ; i < mail->email_len ; i++) {
    if ((mail->email[i] == 0x0d) && (mail->email[i+1] == 0x0a) &&
        (mail->email[i+2] == 0x0d) && (mail->email[i+3] == 0x0a)) {
      i+=4;
      break;
    }
  }

  if (i < mail->email_len) {
    mail->bodyStart = &mail->email[i];
    result = 0;
  }

  return result;
}
```

pop3cDelete

The `pop3cDelete` function simply uses the POP3 `DELE` command to mark an e-mail for deletion. The dialog function returns the status of this operation that we simply return to the user. The pop3cDelete function is shown in Listing 6.12.

LISTING 6.12 pop3cDelete API function.

```
int pop3cDelete ( void )
{
  int result;

  /* Send the USER login */
  sprintf( buffer, "DELE %d\n", retIndex++ );
  result = dialog( sock, buffer );
  if ( result < 0 ) return -1;
  result = -1;

  return( result );
}
```

pop3cDisconnect

Finally, the pop3cDisconnect function is used to disconnect a current session between the POP3 client and server. As discussed, the use of the QUIT command instructs the POP3 server to transition from the Transaction state to the Update state. In this state, the POP3 server removes any e-mails for the session that have been marked for deletion.

The pop3cDisconnect function is provided in Listing 6.13.

LISTING 6.13 pop3cDisconnect function.

```
int pop3cDisconnect ( void )
{
  int result;

  strcpy( buffer, "QUIT\n" );
  result = dialog( sock, buffer );
  if ( result < 0 ) return -1;
  return 0;
}
```

SAMPLE TEST FUNCTION

Now that we've looked at the POP3 client API, let's look at a sample function that uses the API for e-mail collection from a POP3 server. This function is used to connect to the server and collect any e-mails that exist. Upon parsing each e-mail, the subject line is consulted for the action to take. The sample test function is shown in Listing 6.14.

LISTING 6.14 Sample Test main function.

```
int main()
{
  int result, count, index;
  char contents[MAX_MAIL+1];
  mail_t mail;

  /* Load our mail body into the mail structure and clear it
  * out.
  */
  mail.email = contents;
  bzero( contents, sizeof(contents) );
  mail.email_len = MAX_MAIL;

  count = pop3cConnect( SERVER, USER, PASS );

  printf("Connected.  %d emails waiting...\n", count);

  for ( index = 0 ; index < count ; index++ ) {

    result = pop3cRetrieve ( &mail, MAX_MAIL );

    result = pop3cParse ( &mail );

    /* Handlers */
    if (!strncmp(mail.subject, "STATUS", 6)) {
      /* Handle an incoming STATUS email */
    } else {
      /* Silently ignore unknown commands */
    }

    result = pop3cDelete();

  }

  pop3cDisconnect();
  return 0;
}
```

The test function begins by setting up the mail structure. Since we don't know how much space to allocate for a particular application, the developer defines this by creating a character array (which will hold the maximum sized e-mail). The developer then loads a reference to this object into the `mail_t` structure. In environments in which traditional memory management is permitted (Malloc/Free), this object could be allocated on the fly for each e-mail.

We then use the API functions to connect to the POP3 server. The value returned from `pop3cConnect` is the number of e-mails that are currently stored at the server. We use this as our limit in the subsequent loop to gather the e-mails. The `pop3cRetrieve` grabs the next available e-mail, which is promptly parsed by the `pop3cParse` function. The `handlers` section then looks at the subject field to identify the action to take based upon this e-mail. This section is provided as an example only. The application could also interrogate the e-mail body or other header information. Finally, the e-mail is deleted at the server and we continue through the loop to collect other e-mails.

When no more e-mails are available at the server, the test function disconnects from the server using the `pop3cDisconnect` function.

TESTING THE POP3 CLIENT

In order to test or integrate the POP3 client into a design, three parameters must be defined. These parameters are `SERVER`, `USER`, and `PASS` and can be found in the `main.c` source file (on the CD-ROM at ./software/ch6/empop3c/main.c).

The `SERVER` parameter must contain the IP address or fully qualified domain name of a valid POP3 server. It must also be a server on which the `USER` has an account to retrieve e-mail. The `USER` defines the username on the server and the `PASS` symbolic is the password for the user. Examples of `SERVER` include:

```
#define SERVER "192.168.1.1"

#define SERVER "pop.mydomain.com"
```

To verify that a POP3 server actually exists at the defined host, a simple telnet at port 110 to this host can easily identify this.

ADDING EXTENSIONS

The POP3 client presented here provides the foundation for e-mail gathering and simple parsing and server management. Using code from the SMTP server (in Chapter 5), attachments could be parsed and used. While the code currently does nothing with the incoming e-mails, since this is, after all, application specific, the SMTP client code from Chapter 4 could be used to return e-mail to the sender.

SUMMARY

In this chapter, we investigated the POP3 protocol and completed our review of e-mail related protocols. We considered the trade-offs of POP3 to similar protocols (such as the SMTP server) and how it can be utilized in embedded system designs. We then looked in detail at POP3 and its characteristics (text-based, synchronous). Finally, we built an implementation of the POP3 client protocol and discussed ways to utilize the client in an embedded system, as well as extensions using previously demonstrated code.

RESOURCES

Crocker, "Standard for the format of ARPA Internet text messages," RFC 822, August 1982. http://www.landfield.org/rfcs/rfc822.html

Reynolds, "Post Office Protocol,"RFC 918, October 1984. http://www.landfield.org/rfcs/rfc918.html

Kantor & Lapsley"Network News Transfer Protocol—A Proposed Standard for the Stream-Based Transmission of News," RFC 977, February 1986.

Rose, "Post Office Protocol—Version 3," RFC 1081, November 1988. http://www.landfield.org/rfcs/rfc1081.html

Crispin, "Internet Message Access Protocol—Version 4," RFC 1730, December 1994. http://www.landfield.org/rfcs/rfc1730.html

Myers and Rose, "Post Office Protocol—Version 3," RFC 1939, May 1996. http://www.landfield.org/rfcs/rfc1939.html

7 Embedded HTTP Server

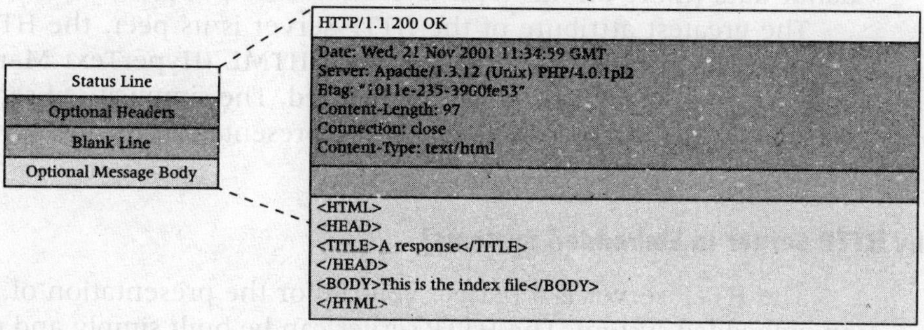

In this chapter, we'll leave the e-mail domain covered in the prior three chapters and look at the HyperText Transfer Protocol (HTTP) and its use in embedded systems as a simple vehicle for remote management and monitoring. Web servers have become the standard for remote management, especially for devices that have no traditional user interfaces (such as Internet routers). Further, we'll look at an implementation that includes dynamic content and dynamic handling of form-based data. Finally, we'll look at how to serve content to nonstandard clients such as Web phones and how our Web server implementation can communicate with them.

INTRODUCTION

The use of Web browsers has become the standard method for communicating with and managing remote embedded devices. The Web browser is a common appliance on networked desktops and provides a rich set of functionality for communication and presentation of data from remote devices.

These days it's commonplace to find HTTP servers on a variety of small embedded devices. Like e-mail, the Web client is a ubiquitous tool and is used by all Internet users. The HTTP server provides the means to export information from the device for remote monitoring as well as permit modification of device parameters via Common Gateway Interface (CGI) forms. With a little work, the HTTP server can provide the means to display dynamic data (more on this topic later in this chapter).

The greatest attribute of the HTTP server is its peer, the HTTP client. Using a very simple tag language called HTML (HyperText Markup Language), a rich presentation can be realized. The simplicity of serving simple files to the client results in simple presentation of possibly complex data.

Why HTTP Server in Embedded Systems?

The HTTP server is a perfect vehicle for the presentation of data from an embedded system. The HTTP server can be built simply and can reside in very small code space. HTTP is very simple and therefore supports the simplicity of implementation. Since the Web browser (HTTP client) provides the rendering of the HTML page to the user, the server need only serve content through a simple socket server to provide the HTTP server functionality. Take for, example, the source code in Listing 7.1.

LISTING 7.1 A very simple static HTTP server.

```
int main( void )
{
  int serverFd, connectionFd, on=1;
  struct sockaddr_in servaddr;
  char timebuffer[MAX_BUFFER+1];
  time_t currentTime;
  const char *page=
      {"HTTP/1.0 200 OK\nContent-Type: text/html\n\n"
         "<HTML><HEAD><TITLE>Welcome</TITLE></HEAD>"
       "<BODY><H1>Welcome!</H1><P><P>"
       "The current time at this device is %s<P>"
       "</BODY></HTML>\n"};

  serverFd = socket(AF_INET, SOCK_STREAM, 0);
```

```
setsockopt(serverFd, SOL_SOCKET, SO_REUSEADDR, &on, sizeof(on));

memset(&servaddr, 0, sizeof(servaddr));
servaddr.sin_family = AF_INET;
servaddr.sin_addr.s_addr = htonl(INADDR_ANY);
servaddr.sin_port = htons(HTTP_SERVER_PORT);

bind(serverFd, (struct sockaddr *)&servaddr, sizeof(servaddr));

listen(serverFd, 5);

while ( 1 ) {

  connectionFd = accept(serverFd,
                        (struct sockaddr *)NULL, NULL);

  if (connectionFd >= 0) {

    read(connectionFd, timebuffer, MAX_BUFFER);

    currentTime = time(NULL);
    snprintf(timebuffer, MAX_BUFFER, page, ctime(&currentTime));

    write(connectionFd, timebuffer, strlen(timebuffer));
    close(connectionFd);

  }

}

}
```

In this very simple server, we await a connection and then emit the "page" as constructed in the `snprintf` function. The page is a simple string that contains the HTML tags that will be rendered by the client. Though very simple, this provides an indication of how easy and powerful HTTP can be for embedded systems. The code for this simpler server can be found on the accompanying CD-ROM at ./software/ch7/shttps/.

HTTP servers can also be disadvantageous in embedded systems design. The traditional HTTP server requires a file system in which the content is stored and then served. A file system, with an API, can be expensive in terms of non-volatile (or volatile) memory usage. For example, a flash-based file system can increase parts count on a device and therefore its cost. The design that is presented here constructs a simple static filesystem that obviates this need through an internal "application" filesystem.

Advanced Uses

While the use of HTTP for retrieval of multimedia files from Web servers is the most common application, HTTP is finding new uses in modern application-layer protocols. HTTP has evolved into an application transport-layer protocol for other application-layer protocols, such as SOAP (Simple Object Access Protocol) and XML-RPC (Extensible Markup Language-Remote Procedure Call). In these applications, the request includes the object of interest along with any parameters and the response is the object or result of computation from that remote object.

As an extensible transport protocol, HTTP is finding new uses outside of the hypertext and content distribution domain.

Origin and Evolution

The HyperText Transfer Protocol was derived from an earlier idea by Ted Nelson in his book, *Literary Machines* (in which the term "hypertext" was coined). A hypertext link provided the ability to tie together ideas or related pieces of knowledge. Therefore, ideas could be linked, allowing a user to identify relations and connections to other pieces of information. Nelson developed this idea in a project called "Xanadu" through the 1960s and early 1970s, but due to a lack of product release, his project was finally dropped.

Using the ideas of Nelson, Tim Berners-Lee of the European Organization for Nuclear Research (CERN) conceived of hypertext links that spanned the network allowing computers to be linked not only by networks but also by information. In 1989, Berners-Lee submitted a proposal that would allow researchers at CERN to gain access to large amounts of stored information.

This information included reports, documentation, online databases, and other information that was useful to a geographically dispersed group that desired to collaborate on a particular subject.

Although useful, the early browsers were limited. In 1994, Marc Andreeson built the first widely used browser called Mosaic at the National Center for Supercomputing Applications (at the University of Illinois). This work led to the first browser company—Netscape.

Since that time, many other browsers have been introduced including Internet Explorer from Microsoft, Communicator from Netscape, Opera from Opera Software, and the open source Galeon (available at sourceforge.net).

PROTOCOL DISCUSSION

HTTP, as described in RFC 2068, is a very simple ASCII-based protocol. HTTP uses a standard synchronous request/response design over the TCP/IP protocol, identical to classical client/server architecture (See Figure 7.1). When a client makes a request to an HTTP server, it sends an HTTP request message. The HTTP request message includes the client request as well as information about the client's capabilities. A single blank line at the end of the request terminates the request message and signals the HTTP server to go to work.

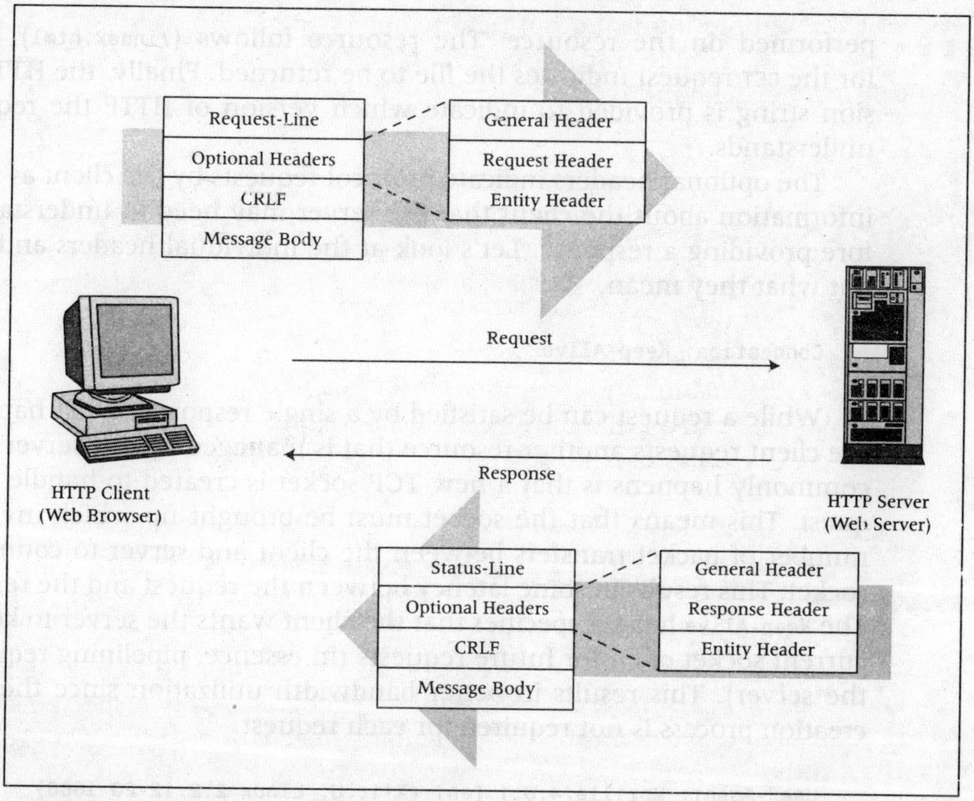

FIGURE 7.1 HTTP protocol architecture.

All HTTP requests follow the basic structure shown in Figure 7.2. The HTTP request message is made up of a number of fields, the request line setting the stage for the activities that follow. The first element is the method token (in this case, `GET`) which indicates the method to be

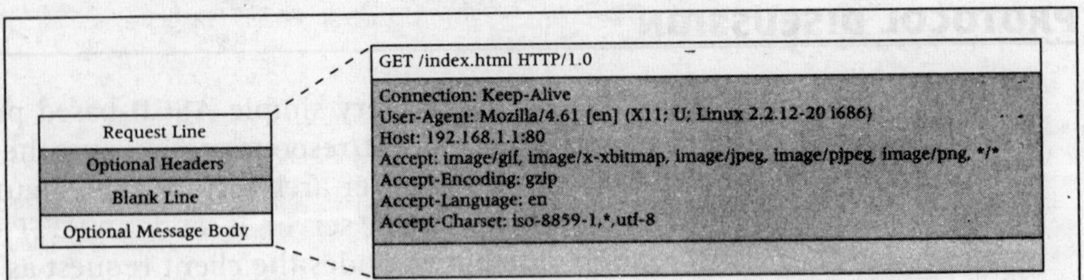

FIGURE 7.2 HTTP request message format.

performed on the resource. The resource follows (`/index.html`), which for the `GET` request indicates the file to be returned. Finally, the HTTP version string is provided to indicate which version of HTTP the requestor understands.

The optional headers indicate protocol requests by the client as well as information about the client that the server may need to understand before providing a response. Let's look at the individual headers and figure out what they mean.

```
Connection: Keep-Alive
```

While a request can be satisfied by a single response, what happens if the client requests another resource that is managed by this server? What commonly happens is that a new TCP socket is created to handle the request. This means that the socket must be brought up which involves a number of packet transfers between the client and server to connect the socket. This results in some latency between the request and the response. The `Keep-Alive` header specifies that the client wants the server to keep the current socket open for future requests (in essence, pipelining requests to the server). This results in better bandwidth utilization since the socket creation process is not required for each request.

```
User-Agent: Mozilla/4.6.1 [en] (X11; U; Linux 2.2.12-20 i686)
```

The `User-Agent` request header field contains information about the User Agent originating the request. Its most common use is in statistical collection of data to identify most common browsers, which present protocol violations, etc. Unfortunately, the field is also used by malicious companies to mangle or refuse to serve content to client browsers that come from different developers.

```
Host: 192.168.1.1:80
```

The `Host` request header is the host URL as specified by the original request. Combining this with our resource results in 192.168.1.1:80/index.html, which is (minus the HTTP:// protocol header) the original URL of the request. The host can be used by hosts that can be referenced by more than one fully qualified domain name (such as www.a.com, www.b.com). By looking at the `Host` header, the server can identify which host was originally requested and serve content appropriately.

```
Accept: image/gif, image/x-xbitmap, image/jpeg, image/pjpeg, image/png,
  */*
```

The `Accept` request header specifies which media types are acceptable within the response. In this case, the client browser informs, among other things, that it can render images of type gif.

```
Accept-Encoding: gzip
```

The `Accept-Encoding` request header indicates which encoding methods are acceptable. In this case, the client indicates that gzip is the only acceptable encoding. If the `Accept-Encoding` request header were followed by an empty field, this would indicate that no encoding method was acceptable.

```
Accept-Language: en
```

`Accept-Language`, like the prior Accept request headers, is used to define the acceptable languages (natural in this case). In the case above, `en` is used to denote that the client browser is interested only in English. A comma delimited list could be provided to identify preferences of languages.

```
Accept-Charset: iso-8859-1,*,utf-8
```

Finally, the `Accept-Charset` request header indicates acceptable character sets to the server.

The HTTP request message contains quite a bit of information to inform the server of its capabilities and preferences. Similarly, the HTTP response follows a similar structure. All HTTP responses follow basic structure shown in Figure 7.3.

The status line identifies the status of the HTTP request. In this case we see a `200 OK` which identifies that the request is satisfied by the message body that follows.

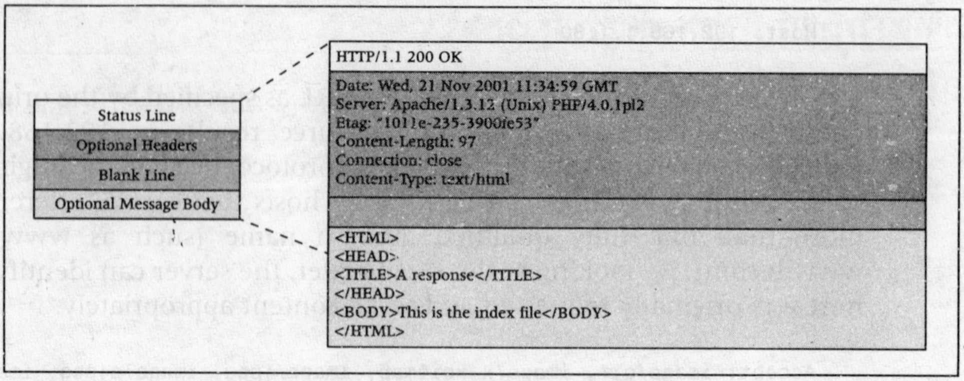

FIGURE 7.3 HTTP response message format.

The response headers then follow and provide some generic and some detailed information about the response. The `Date:` and `Server:` headers are self-explanatory.

The `ETag:` header is an entity tag that can be used (as one service) to identify whether a cached version of a page on a client is the same as that on the server. If the `ETags` match, the page is deemed unchanged and the cached version is used.

The `Content-Length:` header simply represents the number of octets in the message body. This is useful in systems in which memory is dynamically allocated for the body of the message.

The `Connection: close` header indicates that the server, upon emitting the response to the client, will close this socket and that no further requests can be made through it. Recall the discussion of `Keep-Alive` in the request section.

The final header `Content-Type:` indicates the type of data that follows in the message body. The `text/html` type identifies our response as text with an HTML encoding.

Finally, the message body is emitted with a single blank line separating it from the response headers.

We've covered only a few of the many possible headers and variations that can occur in HTTP, but this sampling should indicate the complexity and flexibility of HTTP. Using a simple text-based structure for both requests and responses, data transfer is accommodated as well as feature negotiation.

EMBEDDED HTTP SERVER GOALS

Any good development project begins with a set of criteria that must be met. In this section, we'll look at the functionality requirements for a lightweight, embedded Web server that has some very specific design goals.

Outside of simply serving content via the HTTP protocol, a few other features are desired. These are:

- An application file system for content storage
- Support for dynamic content
- Support for dynamic forms processing (via HTTP POST)
- An embedded log
- Support for Web phone integration

Prior to looking at design, let's better understand what is to be achieved by these features.

Application File System

The HTTP server exists to serve content, which implies that content is stored somewhere in some fashion. Since embedded system architectures can vary greatly, we'll introduce an application file system which is a file system that is bound directly to an application.

A file system can be defined in three parts: a storage medium, a format by which data is stored within the medium, and an API to enable access. These features will be provided in a very compact package to provide content that is directly linkable to the HTTP server application.

Support for Dynamic Content

Serving static content is suitable in many applications, but in an embedded system, the HTTP server is useful as a remote monitoring interface. In this application, the Web server must be able to serve content that changes dynamically with the content that is monitored.

An ideal interface for dynamically altering content is through the static content, in this case the HTML pages. We'll introduce a new tag to provide dynamic data within a static HTML page as well as an API so that user applications can hook into the page to provide their content whenever it's requested.

Support for Dynamic Form Processing

Forms processing is synonymous with CGI forms (Common Gateway Interface). CGI allows a form that accepts data on a Web page to extend to a server-side application for further processing of the data.

This interface is also useful in an embedded system design. The forms interface allows a remote Web user to alter the behavior of an embedded system through the modification of variables extended through a forms interface. We'll present a forms interface that utilizes the HTTP POST method and integrates user-defined forms processors.

Support for Web Phone Presentation

The wireless Web has provided us with a number of other protocols by which to extend content beyond the traditional desktop computer. Protocols such as HDTP (Hypertext Device Transfer Protocol) and HDML (Handheld Device Markup Language) make Web offerings accessible to constrained display devices such as Web phones.

The Web server design will provide support for HDML including integration with the dynamic content support.

Embedded Log

While the ability to log requests to the server is desirable, the space consumed by such logs can quickly overrun small embedded devices. Logs can trace activity to understand device interface use and can help track when the device is being used by unauthorized parties.

Most logs are made up of very repetitive strings that differ in some of the arguments applied to them. The log design presented here will minimize log use to a handful of bytes by separating the static content and the dynamic content.

EMBEDDED HTTP SERVER DESIGN

In this section, the unique design elements of the embedded HTTP server will be discussed.

Application File System

In order to provide typical HTTP services, some kind of file system is necessary. The approach of this design is to aggregate the files (our content) as a compilable data structure. Building an API accessible to the Web server then completes the requirement.

Application File System Structure

The structure of the application file system is a very simple one. Files are aggregated into a sequential structure with headers that identify where files begin in the structure and their length. Each entry in the application file system follows the definition as shown in Table 7.1. The file header is used as a simple synchronization mechanism to know where a file entry starts. The filename is the name of the file in the file system (including directory path) ending with a null terminator. The file size then follows as a four byte integer (big endian). Finally, the contents of the file are provided, up to the length defined by the `file size` field.

TABLE 7.1 Application file system entry.

Element	*Size*	*Description*
File header	2 bytes	Marker bytes to mark beginning of header (0xfa, 0xf3)
File name	Variable	Null terminated file name (with path)
File size	4 bytes	Length of file (in bytes)
File	Variable	Contents of file

File System Builder

A special utility called `buildfs` creates the compilable data structure. The `buildfs` utility takes a directory path as an argument and uses this as the root of the content tree. The content tree is then traversed and each file encountered is accumulated into our application file system structure and written out to the compilable file `filedata.c`. This file can be viewed and includes a hex translation of the contents of each file along with a textual comment for the file that includes its size.

An example of the resulting generated file `filedata.c` is provided in Figure 7.4.

As is illustrated in Figure 7.4, two file entries were created for the two files that were found in the content tree (`/testfile` and `/file2`). Refer to Table 7.1 for a legend that explains how the file entries are encoded.

```
/*
 * filedata.c
 *
 * This file is dynamically generated.
 *
 * mtj@cogitollc.com
 *
 */
unsigned char filedata[]={

  /* File: /testfile, size 5 */

  0xfa, 0xf3, 0x2f, 0x74, 0x65, 0x73, 0x74, 0x66, 0x6c, 0x69, 0x6c, 0x00,
  0x00, 0x00, 0x00, 0x05, 0x41, 0x42, 0x43, 0x44, 0x0a,

  /* File: /file2, size 22 */

  0xfa, 0xf3, 0x2f, 0x66, 0x69, 0x6c, 0x65, 0x32, 0x00, 0x00, 0x00, 0x00,
  0x16, 0x54, 0x68, 0x69, 0x73, 0x20, 0x69, 0x73, 0x20, 0x61, 0x0a, 0x74,
  0x65, 0x73, 0x74, 0x20, 0x66, 0x69, 0x6c, 0x65, 0x2e, 0x0a, 0x0a, 0x00,
  0x00, 0x00, 0x00

};
```

FIGURE 7.4 Sample `filedata.c` containing two files.

Embedded File System API

The file system API is very simple and based around a file header structure. The structure is retrieved through a call to `lookupFilename` and can then be used to push content through a connected client socket back to the requester. Listing 7.2 illustrates the structure and search function.

LISTING 7.2 `fileHdrStruct` and `lookupFilename` prototype.

```
struct fileHdrStruct {
  int hdrStart;
  int size;
  int fileStart;
};

int lookupFilename( char *, struct fileHdrStruct * );
```

The `fileHdrStruct` is made up of three elements. Element `hdrStart` is the index into the `filedata` array to the file entry (as described in Table 7.1). The `size` element is the actual size of the file (again taken from the file entry). Finally, `fileStart` identifies where the actual contents of the file begin in the `filedata` array.

The `lookupFilename` function takes a character string argument as the filename to be found and a `fileHdrStruct` pointer that will hold the information about the filename in the application file system. Since the file system is a simple structure of file entries (see Figure 7.4), locating a file is a simple process of walking through the file headers and comparing the source filename with the file entry file name. When a file is matched, the `fileHdrStruct` is filled in with the elements that optimize later retrieval of the file.

The application file system provides a read-only mechanism to access file-based data. The disadvantage of this approach is that the file system is non-mutable—it can't be changed. Building a read/write file system could have been done here, but with greater complexity. Use of a real read/write file system could also be provided through flash memory devices, but at greater cost. The application file system can be stored with the actual software in a ROM device, and is therefore beneficial from a cost perspective. The HTTP server provides dynamic capabilities, so in many cases, there is no need to change the contents of the file system.

Dynamic Content

Support for dynamic content is surprisingly simple and utilizes the tag concept found in HTML. A new tag has been added to interface to the embedded HTTP server to support this capability. As content is served, it is parsed to search for the new dynamic content tag `<DATA x>` where `x` is the string name of the dynamic content to be inserted into the stream:

```
<P>
The current temperature is <DATA temperature>.
<P>
```

The parser searches for the `<DATA` keyword and then uses the embedded variable name (in this case "temperature") to retrieve the actual content.

Numerous designs were considered for serving dynamic content. The final design that is implemented was chosen for its flexibility. When a developer wants to provide dynamic content, they build an HTML file that includes the dynamic tags that are to be resolved (such as what is shown in Listing 7.21). The code that will provide the dynamic data is then written as a function that returns a null-terminated string. This function is then plugged-in to the HTTP server with the associated variable name that is represented in the HTML file. A sample install is shown in Listing 7.3, along with the code to provide the dynamic content.

LISTING 7.3 Dynamic Data install with corresponding function.

```
addDynamicContent( "temperature", &getTemperature );

...

static char dyndata[81];

char *getTemperature( void )
{
    float temp;

    // read the temperature here...

    sprintf( dyndata, "%5.2f", temp);

    return( dyndata );
}
```

This particular implementation was chosen because the string representation allows for the greatest flexibility in data types (anything can be represented including embedded HTML). Also, by calling a user function to retrieve the data (instead of simply retrieving the content from a stored intermediate array), the developer has the greatest flexibility in data management. For example, the developer's function knows when the data is used because their function is called. This permits synchronization on the available data and its presentation.

Dynamic Forms

The capability to support forms to allow the user to send data to a Web server is also very simple using the HTTP POST method. POST constructs an HTTP request message with the body as the data to be sent to the Web server. Data is assembled in key-value pairs with '&' symbols separating each pair. The job of the forms processor is then to simply receive the HTTP request and then parse the key-value pairs from the body.

A sample forms page that results in an HTTP POST is provided in Listing 7.4 (formtest.html).

LISTING 7.4 Sample form-based HTML page.

```
<HTML>
<HEAD>
<TITLE>
Form Test
</TITLE>
</HEAD>
<BODY>

This is a test.

<FORM ACTION="/control" METHOD="POST">
  <INPUT TYPE=TEXT NAME="Test1" SIZE=10>Test1:
  <INPUT TYPE=TEXT NAME="Test2" SIZE=10>Test2:
  <INPUT TYPE=TEXT NAME="Test3" SIZE=10>Test3:
  <INPUT TYPE="submit" NAME="Go">
</FORM>
</BODY>
</HTML>
```

The `formtest.html` sample file illustrates the use of a `FORM` and the `POST` method. The form contains three text variables of size 10 characters with the names defined by the `NAME` attribute. We install our handler in a fashion similar to the dynamic content handler:

```
addDynamicHandler( "/control", &myHandler);
```

Since the processing is dependent upon the particular Web page (as defined by the `INPUT` variables specified in the page), the API provides for the parsing of the `INPUT` variables to a string value. The dynamic handler is called with the "content" of the `POST`, which is then used to parse the individual variables from the data.

Content-Type Handling

The content-type of an HTTP response specifies how the message body should be treated. For example, a standard HTML page is served with a content-type of `text/html`. A JPEG image is served with a content type of `image/jpeg`. In the absence of a file suffix in an HTTP response, this simply tells the receiver how to treat the data once received (render an HTML page, display a JPEG image, etc.).

Adding new types is as easy as defining a new content-type and then figuring out when to define the content-type from the file suffix in the application file system. We'll investigate adding support for the Hypertext Device Markup Language (HDML) later in this chapter.

When the `content-type` cannot be determined by the HTTP server, the default type to be returned is `application/octet-stream`. This is simply defined as an application-specific stream of bytes.

Dynamic Log

Logs are important not only to understand server usage but can also be useful in debugging. Logs can be resource hogs, and given our design constraints we'll have to identify a more efficient way to store them.

In traditional systems, a log is a file to which processes may write a string and a variable set of arguments. Since we don't have a file system, or much room to store a log, a new approach is required.

To meet our space-constrained requirements, we'll make a few concessions. We won't allow the output of runtime-defined strings (all log strings will be known to the logger at compile-time). All log strings will be defined as scalar indices into a `logString` character array that defines the actual log string output. Supporting a variable number of arguments for a log string is also important and we'll support this with a minimum amount of work for the user.

A log string contains not only the template of the text to emit, but also a declaration of the arguments to embed within it. An example log string is shown here:

```
"Received request for ^."
```

The special character '^' is a replacement symbol that instructs the log constructor to insert a stored argument in its place.

The construction of the log is performed by the developer using two log functions. The first function places a single control byte into the log and the second places a null-terminated string into the log. The following code segment is an example of inserting a log entry:

```
emitByte( PREFIX_BYTE );  emitByte( NORMAL_REQUEST );
emitString ( filename );  emitByte( SUFFIX_BYTE );
```

This snippet of code will place the following data into the log (where `filename` points, in this example, to `file.html`):

```
0xfa, 0x00, 'f', 'i', 'l', 'e', '1', '.', 'h', 't', 'm', 'l', 0x00, 0xf3
```

All compressed log entries start with a prefix byte (`0xfa`) and end with a suffix byte (`0xf3`). This is used for synchronization purposes when constructing an HTML log output for the user. Following the prefix byte is the log entry type byte (in this case `NORMAL_REQUEST`). This byte is an index into the log strings array (more on this to follow). Finally, any arguments are emitted to the log using the `emitString` function. It should be clear from this discussion that the log is simply a circular buffer of bytes that are interpreted as log entries.

The creation of the log is then a dynamic process that is performed when the log is requested. This implies a trade-off of computation for space (we will spend some time to create the log when requested at the savings of a very small and compact log). Log entries are extracted from the circular buffer and then interpreted based upon their type. The type results in an index to the log strings array. The log string is then emitted one character at a time until a replacement symbol is found ('^'). When a replacement symbol is found, the log is consulted again to retrieve a null-terminated string that is promptly emitted (as shown in the previous sample log entry). Emission of the log string then continues until another replacement symbol is found, or the log string is terminated via the null-terminator.

This very simple architecture reduces highly repetitive logs to a handful of bytes that are dynamically created upon user request.

IMPLEMENTATION SUMMARY

The embedded HTTP server implementation is divided into seven segments. These segments are outlined in Figure 7.5.

The implementation segments are divided based upon their place within the module hierarchy, and are:

- HTTP Socket Server (main)
- HTTP Message Protocol
- Internal Application Filesystem API
- Dynamic Content/Handler API
- Log Generator and API
- Compiled Content (`filedata.c`)
- User-defined plug-ins

The implementation discussion with source follows based upon this ordering.

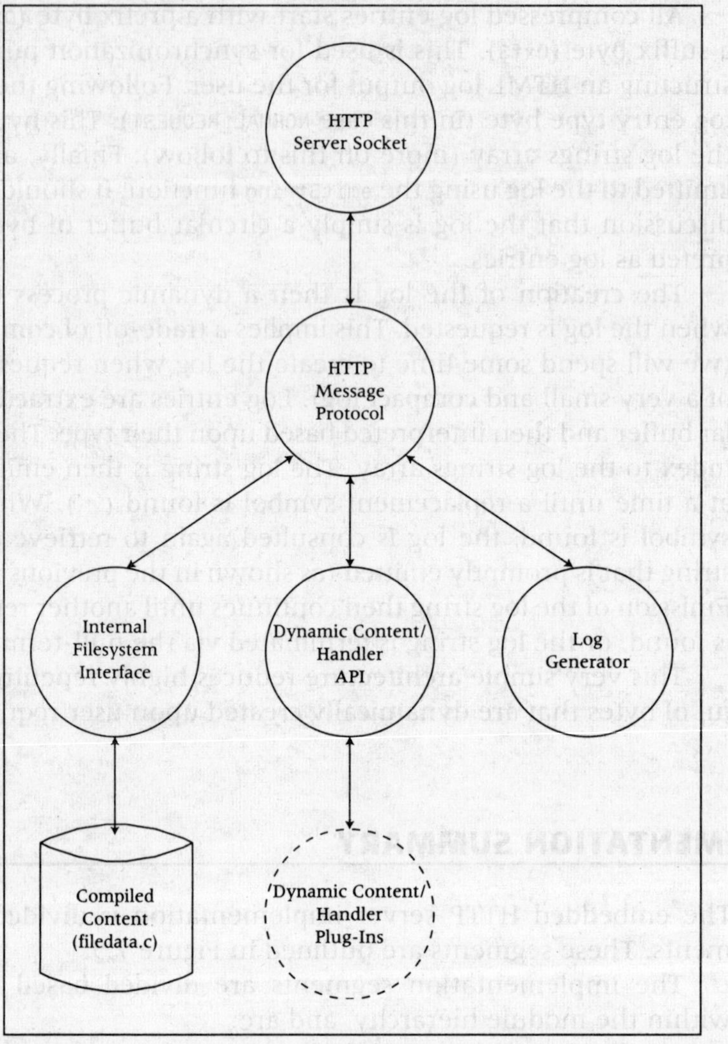

FIGURE 7.5 Embedded HTTP server module hierarchy.

HTTP Socket Server (main)

The HTTP Socket Server is a typical TCP stream socket server implementation (see Listing 7.5). Prior to performing socket related activities, the `userInit` function is called to install any content/handler plug-ins that the user has defined (more on this in the last section of this summary).

LISTING 7.5 HTTP socket server main.

```
int main(int argc, char *argv[])
{
  int listenfd, connfd, on=1;
  socklen_t clilen;
  struct sockaddr_in cliaddr, servaddr;

  extern void userInit();

  /* Init the dynamic content test func */
  userInit();

  listenfd = socket(AF_INET, SOCK_STREAM, 0);

  setsockopt( listenfd, SOL_SOCKET, SO_REUSEADDR,
              &on, sizeof(on) );

  bzero((void *)&servaddr, sizeof(servaddr));
  servaddr.sin_family = AF_INET;
  servaddr.sin_addr.s_addr = htonl(INADDR_ANY);
  servaddr.sin_port = htons(80);

  bind(listenfd, (struct sockaddr *)&servaddr, sizeof(servaddr));

  listen(listenfd, 5);

  for ( ; ; ) {

    clilen = sizeof(cliaddr);
    connfd = accept(listenfd,
                    (struct sockaddr *)&cliaddr, &clilen);
    if (connfd <= 0) break;

    handleConnection(connfd);
    close(connfd);

  }

  close(listenfd);
  return(0);
}
```

The HTTP socket server uses the SO_REUSEADDR socket option to allow immediate reuse of the defined HTTP port (80 as defined here, but can be redefined by the developer). For debugging purposes, SO_REUSEADDR can save quite a bit of time compared to waiting for the socket entry to be reclaimed.

The socket is then bound to the specified port and a queue of five requests is defined using the listen call. This allows us to queue up to five outstanding requests while we fulfill the current one.

The loop then handles each request that is handled by individual sockets (we don't support persistent connections). Once a connection is accepted by the server, the client socket is passed to the function handleConnection to handle the HTTP protocol request message. Upon return, the client socket is closed and we await another request.

HTTP Message Protocol

The HTTP message protocol is implemented in a handful of functions. Request message processing is performed within the handleConnection function, and response message processing is spread across a number of other functions depending upon the particular request.

The handleConnection function is the main entry point to the HTTP message protocol. All request messages are processed by this function, and upon successful parse, lead to a response path. See Listing 7.6 for the handleConnection source.

LISTING 7.6 handleConnection function (request message parser).

```
void handleConnection(int fd)
{
  int len, max, loop;
  char buffer[4096]={0};
  char filename[256]={0};
  int ret;
  struct fileHdrStruct filehdr;

  /*
   * Read in the Request Header
   */
  max = 0;
  loop = 1;
  while (loop) {
    len = read(fd, &buffer[max], 255); buffer[max+len] = 0;
    if (len <= 0) return;
    max += len;
    if (!strncmp(buffer, "POST", 4)) {
```

```
        if (strstr(buffer, "+Query")) loop = 0;
      } else {
        if ((buffer[max-4] == 0x0d) && (buffer[max-3] == 0x0a) &&
            (buffer[max-2] == 0x0d) && (buffer[max-1] == 0x0a)) {
          loop = 0;
        }
      }
    }

    /*
     * Determine request
     */
    if (!strncmp(buffer, "GET", 3)) {
      getFilename(buffer, filename, 4);
      if (!strncmp(filename, "/log", 4)) {
        sendLog(fd);
      } else {
        ret = lookupFilename(filename, &filehdr);
        if (ret > 0) {
          returnFile(fd, &filehdr);
        } else {
          emitByte(PREFIX_BYTE); emitByte(UNKNOWN_FILE);
          emitString(filename);  emitByte(SUFFIX_BYTE);
          write(fd, notfound, strlen(notfound));
        }
      }
    } else if (!strncmp(buffer, "POST", 4)) {
      getFilename(buffer, filename, 5);
      ret = callDynamicHandler(filename, findMsgBody(buffer));
      if (ret == 0) {
        write(fd, created, strlen(created));
      } else {
        write(fd, notfound, strlen(notfound));
      }
      emitByte(PREFIX_BYTE); emitByte(POST_REQUEST);
      emitString(filename);  emitByte(SUFFIX_BYTE);
    } else {
      write(fd, notimplemented, strlen(notimplemented));
    }
  }
```

The first job of `handleConnection` is to read in the HTTP request message. The loop reads from the socket until one of two conditions is met. This function should look for the `Content-Length` header to determine the size of the message body, but instead we look at the end of the buffer for the `<CR><LF><CR><LF>` sequence. If the request is a `POST` method, we simply look for the `+QUERY` text. If either of these two criteria are satisfied, we assume that the request is complete and then move on.

The next step is to handle the type of HTTP request. This is performed by simply identifying the first token from the request message. If the request is a `GET` request, we first parse the filename of the request from the request line. If the request is for the log (identified by a request for `/log`), then we call the function `sendLog` to create the log and emit it to the requester. Otherwise, we search for the filename within the application file system using the `lookupFilename` function. If not found, we send the appropriate status response to the requester (an HTTP 404 status code). Otherwise we call the `returnFile` primitive to emit the requested file through the socket.

Note also the log functions present in the "File not found" case. We emit the `UNKNOWN_FILE` symbol to represent a line in the log of a request of a file that doesn't exist. This case is useful in debugging (or in operation to identify if someone tries to make blind requests to the server).

If the request is an HTTP `POST` request, we again parse for the filename and then call the `callDynamicHandler` function to handle the request. To simplify the job of the dynamic handler, we pass it the pointer to the actual message body of the HTTP `POST` request. This is performed through the `findMsgBody` function.

Finally, if the request is neither a `GET` nor a `POST`, we return a "`not implemented`" status code (HTTP status 501).

Parsing the filename out of the HTTP request is a simple job of returning the first token after the HTTP request method. The function shown in Listing 7.7 accomplishes this task.

LISTING 7.7 `getFilename` **function to parse the filename from the request message.**

```
void getFilename(char *inbuf, char *out, int start)
{
  int i=start, j=0;

  /*
   * Skip any initial spaces
   */
  while (inbuf[i] == ' ') i++;

  for ( ; i < strlen(inbuf) ; i++) {
```

```
      if (inbuf[i] == ' ') {
        out[j] = 0;
        break;
      }
      out[j++] = inbuf[i];
    }

    if (!strcmp(out, "/")) strcpy(out, "/index.html");
  }
```

The getFilename function takes in the input buffer and an output buffer where the filename will be placed. The start argument simply tells us where we can start to look for the filename (since the actual offset is dependent upon the request method). The function skips any additional white space and then copies subsequent characters to the filename buffer. If the resulting filename is simply '/', then we assume that the user is requesting the root index file and we'll define the file as such.

Once we've identified a file to be returned (in the case of the GET request), the returnFile function is called to generate and send the HTTP response. The returnFile function is shown in Listing 7.8.

LISTING 7.8 returnFile **function to perform HTTP response.**

```
void returnFile(int fd, struct fileHdrStruct *filehdr)
{
  int ct;

  extern unsigned char filedata[];

  ct = determineContentType(filehdr->hdrStart);

  returnFileHeader(fd, ct);

  if ((ct == TEXT_HTML) || (ct == TEXT_HDML)) {
    parseAndEmitFile(fd, filehdr);
  } else {
    write(fd, &filedata[filehdr->fileStart], filehdr->size);
  }
}
```

We first determine the type of content to be returned, which is stored as an index to a content-type array. This function is shown in Listing 7.9. Once the content-type is determined, we generate and return the HTTP response message header through the returnFileHeader function.

If the content-type to be returned is an HTML or HDML file, we parse through it to determine if any dynamic content exists. Otherwise, we write the file directly out through the socket.

Determining the type of content is simply the process of extracting the file suffix from the file to be returned and then comparing this to a set of known suffixes that are supported by the server (see Listing 7.9).

LISTING 7.9 Identifying content type via determineContentType.

```
int determineContentType(int fileOffset)
{
  char suffix[20];
  int  i;

  extern unsigned char filedata[];

  fileOffset+=2;

  for ( ; filedata[fileOffset] != 0 ; fileOffset++) {
    if (filedata[fileOffset] == '.') break;
  }

  if (filedata[fileOffset] == 0) return(TEXT_PLAIN);
  else {

    fileOffset++;
    for (i = 0 ; filedata[fileOffset+i] != 0 ; i++) {
      suffix[i] = filedata[fileOffset+i];
    }
    suffix[i] = 0;

    /*
     * Now that we've go the suffix, determine the content type
     */
    if (!strncmp(suffix, "html", 4) ||
        !strncmp(suffix, "HTML", 4) ||
        !strncmp(suffix, "htm", 3)  ||
        !strncmp(suffix, "HTM", 3)) {
      return(TEXT_HTML);
    } else if (!strncmp(suffix, "class", 5) ||
               !strncmp(suffix, "CLASS", 5) ||
               !strncmp(suffix, "jar", 3)   ||
               !strncmp(suffix, "JAR", 3)) {
      return(OCTET_STREAM);
```

```
        } else if (!strncmp(suffix, "jpeg", 4) ||
                   !strncmp(suffix, "JPEG", 4) ||
                   !strncmp(suffix, "jpg", 4)  ||
                   !strncmp(suffix, "JPG", 4)) {
            return(JPEG_IMAGE);
        } else if (!strncmp(suffix, "gif", 3) ||
                   !strncmp(suffix, "GIF", 3)) {
            return(GIF_IMAGE);
        } else if (!strncmp(suffix, "hdml", 4)) {
            return(TEXT_HDML);
        } else {
            return(OCTET_STREAM);
        }
    }
}
```

The symbolic constant returned from `determineContentType` identifies the type and also serves as an index to the `content_types` array for a character string that is returned within the HTTP response. If the `content-type` cannot be determined, the default of `application/octet-stream` is selected.

After the `content-type` is known, the HTTP response header is constructed and returned to the request (see Listing 7.10).

LISTING 7.10 Constructing and returning the HTTP response header via `returnFileHeader`.

```
void returnFileHeader(int fd, int ct)
{
  char line[MAX_LINE+1];

  write(fd, success, strlen(success));

  sprintf(line, "Server: emhttp\n");
  write(fd, line, strlen(line));

  sprintf(line, "Connection: close\n");
  write(fd, line, strlen(line));

  sprintf(line, "Content-Type: %s\n\n", content_types[ct]);
  write(fd, line, strlen(line));
}
```

Recall from Figure 7.3 that all HTTP responses follow the same basic format of status line, optional headers, and response message body. The returnFileHeader function creates and returns the status line (first write shown in Figure 7.3) and then the optional headers. An important header to note is the content-type header that is constructed with the content-type (defined as variable ct) and the content_types array that generates the HTTP textual content type (from TEXT_HTML to text/html).

Finally in returnFile, we call parseAndEmitFile to return an HTML or HDML file. Function parseAndEmitFile (shown in Listing 7.11) simply walks through the file (as defined by the fileHdrStruct passed to it from returnFile) and looks for dynamic content tags (<DATA x>). When one of these tags is found, the variable name specified is passed to getDynamicContent (in Listing 7.12). The string that is returned by getDynamicContent is then simply written through the socket as if it had been part of the original file.

LISTING 7.11 Content file parser.

```
void parseAndEmitFile(int fd, struct fileHdrStruct *filehdr)
{
  int i;
  char content[MAX_LINE+1];

  extern unsigned char filedata[];

  /* Emit the dynamic HTML file replacing the <DATA #> with the
   * appropriate content.
   */

  for (i = 0 ; i < filehdr->size ; i++) {

    if (filedata[filehdr->fileStart+i] == '<') {
      if (!strncmp(
             &filedata[filehdr->fileStart+i+1], "DATA", 4)) {
        i+= 6;
        getDynamicContent(
               &filedata[filehdr->fileStart+i], content);

        /*
         * Emit the dynamic content
         */
        write(fd, content, strlen(content));

        for ( ; filedata[filehdr->fileStart+i] != '>' ; i++);

      } else {
```

```
      write(fd, &filedata[filehdr->fileStart+i], 1);
    }
  } else {
    write(fd, &filedata[filehdr->fileStart+i], 1);
  }

 }
}
```

The getDynamicContent function (see Listing 7.12) simply looks through a structure to find the variable name of the dynamic content. If this name is found, the user-defined function is called to retrieve the current value associated with this content. A string value is returned and simply copied to the content variable to be returned to the content parser. If the variable name is not found, the defaultFunction is called that simply returns an error value that will be visible to the user in the dynamically created Web page.

LISTING 7.12 Dynamic content retrieval function.

```
void getDynamicContent(char *name, char *content)
{
  int j, i;

  if (!init) {
    initContent();
    init=1;
  }

  for (j = 0 ; j < MAX_DYNAMIC_CONTENT ; j++) {

    /* Search for the name in the list, avoid '>' trailing
     * name...
     */
    for (i = 0 ; name[i] != '>' ; i++) {
      if (dynamicContent[j].variableName[i] != name[i]) break;
    }

    if (name[i] == '>') {
      /* We've reached the end, so it was a good match */
      strcpy(content, dynamicContent[j].pfunc());
      return;
    }

}
```

```
    strcpy(content, defaultFunction());
    return;
  }
```

The final element of the HTTP message protocol is the dynamic form handler that is provided by the function `callDynamicHandler`. This function is called from the `handleConnection` function (Listing 7.6) once the method is identified as `POST`. The `callDynamicHandler` function (see Listing 7.13) calls a user-defined function once the form name is parsed from the request and scanned to a matching record.

LISTING 7.13 `callDynamicHandler` **function listing.**

```
int callDynamicHandler(char *name, char *content)
{
  int j, found=-1;

  if (!init) {
    initHandlers();
    init=1;
  }

  for (j = 0 ; j < MAX_DYNAMIC_HANDLERS ; j++) {

    if (!strcmp(name, dynamicHandler[j].fileName)) {
      dynamicHandler[j].pfunc(content);
      found = 0;
      break;
    }

  }

  return found;
}
```

Similar to the `getDynamicContent` function, dynamic handlers are simply called with the message body of the HTTP `POST` method request. The user function is then able to parse the values from the body to use however they're needed. We'll look at an example of this later.

Application File system API

The application file system is interfaced by a single function called `lookup-Filename`. This function is passed a filename that will be searched for in the file system and a structure that will be loaded with information about the file in the application file system.

Function `lookupFilename` (shown in Listing 7.14) is a very simple function that walks through the file system entries comparing the passed filename with the filename present in the entry. When an entry is found that matches, the `fileHdrStruct` structure is loaded with the current entry information.

LISTING 7.14 Application file system API (`lookupFilename`).

```
int lookupFilename(char *filename, struct fileHdrStruct *filehdr)
{
  int offset = 0;
  int size;
  int i, found;
  int ret;

  while (filedata[offset] != 0) {

    ret = offset;
    found = 1;

    if ((filedata[offset] == 0xfa) &&
        (filedata[offset+1] == 0xf3)) {

      /* Skip the header */
      offset+=2;

      /* Search the file name, but don't stop if not found... */
      for (i = 0 ; filedata[i+offset] != 0 ; i++) {
        if (filename[i] != filedata[i+offset]) {
          found = 0;
        }
      }

      /* Skip the filename and null terminator */
      offset += (i+1);

      /* Get the file size */
      size = (filedata[offset  ] << 24) |
             (filedata[offset+1] << 16) |
             (filedata[offset+2] <<  8) |
             (filedata[offset+3]);

      if (found) {
```

```
                filehdr->hdrStart = ret;
                filehdr->size = size;
                filehdr->fileStart = (offset+4);
                emitByte(PREFIX_BYTE); emitByte(NORMAL_REQUEST);
                emitString(filename); emitByte(SUFFIX_BYTE);
                return(1);
            }

            offset += (size+4);
        }

    }
    return(0);
}
```

The lookupFilename function also performs the logging of requests after a file is found (assuming here that the file will be served through the server).

Dynamic Content/Handler API

The API for dynamic content and POST handlers provide for an association between variable name/form name to user-defined function.

In the case of dynamic content, the user provides a variable name (which will be present in the HTML file) and a function that will return the value of the variable as a string. For dynamic handlers, a function is called with the form name (from the HTML file) and the message body that can be parsed by the user-defined function.

The dynamic content installer is shown in Listing 7.15.

LISTING 7.15 Dynamic content plug-in API.

```
int addDynamicContent(char *name, char *(*function)())
{
  int i;

  if (!init) {
    initContent();
    init=1;
  }

  /* First, ensure that the 'name' does not exist in the current
   * list.
   */
```

```
  for (i = 0 ; i < MAX_DYNAMIC_CONTENT ; i++) {
    if (dynamicContent[i].variableName[0] != 0) {
      if (!strcmp(name, dynamicContent[i].variableName)) {
        return(-1);
      }
    }
  }

  /* Next, look for an empty slot */
  for (i = 0 ; i < MAX_DYNAMIC_CONTENT ; i++) {
    if (dynamicContent[i].variableName[0] == 0) {
      strncpy(dynamicContent[i].variableName, name, 80);
      dynamicContent[i].pfunc = function;
      break;
    }
  }

  return(0);
}
```

The function `addDynamicContent` initially ensures that initialization has occurred and that the variable name is then searched for in the `dynamicContent` array. If found, an error is returned immediately (since the variable name must be unique in the array). Otherwise, the name is added along with the function pointer to the function that will provide the content for the named variable.

The dynamic handler installer appears in Listing 7.16.

LISTING 7.16 Dynamic handler plug-in API.

```
int addDynamicHandler(char *name, char *(*function)())
{
  int i;

  if (!init) {
    initHandlers();
    init=1;
  }

  /* First, ensure that the 'name' does not exist in the current
   * list
   */
  for (i = 0 ; i < MAX_DYNAMIC_HANDLERS ; i++) {
    if (dynamicHandler[i].fileName[0] != 0) {
```

```
      if (!strcmp(name, dynamicHandler[i].fileName)) {
        return(-1);
      }
    }
  }

  /* Next, look for an empty slot */
  for (i = 0 ; i < MAX_DYNAMIC_HANDLERS ; i++) {
    if (dynamicHandler[i].fileName[0] == 0) {
      strncpy(dynamicHandler[i].fileName, name, 80);
      dynamicHandler[i].pfunc = function;
    }
  }

  return(0);
}
```

Adding a dynamic content handler is almost identical to adding dynamic content. Rather than associating a variable name to a user-defined function that will return data, instead, the dynamic handler associates a filename with a function that will be passed data from the FORM.

We'll look at examples of these in the customization section.

Log Generator and API

Adding entries to the log is provided by two functions that insert control bytes and strings into the compressed log. The first function `emitByte` is used to insert a control byte and is shown in Listing 7.17.

LISTING 7.17 `emitByte` **function to insert control bytes into the log.**

```
void emitByte(unsigned char byte)
{
  log[curWrite++] = byte;
  if (curWrite == MAX_LOG) curWrite = 0;
}
```

The variable `curWrite` identifies the current position to write into the log. The log is nothing more than a circular buffer of characters (both printable and non-printable).

The second function, `emitString`, is used to insert arguments into the log. The string is used because it can represent any other type (string, integer, float, etc.). The `emitString` function is shown in Listing 7.18.

LISTING 7.18 emitString function to insert arguments into the log.

```
void emitString(char *string)
{
  int i, len = strlen(string)+1;
  for (i = 0 ; i < len ; i++) emitByte(string[i]);
}
```

The emitString function first finds the length of the string argument insert and then adds one to ensure that the null-terminator is also emitted to the log. Each character is then emitted using the emitByte function.

Finally, the sendLog function is used to create the text log from the compressed log format. The sendLog function is shown in Listing 7.19.

LISTING 7.19 The sendLog function is used to create the text log for rendering.

```
void sendLog(int fd)
{
  int count = MAX_LOG;
  int i = curWrite;
  int state = HUNTING_PREFIX_HEADER;
  unsigned char curByte;
  char *logLine;

  extern void returnFileHeader(int, int);
  unsigned char getByte(int *, int *);
  unsigned char peekByte(int *);

  const char *HTML_HDR1={"<HTML><HEAD><TITLE>Log</TITLE></HEAD>"};
  const char *HTML_HDR2={"<BODY><H3>"};
  const char *HTML_HDR3={"</H3></BODY></HTML>\n"};

  /* First, make sure we're on a valid header. */
  i = curWrite;
  while (count > 0) {
    if (peekByte(&i) == PREFIX_BYTE) break;
    (void)getByte(&i, &count);
  }

  /* Emit log header info in HTML format */
  returnFileHeader(fd, TEXT_HTML);

  write(fd, HTML_HDR1, strlen(HTML_HDR1));
  write(fd, HTML_HDR2, strlen(HTML_HDR2));
```

```
    while (count > 0) {
      if (state == HUNTING_PREFIX_HEADER) {
        if (getByte(&i, &count) == PREFIX_BYTE) {
          curByte = getByte(&i, &count);
          logLine = logStrings[(curByte & LOG_TYPE_MASK)].string;
          state = EMIT_STRING;
          write(fd, "\n", 1);
        } else break;
      } else if (state == EMIT_STRING) {
        curByte = *logLine++;
        if      (curByte ==   0) state = HUNTING_SUFFIX_HEADER;
        else if (curByte == '^') state = EMIT_ARGUMENT;
        else write(fd, &curByte, 1);
      } else if (state == EMIT_ARGUMENT) {
        curByte = getByte(&i, &count);
        if (curByte == 0) state = EMIT_STRING;
        else write(fd, &curByte, 1);
      } else if (state == HUNTING_SUFFIX_HEADER) {
        if (getByte(&i, &count) == SUFFIX_BYTE)
          state = HUNTING_PREFIX_HEADER;
        else break;
      }
    }
    write(fd, HTML_HDR3, strlen(HTML_HDR3));
  }
```

The sendLog function uses two other support functions, getByte and peekByte, to grab data from the log. The getByte function acts as the consumer of the current character (incrementing the index pointer passed in) where the peekByte function simply looks at the current character.

We begin by setting up our indices. i represents the index where we'll begin reading (taken from the current write pointer in the log). The count variable is set to the log size, so we'll stop if we reach this point. Since the log is circular, it's quite likely that we'll overwrite old log entries with new ones. For this reason, the sendLog function is written as a state machine to find the prefix header, emit the log entry string (based upon the log entry type byte). While the log string is emitted, we look for the replacement symbol "^". If we find a replacement symbol, we change states to EMIT_ARGUMENT and emit the argument that exists in the log. Once the argument is emitted, we return to the EMIT_STRING to complete emitting the log string. When the log string is complete, we look for the suffix header and continue to the head of the state machine looking for another prefix header.

The state machine appears to be complex, but is quite simple with a quick review. The state diagram in Figure 7.6 illustrates the log emission process.

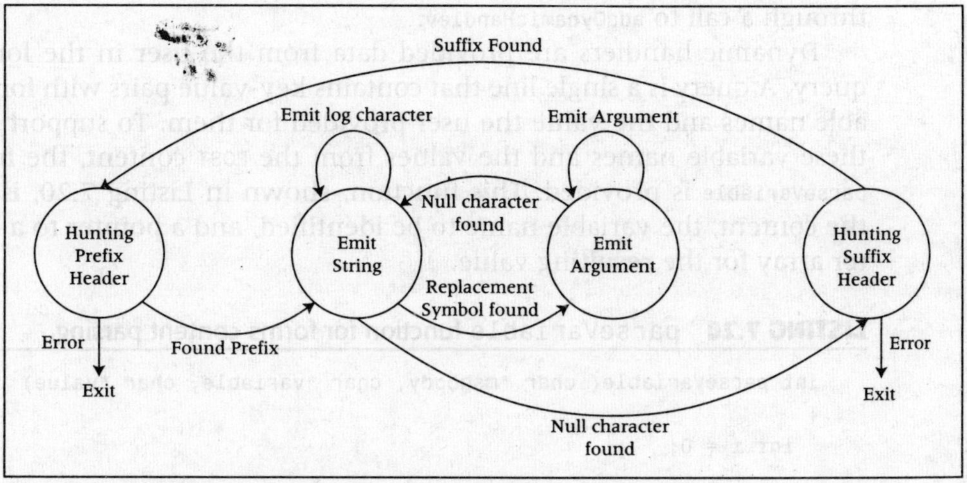

FIGURE 7.6 Compress log emitter state diagram.

One final element to note in `sendLog` is the use of HTML in the output of the log. By emitting HTML headers and footers before and after the log entries, the log is rendered by the client browser with a nicer presentation.

User-Defined Plug-Ins

The user can customize the HTTP server with new content or forms handlers by installing handlers in the `userInit` function of `user.c`. We'll look at specific examples of this in the customizing section.

Developing dynamic content functions are very easy since the function need only return a character string that will be embedded into the content stream. The function must have the basic prototype:

```
char *dynamicContentFunction ( void );
```

The function will be called when the variable associated with the function is encountered within a file being served.

Developing dynamic form handlers is also very easy, following the same model. The form handler is a function that has the following basic prototype:

```
void dynamicHandlerFunction ( char *content );
```

The function is called when the form name is received as a POST method request. The user must have associated the form name with the function through a call to addDynamicHandler.

Dynamic handlers are provided data from the user in the form of a query. A query is a single line that contains key-value pairs with form variable names and the value the user provided for them. To support parsing these variable names and the values from the POST content, the function parseVariable is provided. This function, shown in Listing 7.20, is passed the content, the variable name to be identified, and a pointer to a character array for the resulting value.

LISTING 7.20 parseVariable function for forms content parsing.

```
int parseVariable( char *msgbody, char *variable, char *value)
{
  int i = 0;

  /* First, find the variable in the message body */
  msgbody = strstr(msgbody, variable);

  if (msgbody == NULL) return -1;

  /* Skip the variable and the '=' */
  msgbody += strlen(variable) + 1;

  /* Finally, copy the value into the value string */
  while (msgbody[i] != '&') {
    value[i] = msgbody[i];
    i++;
  }

  value[i] = 0;

  return 0;
}
```

The function parseVariable simply searches the content for the variable name, and once found, the value is copied into the user buffer until the '&' delimiter character is found. We'll look at an example of this function in the customization section.

Compiled Content (`filedata.c`)

Compiled content is a pre-compilation step to convert a tree of content into a single file that contains the content in C structure form. Recall from Table 7.1 that the format of the file is based upon file entries of a specific format.

Our content file is created by a separate application called `buildfs`. This application takes a directory structure as an argument and then accumulates all files found in the tree into the compilable structure.

The `buildfs` application can be found on the accompanying CD-ROM at ./software/ch7/buildfs.

CUSTOMIZING FOR AN APPLICATION

Let's now look at how the embedded HTTP server can be customized for a variety of different applications.

Adding Support for Dynamic Data

Let's first walk through an example of emitting dynamic data through an HTML page. The first task is to write our Web page that contains our `<DATA x>` dynamic tag. The example in Listing 7.21 is a simple page that includes some text data and a single dynamic element called `myvar`.

LISTING 7.21 HTML file with dynamic content.

```
<HTML>
<HEAD>
<TITLE>
Dynamic Content Test
</TITLE>
</HEAD>
<BODY>
The following is a test of dynamic content.
<P>
The myvar entry is <DATA myvar>.
<P>
That was the end of the test...
</BODY>
</HTML>
```

The next step is to write our function to provide the variable identified by myvar. Recall that a dynamic content function simply returns a character string representing our data. The function in Listing 7.22 shows this.

LISTING 7.22 Dynamic Content Function for myvar.

```
static char dataline[80];

char *myvarfunc()
{
  static int myvar = 0;

  myvar++;

  sprintf(dataline, "%d", myvar);

  return(dataline);
}
```

The function myvarfunc simply returns the current count of a statically scoped integer value. Each time the function is called, the counter is incremented.

Finally, we install the handler. This install associates the name myvar, as defined in the HTML file, with the function myvarfunc.

```
addDynamicContent("myvar", &myvarfunc);
```

Therefore, whenever the variable name myvar is encountered in the HTML file, the entire tag is replaced with the string result of the call to myvar function. The resulting display of the HTML file by the browser is then shown in Figure 7.7.

From the example shown in Figure 7.7, the page had been reloaded three times (after the initial load). Therefore, the value of myvar had incremented beyond the initialized value of 0.

Adding Support for Forms Processing

Adding a dynamic forms handler is slightly more complicated than adding dynamic content, but the infrastructure for doing so follows the dynamic content model. First, we'll build the HTML page that will implement our Web form. This page is illustrated in Listing 7.23.

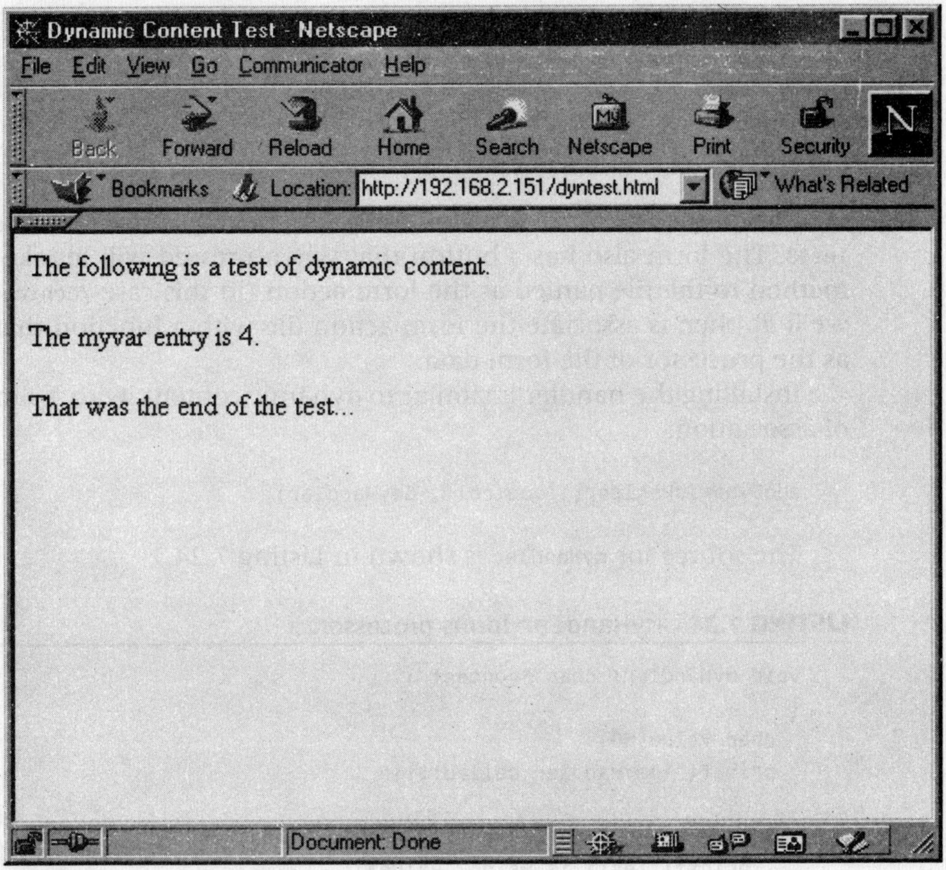

FIGURE 7.7 Browser display for dynamic content test.

LISTING 7.23 HTML file with form (`formtest.html`).

```
<HTML>
<HEAD>
<TITLE>
Form Test
</TITLE>
</HEAD>
<BODY>

This is a test.

<FORM ACTION="/control" METHOD="POST">
  <INPUT TYPE=TEXT NAME="Test1" SIZE=10>Test1:
  <INPUT TYPE=TEXT NAME="Test2" SIZE=10>Test2:
```

```
    <INPUT TYPE=TEXT NAME="Test3" SIZE=10>Test3:
    <INPUT TYPE="submit" NAME="Go">
  </FORM>
  </BODY>
  </HTML>
```

This particular form contains three text fields named `Test1`, `Test2`, and `Test3`. The form also has a button that when pressed will invoke the `POST` method to the file named as the form action (in this case `/control`). What we'll do then is associate the form action file with a function that will act as the processor of the form data.

Installing the handler is similar to dynamic content, with a similar type of association:

```
addDynamicHanlder("/control", &myHandler);
```

The source for `myHandler` is shown in Listing 7.24.

LISTING 7.24 `myHandler` **forms processor.**

```
void myHandler( char *content )
{
  char value[80];
  printf("\nmyHandler called!!!\n");

  if (parseVariable(content, "Test1", value) == 0) {
    printf("Test1 is %s\n", value);
  } else {
    printf("Test1 not found\n");
  }

  if (parseVariable(content, "Test2", value) == 0) {
    printf("Test2 is %s\n", value);
  } else {
    printf("Test2 not found\n");
  }

  if (parseVariable(content, "Test3", value) == 0) {
    printf("Test3 is %s\n", value);
  } else {
    printf("Test3 not found\n");
  }

}
```

When this function is called, we'll emit some data for debugging purposes at the server. The meat of the function is to parse out the values of the variables that are present in the posted request to the server. Recall from Listing 7.23 that each of the text fields has a name. From the source in Listing 7.24, the `parseVariable` function is used to extract the value that is associated with the variable name in the POST content.

The form is rendered as shown in Figure 7.8.

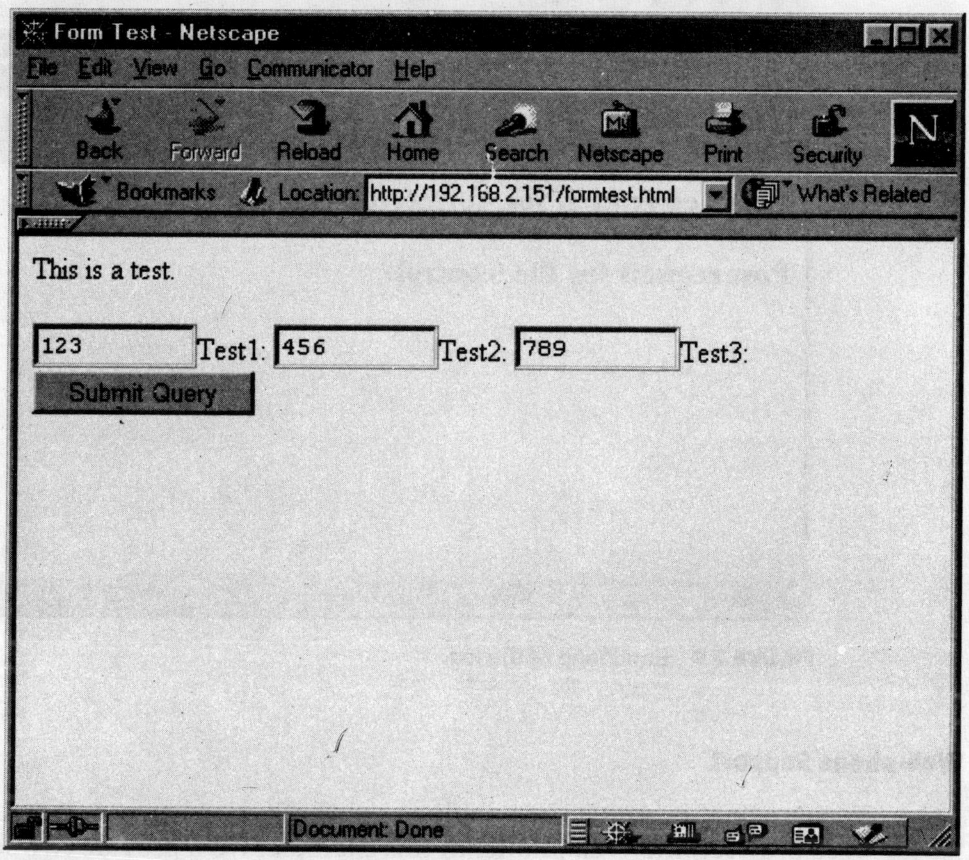

FIGURE 7.8 Browser display for form test.

When the "Submit Query" button is clicked, the shell window running the HTTP server displays the following information:

```
myHandler called!!!
Test1 is 123
```

```
Test2 is 456
Test3 is 789
```

If we now request the log, we'll see two entries. The first is for the `formtest` request and the second for the `POST` (see Figure 7.9).

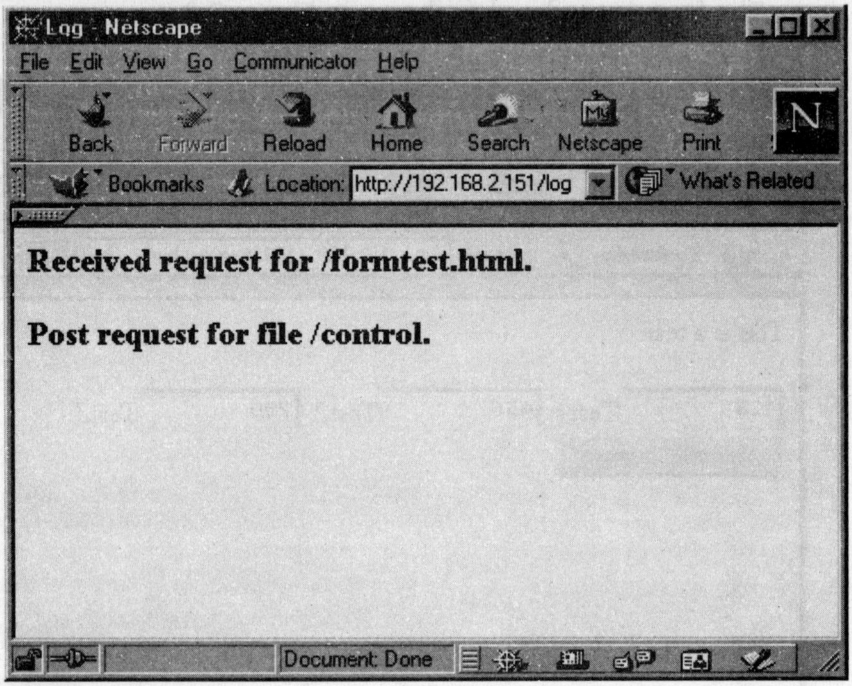

FIGURE 7.9 Rendering of the log.

Web-phone Support

For our final example, let's look at serving content to a non-traditional Web browser, the Web phone. In this example, we'll provide two separate files (one in HTML and one in HDML), but a single set of dynamic content variables that will be requested by each. Listing 7.25 provides the HTML file listing and Listing 7.26 provides the HDML listing.

LISTING 7.25 HTML file with dynamic content (`browser.html`).

```
<HTML>
<HEAD>
</HEAD>
```

```
<BODY>
<CENTER><H2>Device Status</H2></CENTER>
<P>
<PRE>    State    <DATA devstate></PRE>
<PRE>    Temp     <DATA devtemp></PRE>
<PRE>    Accesses <DATA devaccess></PRE>
</BODY>
</HTML>
```

LISTING 7.26 HDML file with dynamic content (`webphone.hdml`).

```
<HDML VERSION="3.0">
<DISPLAY>
<WRAP><CENTER>
Device Status<BR>
<LINE>
<TAB>State<TAB><DATA devstate>
<BR>
<TAB>Temp<TAB><DATA devtemp>
<BR>
<TAB>Accesses<TAB><DATA devaccess>
<BR>
</DISPLAY>
</HDML>
```

Note that each provides the same basic content, but each uses a different markup technology. The first is simple HTML while the second is the Handheld Device Markup Language. This markup language is common among current Web-enabled cellular phones.

Each uses three dynamic variables, whose functions are provided in Listing 7.27

LISTING 7.27 Dynamic functions for `browser.html` and `webphone.hdml`.

```
static char dataline[80];

char *devstateFunc()
{
  /* Dummy return... */
  return( "on" );
}

char *devtempFunc()
{
```

```
    /* Dummy return... */
    return( "25C" );
}

char *devaccessFunc()
{
    static int accesses = 0;

    accesses++;

    sprintf(dataline, "%d", accesses);

    return(dataline);
}
```

The first two functions (`devstateFunc` and `devtempFunc`) simply return a static string. The next indicates the number of times the page has been accessed (`devaccessFunc`). These functions are installed into the server as shown next:

```
addDynamicContent("devstate", &devstateFunc);
addDynamicContent("devtemp", &devtempFunc);
addDynamicContent("devaccess", &devaccessFunc);
```

The browser and Web phone perform rendering differently. While the desktop browser has the ability to provide rich presentation of data (see Figure 7.10), the Web phone has a limited display (see Figure 7.11). Despite this weakness, the Web phone can provide a great platform for remote monitoring.

It's important to note that each file is presented to the requesting device based upon the `content-type`. When the desktop browser requests `browser.html`, the file is sent to the client with a `content-type` of `text/html`. When the Web-enabled cellphone requests webphone.hdml, the file is sent with a `content-type` of `text/hdml`. This permits any device to understand the contents of the transmitted data and either render correctly, or provide an error.

FUTURE

While HTTP has grown to be a very powerful protocol in the domain of serving content to Web clients, its applications are growing outside of this

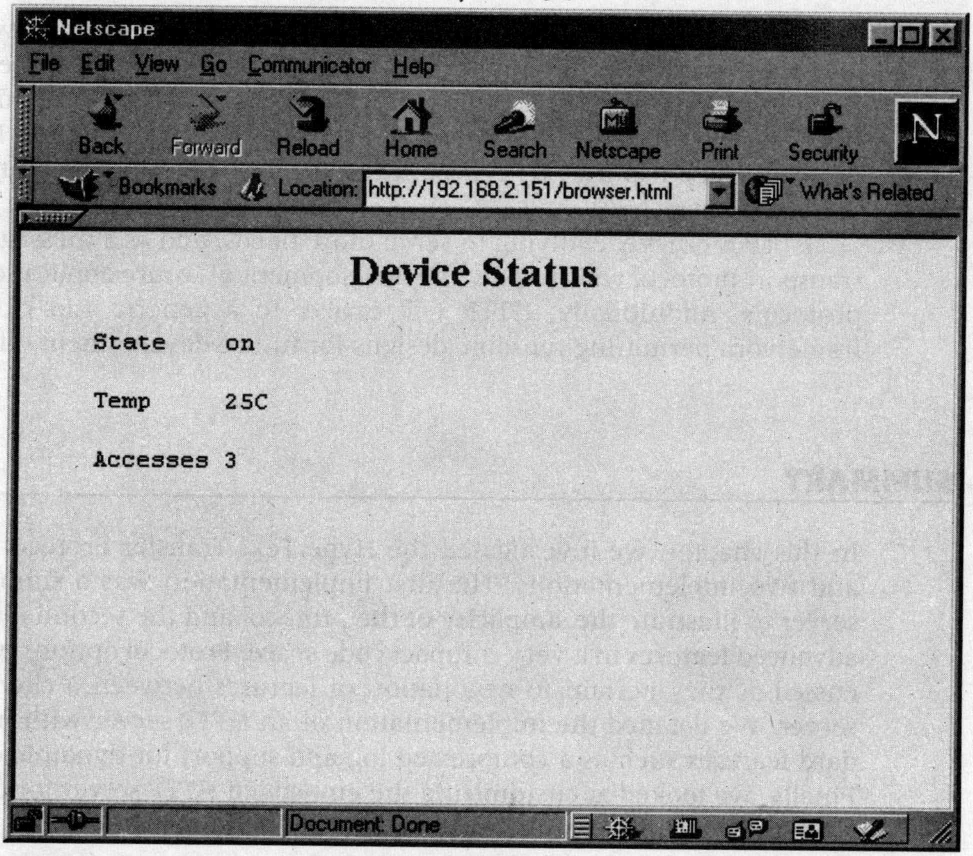

FIGURE 7.10 Browser presentation of `browser.html`.

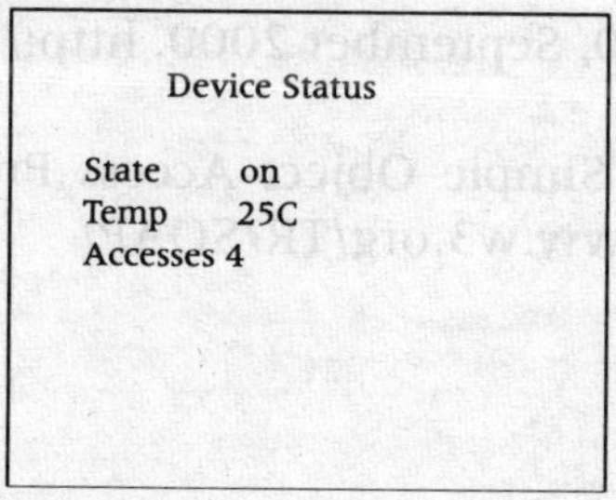

FIGURE 7.11 Web phone presentation of `webphone.hdml`

initial design. HTTP is growing towards a transport protocol that will provide the basis for future application layer protocols. For example, SOAP (Simple Object Access Protocol) and XML-RPC use HTTP as the means to transport their messages between clients and servers. The Internet Printing Protocol (IPP) also uses HTTP as a transport for delivering content to network printers.

HTTP is quickly evolving to serve more needs, and as a message-based transport protocol will simplify the development of future application layer protocols. Additionally, HTTP will evolve to a generic and extensible framework permitting reusable designs for future development efforts.

SUMMARY

In this chapter, we investigated the HyperText Transfer Protocol (HTTP) and two implementations. The first implementation was a simple static server to illustrate the simplicity of the protocol and the second illustrated advanced features in a very compact code space. Protocol options were discussed as they pertain to negotiation of features between a client and a server. We detailed the implementation of an HTTP server with nonstandard features such as a compressed log and support for dynamic content. Finally, we looked at customizing the embedded HTTP server for dynamic content, forms processing, and support for Web-enabled cellular phones.

RESOURCES

Fielding, et al., "Hypertext Transfer Protocol—HTTP/1.1," RFC 2068, January 1997. http://www.landfield.org/rfcs/rfc2068.html

Herriot, et al., "Internet Printing Protocol/1.1: Encoding and Transport," RFC 2910, September 2000. http://www.landfield.org/rfcs/rfc2910.html

Box, et al., "Simple Object Access Protocol (SOAP) 1.1," May 2000. http://www.w3.org/TR/SOAP/

8 Embedded SNMP Agent

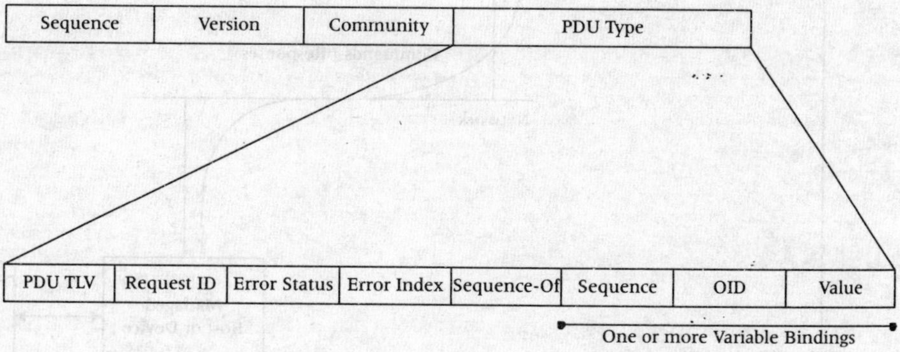

INTRODUCTION

In this chapter, we'll discuss the SNMP architecture, protocol and the development of a very simple SNMP agent targeted towards embedded systems. To demonstrate the agent, we'll configure it to provide command and status information for a remotely controlled antenna.

When it comes to internetworking management, the Simple Network Management Protocol (or SNMP) is the de facto standard protocol. SNMP has provided remote monitoring and management of internetworking equipment since the late 1980s. SNMP is easily extendable, allowing vendors to add their own management functions under a standard framework.

SNMP provides a very simple architecture for monitoring and management. Because of its simplicity and ubiquity, it's hard to find a piece of networking equipment that doesn't support the SNMP.

SNMP SYSTEM ARCHITECTURE

SNMP follows a standard client/server architecture (see Figure 8.1) in which the Network Management System (or NMS) is the client to the many SNMP agents distributed throughout the network.

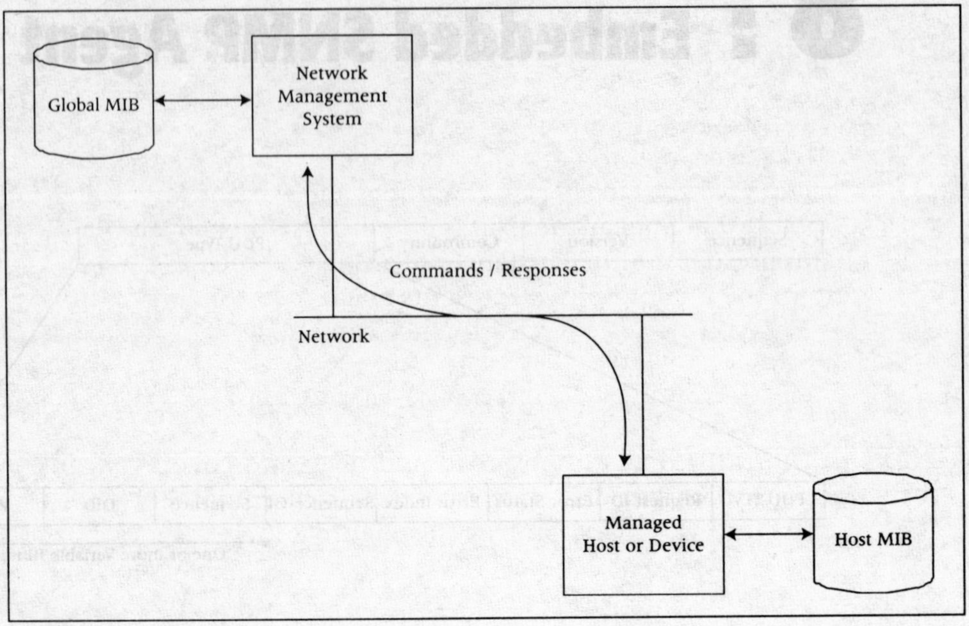

FIGURE 8.1 SNMP architecture.

One of the problems of network management is the perpetual growth of assets on a network that must be managed. This can become a very difficult problem even if the assets are similar (host computers, routers, embedded devices). Without SNMP, the network administrator would have to manually monitor and administer these devices. With SNMP, as new devices are added to a network the NMS can be notified and then routinely monitor them and the parameters they provide. In this way, errors or failures can be quickly identified to maintain network integrity.

SNMP DATA STRUCTURE

Perhaps one of SNMP's greatest strengths is its simplicity. Objects within SNMP are stored in a tree sorted by their Object IDentifier (OID). OIDs are sequences of numbers that identify a particular object within the tree. For example, a standard collection of objects (known in SNMP as a MIB, or Management Information Base) is the System MIB. This MIB contains a number of objects whose values are specific to the device hosting the SNMP agent. One of these objects is known as the System Description (`system.SysDescr.0`). As an OID, this object is uniquely identified by the sequence:

```
{1.3.6.1.2.1.1.1.0}
```

The final zero in this OID identifies this variable as a scalar. A scalar is an object that appears once in the tree. This differs from columnar objects that represent multiple instances of an object (such as a table of values). A zero in the final position represents a leaf (or endpoint) in the tree.

Textually, the previous sequence can also be represented as:

```
iso(1) org(3) dod(6) internet(1) mgmt(2) mib-2(1) system(1) sysDescr(1)
```

The MIB tree is quite broad and deep and covers not only network endpoint data but also data for specialized equipment such as Internet routers, gateways, and bridges (see Figure 8.2).

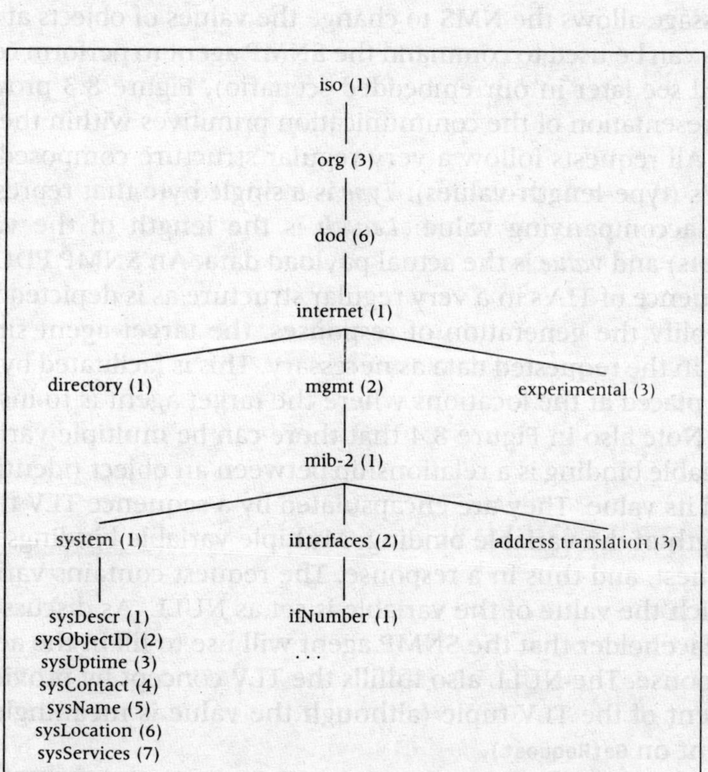

FIGURE 8.2 Sample portion of the MIB-II tree.

Objects in SNMPv1 are typed. The variables can be non-negative INTEGER values, OCTET_STRINGS, or OBJECT_IDENTIFIERS (similar to octet strings). Other specialized types exist such as IPADDRESS for identifying IP addresses and TIMETICKS for representing time.

SNMP PROTOCOL

SNMPv1 provides five basic communication primitives (or Protocol Data Units—PDUs). SNMP provides two synchronous request messages called GetRequest and GetNextRequest. The GetRequest message takes an object identifier and results in a GetResponse message from the SNMP agent. The GetNextRequest yields the object after the named object identifier in the request (again via a GetResponse message). SNMP also provides an asynchronous response called a trap. A trap is a notification of a condition that is sent directly to the NMS. This is used to notify the NMS of errors that may not be able to wait until the next interrogation cycle. Finally, the SetRequest message allows the NMS to change the values of objects at an SNMP agent. This can be used to command the SNMP agent to perform certain actions (as we'll see later in our embedded scenario). Figure 8.3 provides a graphical representation of the communication primitives within the architecture.

All requests follow a very regular structure composed of tuples called TLVs (type-length-values). *Type* is a single byte that represents the type of the accompanying value. *Length* is the length of the value section (in octets) and *value* is the actual payload data. An SNMP PDU is made up of a sequence of TLVs in a very regular structure as is depicted in Figure 8.4. To simplify the generation of responses, the target agent simply parses and fills in the requested data as necessary. This is facilitated by NULL TLVs that are placed at the locations where the target agent is to insert data.

Note also in Figure 8.4 that there can be multiple variable bindings. A variable binding is a relationship between an object (identified by the OID) and its value. They are encapsulated by a sequence TLV that identifies the length of the variable binding. Multiple variable bindings may appear in a request, and thus in a response. The request contains variable bindings in which the value of the variable is set as NULL. As discussed before, this is a placeholder that the SNMP agent will use to fill in the actual data for the response. The NULL also fulfills the TLV concept by providing the final element of the TLV tuple (although the value is meaningless to the SNMP agent on GetRequest).

Now that we've seen conceptually how an SNMP PDU will appear, let's dig into the details of an example of both a request and response. In Figure

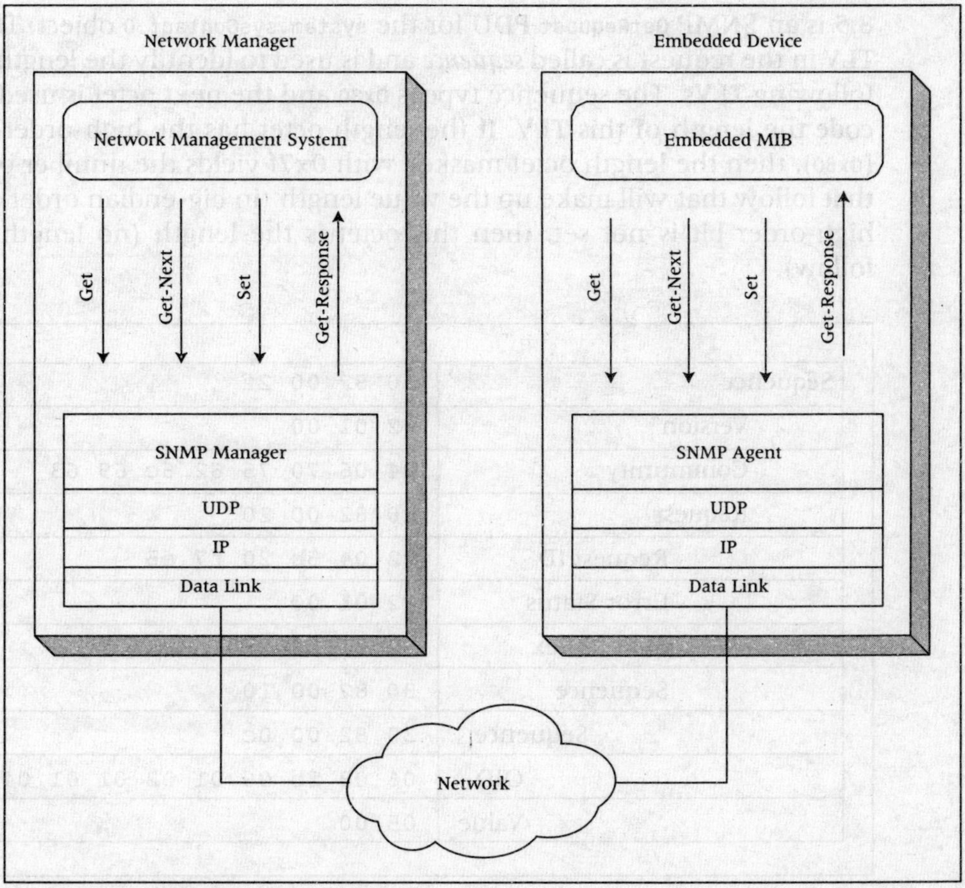

FIGURE 8.3 SNMP system architecture.

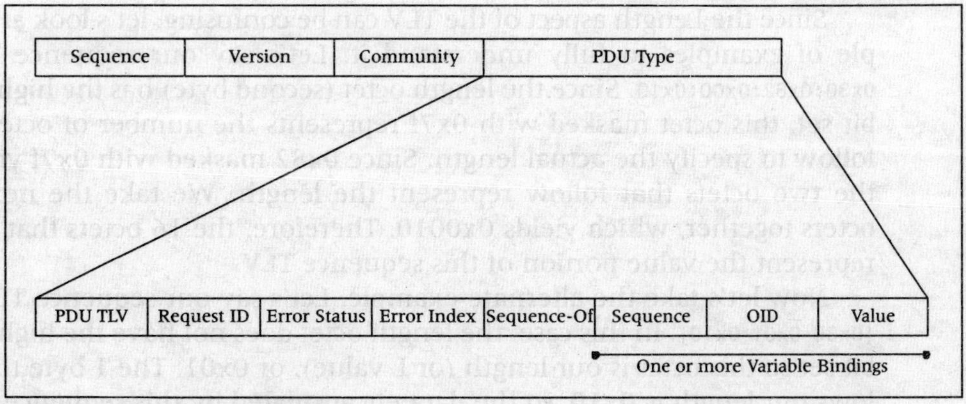

FIGURE 8.4 SNMP PDU format.

8.5 is an SNMP `GetRequest` PDU for the `system.sysContact.0` object. The first TLV in the request is called *sequence* and is used to identify the length of the following TLVs. The sequence type is `0x30` and the next octet is used to decode the length of this TLV. If the length octet has the high-order bit set (`0x80`), then the length octet masked with 0x7f yields the number of bytes that follow that will make up the value length (in big-endian order). If the high-order bit is not set, then this octet is the length (no length octets follow).

Sequence	`30 82 00 2f`
Version	`02 01 00`
Community	`04 06 70 75 62 6c 69 63`
Request	`a0 82 00 20`
Request ID	`02 04 5b 20 f7 e5`
Error Status	`02 01 00`
Error Index	`02 01 00`
Sequence	`30 82 00 10`
Sequence	`30 82 00 0c`
OID	`06 08 2b 06 01 02 01 01 04 00`
Value	`05 00`

FIGURE 8.5 SNMP `GetRequest` PDU for the system.sysContact.0 object.

Since the Length aspect of the TLV can be confusing, let's look at a couple of examples to fully understand it. Let's say our sequence TLV is `0x30:0x82:0x00:0x10`. Since the length octet (second byte) has the high-order bit set, this octet masked with 0x7f represents the number of octets that follow to specify the actual length. Since 0x82 masked with 0x7f yields 2, the two octets that follow represent the length. We take the next two octets together, which yields 0x0010. Therefore, the 16 octets that follow represent the value portion of this sequence TLV.

Now let's take the alternate example. Let's say our sequence TLV was `{0x30 0x01 0x10}`. In this case, the length octet does not have the high-order bit set so this octet is our length (or L value), or 0x01. The 1 byte that follows our length is 0x10, so the data encapsulated by this sequence TLV is 0x10 (or decimal 16 octets).

Back to Figure 8.5, we see the first TLV is a sequence TLV. As discussed before, the sequence TLV includes as its value the length of the TLVs that it encapsulates. In this case, 0x2f (or decimal 47) octets follow this sequence TLV.

The version TLV specifies the version of the SNMP request. In this case, the value is Integer 0 which represents SNMPv1. The Community type specifies the community string which when parsed is an Octet String TLV of value "public." Next is the actual request, which in this case is a `GetRequest` (type 0xA0). The value of this TLV represents the length of the request. A request is always followed by a `Request-ID` TLV to correlate responses to their requests at the manager, and an error status and error index TLV. The error status is filled in on response to inform if any errors occurred. The error index represents the variable binding that the target agent identified as being faulty. Next is a sequence type that encapsulates all variable bindings included in the PDU. Again, the value of this sequence TLV is the length of the remaining octets of the variable binding.

Every variable binding is made up of three TLVs, a sequence type for binding, and OID TLV (to identify the object which we're requesting) and a value TLV. As discussed before, the value in this case is a NULL TLV to be used as a marker for the SNMP agent to insert the actual value.

The SNMP response PDU (`GetResponse`) is modeled very closely to the request (see Figure 8.6). This is because the request is created in a way to

Sequence	30 82 00 3e
Version	02 01 00
Community	04 06 70 75 62 6c 69 63
Request	a2 82 00 2f
Request ID	02 04 5b 20 f7 e5
Error Status	02 01 00
Error Index	02 01 00
Sequence	30 82 00 1f
Sequence	30 82 00 1b
OID	06 08 2b 06 01 02 01 01 04 00
Value	04 0f 6d 74 6a 40 6d 74 6a 6f 6e 65 73 2e 63 6f 6d

FIGURE 8.6 SNMP `GetResponse` PDU for the `system.sysContact.0` object.

minimize the processing required to generate a response. This of course is theory and the practicality of this goal is questionable. The first difference to note in the response is that the lengths have all been updated for any new data added to the response. The essential difference, however, is that the value TLV that has been filled in for the response. The NULL TLV of the variable binding has been filled in with the OID value (as represented in the SNMP MIB table) requested in the binding. The binding value is of type `Octet-String` with a value of `0x04`.

While the TLV structure of SNMP PDUs is conceptually simple, it does offer some complexities. Certain TLVs may be more complicated, depending upon their length, but overall, the structure is both regular and simple.

EXTENDING THE INTERNAL MIB

The MIB is easily extendable by simply adding new MIB entries to the `snmpData` table found in the source file `user.c`. An entry to the table has the following structure (shown in Listing 8.1):

LISTING 8.1 SNMP MIB entry structure.

```
typedef struct {
    unsigned char oidlen;
    unsigned char oid[MAX_OID];
    unsigned char dataType;
    unsigned char dataLen;
    union {
        unsigned char octetstring[MAX_STRING];
        unsigned int intval;
    } u;
    void (*function)(void *, unsigned char *);
} dataEntryType;
```

The field `oidLen` is the length of the `oid` field (object identifier). This is the sequence of digits that uniquely identify the object. The `dataType` field identifies the type of data represented by the OID. This can be one of `INTEGER`, `OCTET_STRING`, `OBJECT_IDENTIFIER`, `COUNTER` or `TIME TICKS`. The `dataLen` field represents the length of the data represented by the OID. A union is used to represent the varying types of data that may exist. In our case, a character string and an integer are all that are needed.

The final element is a pointer to a function. This function is used for user-defined data that is dynamically generated at request time. An example of dynamic data is the system uptime variable. Let's have a look at its initialization. The following structure initialization is based upon the type `dataEntryType` (from Listing 8.1):

```
{8, {0x2b, 6, 1, 2, 1, 1, 3, 0},
   TIME_TICKS, 0, {""},
   currentUptime}
```

The first field (`8`) is the length in bytes of the object identifier. This is followed by the actual `OID` and is represented as a byte array. The next element is the type field of the variable. In this case, the type is `TIME_TICKS` that is used to represent time data with a least significant bit representing 10ms. The next two fields are the length of the data and the value to be returned upon request. These are both set to null since they will be dynamically filled upon requested. Finally, we specify our function that will be called when this particular OID is requested.

All dynamic functions return a void pointer to the data and a byte length of the data (as references to the function). See Listing 8.2 for a dynamic function example.

LISTING 8.2 Example dynamic function for `Uptime`.

```
static void currentUptime(void *ptr, unsigned char *len)
{
  time_t curTime = time(NULL);
  *(unsigned int *)ptr =
       (unsigned int)(curTime - startTime) * 100;
  *len = 4;
}
```

The SNMP agent will determine how to treat the data based upon the type stored in the `dataEntryType`. In the case of `TIME_TICKS`, the SNMP agent knows to treat this return as an integer.

AN EMBEDDED SCENARIO

To further illustrate the use of the SNMP agent in an embedded environment, let's create a scenario and update the agent MIB to support data collection for it. Consider an embedded system controlling a remote antenna. The antenna can be commanded to point to a desired position (using azimuth and elevation) and provides sync status and signal strength from the onboard receiver.

In the SNMP agent, four variables will be used for our interface. These will be grafted to the experimental branch of the MIB tree (shown in Figure 8.7).

OID	Description	Type
1.3.6.1.3.1.0	Azimuth Commanded Position	INTEGER
1.3.6.1.3.2.0	Elevation Commanded Position	INTEGER
1.3.6.1.3.3.0	Receiver Sync Status	OCTET_STRING
1.3.6.1.3.4.0	Receiver Signal Strength	INTEGER

FIGURE 8.7 Antenna MIB elements.

Not having a spare dish and receiver lying around, we'll simulate this code within the user section of the SNMP agent. Our coordinate system will use 0 to 180 degrees to represent the range of movement of the antenna. Therefore, if azimuth and elevation are each set to 90, the antenna is in the zenith position (that is, pointing straight up).

The first step is to create the MIB entries within the SNMP agent. The accompanying source includes the system branch of the MIB, so we'll append this experimental section at the end. In Listing 8.3 is the newly added portion of the MIB.

LISTING 8.3 New MIB entries for the antenna system.

```
/* Antenna Azimuth Commanded Position */
{6, {0x2b, 6, 1, 3, 1, 0},
 INTEGER, 4, {""},
 NULL},

/* Antenna Elevation Commanded Position */
{6, {0x2b, 6, 1, 3, 2, 0},
 INTEGER, 4, {""},
 NULL},

/* Antenna Receiver Sync Status */
{6, {0x2b, 6, 1, 3, 3, 0},
 OCTET_STRING, 0, {""},
 syncStatus},
```

```
/* Antenna Receiver Signal Strength */
{6, {0x2b, 6, 1, 3, 4, 0},
 INTEGER, 0, {""},
 signalStrength}
```

Next, we'll add our functions to generate the dynamic data. For our remotely controlled antenna scenario, two variables are dynamically generated. These are shown in Listing 8.4.

LISTING 8.4 New antenna system dynamic functions.

```
static int sigStr = 0;

static void syncStatus ( void *ptr, unsigned char *len )
{
  if (snmpData[8].u.intval > 90) {
    *len = sprintf((char *)ptr, "detected");
    sigStr = 99;
  } else {
    *len = sprintf((char *)ptr, "no signal");
    sigStr = 0;
  }
}

static void signalStrength ( void *ptr, unsigned char *len )
{
  *(unsigned int *)ptr = sigStr;
  *len = 4;
}
```

The `snmpData` structure represents our MIB table that contains both the data and the descriptions. One item worth note is the use of `snmpData` within function `syncStatus`. To generate simulated data, we specify that when the antenna elevation is greater than 90 degrees, we're pointing to something interesting and a receiver lock is achieved (with associated signal strength). Offset `8` in our MIB table (see Listing 8 4) is the elevation entry and since it's represented as an `INTEGER` type, we use the `intval` element of the union to identify its value.

Now that we've updated our MIB and created our dynamic functions, let's try it out using some of the readily available `snmp` tools. In this experiment, we'll execute our SNMP agent on top of Linux and then use the UC Davis SNMP tools to work with our custom target. As discussed before, developing and testing the protocol on Linux (or any other desktop operating system) is useful to work out any major bugs that may exist before we port to our target environment.

First, let's request our system MIB from the embedded device. The utility `snmpwalk` can be used to perform successive `snmpget` commands to retrieve all objects under the system portion of the MIB tree. An example is provided in Listing 8.5.

LISTING 8.5 Example usage of snmpwalk utility to communicate with the embedded agent.

```
[mtj@plato home]$ ./emsnmp &
[1] 1147
Started the SNMP agent

[mtj@plato home]$ snmpwalk plato public system
system.sysDescr.0 = Embedded Computer
system.sysObjectID.0 = OID: system.sysObjectID.0
system.sysUpTime.0 = Timeticks: (3900) 0:00:39.00
system.sysContact.0 = mtj@mtjones.com
system.sysName.0 = ec.mtjones.com
system.sysLocation.0 = B3B44
system.sysServices.0 = 5
[mtj@plato mtj]$
```

Next, we can interface to our experimental MIB. Since we don't have a MIB compiled with our data, we'll use a numeric object identifier to specify our variables on the target.

```
[mtj@plato mtj]$ snmpget plato public .1.3.6.1.3.3.0
3.0 = "no signal"
[mtj@plato mtj]$
```

The object identified by *.1.3.6.1.3.3.0* is our receiver sync variable, and our simulation is telling us that the receiver sees no signal. We know from our previous discussion regarding the details of the simulation that all we need to do is command the antenna elevation to a value greater than 90 degrees to see a signal. We accomplish this by setting the elevation variable to a threshold value:

```
[mtj@plato] snmpset plato public .1.3.6.1.3.2.0 i 91
2.0 = 91
[mtj@plato mtj]$
```

The `i 91` *represents an integer value of 91. Octet strings may also be set similarly with* `s <string>`.

Finally we read back our sync variable:

```
[mtj@plato mtj]$ snmpget plato public .1.3.6.1.3.3.0
3.0 = "detected"
[mtj@plato mtj]$
```

Note that the `public` argument in the command is the SNMP community name. This is defined in the `emsnmp.h` header file and can be changed for security purposes. Since SNMPv1 traffic is performed in clear text (can be sniffed on the network and spoofed) this should not imply that SNMP is secure.

EMBEDDED SNMP IMPLEMENTATION

The design of the embedded SNMP agent is quite simple. Thinking back to the `GetRequest` and `GetResponse` PDUs, you'll remember that the PDU is made up of a number of constructs (TLVs) that can encapsulate one another. For example, the initial sequence type includes as its value the remaining octets of the message. The same applies for the actual request, and subsequent sequence types. Building a request, or in our case a reply, implies that we descend down to the last TLV and build the message in a sense backwards (since the lengths of initial TLVs depend upon the lengths of all subsequent TLVs).

This problem is reminiscent of the backpatching method used in single-pass assemblers. Consider an assembly file that contains code and declarations of variables. If the variables are declared after their use in the source, then the assembler must either make a first pass through the source to identify where they're located, or it must find another solution. Multiple passes through the source are expensive so something else is needed. Backpatching solves this by building a linked list through the locations that should contain the address of the undefined variable in the generated code. The head pointer of the list is inserted into the symbol table at the address location of the undefined entry. When the symbol is finally defined, we "backpatch" through the generated code and replace the list pointers with the actual address of the symbol.

The problem with SNMP message generation is similar. Instead of forward symbol declaration, we have forward (unknown) TLV lengths. The lengths of the TLVs are dependent upon the lengths of the encapsulated TLVs. Therefore, we must know the length of the last TLV in order to calculate the lengths of all preceding TLVs.

The solution chosen for this problem is to parse the SNMP request using a predictive parser and build the response as we go. The usefulness of a predictive parser is that at any point we can look at our current TLV and know exactly how to process it and what comes next (given the regular structure of SNMP PDUs). We predictively parse through the SNMP PDU, and when we reach the final TLV, we return through our function call chain and update the length values of the TLVs as needed. This method is conceptually simple, efficient, and straightforward to implement.

Now that the basic structure of the design has been outlined, we'll descend into the actual code in the next section.

SNMP SOURCE CODE DISCUSSION

Now we'll look at the embedded SNMP agent source code in detail. This code can be found on the CD-ROM at ./software/ch8/emsnmp/.

Datagram Server Setup

The SNMP agent is a datagram server (UDP) that operates on a synchronous request/response basis. For each request that is received, an attempt to parse the message is made, and if the SNMPv1 request is valid, an SNMPv1 response is generated. Our first step is the creation of a datagram server (see Listing 8.6).

LISTING 8.6 SNMP agent datagram server setup.

```
struct messageStruct {
  unsigned char buffer[1025];
  int len;
  int index;
};

static struct messageStruct request, response;

/*---------------------------------------------------------
 * main() - The embedded SNMP server main
 *-------------------------------------------------------*/
int main(int argc, char *argv[])
{
```

```
struct sockaddr_in servaddr;
struct sockaddr from;
int snmpfd, fromlen, retStatus;

extern void initTable( void );

initTable();

snmpfd = socket(AF_INET, SOCK_DGRAM, 0);

bzero(&servaddr, sizeof(servaddr));
servaddr.sin_family = AF_INET;
servaddr.sin_addr.s_addr = htonl(INADDR_ANY);
servaddr.sin_port = htons(161);

retStatus = bind(snmpfd, (struct sockaddr *)&servaddr,
                  sizeof(servaddr));

if (retStatus < 0) {
  printf("Unable to bind to socket (%d).\n", errno);
  exit(-1);
}

printf("Started the SNMP agent\n");

for ( ; ; ) {

  fromlen = sizeof(from);
  request.len = recvfrom(snmpfd, &request.buffer[0], 1024, 0,
                          &from, &fromlen);

  printf("Received datagram from %s, port %d\n",
         inet_ntoa(((struct sockaddr_in *)&from)->sin_addr),
         ((struct sockaddr_in *)&from)->sin_port);

  if (request.len >= 0) {

    request.index = response.index = 0;
    errorStatus = errorIndex = 0;

    if (parseSNMPMessage() != -1) {
      sendto(snmpfd, response.buffer, response.index, 0,
             (struct sockaddr *)&from, fromlen);
    }
```

```
        }

    }

    close(snmpfd);
    return(0);
}
```

After initializing our SNMP MIB table (via initTable, covered in the next section) we create our server socket. The socket is of type SOCK_DGRAM to represent a datagram socket. We build our sockaddr structure to accept datagrams from any interface (INADDR_ANY) on this host. The port is restricted to 161 which is the reserved port for SNMP communication.

Once the socket is set up, we go into a loop to accept requests through the socket. Requests are received through the recvfrom call. We use this call instead of recv because the datagram socket is unconnected and we need the peer information in order to send back a response.

Next, we do some initialization and call the function parseSNMPMessage. This is our predictive parser for SNMP; it performs all activities for both parsing and generating a valid response. Once this function returns and informs us that a valid response message was constructed, we use sendto to transmit the response back to the requester. Note that in the sendto call, we're using the from and fromlen parameters that we originally received through the recvfrom call (i.e., the source of the request).

At this point, our dialog is complete for this request and we return to the top of the loop to await a new request. It should be clear from this example that SNMP is a stateless protocol; the fact that each request message is performed in isolation of others never alters the behavior of subsequent requests.

A final item to note in this listing is the messageStruct structure. Both the request and response variables are derived from this. The structure simply encapsulates the buffer, length of data contained within the buffer, and the working index that's used within the parser and response generator. These are declared global within this function and are used widely within the parsers.

The SNMP MIB Table

SNMP provides access primarily to a tree of data. A network manager can request the values in an agent's tree and change those values. One example subtree used in this embedded agent is very simple, shown in Figure

8.2. The System MIB, which is a standard element present on all devices, is initialized within `user.c` (see Listing 8.7).

LISTING 8.7 SNMP agent table initialization.

```
time_t startTime;

static void currentUptime(void *, unsigned char *);

dataEntryType snmpData[]={

  /* System MIB */

    /* SysDescr Entry */
    {8, {0x2b, 6, 1, 2, 1, 1, 1, 0},
      OCTET_STRING, 17, {"Embedded Computer"},
      NULL},

    /* SysObjectID Entry */
    {8, {0x2b, 6, 1, 2, 1, 1, 2, 0},
      OBJECT_IDENTIFIER, 8, {"\x2b\x06\x01\x02\x01\x01\x02\x00"},
      NULL},

    /* SysUptime Entry */
    {8, {0x2b, 6, 1, 2, 1, 1, 3, 0},
      TIME_TICKS, 0, {""},
      currentUptime},

    /* sysContact Entry */
    {8, {0x2b, 6, 1, 2, 1, 1, 4, 0},
      OCTET_STRING, 15, {"mtj@mtjones.com"},
      NULL},

    /* sysName Entry */
    {8, {0x2b, 6, 1, 2, 1, 1, 5, 0},
      OCTET_STRING, 14, {"ec.mtjones.com"},
      NULL},

    /* Location Entry */
    {8, {0x2b, 6, 1, 2, 1, 1, 6, 0},
      OCTET_STRING, 5, {"B3B44"},
      NULL},

    /* SysServices */
```

```
    {8, {0x2b, 6, 1, 2, 1, 1, 7, 0},
        INTEGER, 4, {""},
        NULL},

};

const int maxData = (sizeof(snmpData) / sizeof(dataEntryType));


/* MIB Initialization */

void initTable( void )
{

  startTime = time(NULL);

  /* Note:  The C spec permits the auto-initialization of the
   * first member of a union.  Therefore, since the first member
   * of the union is a string, we initialize the 'u.intval' elements
   * here.
   */

  snmpData[6].u.intval = 5; /* System.Services */

}

/* Dynamic Data Functions */

static void currentUptime(void *ptr, unsigned char *len)
{
  time_t curTime = time(NULL);
  *(unsigned int *)ptr =
     (unsigned int)(curTime - startTime) * 100;
  *len = 4;
}
```

Most of the initialization is performed through static initialization upon declaration of the `snmpData` structure array. Each entry in the array is a `dataEntryType` structure and is block initialized. We keep track of the number of elements in the table by simply dividing the total size of the table by the size of a single member.

The `initTable` function performs additional initialization not provided by the table. In `initTable` we initialize a `startTime` variable for use in the uptime MIB entry. Finally, we initialize any `intval` union entries. These entries are initialized here because they cannot be initialized in the table during static initialization. This is due to the way C performs auto-initialization of unions. When a union is statically initialized, only the first element of the union may be set. Therefore, since the intval is the second element of the union, it must be initialized separately and is therefore performed here.

Finally, in this code example there is a dynamic function. This function will be called when an SNMP request arrives for the OID entry that is provided by this function. If we refer back to the structure initialization in Listing 8.7, the SysUptime entry sets a function pointer for currentUptime. This function (as do all dynamic functions in this architecture) passes the value for the OID back through an argument by reference. Dynamic functions allow us to know when a request is made and keeps us from having to update the table every time a value changes (for example, an A/D sensor). Whether string or integer values are returned, all are interpreted as void pointers and the SNMP agent figures out which is appropriate from the type within the SNMP table.

Managing the SNMP MIB Table

Two basic functions are provided for retrieving data and storing data in the SNMP MIB table. These are getEntry and setEntry and are shown in Listing 8.8.

The getEntry function takes as its arguments an id (represents an index into the SNMP table) and then three arguments that are passed by reference to allow their values to be altered. This call is used from within the parser for a GetRequest or GetNextRequest PDU. The dataType argument is the actual type of the SNMP entry (OCTET_STRING, INTEGER, etc.). The argument *ptr* is a void pointer used to return the value of the entry and len is its length. All arguments are simply retrieved from the table and returned.

The only complexity of getEntry is that it must determine what type of data is being returned and then pass it back accordingly. For types OCTET_STRING and OBJECT_IDENTIFIER, the data is passed back as a character string. Types INTEGER, TIME_TICKS, COUNTER, and GAUGE are integer types. Both branches of the case simply cast the void pointer to the type being returned and then copy the data normally.

The function getEntry also supports dynamic data whereby the actual data being returned is created at request time. A row in the table providing dynamic data is identified by its dynamic function variable being non-null (contains a function pointer). In these cases, the dynamic function is called and the function fills in the variable and length by reference (instead of retrieving a value from the table).

The `setEntry` function provides the means to set an SNMP entry to a value specified in the request. It is called from within the SNMP parser in response to an SNMP `SetRequest` PDU. The `setEntry` function has the same basic structure as `getEntry`. Depending upon the type of the SNMP entry, the data is manipulated as either a character string or integer.

Another support function called `getValue` is found here. This function is used to create an integer value from a binary value with a given octet length.

LISTING 8.8 SNMP agent table access functions.

```
static int getValue( unsigned char *vptr, int vlen)
{
  int index = 0;
  int value = 0;

  while (index < vlen) {
    if (index != 0) value <<= 8;
    value |= vptr[index++];
  }

  return value;
}


int getEntry ( int id, unsigned char *dataType,
               void *ptr, int *len )
{

  if (!((id >= 0) && (id < maxData))) return INVALID_ENTRY_ID;

  *dataType = snmpData[id].dataType;

  switch(*dataType) {
    case OCTET_STRING :
    case OBJECT_IDENTIFIER :
      {
        unsigned char *string = ptr;
        int j;

        if (snmpData[id].function != NULL) {
          snmpData[id].function(
                      (void *)&snmpData[id].u.octetstring,
```

```
                    &snmpData[id].dataLen );
        }

        *len = snmpData[id].dataLen;
        for (j = 0 ; j < *len ; j++) {
          string[j] = snmpData[id].u.octetstring[j];
        }
      }
      break;

    case INTEGER :
    case TIME_TICKS :
    case COUNTER :
    case GAUGE :
      {
        int *value = ( int * )ptr;

        if (snmpData[id].function != NULL) {
          snmpData[id].function( (void *)&snmpData[id].u.intval,
                                 &snmpData[id].dataLen );
        }

        *len = sizeof(unsigned int);
        *value = htonl(snmpData[id].u.intval);

      }
      break;

    default :
      return INVALID_DATA_TYPE;
      break;

  }

  return SUCCESS;
}

int setEntry ( int id, void *val, int vlen,
          unsigned char dataType, int index)
{

  int retStatus=OID_NOT_FOUND;
```

```
    int j;

    extern int errorStatus, errorIndex;

    if (snmpData[id].dataType != dataType) {
      errorStatus = BAD_VALUE;
      errorIndex = index;
      return INVALID_DATA_TYPE;
    }

    switch(snmpData[id].dataType) {
      case OCTET_STRING :
      case OBJECT_IDENTIFIER :
        {
          unsigned char *string = val;
          for (j = 0 ; j < vlen ; j++) {
            snmpData[id].u.octetstring[j] = string[j];
          }
          snmpData[id].dataLen = vlen;
        }
        retStatus = SUCCESS;
        break;

      case INTEGER :
      case TIME_TICKS :
      case COUNTER :
      case GAUGE :
        {
          snmpData[id].u.intval =
                          getValue( (unsigned char *)val, vlen);
          snmpData[id].dataLen = vlen;
        }
        retStatus = SUCCESS;
        break;

      default :
        retStatus = INVALID_DATA_TYPE;
        break;

    }

    return retStatus;
  }
```

The Parser and Response Generator

The meat of the SNMP agent is the request PDU parser and response PDU generator. These two elements of the agent are performed together when a response message is generated as the parse progresses through the request message.

The basic structure of the parser is a collection of functions whose job it is to parse a particular kind of TLV. Each of the parser functions is called as a chain and each knows what should follow. From Listing 8.6, we can see that the function `parseSNMPMessage` is called that's responsible for parsing the sequence TLV of which all SNMP PDUs begin. The version TLV always follows the initial sequence TLV, and therefore the `parseSNMPMessage` function calls the `parseVersion` function.

All of the parsing functions follow a very similar pattern. First, the function `parseTLV` is called which does some very simple parsing of the TLV and initializes a TLV structure to identify where the TLV sits within the request message. Next, the TLV is checked to ensure it's what we expect at this point in the parse. We'll then copy the TLV from request message to the response message and record the position in a local variable called `respLoc`. At this point, we've done all of the parsing we can do for this TLV, so the next job is to call the next parsing function in the chain. When the parser returns, we record the length that was returned which represents the total size of the PDU from our position to the end. Finally, we return the length with our `size` added to give the caller an accurate size from its perspective.

One important point to notice here is that while a parser function calls another parser function in line, it can do processing before the function and processing afterward. Processing after the next parser is called allows us to perform the basic backpatching of lengths that we discussed earlier in this chapter. For example, the length returned by the parser is the octet length of all TLVs that follow the current TLV. Therefore, if we need to record a length in the current TLV, that length comes from the return of the called parser function. We in turn pass that length plus our own size up to the previous caller to continue the process. This is the purpose of recording the location of `respLoc`. This is the index in the response message where we insert our length to generate a valid response.

Basic Parsing Primitives

Before jumping into the SNMP parsers, let's first look at some of the basic primitives for parsing unspecified TLVs (see Listing 8.9). The structure tlvStrucType is used to hold the information about a TLV (which is held locally in scope by each parsing function). The structure contains the start index of the TLV, its length (the *L* value of the TLV), the index of the Value (*V* portion of TLV), and the index of the next TLV. We create a local TLV structure and pass it to the function parseTLV. This function performs the TLV parsing and fills in the elements of the structure. Note that this function must understand the type of the TLV since it affects the calculation of the next TLV index.

The parseLength function is also provided here which performs length calculation (computes the *L* portion of the TLV). As discussed earlier in this chapter, a length can be a single byte, or a series of bytes depending upon the high-order bit setting of the *L* byte.

LISTING 8.9 SNMP TLV parsing routines.

```
typedef struct {
  int start;     /* Absolute Index of the TLV */
  int len;       /* The L value of the TLV */
  int vstart;    /* Absolute Index of this TLV's Value */
  int nstart;    /* Absolute Index of the next TLV */
} tlvStructType;

static int parseLength(const unsigned char *msg, int *len)
{
  int i=1;

  if (msg[0] & 0x80) {
    int tlen = (msg[0] & 0x7f) - 1;
    *len = msg[i++];

    while (tlen--) {
      *len <<= 8;
      *len |= msg[i++];
    }

  } else {
    *len = msg[0];
  }

  return i;
}
```

```
static int parseTLV(const unsigned char *msg, int index,
                    tlvStructType *tlv)
{
  int Llen = 0;

  tlv->start = index;

  Llen = parseLength((const char *)&msg[index+1], &tlv->len );

  tlv->vstart = index + Llen + 1;

  switch (msg[index]) {
    case SEQUENCE:
    case GET_REQUEST:
    case GET_NEXT_REQUEST:
    case SET_REQUEST:
      tlv->nstart = tlv->vstart;
      break;
    default:
      tlv->nstart = tlv->vstart + tlv->len;
      break;
  }

  return 0;
}
```

Parsing and Response Generation Functions

Now let's look at the SNMPv1 parser. The first function in the parser is `parseSNMPMessage`. This function is responsible for parsing the initial sequence-of TLV that begins all SNMP request PDUs. Since the basic designs of all TLV parsers are similar, we'll cover this one in more detail and then discuss the other TLV parsers, noting where differences occur.

parseSNMPMessage

In `parseSNMPMessage`, we first call the `parseTLV` function with our local TLV variable along with the request PDU buffer and current index. The current index is always zero at this point because we're just starting the parse phase. When this function returns, we'll have an initialized `tlv` variable that represents the sequence TLV in the request PDU. Our first test of this TLV is just a little sanity checking to make sure that it actually is a `SEQUENCE_OF` type. Note that the `SEQUENCE_OF` and `SEQUENCE` types are the same value (0x30), which doesn't present a problem because we know what to expect at each step of the parse due to the SNMP request's very predictable structure. If the type doesn't match, then we return with a `-1` error return. This could be due to a message received in error (that is, we received something other than an SNMPv1 request).

LISTING 8.10 The SNMP parser entry (`parseSNMPMessage`).

```
static int parseSNMPMessage ( )
{
  int size = 0, seglen, ret, respLoc;
  tlvStructType tlv;

  ret = parseTLV(request.buffer, request.index, &tlv);

  if (request.buffer[tlv.start] != SEQUENCE_OF) return -1;

  seglen = tlv.vstart - tlv.start;
  respLoc = tlv.start;
  COPY_SEGMENT(tlv);

  size = parseVersion();

  if (size == -1) return -1;
  else size += seglen;

  insertRespLen(tlv.start, respLoc, size);

  return ret;
}
```

Next, we determine the segment length (`seglen`) of our TLV. We use this value to determine what to copy to the response message (remember, we build our response as we parse and return later to fill in any necessary elements that are not currently known). In this case, the segment length is (`vstart – start`) which is the length of the beginning of the TLV to the *V* portion. We use this instead of the entire TLV (`nstart - start`) because not doing so would copy the entire PDU to the response since this TLV has a value of the remaining TLVs in the request. Therefore, we copy only the *"TL"* portion and allow the next parse function to deal with the next TLV.

We save the `respLoc` here which is a local index of the location to insert the length when we return. Note that after the `parseVersion` call (to parse the next TLV), we adjust the size for the segment length and then call `insertRespLen` to insert the length into the SNMP response PDU for this TLV.

The COPY_SEGMENT macro is used to copy the request TLV to the response. The macro uses the seglen variable as the length of the TLV to copy only the portion of the TLV that we need.

The next element to parse after the initial sequence TLV is the version TLV. It's important to note here that once this function returns, we have parsed the entire SNMP request PDU. The return value is then the number of octets that followed this TLV in the response. This is important because while there will be a one-to-one correspondence to TLVs in the request and response, there may not be a one-to-one correspondence in their lengths. This is because for GetRequest and GetNextRequest, the NULL TLVs in the request (of two octets in size) will be replaced with the actual value TLV in the response (as retrieved from the SNMPData table).

Finally, we insert the length into the response for this TLV (using insertRespLen) and then return to the UDP server. In all other TLV parsers, we'll return the length thus far except in this case. Since there are no parsers before this function, we'll simply return an error code that will be 0 on success and -1 on error. If the UDP server receives the -1 error code, it will silently ignore the request and not generate a response.

parseVersion

The parseVersion function parses the version TLV. The version TLV is an integer TLV which when reduced results in a single number. In our case, the TLV is represented as {0x02 0x01 0x00} which is an Integer Type (0x02) of Length 1 octet (0x01) with a Value of 0 (0x00).

Once the TLV has been parsed in our tlv structure, we'll do some simple error checking. This agent implementation works only with SNMPv1 PDUs and therefore the version is checked to ensure that the version number (the value of this TLV) is '0' which represents v1. See Listing 8.11.

LISTING 8.11 The SNMP version TLV parser.

```
static int parseVersion ( )
{
  int size = 0, seglen;
  tlvStructType tlv;

  size = parseTLV(request.buffer, request.index, &tlv);

  if (!((request.buffer[tlv.start] == INTEGER) &&
        (request.buffer[tlv.vstart] == SNMP_V1))) return -1;

  seglen = tlv.nstart - tlv.start;
```

```
    size += seglen;
    COPY_SEGMENT(tlv);
    size = parseCommunity();

    if (size == -1) return size;
    else return (size + seglen);
  }
```

Once the VERSION TLV has been successfully parsed the next TLV parser is invoked for the Community string.

parseCommunity

The parseCommunity function parses the community string that is used as a security feature in SNMPv1 (but this should not be imply that SNMPv1 communication is secure). When a request is made of an SNMP agent, a string is inserted into the request. The SNMP agent looks at the string, and if it is not recognized, the agent simply discards the request. The string is commonly the word "public" but can be changed to represent anything else for your environment.

LISTING 8.12 The SNMP community TLV parser.

```
static int parseCommunity ( )
{
  int ret = -1, seglen;
  tlvStructType community;
  int size=0;

  ret = parseTLV(request.buffer, request.index, &community);

  if (!((request.buffer[community.start] == OCTET_STRING) &&
        (community.len == COMMUNITY_SIZE))) return -1;

  if (!bcmp(&request.buffer[community.vstart],
              (char *)COMMUNITY, COMMUNITY_SIZE)) {

    seglen = community.nstart - community.start;
    size += seglen;
    COPY_SEGMENT(community);

    size += parseRequest();

  } else {
```

```
      return -1;
    }

    return size;
  }
```

After the TLV is parsed into the tlv structure, the type and length are checked (see Listing 8.12). The type should be OCTET_STRING (a character string) and the length should match the length of the community string that we've configured into our agent. If these do not match, then we simply return an error. Otherwise we continue and check the request message community string with our configured string. We make this secondary check to minimize our processing of SNMPv1 PDUs that may be unauthorized. Once we match the community strings, we continue with our parse for the request-type.

parseRequest

The parseRequest function is a little more involved than prior parsing functions (see Listing 8.13). This is because we'll be performing more functions than the typical single TLV parser. After parsing what should be the request TLV, we check its type to ensure it's a valid request. We perform the standard copy to the response buffer and then change the response type to GET_RESPONSE (the result of all valid request PDUs). Next, we perform the basic TLV parsing of the request-id TLV, error-status TLV, and error-index TLV. Since there is no error checking done on these values, their parsing (and response generation) is inserted here.

LISTING 8.13 The SNMP request TLV parser.

```
static int parseRequest ( )
{
  int ret = -1, seglen;
  tlvStructType snmpreq, requestid, errStatus, errIndex;
  int size = 0, respLoc, reqType;

  ret = parseTLV(request.buffer, request.index, &snmpreq);

  reqType = request.buffer[snmpreq.start];

  if ( !VALID_REQUEST(reqType) ) return -1;

  seglen = snmpreq.vstart - snmpreq.start;
```

```
    respLoc = snmpreq.start;
    size += seglen;
    COPY_SEGMENT(snmpreq);

    response.buffer[snmpreq.start] = GET_RESPONSE;

    parseTLV(request.buffer, request.index, &requestid);
    seglen = requestid.nstart - requestid.start;
    size += seglen;
    COPY_SEGMENT(requestid);

    parseTLV(request.buffer, request.index, &errStatus);
    seglen = errStatus.nstart - errStatus.start;
    size += seglen;
    COPY_SEGMENT(errStatus);

    parseTLV(request.buffer, request.index, &errIndex);
    seglen = errIndex.nstart - errIndex.start;
    size += seglen;
    COPY_SEGMENT(errIndex);

    ret = parseSequenceOf(reqType);
    if (ret == -1) return -1;
    else size += ret;

    insertRespLen(snmpreq.start, respLoc, size);

    /* Store the error status and index, in the event an
     * error was found
     */
    if (errorStatus) {
      response.buffer[errStatus.vstart] = errorStatus;
      response.buffer[errIndex.vstart] = errorIndex + 1;
    }

    return size;
  }
```

We then continue to parse the Sequence-Of TLV that is the last TLV before we begin variable binding parsing. Note that when we complete parsing and return to this function, we not only insert the length into the response TLV but also error information. Since we've parsed the error-status and error-index TLVs, we manage updating the response buffer for these values at this level. The error information is generated while we parse the variable bindings, so this level of the parse is a good time to fill them in. The error-status simply indicates whether any errors occurred during parse of the variable bindings. The error-index indicates which of the variable bindings resulted in an error. These variables will have already been identified at return of `parseSequenceOf`.

parseSequenceOf

The `parseSequenceOf` function is a basic TLV parser with some error checking to ensure that we are looking at what we expect at the request TLV (see Listing 8.14). The major difference here is that we include the capability to call the next parser function multiple times. Remember that at this level a `Sequence-Of` is included to encapsulate all variable bindings that follow. Multiple variable bindings may be included, so this parser calls the `parsesequence TLV` parser as many times as is necessary. Size is also accumulated to update the length of the response at this level.

LISTING 8.14 The SNMP sequence-of TLV parser.

```
static int parseSequenceOf ( int reqType )
{
  int ret = -1, seglen;
  tlvStructType seqof;
  int size = 0, respLoc;
  int index = 0;

  ret = parseTLV(request.buffer, request.index, &seqof);

  if ( request.buffer[seqof.start] != SEQUENCE_OF ) return -1;

  seglen = seqof.vstart - seqof.start;
  respLoc = response.index;
  COPY_SEGMENT(seqof);

  while (request.index < request.len) {
    size += parseSequence( reqType, index++ );
  }

  insertRespLen(seqof.start, respLoc, size);

  return size;
}
```

parseSequence

The `parseSequence` function is the start of the variable binding parser (see Listing 8.15). Remember that a variable binding is simply a construct that binds an OID (object ID) to a value. This results in three TLVs, one for the sequence, one for the variable (the OID) and one for the value. The `parseSequence` function simply parses the encapsulating sequence TLV and then calls the `parseVarBind` parser to extract the OID and value TLVs.

LISTING 8.15 The SNMP sequence TLV parser.

```
static int parseSequence ( int reqType, int index )
{
  int ret = -1, seglen;
  tlvStructType seq;
  int size = 0, respLoc;

  ret = parseTLV(request.buffer, request.index, &seq);

  if ( request.buffer[seq.start] != SEQUENCE ) return -1;

  seglen = seq.vstart - seq.start;
  respLoc = response.index;
  COPY_SEGMENT(seq);

  size = parseVarBind( reqType, index );
  insertRespLen(seq.start, respLoc, size);
  size += seglen;

  return size;
}
```

parseVarBind

The `parseVarBind` function is the most complex of all of the parser functions (see Listing 8.16). After the OID TLV is parsed into the variable name, we check to make sure that it is an `OBJECT_IDENTIFIER` TLV and then check our SNMP MIB table to see if it's present. We don't abort here if we can't find the OID because we have to complete the parse of this variable binding in order to build a correct response.

We next check the request-type (stored previously at the request parse). If we're dealing with a `GET_REQUEST` or `SET_REQUEST` then we simply copy the OID TLV to the response and continue to the value. If we're dealing with a `GET_NEXT_REQUEST`, then we check to see if the SNMP MIB table contains an OID that follows this OID in the request PDU. As the name suggests, GET_NEXT_REQUEST takes an OID and returns the value (and name) of the next element in the SNMP MIB table. This function is useful for traversing a MIB table when the actual contents may not be known. If the OID is not found in the table, we simply copy the request OID into the response and note that an error occurred. Otherwise, we call the getOID function which copies the next OID found in the SNMP MIB table into the response buffer so that the caller knows which OID is returned in the GET_NEXT_REQUEST response.

Once the OID has been parsed, we move onto the value. We again use the parseTLV function to do our basic parse of the request into the value TLV. We now check to see if the OID was actually found in our SNMP MIB table. If not, we copy the request value to the response (which will be a NULL TLV) and then set the error index and error status to represent the error (NO_SUCH_NAME). If the OID was found, we either get the value of the OID from the SNMP table and load it into the response or in the case of a SET_REQUEST we take the value from the request PDU and store it into the SNMP MIB table.

Finally, we update the size and return to the parseSequence parser. The call chain then either moves forward to parse another variable binding within the loop, or returns through the call chain, updating lengths in the response PDU and ultimately resulting in a correct SNMP response message being returned to the sender.

LISTING 8.16 The SNMP variable-binding parser.

```
static int parseVarBind ( int reqType, int index )
{
  int ret = -1, seglen = 0, id;
  tlvStructType name, value;
  int size = 0;

  extern const int maxData;

  ret = parseTLV(request.buffer, request.index, &name);

  if (request.buffer[name.start] != OBJECT_IDENTIFIER) return -1;

  id = findEntry(&request.buffer[name.vstart], name.len);

  /* For normal GET_REQUEST/SET_REQUEST, we simply copy the NAME
   * tlv over and continue.  But for GET_NEXT_REQUEST, we need to
   * identify the next OID and then copy it in as if it was the
```

```
     * requested object.
     */

    if ((reqType == GET_REQUEST) || (reqType == SET_REQUEST)) {
      seglen = name.nstart - name.start;
      COPY_SEGMENT(name);
      size = seglen;
    } else if (reqType == GET_NEXT_REQUEST) {

      response.buffer[response.index] = request.buffer[name.start];

      if (++id >= maxData) {
        id = OID_NOT_FOUND;
        seglen = name.nstart - name.start;
        COPY_SEGMENT(name);
        size = seglen;
      } else {
        /* Skip the name TLV */
        request.index += name.nstart - name.start;

        getOID(id, &response.buffer[response.index+2],
                  &response.buffer[response.index+1]);

        seglen = response.buffer[response.index+1]+2;
        response.index += seglen ;
        size = seglen;
      }

    }

    /* Parse the value TLV, but then replace with ours if we
     * have it
     */
    ret = parseTLV(request.buffer, request.index, &value);

    if (id != OID_NOT_FOUND) {
      unsigned char dataType;
      int len;

      if ((reqType == GET_REQUEST) ||
          (reqType == GET_NEXT_REQUEST)) {

        getEntry(id, &dataType,
                    &response.buffer[response.index+2], &len);
```

9 Embedded Command-Line-Interface (CLI)

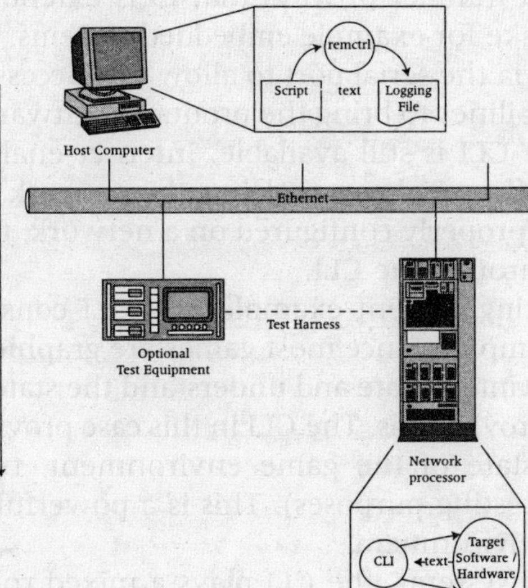

In this chapter, we'll look at the Command Line Interface (CLI) as a network interface. In prior chapters, we've investigated standard protocols and their lightweight implementations. This chapter provides a look at a non-standard protocol that is widespread in deeply embedded systems, and worthwhile for consideration for both remote monitoring and management.

Although the CLI is seen by some as arcane and archaic, it's actually a very useful expert-level interface. After presenting a framework for a network-based CLI, we'll look at some applications of the CLI for automated system testing.

INTRODUCTION

Once upon a time, there was the command line interface. The CLI predates the graphical user interface and was therefore the standard for communicating with computer systems. Going back further (for example, the PDP/8), front-panel switches were the norm. The CLI provided a way for the user to communicate with the machine using some type of language. Commands could be issued to perform activities within the machine or to change its state or behavior. The CLI also provided the means to monitor the activities of the machine.

There are a number of ways that CLIs extend themselves from their host system. Take for example embedded systems. These systems typically provide a CLI via the serial port to allow raw access to the board as well as bootstrap capabilities to bring the product's software to life. Once software is running, the CLI is still available. Internet-enabled devices commonly provide a CLI off a serial port to debug the network environment. If the device cannot be properly configured on a network, there's no way to access it other than through the CLI.

An interesting current example of a CLI console is in game systems (*Quake*, for example). Since most games are graphic-centric, there must be another way to interrogate and understand the state of the system. The CLI is one way to provide this. The CLI in this case provides the capability to investigate the state of the game environment, track resources, modify strategies (for testing purposes). This is a powerful interface, and is quite useful in this environment.

On desktop systems, the CLI plays a mixed role. Linux, for example, still heavily uses the CLI through a variety of shells (command interpreters). DOS uses a CLI, and even the most recent versions of Windows operating systems still maintain non-DOS CLIs for certain functions, although the CLI's use within Windows is waning. Apple has removed the CLI altogether. The CLI is seen too much as an expert-level interface and therefore graphical administration has become the norm. The reason for this is that graphical administration removes the syntax and grammar from the communication with the machine. Instead of building a command line with the commands and options that bring the desired result, boxes are filled in and items are checked.

There are, of course, tradeoffs here. Although in some cases it may be easier to fill in a Web-based form to perform some activity, the time required to do this can be significantly longer than with a CLI. Graphical tools that replace the CLI have their place. Nevertheless, in situations in which the users are required to have some *a priori* knowledge of their control need, or have the ability to provide a wide and varied set of options, the CLI is faster and more flexible. Web forms often reduce the available number of options in order to make the interface easier to deal with. In these cases, having a CLI as an "expert" mode is desirable for complete functionality.

PROTOCOL OVERVIEW

The protocol that is provided by the CLI is by far the simplest presented in this book. The protocol is a custom, string-based protocol that sits on top of TCP (stream based) and provides for synchronous communication (command/response).

Basic Design

As a string based protocol, the CLI server simply awaits a connection and then reads null-terminated ASCII strings. These strings are then parsed to identify the command and any arguments for that command. The CLI then performs the command and responds with a variable amount of data in response. This response data is also in string format. All responses are terminated by a status code that allows the user to understand the status of the command. The status code can be `+OK` for successful parsing and operation or `+ERR` for either unsuccessful parsing or command operation. `+ERR` indicates either that the command made no sense to the CLI (unrecognized command, insufficient arguments, etc.) or the command was recognized but could not be performed (arguments inappropriate, etc.). Once the status code is seen, the response is identified as complete.

An example dialog with the CLI is provided in Listing 9.1.

LISTING 9.1 Example dialog with the embedded CLI.

```
+OK -- Embedded CLI
uptime
5
+OK
hexof
+ERR
hexof 32
0x20
+OK
```

The first line shown ("+OK -- Embedded CLI") is the salutation. This line is emitted from the server immediately upon connection. This provides the client with an indication that it has connected to a valid CLI. The server then awaits commands from the client. The client issues a valid command of `uptime` which is simply a request for the number of seconds that the server has been up. The response is the answer on a separate line followed by a success indicator (+OK). The next command is a test command that can be used to convert a decimal number into hex. The command must be provided with a single argument (the decimal number to convert) and therefore when this command is issued without an argument, an error exists (+ERR result). The final command illustrates the proper use of the `hexof` command with the hex result and success indicator. Therefore, the syntax of commands to the CLI is:

```
<command> [<arg1> [<arg2>] [... [<arg20>]]]
```

A command may have up to twenty arguments that are delimited by white space. The response for a command may take one of the following forms:

```
"+ERR"
"+OK"
<response-lines> "+OK"
```

The status indicator is also used as an end-of-response indicator. When the status indicator is received, no other data will be sent for the previous command. This is useful for external applications that use the CLI in an automated way (more on this later in this chapter).

Simple Command Tokenizer

With the absence of a real parser, we'll perform string tokenization. When the CLI reads a line, it will build a list of individual tokens from the string. To save on space (and time), we'll simply tokenize the string itself and null-terminate the individual tokens within the original string. To identify where the tokens actually begin in the string, we'll keep a array that records the index of the tokens in the string. The tokenizer provides a simple API to also get the arguments from the string (`getArg`) as well as the initial parsing of the command string (`parseCommand`). The prototypes for these functions is provided in Listing 9.2.

LISTING 9.2 Command tokenizer function prototypes.

```
int parseCommand ( char *commandString );
```
— Perform the initial tokenization

```
char *getArg ( int argIndex );
```
— Get an individual argument from the tokenized command string

```
int getArgCount ( void );
```
— Get the total number of arguments for the command string

Command Handlers

After an incoming command string is tokenized, the first token is analyzed to see if it is a valid command (one which the CLI recognizes). A large switch statement is then used within our connection handler to call the individual command handlers that perform the particular action. If a command is not recognized, the `+ERR` status indicator is returned. Otherwise, the command is performed and either the `+OK` or `+ERR` status are emitted after any string data generated as response to the command.

The sample CLI provided here will implement a number of commands for demonstration purposes only. Since the commands are commonly target specific, a few commands are implemented here to illustrate the CLI framework.

IMPLEMENTATION SUMMARY

The embedded CLI implementation is divided into four segments. The first is the TCP stream server that creates the server socket for incoming connections. The second is the tokenizer that splits the command into individual tokens. Third is the connection handler that identifies the recognized commands and then calls the particular handler. Finally, there are individual handlers that implement the commands for the CLI.

Socket Server (Main)

The socket server is very similar to other stream socket servers that we've in this book. This code is provided in Listing 9.3.

LISTING 9.3 Embedded CLI stream socket server.

```
int main(int argc, char **argv)
{
  int listenfd, connfd, on=1;
  socklen_t clilen;
  struct sockaddr_in cliaddr, servaddr;

  listenfd = socket(AF_INET, SOCK_STREAM, 0);

  /* Avoid TIME-WAIT on this socket and allow it to be immediately
   * reused.
   */
  setsockopt( listenfd, SOL_SOCKET, SO_REUSEADDR,
              &on, sizeof(on) );

  bzero(&servaddr, sizeof(servaddr));
  servaddr.sin_family = AF_INET;
  servaddr.sin_addr.s_addr = htonl(INADDR_ANY);
  servaddr.sin_port = htons(EMCLI_PORT);

  bind(listenfd, (struct sockaddr *)&servaddr, sizeof(servaddr));

  listen(listenfd, 1);

  startTime = time(NULL);

  for ( ; ; ) {

    clilen = sizeof(cliaddr);

    connfd = accept(listenfd,
                    (struct sockaddr *)&cliaddr, &clilen);

    if (connfd <= 0) {
      break;
    }

    handleConnection(connfd);

    lastConnect = time(NULL);

    close(connfd);

  }
```

```
  close(listenfd);

}
```

The stream server provides for the setup of the server socket as well as the use of a socket option called SO_REUSEADDR. We enable SO_REUSEADDR here to simplify the execution of the server. Recall that when a socket is closed, on some systems the socket is unavailable for use again for up to two minutes (TIME_WAIT TCP state timeout). When the TIME_WAIT state expires for the socket, the bind may occur for the particular port. Prior to this, the bind will fail with a message referring to the port being unavailable (already in use). Therefore, if we exit our program, we must wait two minutes until restarting it. However, with SO_REUSEADDR, we can start our program right away because the TIME_WAIT restriction has been removed.

Additionally, in the server, we'll record the time that the CLI started (in the startTime variable). We'll also record the last time a connection ended to the CLI (in the lastConnect variable). These two variables are used later by our command handlers.

Command Tokenizer

Tokenizing the command (or splitting it up into its component parts) is a very simple process that's performed by the function in Listing 9.4. This function takes in the string received through the socket and first determines its length. The next task is to skip the command in the string since this will be assumed to be the first contiguous set of characters before the first space. The tokenizer uses space characters as delimiters between the command and arguments and will skip one or more spaces when found.

The vector array is used to identify the index of the arguments within the command string. Note that once we start the loop, we'll record the position as the index off the first argument. This is because the command parse done prior to the loop will set our working index to the first argument. The loop then simply looks for the end of the argument in order to null-terminate it. Then, white space is ignored and if more arguments exist, we continue with the loop.

LISTING 9.4 Command tokenizer.

```
int parseCommand( char *buf )
{
  int i=0;
```

```
    int len = strlen(buf);

    ibuf = buf;
    numArgs = 0;

    /* First, skip the command */
    while ((i < len) && (buf[i] != ' ')) i++;
    buf[i++] = 0;
    while ((i < len) && (buf[i] == ' ')) i++;
    if (i >= len) return 0;

    while (1) {

      if (numArgs >= MAX_ARGS) return -1;

      vector[numArgs] = i;

      if (i >= len) break;

      while ((i < len) && (buf[i] != ' ')) i++;
      buf[i++] = 0;

      while ((i < len) && (buf[i] == ' ')) i++;

      numArgs++;
    }

    return numArgs;
  }
```

The variable numArgs, as shown in Listing 9.4, is a static variable within the parser file that records the number of tokenized arguments for the current command. This variable and vector are used by the API functions getArg and getArgCount. These functions are shown in Listing 9.5.

LISTING 9.5 Tokenizer API functions.

```
  char *getArg( int arg )
  {
    if (ibuf) {
      return &ibuf[vector[arg]];
    } else {
      return NULL;
```

```
  }
}


int getArgCount ( void )
{
  return numArgs;
}
```

The getArg function simply returns a character pointer to the command string at the parsed index. This index, using our vector array, results in the actual index into the command string.

The getArgCount function simply returns the number of arguments that were parsed from the command string.

Connection Handler

The function to manage the individual CLI connections is called, oddly enough, handleConnection. This function is passed a socket descriptor from the socket server that is the actual connection from the remote client. The protocol here is very simple given that we're operating with string-based communication. This function is found in Listing 9.6.

LISTING 9.6 Connection handler function.

```
void handleConnection(int fd)
{
  int i, j, len, done=0, numArgs, status;
  char buffer[MAX_LINE+1];

  /* Send salutation... */
  len = write(fd, salutation, strlen(salutation));

  while (!done) {

    len = read(fd, buffer, MAX_LINE);
    if (len <= 0) return;
    buffer[len] = 0;

    numArgs = parseCommand(buffer);

    if ((buffer[0] == 0) || (buffer[0] == ' ') ||
        (buffer[0] == '#')) {
      ; // Ignore blank/comment lines
```

```
        status = 1;

      } else if ((!strncmp(buffer, "quit", 4)) ||
                 (!strncmp(buffer, "exit", 4))) {
        status = 0;
        done = 1;

      } else if (!strncmp(buffer, "help", 4)) {
        doHelp( fd );
        status = 0;

      } else if (!strncmp(buffer, "verbose", 7)) {
        if (verbose) verbose = 0;
        else verbose = 1;
        len = write(fd,
                    (verbose) ? "Verbose=on\n" : "Verbose=off\n", 13);
        status = 0;

      } else if (!strncmp(buffer, "hexof", 5)) {
        status = convdec(fd);

      } else if (!strncmp(buffer, "decof", 5)) {
        status = convhex(fd);

      } else if (!strncmp(buffer, "uptime", 6)) {
        time_t curTime = time(NULL);
        sprintf(buffer, "%ld\n", curTime-startTime);
        len = write(fd, buffer, strlen(buffer));
        status = 0;

      } else if (!strncmp(buffer, "last", 4)) {
        if (lastConnect != (time_t)0) {
          sprintf(buffer, "%s", ctime(&lastConnect));
          len = write(fd, buffer, strlen(buffer));
        } else {
          len = write(fd, "none\n", 5);
        }
        status = 0;

      } else if (!strncmp(buffer, "who", 3)) {
        status = getpeer(fd);

      } else if (!strncmp(buffer, "push", 4)) {
        status = push(fd);
```

```
        } else if (!strncmp(buffer, "pop", 3)) {
          status = pop(fd);

        } else if ((!strncmp(buffer, "add", 3)) ||
                   (!strncmp(buffer, "sub", 3)) ||
                   (!strncmp(buffer, "mul", 3)) ||
                   (!strncmp(buffer, "div", 3))) {
          status = mathop(fd, buffer[0]);

        } else {
          status = -1;

        }

        if (status == 0) {
            len = write(fd, ready, strlen(ready));
        } else if (status == -1) {
          len = write(fd, notready, strlen(notready));
        }

      }

      return;
    }
```

The first task of the CLI is to emit the salutation string. This notifies the client that it's connected to the CLI server and that it's awaiting commands from the user. The connection handler then accepts commands through the socket, and once a command is received, it's tokenized for later use.

We now have a command buffer that has been tokenized and can now be used by the command handlers. We ignore blank lines and simply respond with no status indicator (performed at the end of the command recognizer). The large `if/then` chain performs string compares to known commands, and upon finding a match, the corresponding command handler is called. In some cases, no command handler is called because the process is simple enough to include directly (`uptime`, for example).

In all cases but blank, a `status` variable is loaded with the status of the operation. If the `status` is '`0`', then the operation was successful and an `+OK` status is returned. A `-1` represents an error condition and a `+ERR` is returned.

The connection handler loops around the command recognizer until the command `quit` or `exit` is received at which point the loop exits and we end up back at the server awaiting another connection. See Listing 9.7 for an example session with the CLI through a telnet connection. User input is shown in bold.

LISTING 9.7 Example dialog with the embedded CLI.

```
 [mtj@plato /mtj]# telnet sartre 9999
Trying 192.168.1.9...
Connected to sartre.mtjones.com.
Escape character is '^]'.
+OK -- Embedded CLI
uptime
34
+OK
who
Peer address 192.168.1.9 port 1042
+OK
push 5
+OK
push 4
+OK
mul
+OK
pop
20
+OK
quit
+OK
Connection closed by foreign host.
[mtj@plato /mtj]#
```

Sample Command Functions

The command handler functions are called from the connection handler to provide some action. A few will be shown here to demonstrate how the command handlers work and how to extend for new commands.

The first function, `convdec`, is used to convert a decimal number into a hex number. This function uses C standard library functions, which may or may not be available in your environment. See Listing 9.8 for the `convdoo` function.

LISTING 9.8 Command handler convdec.

```
int convdec ( int fd )
{
```

```
  char response[81];

  if (getArgCount() < 1) return -1;

  sprintf(response, "0x%x\n", atoi(getArg(0)));
  write(fd, response, strlen(response));

  return 0;
}
```

The convdec command handler first checks to make sure that an argument was tokenized from the command line. One this constraint is satisfied; the sprintf C library function is used to generate a response line containing the hex representation of the decimal value passed with the command. The atoi function converts the string number into an integer. It's important to note that the tokenizer does not alter the string. All tokens are still in their original string format. If the user wishes to use these as integer values, they must first be converted.

Finally, the function emits the newly created response string to the client using the socket descriptor passed by the connection handler.

The next item is important from a process standpoint. If the operation was successful, the command handler function must return a 0. If the operation was not successful, a -1 must be returned. This informs the connection handler which particular status code to return to the user (0 is +OK and '-1 is +ERR).

The next sample function is getpeer that is used to return information about the user that is connected (essentially, the client asks the server to identify us). This action is performed using the getpeername socket API function. See Listing 9.9.

LISTING 9.9 Command handler getpeer.

```
int getpeer ( int fd )
{
  char response[81];
  struct sockaddr_in sockinfo;
  int  len;

  if (getpeername( fd, (struct sockaddr *)&sockinfo, &len ) < 0) {
    return -1;
  } else {

    sprintf(response, "Peer address %s port %d\n",
```

```
                inet_ntoa(sockinfo.sin_addr),
                ntohs(sockinfo.sin_port) );
        write(fd, response, strlen(response));

    }

    return 0;
}
```

This function, as does the first, simply collects some information and emits it back through the socket to the client. In this case, `getpeername` provides us with information on the peer end of the socket (us). The information that we'll return is the IP address and port of the peer. See Appendix A for more information on socket API calls.

It should be clear that these command handling functions could perform any activity. A command could be used to set or read hardware registers. In a multi-tasking system, they could be used to start or stop tasks. They could even be used to reboot the remote hardware. The commands that are shown here are simplistic and provided only for demonstration purposes. The CLI is as powerful as the commands you provide for it and can therefore be a very important interface to a remote system.

AUTOMATED TEST USING THE EMBEDDED CLI

So far, we've looked at the CLI as a user-interface. A user can connect to a remote embedded system through the network to alter the state or monitor an embedded device. This is one use of the CLI, but another is interesting from a verification perspective. If you think of the CLI as a way to provide stimulus to the remote device, the CLI can be used as a test interface. With a test system connected to the embedded device, the CLI can provide commands that change state or perform predefined activities that can be monitored externally (such as setting relay state, reading input status, etc.). In this way, we can close the loop on a test system. If we provide the means to automate the connection and commanding through the CLI, we have an inexpensive way to verify our embedded system in its environment. See Figure 9.1 for a graphical description of this setup.

In this section, we'll expand upon our CLI with an external utility to perform this automated remote test activity.

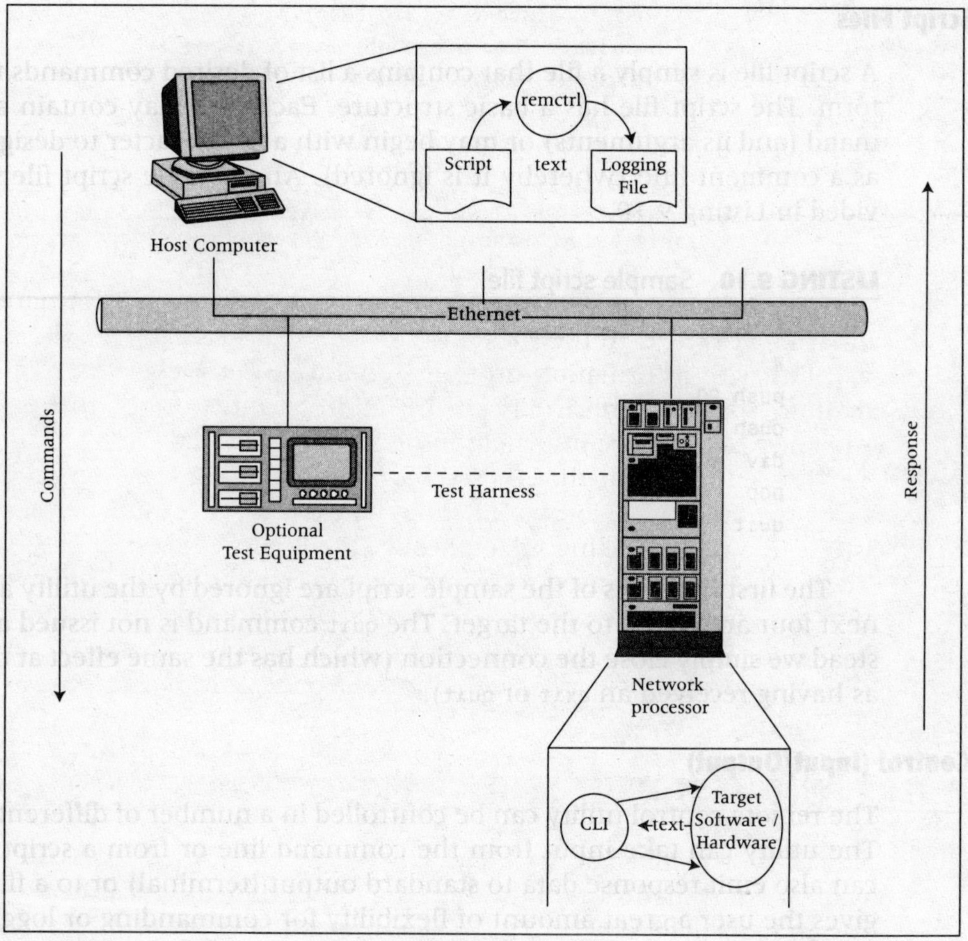

FIGURE 9.1 CLI as an automated test interface.

Remote Control

Our remote test utility, known as `remctrl`, was created as an automated way to issue commands through the socket connection to the CLI and then log the results. The utility is provided with a script file that contains the commands to perform. The utility issues each command found in the script file and then emits the responses that are received from the CLI. The logged data can then be post-processed for validity. As shown in Figure 9.1, test equipment can close the loop on the test and therefore emitted log files from `remctrl` can be correlated with test equipment data for an integrated test.

Script Files

A script file is simply a file that contains a list of desired commands to perform. The script file has a basic structure. Each line may contain a command (and its arguments) or may begin with a '#' character to designate it as a comment line (whereby it is ignored). An example script file is provided in Listing 9.10.

LISTING 9.10 Sample script file.

```
# Sample script file
#
push 20
push 5
div
pop
quit
```

The first two lines of the sample script are ignored by the utility and the next four are issued to the target. The `quit` command is not issued and instead we simply close the connection (which has the same effect at the CLI as having received an `exit` or `quit`).

Control (Input/Output)

The remote control utility can be controlled in a number of different ways. The utility can take input from the command line or from a script file. It can also emit response data to standard output (terminal) or to a file. This gives the user a great amount of flexibility for commanding or logging response data.

For example, if the user wanted to accept commands from the user (otherwise known as standard input) and emit the responses back to the user (standard output), the following command line could be used:

```
./remctrl -t plato.mtjones.com
```

The fact that an input file was not specified (via the `-i` option) and an output file was not specified (via the `-o` option) means that standard in and standard out are used instead. Note that the `-t` option specifies the target for which to connect.

The following code can be used to take input from a script file (named `script`) and emit response data to a file for logging purposes (named `log`):

```
./remctrl -t plato.mtjones.com -i script -o log
```

The user may also omit either of the options. For example, the following line takes input from a script but emits response data to standard output:

```
./remctrl -t plato.mtjones.com -i script
```

In the implementation summary, we'll have a look at how this was accomplished.

Sample Usage

So let's now look at an example using the remote control utility. We'll use the script in Listing 9.10 as our test script file (`sample.tst`) and send our output to standard out. See Listing 9.11 for the utility output.

LISTING 9.11 Sample remote control utility output.

```
[mtj@plato remctrl]# ./remctrl -t plato.mtjones.com -i sample.tst
-- Thu Nov  1 04:48:26 2001
# push 20
+OK
-- Thu Nov  1 04:48:26 2001
# push 5
+OK
-- Thu Nov  1 04:48:26 2001
# div
+OK
-- Thu Nov  1 04:48:26 2001
# pop
4
+OK
-- Thu Nov  1 04:48:26 2001
# quit
[mtj@plato remctrl]#
```

The utility automatically emits the time of the command execution (preceded by the '--' string) and then the actual command being performed (preceded by the '#' character). The response from the embedded CLI is then shown with the status indicator. In all cases, we simply find a `+OK` response indicating that the command was accepted except in the case of the `pop` command. In this case, we receive the result of the operation (in this case `20/4`) and then the `+OK` indication.

IMPLEMENTATION SUMMARY

Let's now take a quick look at the remote control utility. It's implemented as a single function, as it is quite simple. See Listing 9.12 for the full listing.

LISTING 9.12 `remctrl` utility.

```
int main( int argc, char *argv[] )
{
  FILE *infp=NULL, *outfp=NULL;
  char buffer[MAX_LINE+1];
  char inputfile[MAX_ARG+1], outputfile[MAX_ARG+1], target[MAX_ARG+1];
  time_t curTime;
  int  c, in, sock=-1, done=0;
  struct sockaddr_in servaddr;
  time_t theTime;

  if (argc > 1) {

    while (1) {

      c = getopt(argc, argv, "i:o:t:h");

      if (c == -1) {

        if (sock == -1) {
          printf("Must define a target\n");
          exit(-1);
        }

        /* If the user does not specify an input file, use
         * standard input
         */
        if ((infp = fopen(inputfile, "r")) == NULL) {
          infp = fdopen(0, "r");
        }

        /* If the user does not specify an output file, use
         * standard output
         */
        if ((outfp = fopen(outputfile, "w")) == NULL) {
          outfp = fdopen(1, "w");
        }
```

```
        bzero((void *)&servaddr, sizeof(servaddr));
        servaddr.sin_family = AF_INET;
        servaddr.sin_port = htons(CLI_PORT);

        /* Try first as an IP address, then try an FQDN */
        servaddr.sin_addr.s_addr = inet_addr(target);

        if (servaddr.sin_addr.s_addr == 0xffffffff) {
          struct hostent *hptr =
                           (struct hostent *)gethostbyname(target);
          if (hptr == NULL) {
            printf("Can't find %s\n", target);
            exit(-1);
          } else {
            struct in_addr **addrs;
            addrs = (struct in_addr **)hptr->h_addr_list;
            memcpy(&servaddr.sin_addr,
                    *addrs, sizeof(struct in_addr));
          }
        }

        connect(sock,
                (struct sockaddr *)&servaddr, sizeof(servaddr));

        /* Look for the salutation (immediate +OK from the CLI) */
        in = read(sock, buffer, MAX_LINE);

        if (strncmp(buffer, "+OK", 3)) {
          printf("Embedded CLI is not accessible\n");
          exit(-1);
        }

        break;

      } else {

        switch(c) {
          case 'i':
            strcpy(inputfile, optarg);
            break;
          case 'o':
            strcpy(outputfile, optarg);
            break;
          case 't':
```

```
            strcpy(target, optarg);
            sock = socket(AF_INET, SOCK_STREAM, 0);
            break;
          case 'h':
            printf("\n\tremtest -t <target> [-i infile]"
                   " [-o outfile]\n\n");
            exit(-1);
          default:
            printf("unknown argument %c\n", c);
            exit(-1);
        }

      }

    }

  } else {

    printf("Must at least specify a target\n");
    exit(-1);

  }

  while (!feof(infp) && !done) {

    if (fgets(buffer, MAX_LINE, infp) == NULL) break;

    if (buffer[0] == '#') continue;

    theTime = time(NULL);
    fprintf(outfp, "-- %s# %s", ctime(&theTime), buffer);

    if (!strncmp(buffer, "quit", 4) ||
        !strncmp(buffer, "exit", 4)) {
      done=1;
      break;
    }

    /* Send command to the target */
    in = strlen(buffer);
    write(sock, buffer, in);

    for ( ; ; ) {
```

```
            in = read(sock, buffer, MAX_LINE);

            if (in <= 0) {
              done = 1;
              break;
            }

            buffer[in] = 0;

            fwrite(buffer, in, 1, outfp);


            if ((strstr(buffer, "+OK") != NULL) ||
                (strstr(buffer, "+ERR") != NULL)) break;

          }

        }

        close(sock);
        fclose(infp);
        fclose(outfp);
      }
```

The first section of the code performs options parsing from the command line. This is done using the `getopt` library call that is quite useful and simplifies the parsing of command line arguments. The third argument of the `getopt` command identifies the options that are recognized by this command. When an option is followed by the '`:`' character, this tells the `getopt` function that an argument will follow the option. When `getopt` returns a `-1`, the end of the command line options have been found. Prior to this, we collect the arguments (in the switch statement) while waiting for the options to finish.

When we've received all of the options, we do some simple error checking (the target must be specified) and then attempt to open the input and output files. If either of these operations fail, we open standard input (identified by file descriptor `0`) and/or standard output (file descriptor `1`). This permits us to use the same `fgets/fprintf` calls whether we're dealing with a file or simply with terminal I/O.

We then figure out what the target is to which we'll be connecting (whether the specification was an IP address or a fully qualified domain name) and then try to connect. The embedded CLI should immediately emit an +OK status indicator to let us know that we've connected to the CLI, and we'll look for this before continuing.

Our loop at the end of the function provides for the meat of our utility. We get a line from our input file descriptor, and given it is not a comment we emit it to the output file and the socket. Writing to the socket sends our command to the CLI. We'll then go into another loop to read the response data from the CLI until a status indicator is found. All data received through the socket is written to the output file descriptor.

That's it! The remote control utility is a very simple tool that can aid in embedded device testing as well as results logging in a very flexible way.

SUMMARY

In this chapter, we looked at the history of the command line interface and then the development of a simple CLI framework for networked systems. We investigated the use of CLIs in the testing of embedded systems using an automated scripting interface and then discussed an implementation of this very interface.

10 Embedded Service Location Protocol (SLP)

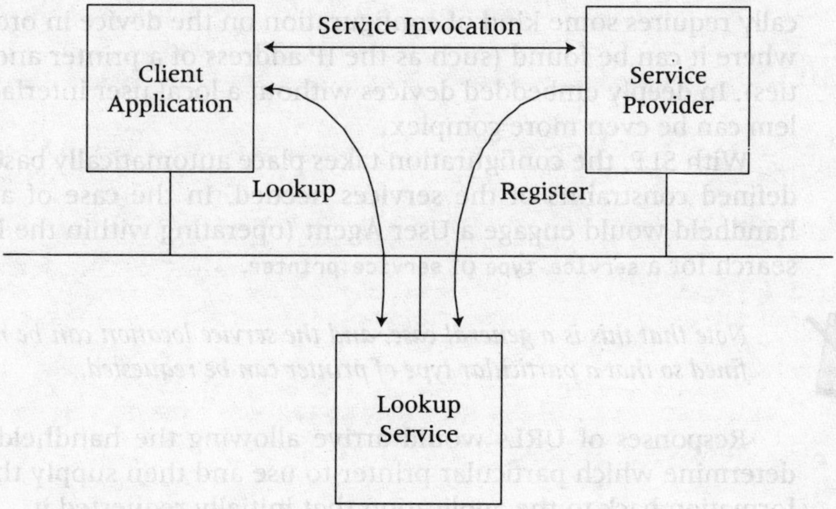

In this chapter, we'll look at the problem of service discovery and the methods available. Specifically, we'll look at the most popular of the discovery protocols, Service Location Protocol (SLP). In addition to SLP, we'll look at the other competing protocols such as Jini and Salutation. Finally, we'll look at a tiny implementation of the SLP protocol and its uses for discovery in networked embedded systems.

INTRODUCTION

Before we discuss service location, let's get a better understanding of the problem that discovery protocols exist to solve. The basic problem that SLP solves is the discovery of assets on a network. These assets can take a variety of forms such as printers (physical hardware) or databases (software).

The Dynamic Host Configuration Protocol (DHCP) provides basic discovery for host configuration but has not successfully branched out for generalized discovery. For this reason, discovery-specific protocols are evolving to satisfy the needs of mobile computing and dynamic networks.

Let's now consider a targeted example of SLP in an embedded scenario. Mobile devices such as wireless handheld computers present unique challenges in the domain of network management. These devices require access to typical resources within a network environment such as printers, databases, network time servers and other resources. Each resource typically requires some kind of configuration on the device in order to specify where it can be found (such as the IP address of a printer and its capabilities). In deeply embedded devices without a local user interface, the problem can be even more complex.

With SLP, the configuration takes place automatically based upon predefined constraints of the services needed. In the case of a printer, the handheld would engage a User Agent (operating within the handheld) to search for a `service-type` of `service:printer`.

Note that this is a general case, and the service location can be much more refined so that a particular type of printer can be requested.

Responses of URLs would arrive allowing the handheld software to determine which particular printer to use and then supply the printer information back to the application that initially requested it.

Even desktop computers benefit from SLP. One of the most primitive problems in networking management is statically defining assets with services. Say, for example, computer A houses a POP3 server that is used for incoming mail. If this machine is changed, all of the devices that point to computer-A must be reconfigured to point to the new POP3 server host. Instead of statically setting where the POP3 server resides in the network, SLP can be used upon boot to dynamically determine where the server resides. At most a reboot would be necessary to reconfigure a host for the change.

An even greater strength of SLP is the capability to explicitly define what is needed from networked assets. For example, in our printer example, the User Agent could specify that not only are we looking for a printer service but that we also desire a color printer. This could be set as the attribute (`type=color`), so that only services that match the scope, `service-type` and attributes will be returned.

Why SLP for Embedded Systems?

For ubiquitous devices, the ability to autoconfigure without system administration is an important requirement. The Holy Grail of autoconfiguration is to deploy a device on a network and have it automatically identify and find the resources it needs. Embedded systems introduce special needs that can be satisfied by SLP. For example, some network devices have no traditional user interfaces. They're black boxes with no traditional user input or output. The primary interfaces are those provided by the network interface. Autoconfiguration, for these devices, can be the defining line between product success and failure.

ALTERNATIVE SERVICE DISCOVERY PROTOCOLS

The service location protocol and the SRVLOC working group have been around only since 1997 (the date at which the SLPv1 IETF specification was introduced). Other discovery protocols compete with SLP, but none provides the simplicity and scalability that SLP offers.

In this section, we'll quickly look at some of the other competing protocols before exploring the details of SLP.

Salutation

The Salutation architecture provides "Find-and-Bind" services on a network. It is an open standard from a consortium of companies (primarily printer vendors). Salutation is not only operating system-independent (like SLP) but is also network protocol-independent (works on non-IP networks). Since the world is IP, this is not a highly motivating argument.

Salutation is implemented as a middleware layer to isolate the developer from the specifics of the protocol. The Salutation Manager performs the discovery functions for the user or registration functions for the service. The Salutation Manager performs these functions through another layer called the "Transport Manager." This layer provides the abstraction of the particular network transport protocol being used. See Figure 10.1 for a graphical depiction of the Salutation architecture.

Although the example shows two transport managers, the actual number is based upon the number of physical networks that will participate in the Salutation protocol (or are available on the device). Commonly, a device such as a cell phone, which has a limited number of interfaces, will contain only one.

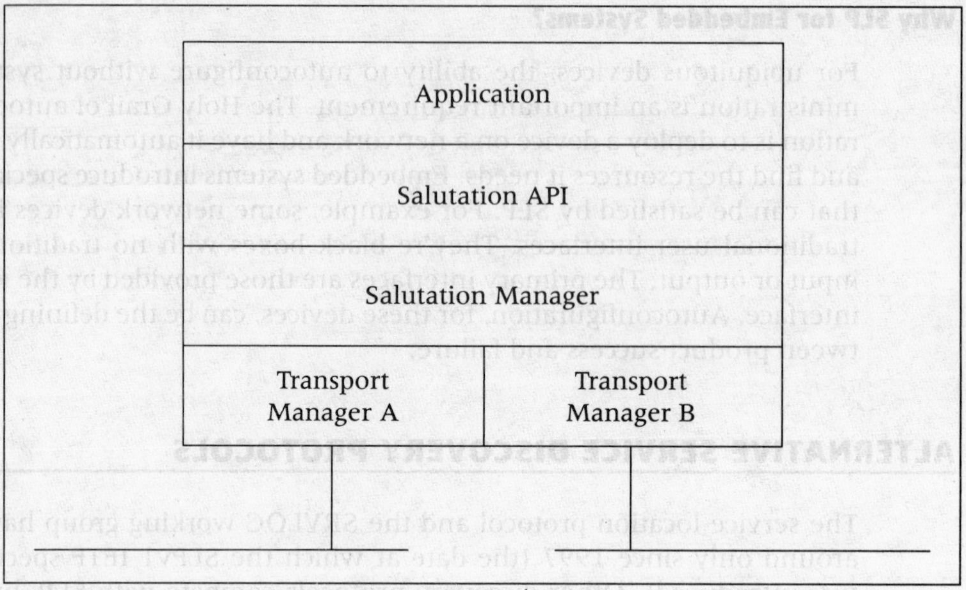

FIGURE 10.1 Salutation Discovery Protocol architecture.

Jini

The Jini architecture from Sun Microsystems is a distributed system architecture that provides the capability to virtually connect services on distributed nodes together. The grouping of nodes is called a "federation" and consists of devices, software, and users.

Since Jini is a method by which multiple computers on a network appear as one, the process of discovery is very important. For this reason, discovery is an integral part of the architecture. A Lookup Service exists as the network directory for services. Service providers register services (and the attributes of the services) to the Lookup Service. Client applications can then query the Lookup Service to discover services that are needed. Once a suitable service is found, a Service Object is loaded from the Lookup Service. This object is used by the client application to communicate with the service provider (all via Java's Remote Method Invocation, or RMI). The object contains the methods that define the API for the particular service.

Noted drawbacks of Jini are that it is Java specific. Despite this issue, the Jini architecture provides a very powerful infrastructure for distributing and connecting applications to the services they need. The Jini discovery architecture is shown in Figure 10.2.

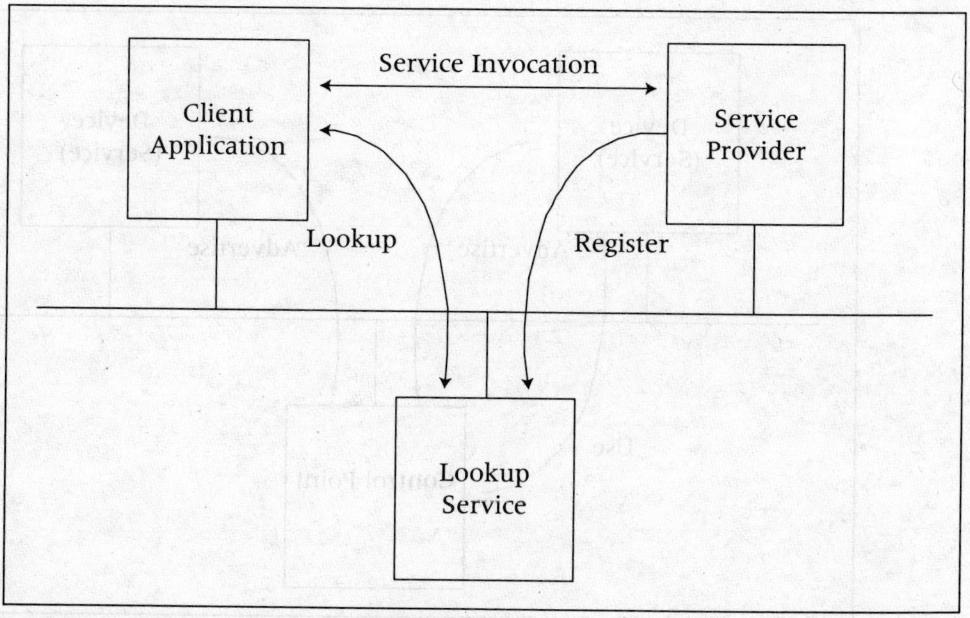

FIGURE 10.2 Jini discovery protocol architecture.

UPnP

Microsoft's Universal Plug and Play (UPnP) is a peer-to-peer architecture for networked systems. UPnP includes a very similar architecture to other discovery models, but differs in the protocols used. UPnP includes what is called a control point as a controller (user needing services). When a new device connects to a network, it advertises its services to all connected control points. A control point may then communicate with a device to utilize an advertised service.

UPnP uses the HTTP protocol over TCP/IP for communication. Communication can occur through HTTPU (HTTP Unicast UDP) or HTTPMU (HTTP Multicast UDP). The payloads of the HTTP transfers are Simple Object Access Protocol (SOAP) messages.

A drawback of UPnP is its bloat. For very small devices that want either to simply advertise services or locate them, the need for HTTP and SOAP on the device can limit its deployment. See Figure 10.3 for a graphical view of the UPnP architecture. UpnP is also the protocol responisible for a well-known security hole in Windows 98, 2000, Me, and XP.

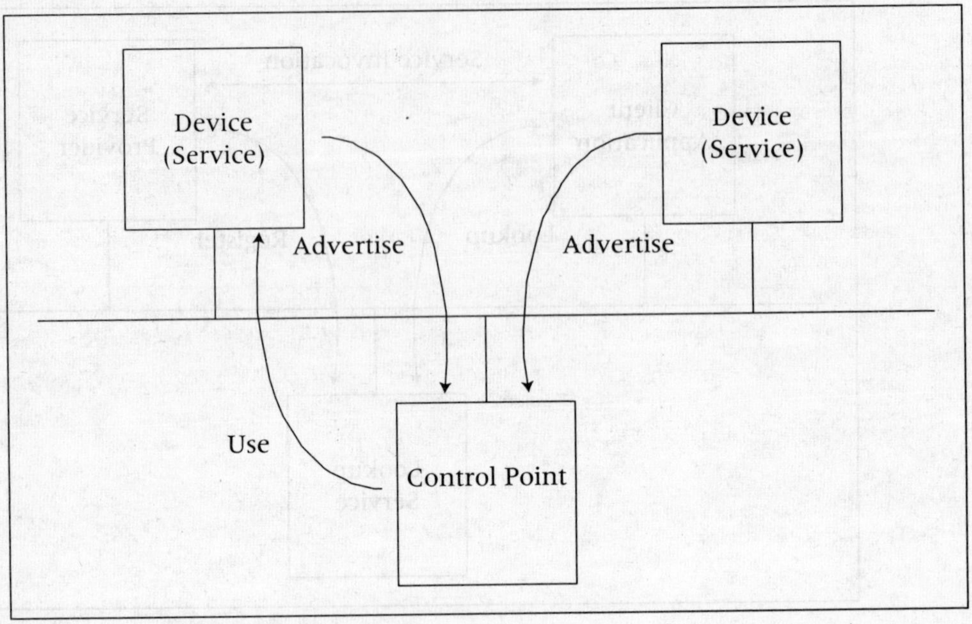

FIGURE 10.3 UPnP discovery protocol.

SLP ARCHITECTURE

The Service Location Protocol is a very simple protocol with a very simple architecture for the discovery of services on an IP network in an operating system-independent fashion. In this section we'll look at the SLP architecture and the agents involved.

Agents of SLP

SLP involves three agents in the process of service advertisement and discovery. These are the Directory Agent (DA), Service Agent (SA), and User Agent (UA). See Figure 10.4 for the diagram of SLP agent relationships.

From Figure 10.4, User Agents act on behalf of a device to request services from a network. Service Agents act on behalf of a device to advertise a server. Directory Agents act as a proxy between User and Service Agents and help reduce SLP network traffic.

Directory Agent

The DA is an optional agent within the SLP architecture and can be deployed for SLP scalability. The DA can simplify the SLP architecture by providing an

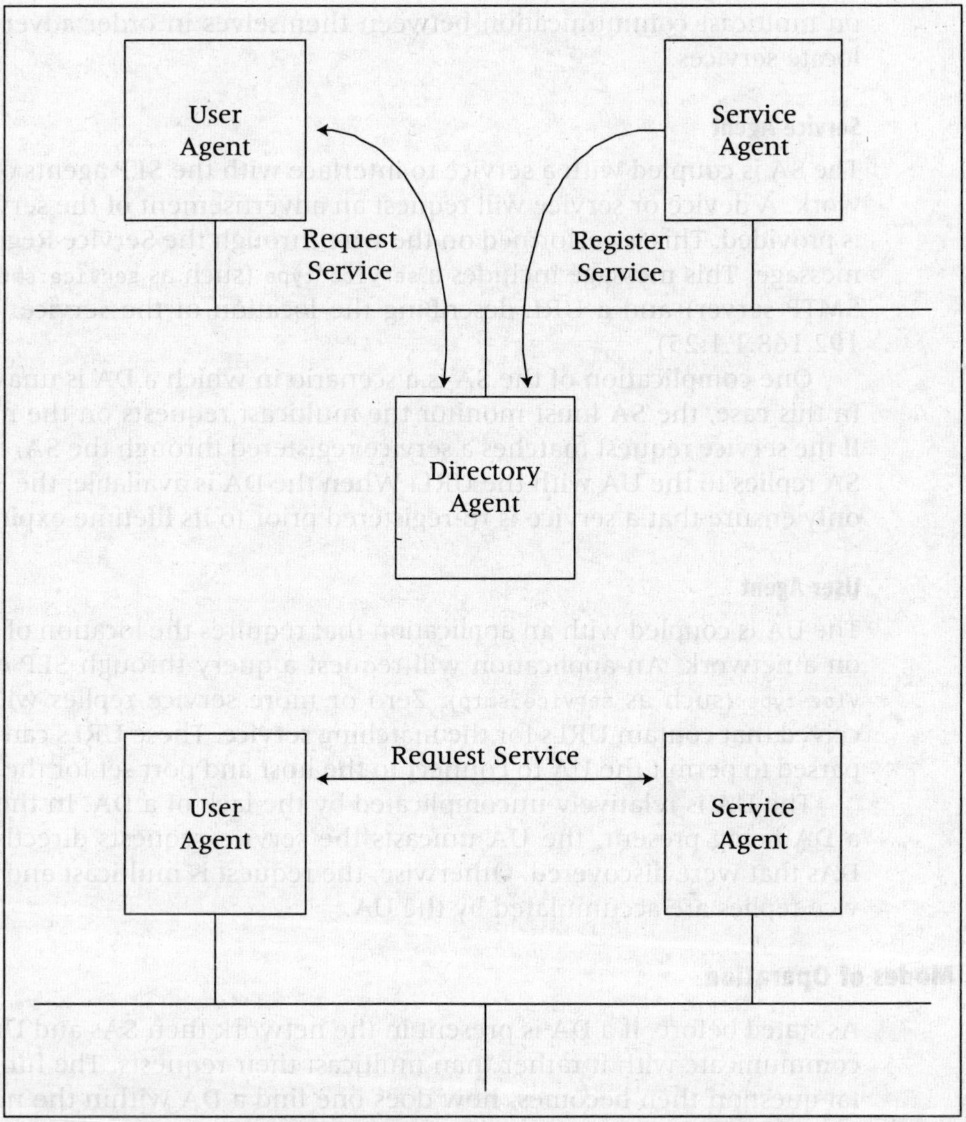

FIGURE 10.4 SLP agent relationships.

entity that caches service location information. In this way, SAs can register services with the DA and UAs can query the DA for information.

When one or more DAs are present, UAs and SAs must communicate directly with them. In this way, the network is not cluttered with SLP traffic. When a DA is not present within the network, UAs and SAs must rely on multicast communication between themselves in order advertise and locate services.

Service Agent

The SA is coupled with a service to interface with the SLP agents on a network. A device or service will request an advertisement of the service that is provided. This is performed on the wire through the Service Registration message. This message includes a `service type` (such as `service:smtp` for an SMTP server) and a URL describing the location of the service (such as 192.168.1.1:25).

One complication of the SA is a scenario in which a DA is unavailable. In this case, the SA must monitor the multicast requests on the network. If the service request matches a service registered through the SA, then the SA replies to the UA with the URL. When the DA is available, the SA need only ensure that a service is re-registered prior to its lifetime expiring.

User Agent

The UA is coupled with an application that requires the location of services on a network. An application will request a query through SLP of a `service-type` (such as `service:smtp`). Zero or more service replies will be received that contain URLs for the matching service. These URLs can then be parsed to permit the UA to connect to the host and port set for the service.

The UA is relatively uncomplicated by the lack of a DA. In the case of a DA being present, the UA unicasts the service requests directly to the DAs that were discovered. Otherwise, the request is multicast and the service replies are accumulated by the UA.

Modes of Operation

As stated before, if a DA is present in the network then SAs and UAs must communicate with it rather than multicast their requests. The fundamental question then becomes, how does one find a DA within the network? SLP provides a very simple solution to this problem, in which SLP is used to discover the DA.

By default, the SLP agent software is first initialized to operate in multicast mode (SLP assumes initially that no DA is present). Discovery is then performed to find a DA (via multicast). Any DAs that are present on the network will unicast a DA advertisement to the sender for the request. The agent will then use these DA URLs for future discovery or advertisement requests.

The two modes supported by SLP then are unicast mode (when a DA is present) and multicast mode (when a DA is not present). The SLP specification states that when a DA is present, the agent must use it rather than perform multicast requests.

Agent Communication

All replies within the SLP architecture are unicast. Regardless of the SLP architecture (with or without a DA) a request received by either multicast or unicast means always elicits a unicast response. This method exists to minimize the traffic on a network and avoid uninterested hosts from receiving the responses.

SLP PROTOCOL

In this section, we'll explore the SLP protocol. SLP is a synchronous UDP-based message protocol in which a request message is sent and response messages are returned. This section will discuss the messages that are supported within this embedded SLP implementation.

Messages

All SLP messages are prefixed with an SLP header. This header contains general information about the particular request as well as protocol options. See Figure 10.5 for the protocol header.

The SLP header contains a version number that represents the SLP protocol version of this message. This is used for compatibility reasons. The Function Code is the actual message type (`SrvReg`, `DAAdvert`, etc.). The Length

Byte 0	Byte 1	Byte 2	Byte 3
0 1 2 3 4 5 6 7	0 1 2 3 4 5 6 7	0 1 2 3 4 5 6 7	0 1 2 3 4 5 6 7
Version	Function Code	Length	
Length cont.	C F R Reserved		Ext. Offset
Ext. Offset cont.		Transaction Identifier (XID)	
Language Tag Length		Language Tag	

FIGURE 10.5 SLP protocol header.

field is the length of the entire SLP message (including the SLP header). A number of flags exist to specify whether the request is multicast and/or whether the message is a first request or subsequent response due to timeout. The next extension offset is used for adding extensions to the protocol header. The XID field is a request identifier. Each time a new request is made, the XID is initialized with a new value. Responses include this XID to allow agents in the network to correlate message responses back to their individual request.

Finally, the language tag and length are used to identify the language used in protocol transfers. This is defined as `en` by default in the implementation that will follow, but can be changed based upon RFC 1766 "Tags for the Identification of Languages."

Another common structure that is used in several of the SLP messages is the URL entry. This structure specifies a URL and the lifetime associated to it. When the structure is used in a registration, the lifetime is the time in seconds that the registration should be active. When the URL entry is provided by a request, the lifetime is the number of seconds until the entry expires. No services can be advertised as permanently available—routine re-registration is required. See Figure 10.6 for the URL entry structure.

Byte 0	Byte 1	Byte 2	Byte 3
0 1 2 3 4 5 6 7	0 1 2 3 4 5 6 7	0 1 2 3 4 5 6 7	0 1 2 3 4 5 6 7
Reserved	Lifetime (seconds)		URL String Len
URL Str Len cont.	URL String (variable)		
Num Auth Blocks	Authentication Blocks (optional)		

FIGURE 10.6 URL entry structure within SLP messages.

The Lifetime field is the first valid field (of Figure 10.6) and was discussed in the prior section. The URL String Length field contains the number of characters (excluding any null terminator, which does not exist in the URL string). Next is the actual URL string. Finally, a single byte contains the number for Authentication Blocks (Num Auth Blocks). This optional field is ignored in the following implementation since security is not included.

The following sections will outline the format and usage of the SLP messages that are used within this implementation.

Service Request (`SrvRqst`)

The `SrvRqst` message is sent from a UA to request the location of services as specified in the message. See Figure 10.7 for the format of the service request message.

Byte 0 (bits 0 1 2 3 4 5 6 7) Byte 1 (bits 0 1 2 3 4 5 6 7)	Byte 2 (bits 0 1 2 3 4 5 6 7) Byte 3 (bits 0 1 2 3 4 5 6 7)
SLP Header (SrvRqst)	
PRList String Length	PRList String (variable)
Service Type String Length	Service Type String (variable)
Scope List String Length	Scope List String (variable)
Query String Length	Query String (variable)
SPI String Length	SPI String (variable)

FIGURE 10.7 Service Request message format.

All messages within SLP begin with the SLP header (shown in Figure 10.5), although in this case the function ID of the message will be `1 (SRV_RQST)`.

The PRList is the Previous Responder List. This is the list of addresses of Directory Agents or Service Agents that have already responded to the request. In the case of multiple requests for the same service, the address of a responder will be added to this comma-delimited list. When a DA or SA receives this message and finds its address on the list, the message is silently dropped to avoid cluttering the network with repeated responses to the same request. The PRList String Length is the string length of the PRList.

The `service-type` is the type of service to be located. Examples of this are `service:http` to locate an HTTP service or `service:directory-agent` to locate Directory Agents on the local network.

The scope list is the scope of the search. All agents within the SLP architecture are initialized with one or more scopes. These scopes partition the agents into logical groups based upon the function. For example, a scope of "devices" could include physical devices on a network where "services" could refer to software services. The scope limits the search to only the partition that is useful to the requesting agent, although multiple scopes may be set.

The Query String is an LDAP search filter. To further refine a search, an application could specify a predicate of `(type=color)` for a service type of `service:printer`. This would refine the search of printers to only those that provide a color printing capability.

LDAP is the Lightweight Directory Access Protocol and is used to access online directory services.The SLP SPI pertains to authentication, and is not supported by this implementation.

Service Reply (SrvRply)

The `SrvRply` message is sent from a DA or SA to a UA in response to a service request message. Figure 10.8 provides the format for the service reply message.

Byte 0	Byte 1	Byte 2	Byte 3
0 1 2 3 4 5 6 7	0 1 2 3 4 5 6 7	0 1 2 3 4 5 6 7	0 1 2 3 4 5 6 7
SLP Header (SrvRply)			
Status Code		URL Entry Code	
URL Entry 1 (variable length)			
URL Entry N (variable length)			

FIGURE 10.8 Service Reply message format.

The `SrvRply` message starts with an error code to indicate the success or failure of the preceding `SrvRqst`. This is followed by the number of URL entries that are contained within the reply. Finally, zero of more URL entries are provided. The format of the URL entry is provided in Figure 10.6.

The `SrvRply` message is iterated based upon the URL entry count to retrieve the URLs that matched the search request.

Directory Agent Advertisement (DAAdvert)

The `DAAdvert` message is a message that is generated asynchronously as the DA starts up but can also result from a `service-reply`. For example, when a `SrvRqst` is emitted with a `service-type` of `service:directory-agent`, then the DA will respond with a `DAAdvert`. Searching for the particular `service-type` is called *Active Discovery* and is used to identify the DAs operating within the local subnet. See Figure 10.9 for the message format of `DAAdvert`.

Byte 0	Byte 1	Byte 2	Byte 3
0 1 2 3 4 5 6 7	0 1 2 3 4 5 6 7	0 1 2 3 4 5 6 7	0 1 2 3 4 5 6 7
SLP Header (DAAdvert)			
Status Code		DA Stateless Boot Timestamp	
DA Stateless Boot Timestamp (cont)		DA URL String Length	
DA URL String (variable)			
Scope List String Length		Scope List String (variable)	
Attribute List String Length		Attribute List String (variable)	
SPI String Length		SPI String (variable)	
Num Auth Blocks	Authentication Blocks (optional)		

FIGURE 10.9 Directory Agent Advertisement message format.

The format of the `DAAdvert` is different from that of a `SrvRply`, and therefore `SrvRqsts` must tolerate the receipt of both types of responses. Instead of a URL entry, the `DAAdvert` responds with a length and string for of the URL embedded within the message. A scope list is also returned which represents the scopes that the DA supports. The DA may also provide a list of attributes in the `DAAdvert` to further define the DA.

Service Registration (SrvReg)

The `SrvReg` message provides the capability to register a service with a DA. Recall that in the absence of a DA, the SA must listen and respond to `SrvRqst` messages. The `SrvReg` message format is provided in Figure 10.10.

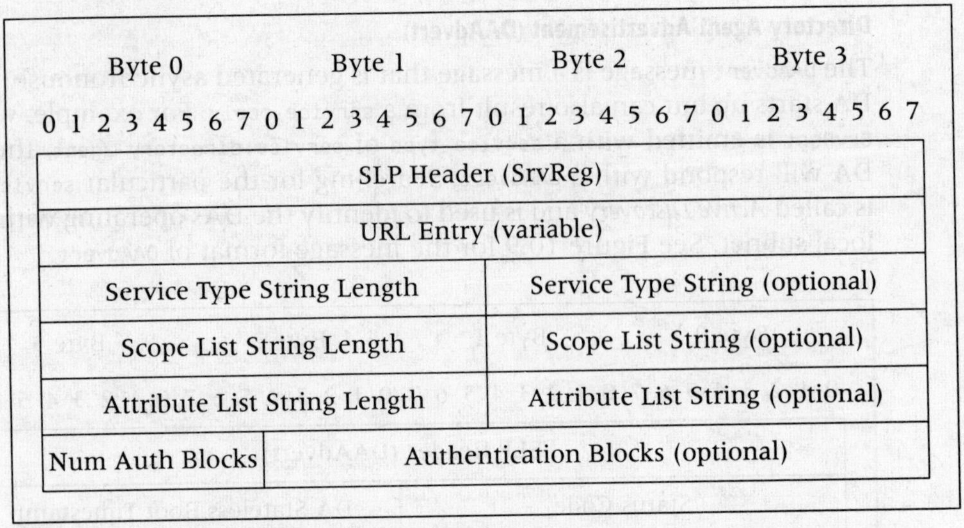

FIGURE 10.10 Service Registration message format.

The first element of a `SrvReg` message after the SLP protocol header is a URL entry. This contains the URL and lifetime being registered (see Figure 10.6 for the URL entry format). The `service-type` string represents the type of service being registered and the scope list specifies the scopes under which this registration can be found. The attribute list lists any special attributes that are to be integrated with this registration for providing additional information about the service. These are used within the DA to help refine the search and provide only results that are meaningful.

Service Acknowledge (SrvAck)

The `SrvAck` message is returned by the DA to an SA in response to a `SrvReg` (see Figure 10.11). This message contains only an error code to indicate the status of the service register.

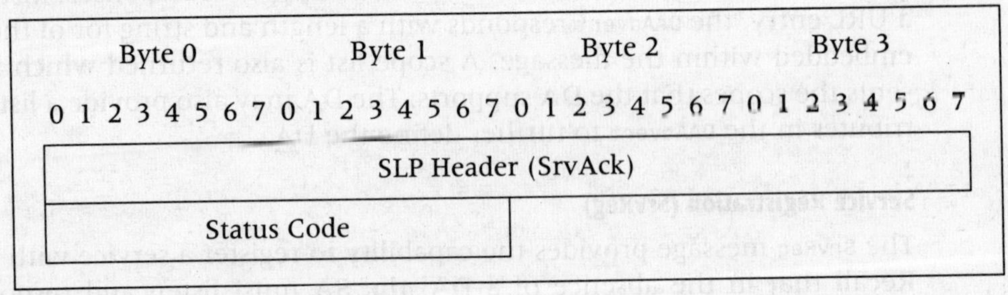

FIGURE 10.11 Service Acknowledge message format.

A value of zero is the common no-error case, non-zero represents one of 15 error types.

Service De-Registration (SrvDeReg)

The `SrvDeReg` message is used by an SA to deregister a previously registered service (see Figure 10.12). The message includes the service URL that was registered.

Byte 0 | Byte 1 | Byte 2 | Byte 3

0 1 2 3 4 5 6 7 0 1 2 3 4 5 6 7 0 1 2 3 4 5 6 7 0 1 2 3 4 5 6 7

SLP Header (SrvDeReg)	
Scope List String Length	Scope List String (optional)
URL Entry (variable)	
Attribute Query String Length	Attribute Query String (variable)

FIGURE 10.12 Service Deregistration message format.

A `SrvAck` message is returned by the DA to acknowledge deregistration or to report an error.

Service-Type Request (SrvTypeRqst)

The `SrvTypeRqst` message interrogates the DAs in the network for the `service-types` that are currently registered. This command is useful for the process of browsing the services that are available (see Figure 10.13).

The message includes a PRList so that DAs that have already been heard from can silently ignore the message. The naming authority is specified as 0xffff (rather than a 0 string length or actual length of an included string). The `-1` value in the naming authority instructs the DA to return all `service-types` regardless of naming authority. Finally, the scope list is included which must match any registered services of the specified `service-type`.

Service-Type Reply (SrvTypeRply)

The `SrvTypeRply` message is sent by the DA in response to a `SrvTypeRqst` message (see Figure 10.14). The `SrvTypeRply` includes a status code indicating the status of the response and a string with an accompanying length.

Byte 0	Byte 1	Byte 2	Byte 3
0 1 2 3 4 5 6 7	0 1 2 3 4 5 6 7	0 1 2 3 4 5 6 7	0 1 2 3 4 5 6 7
SLP Header (SrvTypeRqst)			
PRList String Length		PRList String (optional)	
Naming Authority String Length		Naming Authority String (optional)	
Scope List String Length		Scope List String (optional)	

FIGURE 10.13 Service Type Request message format.

The string contains a comma-delimited series of `service-types` (such as `service:http`).

These `service-types` can then be used with a `SrvRqst` to iterate from a type to the available services of this type on the network. The `service-type` messages are useful for browsing all services on a network.

Byte 0	Byte 1	Byte 2	Byte 3
0 1 2 3 4 5 6 7	0 1 2 3 4 5 6 7	0 1 2 3 4 5 6 7	0 1 2 3 4 5 6 7
SLP Header (SrvTypeRqst)			
Status Code		Service Type String Length	
Service Type String (variable)			

FIGURE 10.14 Service Type Reply message format.

Sample Dialogs

Let's now look at a few message dialogs between the SLP agents in binary (wire) format.

In the following on-the-wire examples, we'll use the following legend to illustrate the contents of the messages. The SLP Header will be presented in **bold**, the service-type in *italic*, and the URL entry <u>underlined</u>.

Active DA Discovery

Active DA discovery is the process by which an SLP agent initially interrogates the network to find any DAs that may exist. The request takes the form of a service request (`SrvRqst`) and the reply from the DA is a Directory Agent advertisement (`DAAdvert`) (see Listing 10.1 and Figure 10.15).

LISTING 10.1 Active DA discovery messages.

Service Request (`SrvRqst`):

```
0000 : 02 01 00 00 38 60 00 00 00 00 00 00 00 02 65 6e    ....8`........en
0010 : 00 00 00 17 73 65 72 76 69 63 65 3a 64 69 72 65    ....service:dire
0020 : 63 74 6f 72 79 2d 61 67 65 6e 74 00 07 64 65 66    ctory-agent..def
0030 : 61 75 6c 74 00 00 00 00                            ault....
```

Directory Agent Advertisement (DAAdvert):

```
0000 : 02 08 00 00 51 00 00 00 00 00 01 00 02 65 6e       ....Q.........en
0010 : 00 00 00 00 00 04 00 2b 73 65 72 76 69 63 65 3a    .......+service:
0020 : 64 69 72 65 63 74 6f 72 79 2d 61 67 65 6e 74 3a    directory-agent:
0030 : 2f 2f 70 6c 61 74 6f 2e 6d 74 6a 6f 6e 65 73 2e    //plato.mtjones.
0040 : 63 6f 6d 00 07 64 65 66 61 75 6c 74 00 00 00 00    com..default....
0050 : 00
```

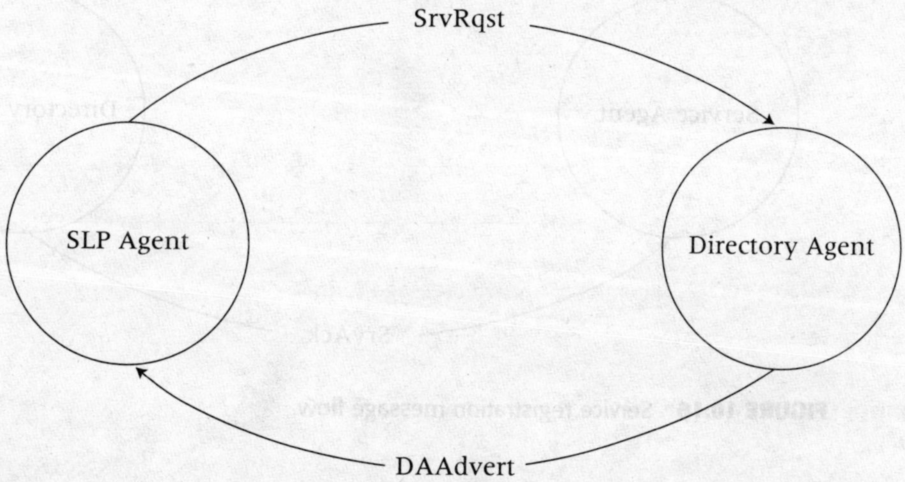

FIGURE 10.15 Active DA discovery message flow.

Unicast Service Registration

Service registration is performed through an SA by means of the `SrvReg` message. A DA, if present, will respond with a SrvAck message upon successful registration (see Listing 10.2 and Figure 10.16).

LISTING 10.2 Service registration messages.

Service Registration (SrvReg):

```
0000 : 02 03 00 00 4f 40 00 00 00 00 00 00 00 02 65 6e   ....O@........en
0010 : 00 2a 30 00 1f 73 65 72 76 69 63 65 3a 68 74 74   .*0..service:htt
0020 : 70 3a 2f 2f 6d 74 6a 6f 6e 65 73 2e 63 6f 6d 3a   p://mtjones.com:
0030 : 38 30 38 30 00 00 0c 73 65 72 76 69 63 65 3a 68   8080...service:h
0040 : 74 74 70 00 07 64 65 66 61 75 6c 74 00 00 00      ttp..default...
```

Service Acknowledgement (`SrvAck`):

```
0000 : 02 05 00 00 12 00 00 00 00 00 00 01 00 02 65 6e   ..............en
0010 : 00 00                                             ..
```

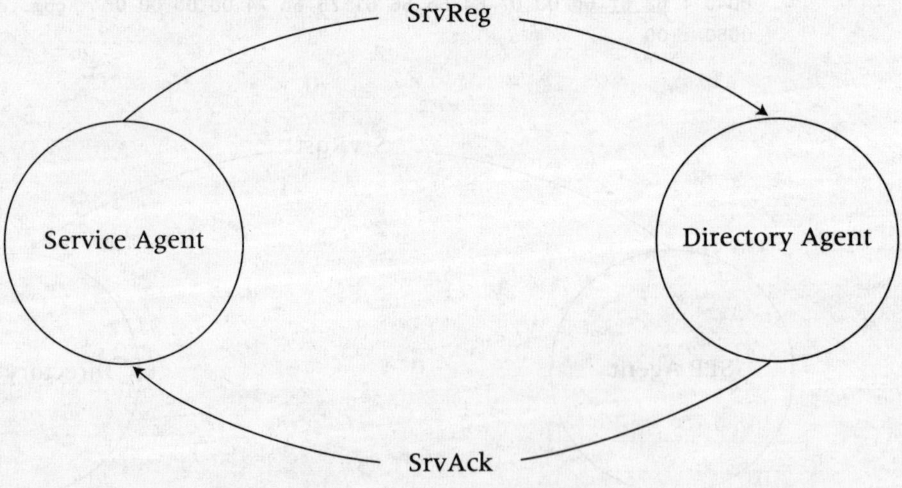

FIGURE 10.16 Service registration message flow.

Unicast Service Request

A service request is issued by a UA to find URLs for a particular `service-type`. The request includes the `service-type` and the response includes the

URLs that match the `service-type` (and scope). See Listing 10.3 and Figure 10.17.

LISTING 10.3 Unicast service request messages.

Service Request (`SrvRqst`):

```
0000 : 02 01 00 00 2d 40 00 00 00 00 00 00 02 65 6e    ....-@........en
0010 : 00 00 00 0c 73 65 72 76 69 63 65 3a 68 74 74 70    ....service:http
0020 : 00 07 64 65 66 61 75 6c 74 00 00 00 00    ..default....
```

Service Reply (`SrvRply`):

```
0000 : 02 02 00 00 39 00 00 00 00 00 00 01 00 02 65 6e    ....9.........en
0010 : 00 00 00 01 00 1e d2 00 1f 73 65 72 76 69 63 65    .........service
0020 : 3a 68 74 74 70 3a 2f 2f 6d 74 6a 6f 6e 65 73 2e    :http://mtjones.
0030 : 63 6f 6d 3a 38 30 38 30 00    com:8080.
```

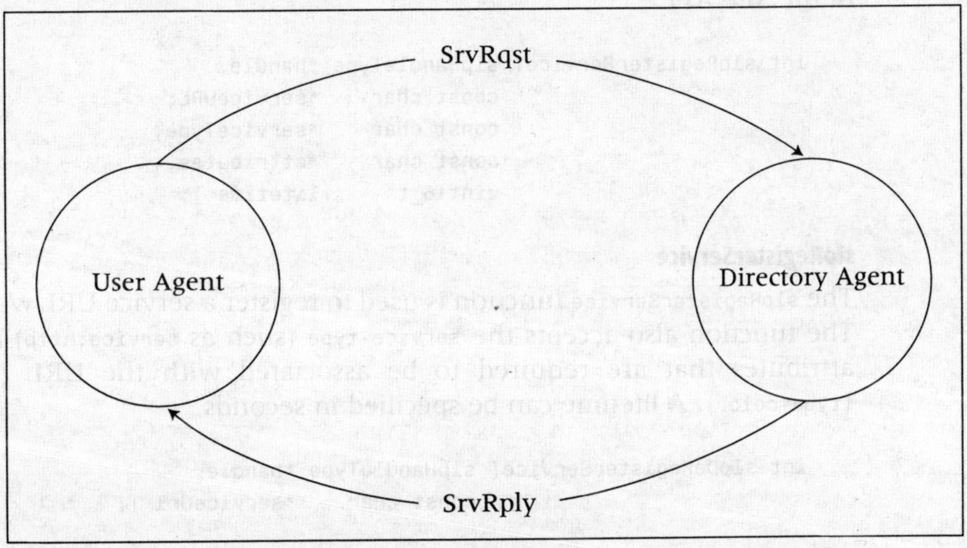

FIGURE 10.17 Unicast service request message flow.

SLP API

SLP is commonly implemented as an API that is extended to user applications. The User Agents and Service Agents are abstracted by the APIs to the applications that require the services.

SLP is defined specifically as a protocol, although RFC 2614 also defines an API that is recommended to interface to SLP. The implementation provided next is not compliant with the API RFC, even though the interfaces are very similar. In all cases, a -1 return indicates an error.

```
int slpInit( void );
```

slpInit

The `slpInit` function is used for boot-time initialization of the SLP layer. Active DA discovery is performed here to determine whether the SLP messages should be unicast (if the DA is present) or multicast out to whomever is listening.

```
int slpOpen( slpHandleType *handle );
```

slpOpen

The `slpOpen` function is used to create an SLP handle. The handle contains information about the particular SLP session and must be passed to any call of the SLP API.

```
int slpRegisterService( slpHandleType *handle,
                        const char    *serviceURL,
                        const char    *serviceType,
                        const char    *attributes,
                        uint16_t      lifetime );
```

slpRegisterService

The `slpRegisterService` function is used to register a service URL with a DA. The function also accepts the `service-type` (such as `service:http`) and any attributes that are required to be associated with the URL (such as `(type=color)`. A lifetime can be specified in seconds.

```
int slpDeRegisterService( slpHandleType *handle,
                          const char    *serviceUrl );
```

slpDeRegisterService

The `slpDeRegisterService` function deregisters a previously registered service from a DA. This function requires only the handle and the service URL that was previously used in registration.

```
int slpRequestService( slpHandleType *handle,
                       slpParsedServiceReplyType *slpPReply,
                       const char *serviceType,
                       const char *predicates );
```

slpRequestService

The `slpRequestService` function permits the UA to find services within a network. The `service -type` is passed in as well as predicates (search criteria) and the result is a parsed reply (of type `slpParsedServiceReplyType`).

```
int slpRequestAllServices( slpHandleType *handle,
                           slpParsedServiceTypeReplyType *slpPReply );
```

slpRequestAllServices

The `slpRequestAllServices` function is used to identify all service types that are registered within a network. The result is returned in the `slpParsedServiceTypeReplyType` and contains the number of services found with a list of `service-types`.

```
int slpClose( slpHandleType *handle );
```

slpClose

The `slpClose` function is used to close out an SLP session. This function must be called when no further SLP functions are to be called. In order to start a new session, the `slpOpen` must be called again for a new handle.

```
int slpParseServiceURL( char *url,
                        char *serviceType,
                        char *addrSpec,
                        char *port );
```

slpParseServiceURL

The `slpParseServiceURL` function takes in a URL (received the `slpRequestService` function) and parses out the individual elements. For example, the URL:

```
service:smtp://192.168.1.1:25
```

would be parsed into a `ServiceType service:smtp`, `addrSpec` 192.168.1.1 and port 25.

IMPLEMENTATION SUMMARY

Let's now walk through a small SLP implementation based upon the previously outlined API. We'll first look at the support functions used by the SLP API functions and then the API functions themselves.

Support Functions

SLP messages are created from the `slpMsgType`. This type is shown in Listing 10.4.

LISTING 10.4 SLP message type.

```
typedef struct {
     int index;
     int len;
     char buffer[MAX_BUFFER+1];
} slpMsgType;
```

The SLP message structure is made up of not only the buffer that contains the SLP message, but other values that support the construction and parsing of the message. The message is contained in the `buffer` variable. When constructing or parsing a message, the `index` represents the current index in the process. The `len` variable is the total length of the message contained in the buffer.

Constructing an SLP message is then abstracted by three functions that emit a byte, a short (two bytes) and a string (variable number of bytes). These functions are shown in Listing 10.5.

LISTING 10.5 Functions to help create SLP messages.

```
void slpCreateHeader( slpMsgType *slpMsg,
                      int type,
                      const char *lang,
                      uint8_t flags )
{
  int len = strlen(lang);

  extern int archType;

  if ((slpMsg == NULL) || (lang == NULL)) return;

  bzero( (void *)slpMsg, sizeof(slpMsgType) );

  if (archType == MULTICAST_ARCH) flags |= REQUEST_MCAST;

  emitByte(slpMsg, SLP_VERSION);
  emitByte(slpMsg, (unsigned char)type);
  emitShort(slpMsg, 0); emitByte(slpMsg, 0); // Fake length
  emitByte(slpMsg, flags);
```

```
  emitShort(slpMsg, 0);           // Rsvd / Next Ext Offset
  emitShort(slpMsg, 0);           // Next Offset Continued
  emitShort(slpMsg, 0);           // Fake XID
  emitShort(slpMsg, len);         // Language Tag Length
  emitString(slpMsg, lang);       // Language Tag
}


void emitByte( slpMsgType *slpMsg, uint8_t value)
{
  if (slpMsg == NULL) return;
  slpMsg->buffer[slpMsg->index++] = value;
  slpMsg->len++;
}


void emitShort( slpMsgType *slpMsg, uint16_t value)
{
  if (slpMsg == NULL) return;
  slpMsg->buffer[slpMsg->index++] = (unsigned char)(value >> 8);
  slpMsg->buffer[slpMsg->index++] = (unsigned char)(value & 0xff);
  slpMsg->len+=2;
}


void emitString( slpMsgType *slpMsg, const char *string)
{
  int i, len = strlen(string);

  if ((slpMsg == NULL) || (string == NULL)) return;
  for (i = 0 ; i < len ; i++) emitByte(slpMsg, string[i]);
}
```

Each of the functions accepts an `slpMsgType` pointer (per Listing 10.4) and the object to insert into the message stream. The `slpCreateHeader` function takes a `slpMsgType` reference and fills in the initial values for the header fields. The `emitByte` function takes the message and the octet value and simply inserts this value at the current offset specified by the `slpMsg` index. The index is incremented so that on the next call, subsequent data will occupy the next available byte to fill. The length field of the message is then incremented. The `emitShort` and `emitString` functions are then simply variations on this theme. We'll see later that the antithesis of the `emitX` functions are the `getX` functions.

Basic message parsing follows a similar design to the functions in Listing 10.5. The reverse functions are provided in Listing 10.6. These functions provide the capability to extract data from an SLP message, based upon what's expected from the higher level parser. It should be noted that the overall design of SLP message parsing is based upon a predictive parser. The high level parser knows the format of a given SLP message type, and the parser simply extracts the elements based upon this knowledge.

LISTING 10.6 Functions to help parse SLP messages.

```
int getByte( slpMsgType *slpMsg, uint8_t *value)
{
  int ret = -1;
  if (slpMsg == NULL) return -1;
  if (slpMsg->index < slpMsg->len) {
    if (value) {
      *value = slpMsg->buffer[slpMsg->index++];
    } else {
      slpMsg->index++;
    }
    ret = 0;
  }

  return ret;
}

int getShort( slpMsgType *slpMsg, uint16_t *value)
{
  int ret = -1;
  if (slpMsg == NULL) return -1;
  if (slpMsg->index+1 < slpMsg->len) {
    if (value) {
      *value  = slpMsg->buffer[slpMsg->index++] << 8;
      *value |= slpMsg->buffer[slpMsg->index++];
    } else {
      slpMsg->index+=2;
    }
    ret = 0;
  }

  return ret;
}

int getTriOctet( slpMsgType *slpMsg, uint32_t *value)
```

```
{
  int ret = -1;
  if (slpMsg == NULL) return -1;
  if (slpMsg->index+2 < slpMsg->len) {
    if (value) {
      *value  = slpMsg->buffer[slpMsg->index++] << 16;
      *value |= slpMsg->buffer[slpMsg->index++] <<  8;
      *value |= slpMsg->buffer[slpMsg->index++];
    } else {
      slpMsg->index+=3;
    }
    ret = 0;
  }

  return ret;
}

int getString( slpMsgType *slpMsg, int len, char *string)
{
  int i, ret = -1;

  if (slpMsg == NULL) return -1;

  if (slpMsg->index+len < slpMsg->len) {
    if (string) {
      for (i = 0 ; i < len ; i++) {
        string[i] = slpMsg->buffer[slpMsg->index+i];
      }
      string[i] = 0;
    }
    slpMsg->index += len;

    ret = 0;
  }

  return ret;
}
```

These functions are very similar to their `set` cousins except for certain special cases. In these cases, parsing a message may result in data for which the parser is not interested. In these cases, the parser provides a null pointer where it could commonly provide a pointer to a variable to store the retrieved data. By sending a null pointer, the value is ignored in the message stream but the index parameter is updated to permit parsing to continue.

SLP Communication Layer

Since SLP requires a layer for communication with the network, these functions are implemented as a separate object. These functions are primarily hidden from the user API (except for `open`, `close`, and `initialization`).

All SLP tasks are performed with a handle. The handle contains specific information about an SLP session. This information is collected within a handle (shown in Listing 10.7).

LISTING 10.7 SLP communication handle.

```
typedef struct {
    int sock;
    uint16_t curXid;
    struct sockaddr_in peerAddr;
} slpHandleType;
```

The SLP handle contains a socket descriptor for communication to other SLP peers, an XID (unique identifier for SLP messages) and a `sockaddr_in` structure that specifies the peer information (to whom the SLP agent speaks).

The first SLP call made is to `slpInit`. This function performs host-level initialization of the SLP software. The primary function of `slpInit` is active DA discovery that is used to determine whether the agent speaks multicast to SLP peers or to a particular DA. See Listing 10.8 for the `slpInit` function.

LISTING 10.8 `slpInit` API function.

```
static struct sockaddr_in daSockAddr;
int archType = MULTICAST_ARCH;

int slpInit( void )
{
  slpHandleType initHandle;
  slpParsedServiceReplyType reply;
  int ret;

  int slpOpen( slpHandleType * );

  archType = MULTICAST_ARCH;

  /* Perform Active DA Discovery */

  slpOpen( &initHandle );
```

```
    ret = slpRequestService( &initHandle, &reply,
                             "service:directory-agent",
                             "" );

    slpClose( &initHandle );

    if ( ret != 0 ) {
      char serviceType[MAX_STRING];
      char addrSpec[MAX_STRING];
      char port[MAX_STRING];

      if (reply.urlCount > 0) {

        slpParseServiceURL( reply.urls[0].url, serviceType,
                            addrSpec, port );

        daSockaddr.sin_family = AF_INET;
        daSockaddr.sin_addr.s_addr = inet_addr(addrSpec);

        if (daSockaddr.sin_addr.s_addr == 0xffffffff) {
          struct hostent *hptr =
                        (struct hostent *)gethostbyname(addrSpec);
          if (hptr == NULL) {
            /* Can't figure it out, must be a bad addrSpec */
            archType = MULTICAST_ARCH;
            return 0;
          } else {
            struct in_addr **addrs;
            addrs = (struct in_addr **)hptr->h_addr_list;
            memcpy(&daSockaddr.sin_addr,
                     *addrs, sizeof(struct in_addr));
          }
        }

        daSockaddr.sin_port = htons(atoi(port));
        if (daSockaddr.sin_port == 0) {
          daSockaddr.sin_port = htons(PORT_NUMBER);
        }

        archType = UNICAST_ARCH;

      }
```

```
  }

#ifdef SLP_DEBUG

  printf("architecture is %s\n",
          (archType == UNICAST_ARCH) ? "Unicast" : "Multicast" );
  if (archType == UNICAST_ARCH) {
    printf("DA Host : %s\n", inet_ntoa(daSockaddr.sin_addr) );
    printf("DA Port : %d\n", ntohs(daSockaddr.sin_port) );
  }

#endif

  return 0;
}
```

The first three functions of `slpInit` provide active DA discovery. A handle is first created through a call to `slpOpen`. Next, the handle is used to find the service of type `service:directory-agent`. Finally, the handle is closed through a call to `slpClose`. If any DAs were discovered on the network, they would now be contained within the `slpParsedServiceReplyType` local to this function called *reply* .

If the return value of `slpRequestService` is non-zero then DAs were found (since this function returns the number of URLs that are contained within the reply structure). The first URL in the reply structure is then passed to the URL parser (`slpParseServiceURL`). There should be only one in this case, since the response was a `DAAdvert`. We then determine if the response was an IP address or a fully qualified domain name and load the result into the `sockaddr` structure. The global `daSockaddr` structure contains the peer information for the peer DA. The `archType` is also set here depending upon the architecture. If a DA was found, then the architecture is Unicast. Otherwise, it's Multicast and requests are multicast on the network.

The `slpInit` function is typically called once when the application is started, but it can be run at any time. The purpose of running this function more than once is to re-interrogate the network to see if the architecture has changed (whether a DA was started or it disappeared).

Listing 10.9 shows the `slpOpen` function that is used to open an SLP session. This function uses information gathered by the `slpInit` function to determine how to communicate in the network. One of the primary functions of `slpOpen` is to create an SLP socket that is used for communication. See Listing 10.9 for the `slpOpen` function.

LISTING 10.9 slpOpen API function.

```
int slpOpen( slpHandleType *handle )
{
  int on=1, ret=-1;
  struct ip_mreq mreq;
  struct sockaddr_in localAddr;

  if (handle == NULL) return -1;

  bzero( (void *)handle, sizeof(slpHandleType) );

  do {

    handle->sock = socket(AF_INET, SOCK_DGRAM, 0);
    if (handle->sock < 0) {
      printf("Can't create socket\n");
      break;
    }

    ret = setsockopt(handle->sock, SOL_SOCKET, SO_REUSEADDR,
                      (char *)&on, sizeof(on));
    if (ret) break;

    localAddr.sin_family = AF_INET;
    localAddr.sin_addr.s_addr = htonl( INADDR_ANY );
    localAddr.sin_port = htons( 0 );

    if (bind(handle->sock, (struct sockaddr *)&localAddr,
            sizeof(localAddr)) < 0) {
      printf("Can't bind to port %d\n", PORT_NUMBER);
      break;
    }

    if (archType == MULTICAST_ARCH) {

      ret = setsockopt(handle->sock, IPPROTO_IP, IP_MULTICAST_TTL,
                        (char *)&on, sizeof(on));

      if (ret) break;

      bzero( (void *)&mreq, sizeof(mreq) );
      mreq.imr_multiaddr.s_addr = inet_addr( GROUP_IP );
      mreq.imr_interface.s_addr = htonl( INADDR_ANY );
```

```
      ret = setsockopt(handle->sock, IPPROTO_IP,
                       IP_ADD_MEMBERSHIP,
                       (char *)&mreq, sizeof(mreq));

      if (ret) {
        printf("can't join multicast group (%d)\n", errno);
        break;
      }

      handle->peerAddr.sin_family = AF_INET;
      handle->peerAddr.sin_port = htons(PORT_NUMBER);
      handle->peerAddr.sin_addr.s_addr = inet_addr( GROUP_IP );

    } else {

      memcpy(&handle->peerAddr,
              &daSockaddr, sizeof(struct sockaddr) );

    }

  } while (0);

  return ret;
}
```

Most of the socket initialization code in `slpOpen` should be familiar by now. Some of the different features of this code are the configuration required for a multicast socket (when the DA is absent). The first multicast-related configuration is the setting of the multicast TTL (time-to-live). This value is set to `1` to ensure that our mulitcast packets do not leave the current subnetwork (will not go further than a gateway or router on the current subnetwork). We then configure our socket to be a member of a multicast group through the `IP_ADD_MEMBERSHIP` socket option. This allows us to receive multicast packets through the socket.

Note that if the architecture is Unicast (a DA was found), then we simply copy the information over into our `peerAddr` structure in the handle that was collected in the `slpInit` function.

Sending messages, though not an API function, is a simple socket call for UDP (via `sendto`). See Listing 10.10 for the `slpSendMessage` listing.

LISTING 10.10 `slpSendMessage` **primitive.**

```
int slpSendMessage( slpHandleType *handle,
                    slpMsgType *slpMsg
```

```
                )
{
  int rc;

  if ((handle == NULL) || (slpMsg == NULL)) return -1;

  setSlpXID( slpMsg, ++handle->curXid );

  rc = sendto( handle->sock, slpMsg->buffer, slpMsg->len, 0,
                (struct sockaddr *)&handle->peerAddr,
                 sizeof(handle->peerAddr) );

  if (rc < 0) printf("slpSendMessage failed (%d)\n", errno);

  return rc;
}
```

The `slpSendMessage` function sends a message to the peer as specified by the initialization. An XID is also set to allow us to determine which responses were for us. The XID is a unique ID that is returned by the DA (or SA) in the SLP response. This allows us to correlate a request with a response.

The `slpReceiveMessage` is a little more complicated due to the blocking nature of the socket. Since the socket is blocking, we want to call `recv` only if there is actually data there to receive. To solve this problem we use the select call that notifies us of two events. Data is available either in the socket (as configured through the `rfds` structure) or a timeout occurred (via the `tv` structure).

For a complete discussion of the `select` *call, see the Stevens text listed under RESOURCES in this chapter.*

See Listing 10.11 for the `slpReceiveMessage` listing.

LISTING 10.11 `slpReceiveMessage` **primitive.**

```
int slpReceiveMessage( slpHandleType *handle,
                       slpMsgType *slpMsg,
                       int timeout
                     )
{

  fd_set rfds;
```

```
    struct timeval tv;
    int ret=-1;

    if ((handle == NULL) || (slpMsg == NULL)) return -1;

    do {

      bzero((void *)slpMsg, sizeof(slpMsgType));

      FD_ZERO(&rfds);
      FD_SET(handle->sock, &rfds);

      tv.tv_sec = 1;
      tv.tv_usec = 0;

      ret = select(handle->sock+1, &rfds, NULL, NULL, &tv);

      if (ret > 0) {

        if (FD_ISSET(handle->sock, &rfds)) {

          slpMsg->len = recv( handle->sock, slpMsg->buffer,
                                  MAX_BUFFER, 0 );

          ret = 0;
          if (peekXid(slpMsg) == handle->curXid) break;

          ret = -1;

        } else {
          /* Error... */
          ret = -1;
        }

      } else {
        /* Timeout */
        ret = -1;
      }

    } while (timeout--);

    return ret;
  }
```

Once we set our parameters to the select call, we call select and wait for an event to occur. The select call blocks until something occurs that we've set. Either data is available which is indicated to us by a set bit in the `rfds` structure, or a timeout occurs (a `-1` return from `select`). When a timeout occurs, we'll set a timeout return and then loop back for as many times as is set by the timeout variable (user-defined parameter). This allows us to wait for some amount of time for a message, and if a message does not arrive then we finally exit.

When a message does arrive, we load the length into the `slpMsgType` structure (from the return value of `recv`) and then check the XID of the message. If the XID of the SLP response message matches our XID (the last one transmitted via this handle) then we have a response message for us and simply pass it back to the caller. The upper layer performs the actual message parsing and determines if the response message is a valid response for our request.

The final communication layer primitive is the `slpClose` function (see Listing 10.12). This function closes out an SLP session.

LISTING 10.12 `slpClose` **API function.**

```
int slpClose( slpHandleType *handle )
{
  struct ip_mreq mreq;
  int ret = -1;

  if (handle == NULL) return -1;

  if (handle->sock >= 0) {

    if ( archType == MULTICAST_ARCH) {
      bzero( (void *)&mreq, sizeof(mreq) );
      mreq.imr_multiaddr.s_addr = inet_addr( GROUP_IP );
      mreq.imr_interface.s_addr = htonl( INADDR_ANY );

      ret = setsockopt(handle->sock, IPPROTO_IP,
                       IP_DROP_MEMBERSHIP,
                       (char *)&mreq, sizeof(mreq));
    }

    close(handle->sock);

    handle->sock = -1;
```

```
  }

  return ret;
}
```

The primary purpose of this function is to close the socket associated with the SLP handle. Another important task is to remove membership from the multicast group. This is performed through the `IP_DROP_MEMBERSHIP` socket option. While this is not actually required (since closing the socket will have this done for us), it's good design to do it just in case the underlying socket layer is not implemented in this way.

SLP Registration (slpRegisterService)

This is our first look at one of the SLP API functions for SLP services. SLP registration is the process of registering a service URL and type with a DA so that UAs can find and then utilize our service. Note that SAs can also use services, and therefore the function of an SLP agent can change based upon what function it currently performs. See Listing 10.13 for the `slpRegisterService` implementation.

LISTING 10.13 `slpRegisterService` API function.

```
int slpRegisterService( slpHandleType *handle,
                        const char *serviceURL,
                        const char *serviceType,
                        const char *attributes,
                        uint16_t   lifetime
                      )
{
  slpMsgType slpMsg;
  int ret, i;

  if ((handle == NULL) || (serviceURL == NULL) ||
      (serviceType == NULL) || (attributes == NULL)) return -1;

  slpCreateHeader(&slpMsg, SRV_REG, "en", FRESH);

  /* First, emit the <URL-Entry> */
  emitByte(&slpMsg, 0);                         /* Reserved Field */
  emitShort(&slpMsg, lifetime);                 /* Lifetime       */
  emitShort(&slpMsg, strlen(serviceURL));       /* URL Length     */
  emitString(&slpMsg, serviceURL);              /* URL            */
  emitByte(&slpMsg, 0);                         /* # of URL Auths */
```

```
    /* Next, the service string */
    emitShort(&slpMsg, strlen(serviceType));
    emitString(&slpMsg, serviceType);

    /* Emit the scope string */
    emitShort(&slpMsg, 7);
    emitString(&slpMsg, "default");

    /* Emit the attribute List */
    emitShort(&slpMsg, strlen(attributes));
    emitString(&slpMsg, attributes);

    /* Emit null AttrAuths */
    emitByte(&slpMsg, 0);

    setSlpHeaderLength( &slpMsg );

    slpPrintMessage( &slpMsg );

    ret = slpSendMessage( handle, &slpMsg );

    for (i = 0 ; i < 5 ; i++) {

      ret = slpReceiveMessage( handle, &slpMsg, 1 );

        if (slpMsg.buffer[2] == SRV_REPLY) {
          ret = 0;
          break;
        }

    }

    return 0;
}
```

Once some error checking is performed on the passed parameters, we create an SLP message header using the function `slpCreateHeader`. This function creates a clean SLP header and fills it with the parameters passed on the command line. This function also uses our message creation functions and therefore, subsequent calls to the `emit` functions will place the data in the proper place (our current index will be the first byte after the header).

Since we're creating a `SrvReg` message, we start with a URL entry (from Figure 10.6). We then emit the service string, scope string, and the attribute list (based upon the parameters passed in by the user). Next, we emit a single octet of value zero as the `Attribute Auth` blocks. Since the octet is zero, no `auth` blocks are provided. Finally, we call the `setSlpHeaderLength` function that emits the total length of the message into the proper place in the SLP header.

Finally, for debug purposes, we emit the message to the console and then send it using the `slpSendMessage` primitive. A call to `slpReceiveMessage` causes us to wait for responses. When `slpReceiveMessage` returns, a message has been received. A return of '`0`' represents successful message receipt. We simply check the message type in the `slpMsg` buffer and if it matches our expectations (in this case a `SRV_REPLY`) we exit and return success to the caller. Otherwise, we await our response. This is because in multicast mode we can receive other requests from other agents on the network, but no replies. Replies are always unicast back to the requester.

SLP Deregistration (slpDeRegisterService)

If an application wants to revoke a registration from a DA, the deregistration function is called to remove the service reference. The format of the deregister message is slightly different than the registration, including the type (`SrvDeReg`). In our minimal implementation, the caller provides the handle and service URL to be deregistered. We assume that all deregistration is to occur for all language tags, and therefore this parameter is not accepted from the caller. See Listing 10.14 for the `slpDeRegisterService` implementation.

LISTING 10.14 `slpDeRegisterService` **API function.**

```
int slpDeRegisterService( slpHandleType *handle,
                          const char *serviceURL
                        )
{
  slpMsgType slpMsg;
  int ret, i;

  if ((handle == NULL) || (serviceURL == NULL)) return -1;

  slpCreateHeader(&slpMsg, SRV_DEREG, "en", FRESH);

  /* First, emit the scope */
  emitShort(&slpMsg, 7);
  emitString(&slpMsg, "default");
```

```
    /* Next, emit the <URL-Entry> */
    emitByte(&slpMsg, 0);                        /* Reserved Field */
    emitShort(&slpMsg, SLP_LIFETIME);            /* Lifetime       */
    emitShort(&slpMsg, strlen(serviceURL));      /* URL Length     */
    emitString(&slpMsg, serviceURL);             /* URL            */
    emitByte(&slpMsg, 0);                        /* # of URL Auths */

    /* Next, the null tag list (deregister in all languages) */
    emitShort(&slpMsg, 0);

    /* Emit null AttrAuths */
    emitByte(&slpMsg, 0);

    setSlpHeaderLength( &slpMsg );

    slpPrintMessage( &slpMsg );

    ret = slpSendMessage( handle, &slpMsg );

    for (i = 0 ; i < 5 ; i++) {

      ret = slpReceiveMessage( handle, &slpMsg, 1 );

      if (slpMsg.buffer[2] == SRV_REPLY) {
        ret = 0;
        break;
      }

    }

    return 0;
}
```

Notice that the `slpRegisterService` and `slpDeRegisterService` functions are very similar in layout. What is different about the functions is that the formats created using the `emit` functions are tailored specifically to the format of the actual message. The basic flow of the functions is identical.

SLP Find Services (slpRequestService)

Finding services in the network is performed through the `slpRequestService` API function. This function is slightly different than the previous two functions because as well as emitting an SLP message and awaiting a response, the function also performs parsing of the response to provide the URL data. The function is provided in Listing 10.15.

LISTING 10.15 `slpRequestService` **API function.**

```
int slpRequestService( slpHandleType *handle,
                       slpParsedServiceReplyType *slpPReply,
                       const char *serviceType,
                       const char *predicates
                 )
{
  slpMsgType slpMsg;
  int ret, i;

  if ((handle == NULL) || (slpPReply == NULL)) return -1;

  bzero( (void *)slpPReply, sizeof(slpParsedServiceReplyType) );

  slpCreateHeader(&slpMsg, SRV_RQST, "en", FRESH);

  /* Emit the PRLIST */
  emitShort(&slpMsg, 0);

  /* Next, the service string */
  emitShort(&slpMsg, strlen(serviceType));
  emitString(&slpMsg, serviceType);

  /* Emit the scope string */
  emitShort(&slpMsg, 7);
  emitString(&slpMsg, "default");

  /* Emit the predicates List */
  emitShort(&slpMsg, strlen(predicates));
  emitString(&slpMsg, predicates);

  /* Emit null <SLP SPI> */
  emitShort(&slpMsg, 0);

  setSlpHeaderLength( &slpMsg );

  slpPrintMessage( &slpMsg );

  ret = slpSendMessage( handle, &slpMsg );
```

```
    for (i = 0 ; i < 5 ; i++) {

      ret = slpReceiveMessage( handle, &slpMsg, 1 );

      if (ret == 0) {
        slpPrintMessage( &slpMsg );

        ret = slpParseServiceReply( &slpMsg, slpPReply );

      }

    }

    return slpPReply->urlCount;
  }
```

In our receive loop (Listing 10.15) after receiving a message, we pass the received message to the function `slpParseServiceReply`. This function extracts the URL entries (if present) in the response and places them in the reply structure. This structure is then further parsed by the user to decompose the URL entries into their individual elements.

The `slpRequestService` function returns the number of elements parsed from the responses. Note that more than one response may be received. Because of this, the `slpParseServiceReply` function appends newly parsed URLs into the reply.

SLP Find Services Types (slpRequestAllServices)

This function permits the interrogation of the network for `service-types`. These `service-types` take the form (`service:<protocol>`). This function is similar to the `slpRequestServices` API function, but instead of URL replies, we will receive a `service-type` reply. The `slpRequestAllServices` API function is shown in Listing 10.16.

LISTING 10.16 `slpRequestAllServices` **API function.**

```
  int slpRequestAllServices(slpHandleType *handle,
                            slpParsedServiceTypeReplyType *slpPReply
                            )
  {
    slpMsgType slpMsg;
    int ret, i;
```

```
    if ((handle == NULL) || (slpPReply == NULL)) return -1;

    bzero( (void *)slpPReply,
            sizeof(slpParsedServiceTypeReplyType) );

    slpCreateHeader(&slpMsg, SRV_TYPE_RQST, "en", FRESH);

    /* Emit the PRLIST */
    emitShort(&slpMsg, 0);

    /* Emit the Naming Authority */
    emitShort(&slpMsg, 0xffff);

    /* Emit the scope string */
    emitShort(&slpMsg, 7);
    emitString(&slpMsg, "default");

    setSlpHeaderLength( &slpMsg );

    slpPrintMessage( &slpMsg );

    ret = slpSendMessage( handle, &slpMsg );

    for (i = 0 ; i < 5 ; i++) {

      ret = slpReceiveMessage( handle, &slpMsg, 1 );

      if (ret == 0) {
        slpPrintMessage( &slpMsg );

        ret = slpParseServiceTypesReply( &slpMsg, slpPReply );

        printf( "slpReply resulted in %d elements\n",
                 slpPReply->srvCount );

      }

    }

    return slpPReply->srvCount;
  }
```

For `slpRequestAllServices`, we create our SLP request message and then await responses. Once a response is received, we parse it using the `Ser-`

viceTypes parser and return the number of service-types found. We'll see a demonstration of this function later and its usefulness as a service browser.

SLP Message Parsers

A number of parsers exist to parse the needed elements from SLP message responses. Most are hidden within the API functions, with slpParseServiceURL being provided to the user for individual URL parsing.

SLP Service Reply Parser

The first parser function takes an SLP service reply (SrvRply) message and parses the URL elements from it (see Listing 10.17).

LISTING 10.17 slpParseServiceReply parser primitive.

```
int slpParseServiceReply( slpMsgType *slpMsg,
                          slpParsedServiceReplyType *reply
                        )
{
  uint8_t version, messageType;
  uint16_t xid, langLen, numUrls;
  int len;

  if ((slpMsg == NULL) || (reply == NULL)) {
    return -1;
  }

  /*
   *  First, verify that the version is correct and that the response
   *  is a service reply.
   */
  getByte(slpMsg, &version);
  getByte(slpMsg, &messageType);
  if (version != 2) {
    return -2;
  }

  getTriOctet(slpMsg, (uint32_t *)&len);

  /* Skip some unused portions of the header */
  getTriOctet(slpMsg, NULL);
  getShort(slpMsg, NULL);

  getShort(slpMsg, &xid);
```

```
getShort(slpMsg, &langLen);
getString(slpMsg, langLen, NULL);

if (messageType == SRV_REPLY) {

  /* Store the error code and URL count into the reply */
  getShort( slpMsg, &reply->errorcode );
  getShort( slpMsg, (uint16_t *)&numUrls );

  if ((reply->errorcode != 0) || (numUrls == 0)) return -3;

  while ((numUrls--) && (reply->urlCount < MAX_URLS)) {

    getByte( slpMsg, NULL );                    // Reserved Field
    getShort( slpMsg, &reply->urls[reply->urlCount].lifetime );
    getShort( slpMsg, (uint16_t *)&len );
    getString( slpMsg, len,
                (char *)&reply->urls[reply->urlCount].url[0] );
    getByte( slpMsg, NULL );                    // Num Auth Blocks

    reply->urlCount++;

  }

} else if (messageType == DA_ADVERT) {

  /* Store the error code count into the reply */
  getShort( slpMsg, &reply->errorcode );

  getShort( slpMsg, NULL );
  getShort( slpMsg, NULL );

  /* Get the directory-agent URL */
  getShort( slpMsg, (uint16_t *)&len );
  getString( slpMsg, len,
              (char *)&reply->urls[reply->urlCount].url[0] );

  if (len) reply->urlCount++;
}

return 0;

}
```

Note the use of the get functions in the parser. The parser functions act as predictive parsers and extract the elements out of the message, based upon the expected format of the message. Since the format is known (based upon the message type), the predictive parser method works flawlessly.

The service reply message can be either a SRV_REPLY message, or a DA_ADVERT. This is because when the slpRequestService message is emitted, the user may be looking for a service response from the DA of services it has cached, or it may be the DA responding with a DA_ADVERT. For this reason, the parser looks for either response and parses them each accordingly. For the DA_ADVERT, only one URL will be provided. For the SRV_REPLY, multiple services may be provided in the response and therefore the contents are iterated to gather each one.

When parsing is complete, the function returns a zero to represent a successful parse and a negative value to represent an error. The reply field will also be loaded with the number of URLs parsed within the urlCount field.

slpServiceTypesReply PARSER

The service types parser parses a response message of type SRV_TYPE_REPLY. This message contains service-types that are available within the DA. From these service-types, the UA can iterate and request each type and thus browse all services available on the network. See Listing 10.18 for the parser source.

LISTING 10.18 slpParseServiceTypesReply **parser primitive.**

```
int slpParseServiceTypesReply(
              slpMsgType *slpMsg,
              slpParsedServiceTypeReplyType *reply )
{
  uint8_t version, messageType;
  uint16_t xid, langLen, serviceOctets;
  int len, curOctet, srvIndex, srvChar;

  if ((slpMsg == NULL) || (reply == NULL)) {
    return -1;
  }

  /*
   *  First, verify that the version is correct and that the response
   *  is a service-type reply.
```

```
  */
  getByte(slpMsg, &version);
  getByte(slpMsg, &messageType);
  if ((version != 2) || (messageType != SRV_TYPE_REPLY)) {
    return -2;
  }

  getTriOctet(slpMsg, (uint32_t *)&len);

  /* Skip some unused portions of the header */
  getTriOctet(slpMsg, NULL);
  getShort(slpMsg, NULL);

  getShort(slpMsg, &xid);

  getShort(slpMsg, &langLen);
  getString(slpMsg, langLen, NULL);

  /* Store the error code and Services count into the reply */
  getShort( slpMsg, &reply->errorcode );
  getShort( slpMsg, (uint16_t *)&serviceOctets );

  if ((reply->errorcode != 0) || (serviceOctets == 0)) return -3;

  curOctet = 0;
  srvIndex = 0;
  srvChar = 0;

  while ((curOctet < serviceOctets) &&
         (reply->srvCount < MAX_SERVICE_TYPES)) {

    if (slpMsg->buffer[slpMsg->index] == ',') {
      reply->service[srvIndex][srvChar] = 0;
      slpMsg->index++;
      srvChar = 0;
      srvIndex++;
    } else if (slpMsg->buffer[slpMsg->index] == 0) {
      srvIndex++;
      break;
    } else {
      reply->service[srvIndex][srvChar++] =
               slpMsg->buffer[slpMsg->index++];
    }
```

```
    }

    reply->srvCount = srvIndex;

    return 0;
}
```

The `slpParseServiceTypesReply` parser works with string list. The SLP string list is a comma-delimited list of `service-types`. The `while` loop at the end of the parser in Listing 10.18 illustrates the parsing function and decomposing the list of `service-types` into an array of `service-types`.

slpparseServiceURL

The final parser function is an API function that is used by the client application to parse a URL to its basic elements (`service-type`, address and port number). The client passes in the URL and pointers to elements that will be loaded with the parsed components. See Listing 10.19 for the parser listing.

LISTING 10.19 `slpParseServiceURL` **API function.**

```
int slpParseServiceURL ( char *url,
                         char *serviceType,
                         char *addrSpec,
                         char *port )
{
  int i, j, len;

  if ((url == NULL) || (serviceType == NULL) ||
      (addrSpec == NULL) || (port == NULL)) {
    return -1;
  }

  serviceType[0] = 0;
  addrSpec[0] = 0;
  port[0] = 0;

  if (strncmp(url, "service:", 8)) return -1;

  len = strlen(url);

  j = 0;
  i = 8;
```

```
while ((i < len) && (url[i] != ':') && (url[i] != 0)) {
  serviceType[j++] = url[i++];
}
serviceType[j] = 0;

if (!((url[i] == ':') && (url[i+1] == '/'))) {
  return -1;
}

j = 0;
i+=3;
while ((i < len) && (url[i] != ':') && (url[i] != 0)) {
  addrSpec[j++] = url[i++];
}
addrSpec[j] = 0;

if (url[i] == 0) return 0;
j = 0;
i++;
while ((i < len) && (url[i] != 0)) {
  port[j++] = url[i++];
}
port[j] = 0;

return 0;
}
```

The function simply uses the ':' delimiter to identify the structure of the URL and which components should be stored away for return to the caller. The final port number is an optional item, and as shown is detected and the function returns if it's not present.

SLP TOOLS

The implementation provided here is an API for the construction of User Agents and Service Agents. The Directory Agent is not provided, though it could be implemented using the API functions.

For verification of the source, the `OpenSLP` implementation that provides a DA (`slpd`) was utilized. This can be downloaded at http://www.openslp.org. The DA also provides a log (in Linux, /var/log/slpd.log) which is useful for testing SLP applications.

Also provided in the *OpenSLP* distribution is an `slptool` that provides a command line interface to the DA. Using `slptool`, services can be registered and searched. Listing 10.20 provides a sample dialog by `slptool` with the DA. In this dialog, a service is registered and then located.

LISTING 10.20 Using `slptool` for SLP testing.

```
[root@plato emslp]# slptool register service:http://192.168.1.1:8080
[root@plato emslp]# slptool findsrvs service:http
service:http://192.168.1.1:8080,65535
[root@plato emslp]#
```

`OpenSLP's slptool` has numerous other uses for testing and verifications. In addition to `OpenSLP`, a number of other implementations exist for Version 1 and the current Version 2.

SLP TEST PROGRAMS

Let's now look at the use of the presented SLP API. In the following example applications, we'll use each of the API functions to illustrate how easy it is to enable any embedded application with SLP functionality.

Registering a Service

Registering a service within the network is the job of the SA. In this test example, our application calls the function `registerTest` to register our service to the network. Note that in this implementation, the SA requires a DA for proper function. The UA has no such constraints.

The register test function is provided in Listing 10.21.

LISTING 10.21 Service registration test.

```
void registerTest( void )
{
  int ret;
  slpHandleType handle;

  ret = slpInit();

  ret = slpOpen(&handle);

  ret = slpRegisterService( &handle,
                            "service:http://mtjones.com:8081",
```

```
                              "service:http",
                              "",
                              10800);

    ret = slpClose( &handle );

    return;
  }
```

Note that the first task is always to initialize the SLP layer via the `slpInit` call. This need only be done once at startup, but can be done for every call thereafter. We next open an SLP handle to gain access to the SLP entities on the network. We register our service with the `slpRegisterService` call. This includes our handle, the service URL, the `service-type`, a null attribute list, and our lifetime (in seconds). Finally, we close the SLP handle since we've finished our task.

Having run this test, we can use the `OpenSLP` `slptool` to look interrogate the DA for services. A session looking for our previously registered service is provided in Listing 10.22.

LISTING 10.22 Testing the registration using `slptool`.

```
[root@plato emslp]# slptool findsrvs service:http
service:http://mtjones.com:8081,10785
```

As shown, the `slptool` responds with the service that we previously registered. Note that the lifetime in this example is different from what we registered. This is because the DA responds with the remaining lifetime of the service registration. Here we find that the service has aged 15 seconds.

Finding a Service

Locating a service is typically done by a UA. To locate a service, the agent need only provide the `service-type`. The DA then responds with all services that match that type. The `slpRequestService` function also performs the job of parsing the results to simplify the user's utilization of the URLs. See Listing 10.23 for the service location test.

LISTING 10.23 Service location test.

```
void findTest( void )
{
  int ret;
```

```
    slpHandleType handle;
    slpParsedServiceReplyType reply;
    char serviceType[80], addrSpec[80], port[80];
    int i;

    ret = slpInit();

    ret = slpOpen(&handle);

    ret = slpRequestService( &handle, &reply,
                             "service:http",
                             "");

    printf("url count   : %d\n", reply.urlCount);
    for (i = 0 ; i < reply.urlCount ; i++) {
      slpParseServiceURL( reply.urls[i].url,
                          serviceType, addrSpec, port );
      printf("url         : %s\n", reply.urls[i].url);
      printf("serviceType : %s\n", serviceType);
      printf("addrSpec    : %s\n", addrSpec);
      printf("port        : %s\n", port);
    }

    ret = slpClose( &handle );

    return;
}
```

What's unique about this test is the use of the `slpRequestService` result. The reply structure will be filled with the URLs that resulted from the query. A call to `slpParseServiceURL` parses the URL to its basic elements for display. A sample run of this test is shown in Listing 10.24.

LISTING 10.24 Testing the `slpRequestService` function with `findTest`.

```
url count   : 1
url         : service:http://192.168.1.1:8080
serviceType : http
addrSpec    : 192.168.1.1
port        : 8080
```

From a user application perspective, all of the information is available to connect to the found service through the reply URLs.

Browsing All Services on a Network

Our final example looks at a combination of a new SLP API function and use of prior services. An important aspect of SLP is the capability to browse the services that are available on a network (given proper scope). The function to do this is surprisingly simple, and is shown in Listing 10.25.

LISTING 10.25 Service browsing test.

```
void browseNetwork( void )
{
  int ret;
  slpHandleType handle;
  slpParsedServiceReplyType reply;
  slpParsedServiceTypeReplyType sreply;
  int i, j;

  ret = slpInit();

  ret = slpOpen(&handle);

  slpRequestAllServices( &handle, &sreply );

  for (j = 0 ; j < sreply.srvCount ; j++) {

    printf("Service %s\n", sreply.service[j]);

    slpRequestService( &handle, &reply,
                       sreply.service[j], "");

    for (i = 0 ; i < reply.urlCount ; i++) {
      printf("\t%s\n", reply.urls[i].url);
    }
    printf("\n");

  }

  ret = slpClose( &handle );

  return;
}
```

In this function, we first use the `slpRequestAllServices` API function to retrieve all of the `service-types` that are active on the network. Then we iterate through these services and request the services that match the prior collected `service-types`. The types `slpParsedServiceReplyType` and `slpParsedServiceTypeReplyType` are provided on the CD-ROM in file `slpTypes.h`.

This test application results in Listing 10.26. Note that for test purposes, we prime the DA with a number of services to make the output interesting.

LISTING 10.26 Sample output of the service browsing test.

```
slptool register service:http://192.168.1.1:8080
slptool register service:http://192.168.1.2:8082
slptool register service:smtp://192.168.15.3:25
slptool register service:ntp://192.168.15.8

Service service:http
    service:http://192.168.1.1:8080
    service:http://192.168.1.2:8082

Service service:smtp
    service:smtp://192.168.15.3:25

Service service:ntp
    service:ntp://192.168.15.8
```

The SLP API functions are very simple to use and integrate easily to embedded applications. The strength of SLP is its simplicity and its genericness. SLP is a big step forward for zero-configuration of embedded network devices.

SUMMARY

In this chapter, we've investigated the Service Location Protocol, its architecture, and messaging primitives. While the SLP is simple compared to its competitors, its simplicity makes it usable by a wider audience of varying applications. We looked at the competing protocols for service location and then dug down into the SLP architecture and messages. We then presented a simple API for service location and SLP's implementation. Finally, we looked at sample programs that utilized the defined API in conjunction with an open source DA.

RESOURCES

Salutation Consortium. http://www.salutation.org

Jini Architecture. http://www.sun.com/jini/

Universal Plug-and-Play Forum. http://www.upnp.org/

Alvestrand, "Tags for the Identification of Languages," RFC 1766, March 1995. http://www.landfield.org/rfcs/rfc1766.html

Guttman, et al., "Service Location Protocol, Version 2," RFC 2608, June 1999. http://www.landfield.org/rfcs/rfc2608.html

Kempf, Guttman, "An API for Service Location," RFC 2614, June 1999. http://www.landfield.org/rfcs/rfc2614.html

Stevens, W. Richard, *Unix Network Programming—Networking APIs: Sockets and XTI Volume 1*, W. Richard Stevens, Prentice Hall PTR, 1998.

11 Embedded NNTP Client

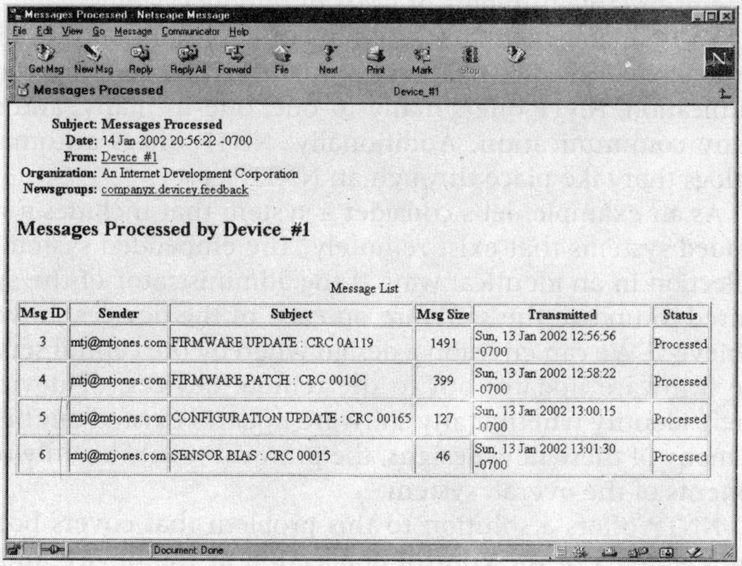

In this chapter, we look at the Network News Transfer Protocol (NNTP) as a communication medium for embedded systems. NNTP offers some interesting variations and similarities to previously discussed protocols such as POP3 and SMTP. We'll look at the architecture of NNTP, some novel uses in embedded systems, and finally an implementation of an NNTP client suitable for an embedded design.

INTRODUCTION

NNTP is a text-based protocol used to distribute Usenet news on the Internet. It is used as a client/server protocol to distribute news between a user and a server as well as between servers to propagate news around the Internet. It is very similar to the POP3 and SMTP protocols in that the protocol is text-command based. SMTP/POP3 is also very similar in the data formats transported through NNTP.

Why NNTP for Embedded Systems?

While NNTP is traditionally used as an archival group messaging system, it can be very useful in designs that employ either large numbers of remote systems or large numbers of users of remote systems.

NNTP enables a different architecture for remote communications than we looked at in prior chapters. While SMTP is good for one-to-one communication, NNTP offers many-to-one, one-to-many, and even many-to-many communication. Additionally, NNTP offers automatic archival of dialogs that take place through an NNTP server.

As an example, let's consider a system that includes a number of embedded systems that exist remotely. The embedded systems perform data collection in an identical way. If the administrator of the system were required to update the software on each of the devices, how would this be achieved? We can envision a design whereby the central server would push the firmware updates out to the remote devices, or devices would routinely identify whether any software updates existed on the central server. In many of these new designs, the protocol would be only one of the components of the overall system.

NNTP offers a solution to this problem that covers both the protocol and elements of the control application at the device and central server (see Figure 11.1). Using NNTP, a group would be created at the central server for whom the administrator could post software updates (via a standard news client). The software update would be automatically encoded in a form that could be transferred over the ASCII-based protocol (such as Base64 or Quoted-Printable). The software update would then be available at the NNTP server for download by the embedded devices.

Note the difference here with SMTP. SMTP is directed to a particular endpoint (or multiple endpoints, if configured on the recipient list). With NNTP, the message is posted to the NNTP group at the server and is then available to any device that wants to access it. Additionally, NNTP messages can be retained forever which means that devices will always have access to patches and other information for their product life. Once an SMTP message is consumed at the server, it is removed.

When the embedded device connects to the central server through its available communications link, it connects to the NNTP server to see if any

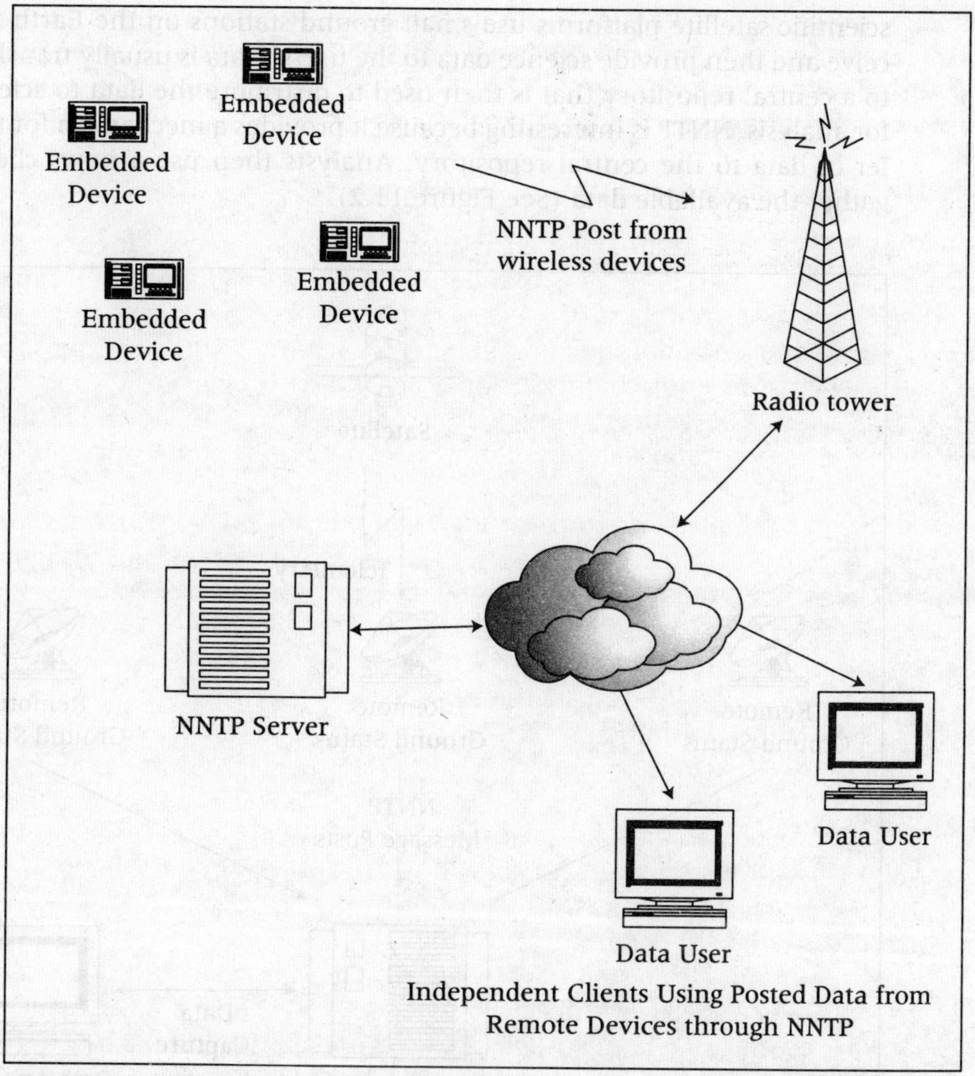

FIGURE 11.1 Using NNTP for communication with numerous remote embedded devices.

new posts have been made. Upon finding that a new post exists, the device grabs the post through NNTP. Reviewing the post would identify it as a software update (possibly through the subject of the message) and the attachment of the post would be decoded and applied to the device.

The reverse situation also presents an interesting option with NNTP. Take for example one or more embedded systems that emit data. Small scientific satellite platforms use small ground stations on the Earth to receive and then provide science data to the users. Data is usually transferred to a central repository that is then used to distribute the data to scientists for analysis. NNTP is interesting because it provides a mechanism for transfer of data to the central repository. Analysts then use a news client to gather the available data (See Figure 11.2).

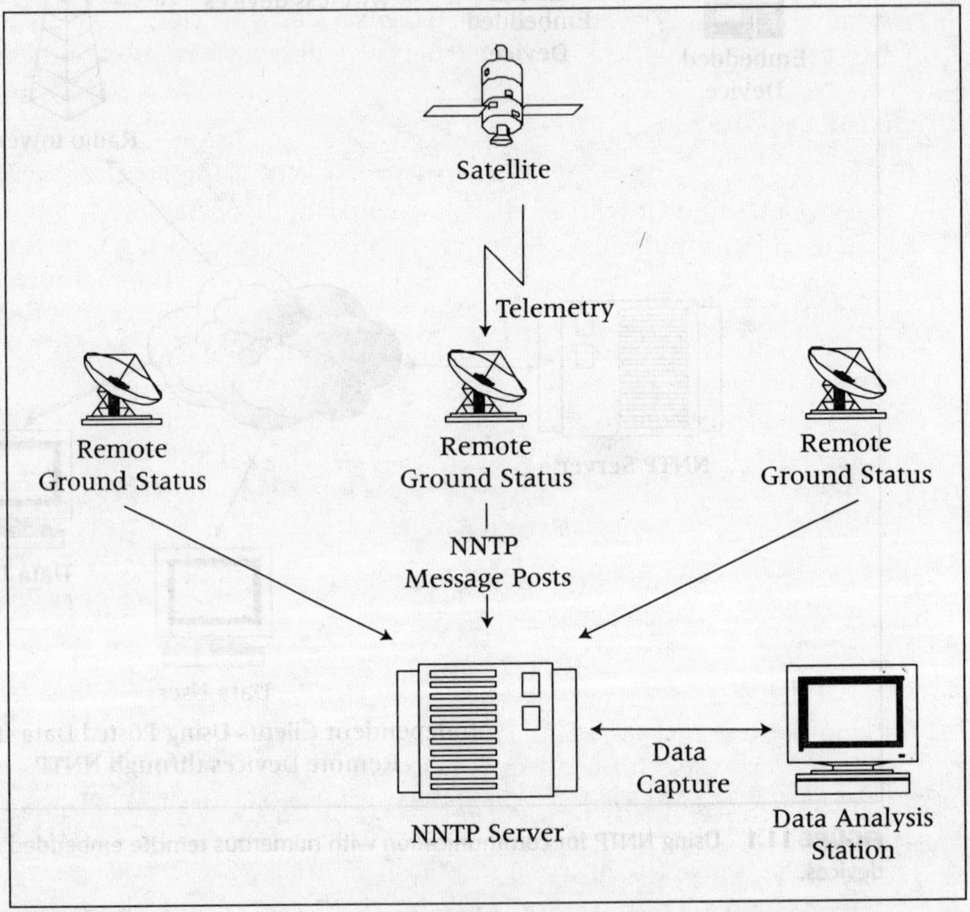

FIGURE 11.2 Using NNTP for communication from a single device to many users.

An important point to note regarding the NNTP server is that since the messages remain for sometimes long periods of time, the need for large (and reliable) archival storage is needed. When messages are no longer needed, the NNTP server administrator can purge these messages.

Security can also be an important element. In this implementation, an insecure client is provided. NNTP provides for username and password authentication that could be easily integrated using the POP3 client source as a model.

Advanced Uses

NNTP is useful to transport ASCII data, but given encoding strategies such as Base64 or Quoted-Printable encoding, rich content can also be distributed including audio or video data. As NNTP is a transport closely related to SMTP, it offers some of the advantages that were discussed in the SMTP chapters.

Origin and Evolution

NNTP began as a UUCP-based (UNIX to UNIX Copy Program) protocol in 1979 at Duke University. It was created by two graduate students (Tom Truscott and Jim Ellis). Seven years later, the protocol NNTP was available over the TCP/IP suite of protocols and an explosion of popularity occurred.[1]

DELETE MENNTP provides not only the means to communicate with the end user, but also with intermediate systems to receive news feeds and to propagate feeds. NNTP takes care of accepting posts from a user and propagating them to the network of NNTP servers running worldwide.

Recently, Google (www.google.com) has offered access to the complete Usenet archive. In this archive, over 700 million messages spanning the 20 year life of the Usenet can be found.[2]

PROTOCOL OVERVIEW

NNTP is a simple dialog-based protocol that operates in the ASCII text domain (that is, human-readable protocol). NNTP is a synchronous command/response protocol in which a command is issued and a resulting response is generated by the NNTP server. Responses follow a very specific format that makes the protocol very easy to implement.

The entire NNTP specification (as defined by RFC 977) is less than 20 pages long and provides a small set of commands for news transport. In the implementation discussed here, we'll use an even smaller subset of commands to provide a basic NNTP client API.

[1]Usenet Software: History and Sources, http://www.faqs.org/faqs/usenet/software/part1/
[2]The Google Search Engine (Copyright 2001 Google), http://www.google.com

NNTP ARCHITECTURE

NNTP is a text-based client/server protocol that also offers server/server communication. The client/server model is used for user dialog with the NNTP server using a newsreader (commonly provided by Web browsers). The server/server model is used as the news propagation mechanism to ensure that the news is consistent among all news sites around the world (see Figure 11.3).

The news client initiates communication with the NNTP server to receive news. A news client may authenticate itself, but this is not necessary

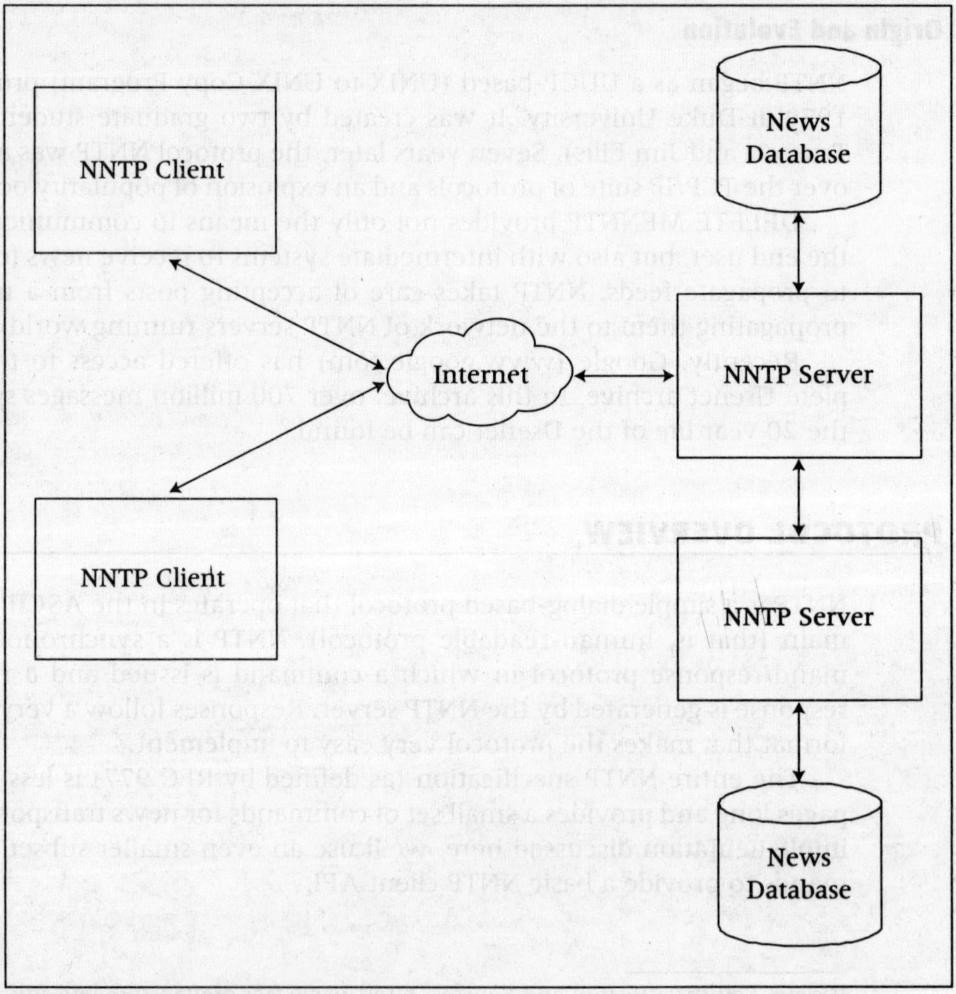

FIGURE 11.3 NNTP architecture.

in the NNTP model. The news client will commonly cache a list of newsgroups that the user has interest in as well as the messages that have been read thus far. The news client will then iterate through each of the cached newsgroups to see if any new messages are available. If any messages are available, a special command is performed to grab basic information about the messages (such as the subject, sender, and date) and make this available to the user. The user may then request the entire article associated with a header to be downloaded for review. When the user is finished with a group, it may be marked as "read" which increments the message index to identify new messages on the next connect. A user may also post to a newsgroup to send a new message.

The NNTP server also communicates with other NNTP servers for which it has been configured. The NNTP server may provide posts that it has received (known as a feed) to other servers or may request a feed from the server to which it has connected.

In our embedded model, we'll implement only the client portion since it is ultimately fits our requirement and is very scalable to a deeply embedded system.

Sample Dialog

Let's now look at a simple dialog with an NNTP server as performed through a simple telnet session. We'll use the `dnews` server in the following examples because it's very easy to configure and it works.[3] Many heavy-duty news sites use the InterNetNews (INN) from the Internet Software Consortium.[4] INN is the descendent of the earliest news servers and is feature rich. INN can be overwhelming for configuration due to its complexity, but it is the standard.

By opening a simple telnet session to port 119 of the NNTP server (see Listing 11.1), we can carry out a dialog with the server. User input is shown in bold.

LISTING 11.1 Sample NNTP client/server dialog.

```
root@plato /root]# telnet localhost 119
S: 200 plato.mtjones.com DNEWS Version 5.5d1, SO, posting OK
C: list
S: 215 list of newsgroups follows
```

[3]Dnews News Server—NetWin, http://netwinsite.com/dnews.htm

[4]INN: InterNetNews, Internet Software Consortium, http://www.isc.org/products/INN/

```
S: control 2 3 y
S: control.cancel 2 3 y
S: my.group 10 3 y
S: new.group 6 3 y
S: .
C: group my.group
S: 211 8 3 10 my.group selected
C: article 3
S: 220 3 <3C36AF8E.1BD3047E@mtjones.com> article retrieved
S: Message-ID: <3C36AF8E.1BD3047E@mtjones.com>
S: Date: Sat, 05 Jan 2002 00:47:27 -0700
S: From: "M. Tim Jones" <mtj@mtjones.com>
S: X-Mailer: Mozilla 4.74 [en] (Win98; U)
S: X-Accept-Language: en
S: MIME-Version: 1.0
S: Newsgroups: my.group
S: Subject: this is my post
S: Content-Type: text/plain; charset=us-ascii
S: Content-Transfer-Encoding: 7bit
S: NNTP-Posting-Host: sartre.mtjones.com
S: X-Trace: plato.mtjones.com 1010328764 sartre.mtjones.com
S: Lines: 6
S: Path: plato.mtjones.com
S: Xref: plato.mtjones.com my.group:3
S:
S:
S: Hello
S:
S: This is my post.
S:
S:
S: .
C: date
S: 111 20020112122419
C: quit
S: 205 closing connection - goodbye!
```

Let's now walk through this sample dialog to understand how the client/server side of NNTP works.

Recall that the server responds with a status response line that includes a three-digit numeric code along with additional textual information. The three-digit numeric code follows a strict standard as shown in Table 11.1

TABLE 11.1 NNTP status response line numeric codes.

Code	*Description*
1xx	Informational message
2xx	Command was successful.
3xx	Command thus far is successful – send the rest of it.
4xx	Command was correct but could not be performed.
5xx	Command unimplemented

We first telnet to the NNTP server which is by default located at port 119. The NNTP server immediately responds with a salutation preceded by the successful status code `200`.

```
S: 200 plato.mtjones.com DNEWS Version 5.5d1, SO, posting OK
```

The salutation provides some information in addition to the fact that we've successfully connected to an NNTP server. After the numeric status code is the fully qualified domain name of the server (`plato.mtjones.com`). Next is the NNTP server implementation and version (`dnews`, 5.5d1). The salutation ends with `posting OK` which means that the client may post news messages to the server.

We next issue a simple command requesting that the server identify any new groups that are available.

```
C: list
S: 215 list of newsgroups follows
S: control 2 3 y
S: control.cancel 2 3 y
S: my.group 10 3 y
S: new.group 6 3 y
S: .
```

The `list` command is sent by the client to the server who responds with a list of the currently available newsgroups. The list is preceded by the status response line (`215` represents receipt and processing of a successful command). Each of the available newsgroups are then iterated with the list completing with the '.'. Recall that SMTP and POP3 use this convention for the transfer of e-mail messages. NNTP uses the '.' end-of-list indicator for all potential multi-line server output.

We then issue a group command with the argument `my.group`. This instructs the NNTP server that we're interested in the group `my.group` and allows us to read or write messages to that group.

```
C: group my.group
S: 211 8 3 10 my.group selected
```

The NNTP server responds with a successful response code and then a number of other arguments. The first, `8`, is the number of messages that are available within this group to be read. The second two arguments, `3` and `10`, represent the range of article IDs that may be read. The next arguments are the group that we requested and an indication that it has been selected. Once the `group` command is successfully issued, all article-related actions are focused on that particular group. The user may specify a new group at any time while in the command mode.

Since article 3 is the first available in the group, we issue the command `article` with the Message-ID to request that particular message. The `article` command retrieves the head and body of the specified message. We could have also split this transfer by first performing a `head` command and then a `body` command.

```
C: article 3
S: 220 3 <...@mtjones.com> article retrieved
S: Message-ID: <3C36AF8E.1BD3047E@mtjones.com>
S: Date: Sat, 05 Jan 2002 00:47:27 -0700
S: From: "M. Tim Jones" <mtj@mtjones.com>
S: X-Mailer: Mozilla 4.74 [en] (Win98; U)
S: X-Accept-Language: en
S: ...
S: .
```

After processing our article command, the NNTP server emits the status response line and then the entire message. We know when the client is complete because a single '.' on a line by itself identifies the end-of-message condition. Recall that the message head and body are separated by a single blank line (see Listing 11.1).

If the message headers look familiar, it's because they're the standard headers that can be found in an SMTP message. This similarity allows an NNTP client to utilize a standard mail user agent (MUA) functionality with the NNTP command structure.

The NNTP server provides a number of other commands, such as the `date` command illustrated below. From the numeric code in the status response line, we can see that this response is an informational message. The date and time are encoded within the next string (January 12, 2002 12:24:19).

```
C: date
S: 111 20020112122419
```

Finally, when we want to end our dialog with the NNTP server, we issue the `quit` command.

```
C: quit
S: 205 closing connection - goodbye!
```

The server then provides us with a success response and closes the connection.

BASIC DESIGN

The NNTP client implementation presented here uses a minimal number of API functions to support NNTP server connectivity. Since accessing an NNTP server will be different for each embedded application, the API provides a generalized set of features. An embedded client can connect, define a group, read and post messages, and disconnect. Despite the minimum number of primitives, the API is very flexible as will be demonstrated later in this chapter.

In the next section, we'll discuss each of the API functions. This precedes a detailed discussion of the NNTP client API implementation.

NNTP Client API

The NNTP client API provides six functions to manage news messages on a remote server. These functions are shown in Listing 11.2.

LISTING 11.2 NNTP client API functions.

```
int  nntpConnect ( char *nntperver );
int  nntpSetGroup ( char *group, int lastMessage );
int  nntpPeek ( news_t *msg, int totalLen );
int  nntpRetrieve ( news_t *msg, int totalLen );
void nntpSkip ( void );
```

```
int nntpParse ( news_t *msg, unsigned int flags );
int nntpPost ( news_t *msg );
int nntpDisconnect ( void );
```

The API mimics common user interactions with an NNTP server (through a news client) and is therefore very intuitive. Many of the unnecessary details of news management have been abstracted away so that the embedded software developer can concentrate on the actual task at hand.

Most of the NNTP API functions use a news structure that defines a single message. The type is visible to the user and contains not only raw message buffers but also separate elements that are used in parsing. The `news_t` structure is shown in Listing 11.3.

LISTING 11.3 news_t structure type.

```
typedef struct {
  char *msg;
  int  msgLen;
  int  msgId;
  char subject[MAX_STRING+1];
  char sender[MAX_STRING+1];
  char msgDate[MAX_STRING+1];
  char *bodyStart;
} news_t;
```

The `msg` field of the `news_t` structure is a pointer to the buffer that will contain the news message. This is provided by the user for maximum flexibility. Some systems may utilize very small messages while others may support large Base64-encoded messages. For space efficiency, the user provides the buffer and its length in the `msgLen` field. The `msgId` field is loaded by the `nntpRetrieve` function to identify the actual Message-ID (more on this in the `nntpRetrieve` function discussion). Fields `subject` and `sender` are filled in by the parser or by the user if an `nntpPost` is being performed. The `bodyStart` field is a pointer to the start of the actual body of the message (skipping the header portion and blank line that separates the header and body). This is initialized by the `nntpParse` function, but must also be provided by the user for a new message that is being emitted through the `nntpPost` function.

The `nntpConnect` function is used to connect to an NNTP server. The caller must provide the IP address or fully qualified domain name of an NNTP server. The function performs all functions necessary to connect to the server and flow to a state in which the system may send or receive news messages. The function returns a status code (0 for success and -1 for error).

The nntpSetGroup function specifies the current group for the NNTP connection. The client may read or post a message only once a valid group has been specified. This function takes the group name (for example, company.device.patches) and identifies if any new messages exist based upon the lastMessage argument passed from the user. The NNTP server does not keep track of the messages a client has read or which groups a client may subscribe to; this information is kept locally with the client. Therefore, when a client downloads messages from a server for a particular group, it must keep track of the last message read, otherwise it will download all messages available on the next connect.

The nntpPeek function is used to peek at the next available message. Only the headers are downloaded from the server. This is advantageous because not all devices may need every message in a group. This function allows a device to look at the headers of the message to determine if the rest of the message needs to be downloaded.

API function nntpRetrieve provides the message download capability for the client. The application must provide a pre-initialized news_t message structure along with the size of the message buffer within the structure. The function automatically retrieves the next available message. The next message available is defined by the nntpSetGroup call and is retained for the connection by the API.

While nntpRetrieve downloads a message into the news_t message structure, only the msg, msgLen, and msgId fields will be set by the function. The user must call the nntpParse function to physically parse the message into its component parts. If a full parse is requested, the nntpParse function identifies the start of the body and initializes the bodyStart field with a pointer to the body of the msg field. The subject and sender fields are also parsed into separate fields within the news_t structure.

To post a message to a group, the client can use the nntpPost function. This function accepts a news_t structure. The caller must pre-initialize the msg field and fill it with the body of the message to be posted. The bodyStart field must also point to the msg (commonly the start, since the msg in this instance is the body of the message rather than both the header and body). As with nntpRetrieve, the application must specify the group of interest prior to this using the nntpSetGroup primitive.

Finally, the nntpDisconnect API function is used to close out an NNTP connection. This function closes the socket for the connection and initializes the internal state variables to default values indicating that no connection exists.

All primitives discussed here (except for `nntpSkip`) return `0` on success and `-1` on error.

COMMUNICATION STRUCTURE

Messages posted and retrieved through NNTP follow the same basic structure as previously discussed with SMTP and POP3. Messages are composed of 7-bit ASCII text with optional binary attachments encoded using a binary encoding method such as Base64 or Quoted-Printable (see Chapter 5 for more details on these encoding methods).

Recall the header formats observed in Chapter 5 with the headers presented here (in Listing 11.1). NNTP adds extensions to support special communication between the server and client. Most extensions listed are identical to those found for the SMTP and POP3 protocols. Headers and message bodies are separated by a single blank line and the end of message is indicated by a single period on a line by itself (again, identical to SMTP-related protocols).

The headers available and their descriptions can be found in RFC 822. Additional information can be found in RFC 1036 (NNTP specific).

A client may include special headers for client-to-server (or client-to-client) communication. User-specified headers can be have an 'X-' prefix to denote a special header that may not be meaningful to all applications. For example, the NNTP server includes the following header:

```
S: X-Trace: plato.mtjones.com 1010328764 sartre.mtjones.com (6 Jan 2002
   07:52:44 -0700)
```

This audit trail identifies the host that originated the message (`plato.mtjones.com`) and the server that received it (`sartre.mtjones.com`) along with the date and time of receipt. Most clients and servers will simply pass this header through without notice. Specialized applications can utilize these headers and their data in such a way that they are hidden and do not appear anywhere in the body of the message.

Characteristics

While NNTP shares many of the concepts created for SMTP and POP3, it also combines them in a novel way. NNTP provides for client communication with a server as well as server-to-server communication (similar to SMTP). NNTP also provides for message retrieval, commonly a function provided by POP3. NNTP differs from SMTP and POP3 in that it is a group communication protocol and provides for persistence in messages at the servers.

Like SMTP and POP3, NNTP is a text-based synchronous command/response protocol. While not as efficient as binary protocols (such as SNMP), developing clients and servers for text-based protocols is much easier, and simpler to validate.

IMPLEMENTATION SUMMARY

Let's now look at the implementation of the NNTP API. From Listing 11.2, we can see that the API functions are split into a well-defined set of capabilities available from the NNTP server. Each of the functions is stateful, meaning some state is retained within the API for the user until the `nntpDisconnect` function is called. Once `nntpDisconnect` is called, all internal state information is discarded.

Support Functions

Before jumping into the API functions, let's first look at one of the support functions that simplifies communication with the NNTP server. This is a variation on the dialog function that we've used in the past for the POP3 server and SMTP client (see Listing 11.4).

LISTING 11.4 Dialog function for client/server communication.

```
int dialog( int sd, char *buffer, char *resp )
{
  int ret, len;

  if ((sd == -1) || (!buffer)) return -1;

  if (strlen(buffer) > 0) {
    len = strlen( buffer );
    if ( write( sd, buffer, len ) != len ) return -1;
  }

  if (resp != NULL) {
    ret = read( sd, buffer, MAX_LINE );
    if (ret >= 0) {
```

```
            buffer[ret] = 0;
            if (strncmp( buffer, resp, 3 )) return -1;
        } else {
            return -1;
        }
    }

    return 0;
}
```

Once we have a connection with the NNTP server, the dialog function is used to send a command and then await a response. When a response is received, the status code is compared to the expected code (contained within `resp`). If it does not match, an error return is generated; otherwise, the user receives a successful return. Note that in both cases, the incoming command is optional and the response is optional. Note also that the `buffer` used to contain the command is used to accept the response. This is done so that the user has access to the return buffer. In some cases, the status response line contains additional information of interest to an API function. By using the buffer provided by the user, the contents of the status response line are available upon return.

nntpConnect

`nntpConnect` is a very simple function that initiates communication with the NNTP server. It creates the socket and binds the peer to port 119 (the NNTP server port). The caller passes in either an IP address or a fully qualified domain name of an NNTP server. The function will internally figure out through trial and error which one is represented (see Chapter 6 on POP3 for a more detailed discussion of this process). See Listing 11.5 for the `nntpConnect` source.

LISTING 11.5 `nntpConnect` API function.

```
int nntpConnect ( char *nntpServer )
{
  int result = -1;
  struct sockaddr_in servaddr;

  if (!nntpServer) return -1;

  curGroup[0] = 0;
```

```
    sock = socket( AF_INET, SOCK_STREAM, 0 );

    bzero( &servaddr, sizeof(servaddr) );
    servaddr.sin_family = AF_INET;
    servaddr.sin_port = htons( 119 );

    servaddr.sin_addr.s_addr = inet_addr( nntpServer );

    if ( servaddr.sin_addr.s_addr == 0xffffffff ) {
      struct hostent *hptr =
                    (struct hostent *)gethostbyname( nntpServer );
      if ( hptr == NULL ) {
        return -1;
      } else {
        struct in_addr **addrs;
        addrs = (struct in_addr **)hptr->h_addr_list;
        memcpy( &servaddr.sin_addr,
                  *addrs, sizeof(struct in_addr) );
      }
    }

    result = connect( sock,
                  (struct sockaddr *)&servaddr, sizeof(servaddr) );

    if ( result >= 0 ) {

      buffer[0] = 0;
      result = dialog( sock, buffer, "200" );

      if (result < 0) nntpDisconnect();

    }

    return ( result );
}
```

Once the socket connect is performed, we immediately check for the salutation. Note that we initialize the buffer as a null string that tells the dialog function that no command is to be sent out. In this case, we're looking only for a response that is a server salutation. We know that the status code for a successful salutation is 200, so we pass this to dialog. The connection is automatically closed if the dialog with the server is unsuccessful which means that the application need only perform a nntpDisconnect if the connect was successful.

nntpSetGroup

Before the application can post or retrieve messages, it must have defined a group. Groups contain messages (and some allow posting of messages), so the application must define one prior to any message activity. The `nntpSetGroup` function is shown in Listing 11.6.

LISTING 11.6 nntpSetGroup API function.

```
int nntpSetGroup( char *group, int lastRead )
{
  int result = -1;
  int numMessages = -1;

  if ((!group) || (sock == -1)) return -1;

  snprintf( buffer, 80, "group %s\n", group );

  result = dialog( sock, buffer, "211" );

  if (result == 0) {
    sscanf( buffer, "211 %d %d %d ",
              &numMessages, &firstMessage, &lastMessage );

    if (lastRead == -1) {
      curMessage = firstMessage;
    } else {
      curMessage = lastRead+1;
      numMessages = lastMessage - lastRead;
    }

    if (result == 0) {
      strcpy( curGroup, group );
    }

  }

  return( numMessages );
}
```

The `nntpSetGroup` function issues the NNTP `group` command to define a group for the connection (this can be changed at any time in this connection). The response to the command, through the dialog function, contains not only the status code but also some information that is of interest to us.

The three numbers that follow the status code on the response line are defined as the number of available messages within the group, the first available message, and the last. We initialize some internal variables with this information so that they are available when the application performs an `nntpRetrieve`.

One important point to note is that NNTP messages can be persistent, which means that once a post is made it never disappears. Given this, we don't want our system receiving the same messages repeatedly, so we must keep some state information for each group at the application. The application must keep track of the last message read for each group. When the `nntpSetGroup` call is made, the application passes in the numeric ID of the last message read. The `nntpSetGroup` function considers this when determining the number of messages available and the range of those messages (using variable `lastRead` as an offset). If the application passes in a `-1` for the last read message, the function assumes that no messages have been read (all messages are new).

Along with the stateful variables kept for the connection, a variable called `curGroup` is initialized. This variable defines the currently set group that is the target for all retrieve and post requests.

The `nntpSetGroup` function returns the number of new messages that are available or `-1` on error.

nntpPeek

The `nntpPeek` API function allows us to peek at the message without downloading it in its entirety (see Listing 11.7). The peek function is provided by the NNTP command `head`, which provides the capability to download the headers of the message but not the body. Most NNTP clients use this capability. When the list of messages available in a Usenet group is displayed, this is more often than not a list captured from the headers. When the user selects the message, the actual message is downloaded either through the `article` command or the `body` command.

LISTING 11.7 nntpPeek API function.

```
int nntpPeek ( news_t *news, int totalLen )
{
  int result = -1, i, len=0, stop, state, bufIdx=0;

  if ((!news) || (sock == -1)) return -1;

  if ((curMessage == -1) || (curMessage > lastMessage)) return -1;
```

```
    /* Save the message id for this particular message */
    news->msgId = curMessage;

    snprintf( buffer, 80, "head %d\n", curMessage );

    result = dialog( sock, buffer, "221" );

    if (result < 0) return -1;

    state = stop = 0;

    while (!stop) {

      if (bufIdx+len > totalLen - 80) break;

      len = read( sock, &news->msg[bufIdx], (totalLen-bufIdx) );

      /* Search for the end-of-mail indicator in the current buf */
      for ( i = bufIdx ; i < bufIdx+len ; i++ ) {
        if      ((state == 0) && (news->msg[i] == 0x0d) ) state = 1;
        else if ((state == 1) && (news->msg[i] == 0x0a) ) state = 2;
        else if ((state == 2) && (news->msg[i] == 0x0d) ) state = 1;
        else if ((state == 2) && (news->msg[i] ==  '.') ) state = 3;
        else if ((state == 3) && (news->msg[i] == 0x0d) ) state = 4;
        else if ((state == 4) && (news->msg[i] == 0x0a) ) {
          stop = 1; break;
        }
        else state = 0;
      }

      bufIdx += len;

    }

    bufIdx -= 3;
    news->msg[bufIdx] = 0;
    news->msgLen = bufIdx;

    return bufIdx;
  }
```

While the NNTP `head` command emits only the headers and not the body of the message, the end-of-message indicator is the same. The nntpPeek and nntpRetreive commands are therefore very similar. We'll discuss a few more details of this code in the nntpSkip and nntpRetrieve sections that follow.

nntpSkip

The nntpSkip API function is used to skip over a message at the server. The nntpRetrieve function automatically provides this, so this function is used solely in conjunction with nntpPeek. The nntpPeek function looks only at the headers, but does not automatically increment the message ID. If the user is not interested in downloading the message last peeked at, the nntpSkip message is used to ignore the message and go on to the next (see Listing 11.8).

LISTING 11.8 nntpSkip API function.

```
void nntpSkip( void )
{
  curMessage++;
}
```

nntpRetrieve

Receiving messages from a group is provided by the nntpRetrieve API function (shown in Listing 11.9). The nntpRetrieve function is actually very simple given NNTP's mechanism for retrieving news. The article command is issued with the id of an article to retrieve (in this case, our stateful curMessage is the next message to retrieve). If the response line indicates success (with a 220 status code), the entire message will follow and end with a period on a line by itself.

LISTING 11.9 nntpRetrieve API function.

```
int nntpRetrieve ( news_t *news, int totalLen )
{
  int result = -1, i, len=0, stop, state, bufIdx=0;

  if ((!news) || (sock == -1)) return -1;

  if ((curMessage == -1) || (curMessage > lastMessage)) return -1;

  /* Save the message id for this particular message */
  news->msgId = curMessage;
```

```
snprintf( buffer, 80, "article %d\n", curMessage++ );

result = dialog( sock, buffer, "220" );

if (result < 0) return -1;

len = strlen(buffer);
for ( i = 0 ; i < len-1 ; i++ ) {
  if ( (buffer[i] == 0x0d) && (buffer[i+1] == 0x0a) ) {
    len -= i-2;
    memmove( news->msg, &buffer[i+2], len );
    break;
  }
}

state = stop = 0;

while (!stop) {

  if (bufIdx+len > totalLen - 80) break;

  /* Search for the end-of-mail indicator in the current buffer */
  for ( i = bufIdx ; i < bufIdx+len ; i++ ) {
    if      ((state == 0) && (news->msg[i] == 0x0d) ) state = 1;
    else if ((state == 1) && (news->msg[i] == 0x0a) ) state = 2;
    else if ((state == 2) && (news->msg[i] == 0x0d) ) state = 1;
    else if ((state == 2) && (news->msg[i] ==  '.') ) state = 3;
    else if ((state == 3) && (news->msg[i] == 0x0d) ) state = 4;
    else if ((state == 4) && (news->msg[i] == 0x0a) ) {
      stop = 1; break;
    }
    else state = 0;
  }

  bufIdx += (i-bufIdx);

  if (!stop) {

    len = read( sock, &news->msg[bufIdx], (totalLen-bufIdx) );

    if ( (len <= 0) || (bufIdx+len > totalLen) ) {
      break;
    }
```

```
        }

    }

    bufIdx -= 3;
    news->msg[bufIdx] = 0;
    news->msgLen = bufIdx;

    return bufIdx;
}
```

Almost half of the code of the nntpRetrieve is the state machine to identify the end of the message. The rest is basic housekeeping to identify the end of the message and then to null-terminate it. The news structure message length is loaded into the field msgLen. The nntpRetrieve function returns the length of the message or -1 on error.

Note that after nntpRetrieve is called, the only elements that will be initialized within the news structure are as follows: the msg field (contains the actual message), the msgLen (representing the total length of the raw message), and the msgId (the NNTP ID of the message). The application can use the msgId to identify the last message read which is used on the next call with the nntpSetGroup API function.

nntpParse

Once a message is received, we may want to know the sender, subject, or the contents of the body of the message. The nntpParse API function is used to find these elements in the raw message and then cache them within the news structure (see Listing 11.10).

LISTING 11.10 nntpParse API function.

```
int nntpParse( news_t *news, unsigned int flags )
{
  int result;

  if (!news) return -1;

  result = parseEntry( news, "Subject:", news->subject );
  if (result < 0) return result;

  result = parseEntry( news, "Date:", news->msgDate );
  if (result < 0) return result;
```

```
    result = parseEntry( news, "From:", news->sender );
    if (result < 0) return result;
    fixAddress( news->sender );

    if (flags == FULL_PARSE) {
      result = findBody( news );
    }

    return result;
}
```

Two methods of parsing are provided by `nntpParse`. The first is a full parse (the caller passes in `FULL_PARSE` for flags) which means that all parsing is performed. The second method consists only of a header parse (`HEADER_PARSE`) which does not identify the beginning of the body of the message. This could be important depending upon the method used to download the message from the server. If an `nntpPeek` was used, only the headers are available and therefore only a header parse may be performed. If an `nntpRetrieve` was used, the full parse may be performed since the body was downloaded as well as the headers.

The function `parseEntry` is used to find the named header (in the first case `Subject:`) and then retrieve and store the value associated with that header. The function `fixAddress` takes an e-mail address in the form `<xxx@yyy.zzz>` and converts it to the form `xxx@yyy.zzz`. Finally, the `findBody` function searches for the body of the message. The body begins after the first blank line of the headers.

Upon calling the `nntpParse` function, the subject and sender fields of the `news` structure will be initialized to the parsed values. If a full parse is requested, the `bodyStart` field is loaded with a pointer to the body of the message within the `msg` field.

The `nntpParse` function is provided as an aid to the application developer to simplify the parsing of the message and provide the most common elements that the developer may need to access.

nntpPost

The `nntpPost` API function allows an application to post a message to the currently defined newsgroup (see Listing 11.11). The application provides an initialized *news* message. The message must contain the body of the message to be posted (within the `msg` field) as well as the `bodyStart` field pointing to the body (typically the first octet of the `msg` field). The application may provide the sender of the message in the `sender` field and the subject within the `subject` field.

LISTING 11.11 nntpPost API function.

```
int nntpPost( news_t *news )
{
  int result = -1;

  if (sock == -1) return -1;

  strcpy( buffer, "POST\n" );

  result = dialog( sock, buffer, "340" );

  if (result == 0) {

    /* Emit the header elements */
    if (strlen(news->sender) > 0) {
      snprintf( buffer, MAX_LINE, "From: %s\n", news->sender );
      if (dialog( sock, buffer, NULL )) return -1;
    }

    snprintf( buffer, MAX_LINE, "Newsgroups: %s\n", curGroup );
    if (dialog( sock, buffer, NULL )) return -1;

    if (strlen(news->subject) > 0) {
      snprintf( buffer, MAX_LINE, "Subject: %s\n",
                news->subject );
      if (dialog( sock, buffer, NULL )) return -1;
    }

#ifdef ORGANIZATION
    if (strlen(ORGANIZATION)) {
      snprintf( buffer, MAX_LINE, "Organization: %s\n",
                ORGANIZATION );
      if (dialog( sock, buffer, NULL )) return -1;
    }
#endif

    /* Emit the blank line separating the header and body */
    if (dialog( sock, "\n\r", NULL)) return -1;

    /* Emit the body of the message */
```

```
    if (dialog( sock, news->bodyStart, NULL)) return -1;

    /* Emit the final end of message indicator */
    strcpy(buffer, "\n\r.\n\r");
    if (dialog( sock, buffer, "240")) return -1;

  }

  return result;
}
```

The `nntpPost` function first emits the post command and then awaits a response from the NNTP server. In this case, the response is a status-code `340`. Recall from Table 11.1 that this type of code indicates an intermediary status and instructs the client that everything is correct thus far and to continue.

The header elements of the message are then emitted (when provided by the client) followed by a blank line to distinguish the header and body of the message. After the body of the message is emitted (as defined by the `bodyStart` field) the function emits the end-of- message indicator and awaits a successful status indicator.

The `nntpPost` function returns either a `0` on success or a `-1` on failure.

nntpDisconnect

The final function for the NNTP API is used to close a session with the NNTP server (see Listing 11.12).

LISTING 11.12 `nntpDisconnect` **API function.**

```
int nntpDisconnect ( void )
{
  if (sock == -1) return -1;
  close(sock);
  sock = curMessage = firstMessage = lastMessage = -1;
  curGroup[0] = 0;
  return 0;
}
```

Once the client socket is closed, we initialize the internal stateful variables that are kept for the connection. The current group is also cleared indicating that no group is currently defined (for the next connection).

SAMPLE TEST FUNCTION

Now that we've looked at the NNTP API in detail, let's look at a sample application that uses the API. In this example embedded application, we have a number of embedded devices in the field. Each of the devices performs data collection in a uniform way. NNTP is used to provide firmware updates and/or configuration to the embedded devices. The advantage here is that for similar devices in the field, we can globally change every device by sending one message. If the devices differ in some way, we can either insert code into the message to indicate to whom the message is directed (using a device number pattern) or by segmenting the devices into different newsgroups.

Our sample test function is shown in Listing 11.13. This source and the NNTP API can be found on the CD-ROM at `/software/ch11/emnntp/`.

LISTING 11.13 Sample NNTP API test function.

```
int main()
{
  int result, count, index = 0;
  int lastMessage = -1;
  char contents[MAX_MSG+1];
  news_t news;

  /* Load our news body into the mail struct and clear it out. */
  news.msg = contents;
  bzero( contents, sizeof(contents) );
  news.msgLen = MAX_MSG;

  while (1) {

    /* Connect to the NNTP Server */
    count = nntpConnect( SERVER );

    if (count == 0) {

      /* Set our incoming message group */
      count = nntpSetGroup( GROUP, lastMessage );

      index = 0;

      while (count-- > 0) {
```

```
        result = nntpRetrieve( &news, MAX_MSG );

        if (result > 0) {

          result = nntpParse ( &news, FULL_PARSE );

          if (result == 0) {

            /*--------------------*/
            /* Process the Message */
            /*--------------------*/

            /* Save some data about the processed message */
            strncpy( messages[index].msgSubject,
                     news.subject, MAX_STRING );
            strncpy( messages[index].msgSender,
                     news.sender, MAX_STRING );
            strncpy( messages[index].msgDate,
                     news.msgDate, MAX_STRING );
            messages[index].msgId = news.msgId;
            messages[index].msgSize = strlen(news.bodyStart);
            index++;

            lastMessage = news.msgId;

          }

        }

      }

      /* Send back feedback */

      result = nntpSetGroup( FEEDBACK_GROUP, -1 );

      if (result >= 0) {

        strcpy(news.sender, MYNAME);
        strcpy(news.subject, "Messages Processed");

        bzero(news.msg, MAX_MSG);

        sprintf( news.msg,
                 "<HTML><BODY><H2>Messages Processed by %s</H2>"
```

```
                    "<BR><CENTER>"
                    "<TABLE BORDER><CAPTION>Message List</CAPTION>",
                    MYNAME );

        sprintf( &news.msg[strlen(news.msg)],
                    "<TR><bold><TH>Msg "
                    " ID</TH><TH>Sender</TH><TH>Subject</TH>"
                    "<TH>Msg Size</TH><TH>Transmitted</TH>"
                    "<TH>Status</TH></bold></TR>");

        for ( count = 0 ; count < index ; count++ ) {

          sprintf( &news.msg[strlen(news.msg)],
                    "<TR><TD><CENTER>%d</CENTER>"
                    "</TD><TD>%s</TD><TD>%s</TD>"
                    "<TD><CENTER>%d</CENTER></TD>"
                    "<TD>%s</TD><TD>%s</TD></TR>",
                    messages[count].msgId,
                    messages[count].msgSender,
                    messages[count].msgSubject,
                    messages[count].msgSize,
                    messages[count].msgDate, "Processed" );

        }

        sprintf( &news.msg[strlen(news.msg)],
                    "</TABLE></CENTER></BODY></HTML>" );

        news.bodyStart = news.msg;

        result = nntpPost( &news );
      }
    }

    nntpDisconnect();

    sleep(60);

  }

  return 0;
}
```

In this example, two different groups are used by the device. The first group is the one from which the device gets its control messages; the second group is where the device will post its results (in this case, the control messages that have been processed). The groups are defined as symbolic constants within the main file and are shown in Listing 11.14 (with other useful defines).

LISTING 11.14 Sample test function configuration parameters.

```
#define SERVER          "192.168.2.151"
#define GROUP           "companyx.devicey.control"
#define FEEDBACK_GROUP  "companyx.devicey.feedback"
#define MYNAME          "Device_#1"
```

The first task in our sample test function is the initialization of the news message. We create our separate buffer and load it into the news structure as the `msg` field. We then attempt an NNTP connection using the `nntpConnect` API call. If this is successful, our `count` variable will contain the number of new messages that are available (based upon our `lastMessage` internal state variable). We initialize this to `-1` in this function for the first call, but subsequent calls will contain the actual last message that was processed.

We then loop through the number of new messages, retrieving with the `nntpRetrieve` API call. We could have also used the `nntpPeek` call to determine if we actually wanted to download the entire message, but for this example, we'll assume that every message is useful to us. Once the message is retrieved, we call the `nntpParse` function indicating that we want a full parse of the message (since the message body is present in the news message buffer). If the `nntpParse` returns a successful response, we have a good message that has been parsed within the `news` structure.

The processing portion of the message has been omitted (since it will be different for each application). Where the comment "`Process the Message`" is placed is the point at which the actual message would be processed by the application. At this point, we save some data about the message for later use.

The final point to notice about incoming messages is the update of the `lastMessage` variable with the `msgId` field of the message. The `msgId` field is loaded within the `nntpRetrieve` API function with the actual ID of the message. By setting our `lastMessage` variable with this value, we indicate that we've processed this message. On the next call to the `nntpSetGroup` function, we use this value to ignore all but the new messages.

One the device has processed all of the new messages, we'll require it to provide feedback of its actions. A new group is used for this purpose. The application first defines the new group as our target using the `nntpSetGroup` API function. The message is then built, using an HTML table to format the information. Before we post our message, we set the `bodyStart` field of the news message to the beginning of the `msg` field. We then post the `news` message using the `nntpPost` API function. Figure 11.4 shows the rendering of the resulting message through a standard Netscape browser.

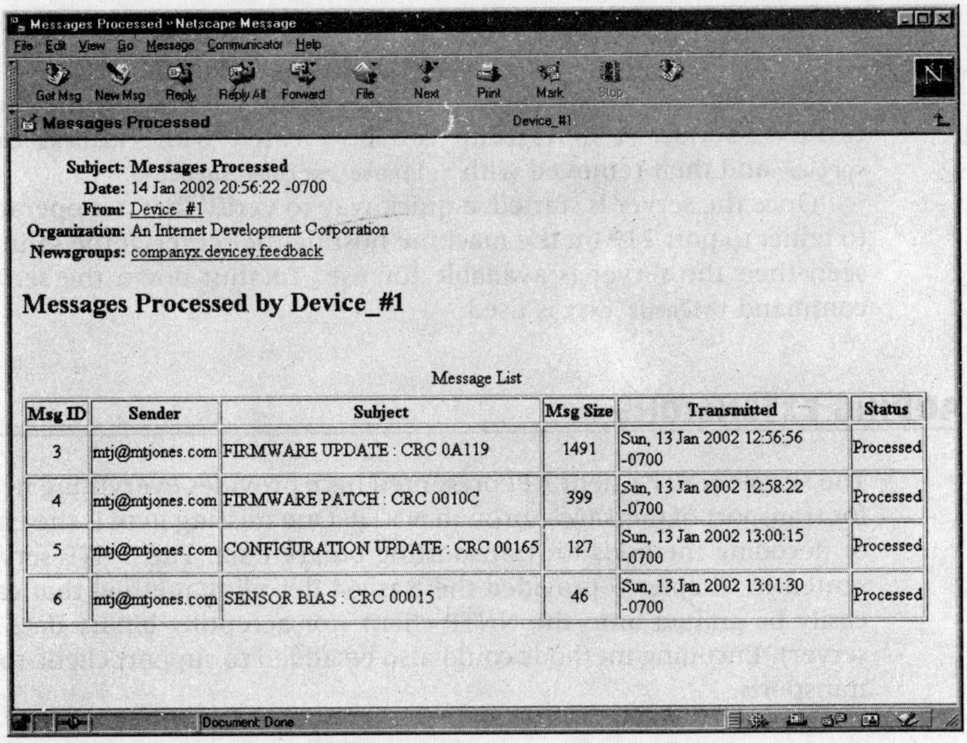

Subject: Messages Processed
Date: 14 Jan 2002 20:56:22 -0700
From: Device_#1
Organization: An Internet Development Corporation
Newsgroups: companyx.devicey.feedback

Messages Processed by Device_#1

Message List

Msg ID	Sender	Subject	Msg Size	Transmitted	Status
3	mtj@mtjones.com	FIRMWARE UPDATE : CRC 0A119	1491	Sun, 13 Jan 2002 12:56:56 -0700	Processed
4	mtj@mtjones.com	FIRMWARE PATCH : CRC 0010C	399	Sun, 13 Jan 2002 12:58:22 -0700	Processed
5	mtj@mtjones.com	CONFIGURATION UPDATE : CRC 00165	127	Sun, 13 Jan 2002 13:00:15 -0700	Processed
6	mtj@mtjones.com	SENSOR BIAS : CRC 00015	46	Sun, 13 Jan 2002 13:01:30 -0700	Processed

FIGURE 11.4 Example of a posted message.

When we've finished with our connection, we use the `nntpDisconnect` API function to close out the connection, and then for demonstration purposes we put our application to sleep for a short time. If any new messages have been posted to the control group, they'll be processed at the next cycle.

TESTING THE NNTP CLIENT

In order to test the NNTP client, we must have access to an NNTP server. Rather than clutter the global Usenet, we've configured a local NNTP server for our use. The dnews server from NetWin is a very configurable server.

The dnews server uses an application called tellnews to communicate with and control the NNTP server. You can start with a standard configuration:

```
/usr/local/dnews/dnews_start
```

Once started, we can check the status of the server using the command tellnews status. A newsgroup can be created with tellnews newsgroup <group> and then removed with tellnews rmgroup <group>.

Once the server is started, a quick way to verify that it is operational is to telnet to port 119 on the machine hosting the server. If the salutation is seen then the server is available for use. To shut down the server, the command tellnews exit is used.

ADDING EXTENSIONS

The simple NNTP Client API presented here provides everything necessary for transport of messages through NNTP. One missing item is the encoding or decoding methods for transporting binary data. The SMTP server presented in Chapter 5 provided the Base64 decoding method that can very easily be grafted onto the NNTP client (for accepting binary data from a server). Encoding methods could also be added to support client-to-server transports.

SUMMARY

In this chapter, we've presented the Network News Transfer Protocol and the architecture over which it operates. We've discussed some of the interesting possibilities of NNTP with embedded systems and identified its strengths in managing communication among a large number of players. Finally, we presented the implementation of an NNTP client API with a test application that utilized two Usenet groups for receiving and transmitting information.

RESOURCES

"Usenet Software: History and Sources." http://www.faqs.org/faqs/usenet/software/part1/

The Google Search Engine (Copyright 2001 Google). http://www.google.com

Dnews News Server—NetWin. http://netwinsite.com/dnews.htm

INN: InterNetNews, Internet Software Consortium. http://www.isc.org/products/INN/

RFC 822, Standard for the Format of ARPA Internet Text Messages, Crocker, August 1982. http://www.landfield.org/rfcs/rfc822.html

RFC 977, Network News Transfer Protocol: A Proposed Standard for the Stream-Based Transmission of News, Kantor and Lapsley, February 1986. http://www.landfield.org/rfcs/rfc977.html

RFC 1036, Standard for Interchange of USENET Messages, Horton and Adams, December 1987. http://www.landfield.org/rfcs/rfc1036.html

RFC 1123, Requirements for Internet Hosts—Application and Support, R. Braden, Editor, October 1989. http://www.landfield.org/rfcs/rfc1123.html

RFC 1153, Digest Message Format, F. Wancho, April 1990. http://www.landfield.org/rfcs/rfc1153.html

12 Designing New Application Layer Protocols

In this chapter we'll look at software reuse issues for the design of application layer protocols and limitations that may be imposed by the different types of software licenses. We'll investigate some of the design options available to get a new application layer protocol up and running quickly. We'll also look at some of the issues of reusing existing software (or pieces of the software) due to the licenses under which they're covered.

INTRODUCTION

Since there are as many design methods as there are designers, this chapter will focus on methods that take advantage of existing protocol and design resources. This is by no means a chapter on design, but on reuse as a way to simplify the development process.

Design Methods

Although there are many ways to design application layer protocols, this section will look at a number of broad categories for ways to simplify their construction. One point to consider when using an existing protocol (or using code elements of a protocol implementation) is the license under which the protocol is released. A brief discussion of the different types of licenses that open source protocols are released under is provided in the next section.

In the following sections, we'll discuss four broad methods for protocol development.

- Using an existing protocol
- Reusing pieces from an existing protocol
- Tailoring an existing protocol
- Designing a brand new protocol

Using an Existing Protocol

The first question to ask when designing a new application layer protocol is if the protocol requirement can be satisfied by an existing protocol. In many cases, the answer is yes. For example, the Simple Object Access Protocol (SOAP) uses HTTP as its underlying protocol. HTTP provides a number of useful transport features for communicating SOAP messages. Therefore, SOAP need not worry about the transport of messages over a network since this function is provided by HTTP.

As we've discussed in prior chapters, protocols such as SMTP and NNTP provide the capability to transport data through a network using the existing mail and Usenet infrastructure. This allows the developer to concentrate on their application and not on lower-level transport features.

Consequently, using an existing protocol simply requires the system designer to frame the problem in terms of the desired protocol, if possible. Otherwise, another method must be used.

Tailoring an Existing Protocol

The next question to ask is whether an existing protocol can be modified to solve the particular requirements of your application. Note that all of the application layer protocols presented in the prior chapters were protocols tailored for embedded systems (rewritten from the specification, not from other code sources). While the implementations presented in this book were not fully compliant with the RFCs for the protocols, they provided enough functionality to successfully communicate with peer servers or clients.

Tailoring existing protocols offers a quick way to get a system off the ground without writing lower-level transport features. In many cases, the tailored protocol can reuse the protocol infrastructure that amounts to less work for the system designer. For example, using a POP3 client as an embedded protocol also takes advantage of the external POP3 storage structure. Adhering to standard protocols provides communication compatibility that often results in great reduction in development costs.

Just as reusing an existing protocol does, tailoring an existing protocol requires the designer to frame the problem in terms of the selected protocol. Then the protocol is dissected to remove or add the necessary elements to satisfy the requirements of the given application.

Reusing Pieces from an Existing Protocol

If a protocol cannot be reused or tailored for the given application, the next step is to identify the closest protocol and reuse elements of it that will satisfy the application requirements.

Throughout this book, elements of protocols have been reused where possible. For example, in Chapter 11, the message retrieval and parsing functions were reused (and slightly tailored) from Chapter 5 (Embedded SMTP Server). Many of the server-socket initialization elements were reused in various protocols.

Although reuse has not lived up to the claims that were made for it in software engineering circles, reuse has a place in the variety of ways that it can be used. The protocol implementations discussed in this book have reused functions in their entirety and design elements have been reused. Concepts have also been reused (such as the transmission of HTML tables through NNTP following the SMTP client protocol in Chapter 4).

One final important issue for reuse is that in many cases you'll not only save time and effort, but also increased system reliability. Reusing software elements that have been field tested mean that the overall reliability of the software will increase. This important factor is sometimes overlooked.

One might inquire as to how to determine if elements can be reused from a particular protocol or arbitrary piece of software for that matter. If an existing protocol exhibits behavior that is useful to your application requirements, then elements may be reused from that protocol. One can also determine if elements can be reused by having an *a priori* understanding of existing protocol implementations. This can be achieved only by reading the source code of existing protocols. Reading the source for existing protocols can serve multiple purposes. For example, we can understand different design methodologies or code implementations. We can also learn different coding methods (both good and bad). Understanding the difference can be very beneficial. Reading open source can be very beneficial and is the next best thing to the experience gained from doing it yourself.

Designing a Protocol from Scratch

Last, but not least, is the last resort for protocol development: starting from scratch. It's not surprising how often this does occur, since we always assume that the requirements for our development are somehow special. We may also assume that our project is without precedent. Despite all this, there's rarely an occasion when reusing an existing protocol or tailoring one for our application will not satisfy at least some of our requirements.

The point to keep in mind is this. When we develop software, we must consider why we're doing it. If we're developing a piece of software because we want to learn more about a protocol or algorithm, then we can address the problem any way we want. However, if we're developing software with a schedule or cost constraints, we should try to simplify our job in any way we can. Reusing or tailoring software is certainly a good step towards this and supports compatibility with other systems.

LICENSES

While many open source licenses exist, the two main licenses are the GPL and BSD. While both have the goal of using a community of developers to improve the software in both functionality and stability, they go about it in very different ways.

GNU Public License

The GNU Public License (GPL), is one of the most common licenses in the open source domain. The license says that if you use GPL source in your application, the source to your application is then GPL source. This doesn't work very well if you have an application that represents intellectual property (IP) to you or your company. If your application uses GPL and you release it in any way, then your IP becomes part of the GPL, which may not always desirable. For this reason, releasing or using GPL software must be carefully considered.

Despite these limitations, the GPL is one of the most widely used open source licenses. The GNU/Linux operating system is GPL source and GPL is likely one of the primary reasons that so much open source software exists for the Linux platform.

One important factor of the GPL is the use of the source for competitive reasons. If you release source under GPL, only those who also release their source under the GPL can use it. Therefore, your code cannot find its way into a closed-source system that competes against you. Since cooperation is not at the heart of competition, very few organizations release source under the GPL.

BSD and BSD-Like Licenses

The Berkeley Software Distribution, or BSD, is probably the next most common open source license. BSD takes a kinder road to source sharing. The BSD license encourages you to use the source (in commercial or non-commercial licenses) and to provide back useful changes. If you don't, that's okay. Nevertheless, for the good of the source in question, providing source updates back means that the source will evolve for the better. BSD requires that source headers (including license information) remain with the source and binary image, but other than that, it's free.

There's an interesting difference here with the word "free" when discussing these two open source licenses. Free with BSD means free of cost while in GPL it refers to freedom to view and change source, as long as you provide any changes back to the community. Therefore, while GPL forces developers to return source, BSD simply encourages it.

One might think that this would make GPL software of a higher caliber than BSD software. While Linux is the most common open source operating system in use today, BSD is viewed as the most stable and reliable. BSD is also the platform that yields the most interesting TCP/IP protocol suite advancements. Some view the use of GPL as losing freedom and therefore prefer BSD as an alternative in this regard.

License for Software in this Book

The license that covers the software in this book, with the exception of the SMTP server, is a BSD-style license. This means that you can use the software for any purpose, in commercial and non-commercial settings, without prior approval of the author. All that is required is that the headers remain on the source and be available for display in binary form. It's also nice if you feed any changes you make back to the author, but this isn't necessary. Otherwise, the sources can be used and/or modified in any way without prior permission from the author. The SMTP Server is GPL because of the use of a GPL Base64 decoder. The GPL requires that any software that is integrated (linked) with the SMTP server must be opened up under the GPL. Many developers avoid the GPL for this reason; it forces them to publicize their intellectual property.

LEARNING MORE

In a prior section, the method of reading source code was presented as a way to learn protocol development as well as understand different coding methodologies. We can also learn much about protocols and the rationale for their design by reading the RFCs. RFCs are a great resource for not only understanding protocol design but also the evolution of protocols. For example, reading the NNTP RFC by itself can be somewhat confusing, but by reading the previously published SMTP related protocol RFCs, NNTP becomes very clear and readable. Reading RFCs also permits a better understanding of the similarities and differences of competing or complementary protocols. Reading RFCs is also a great way to understand the new directions that protocols will take in the future. In short, reading RFCs is yet another way to gain a clear understanding of protocols and their design and can be beneficial when designing new application layer protocols.

SUMMARY

In this chapter, a number of broad design methods were discussed for the development of new application layer protocols. While starting from scratch is a common approach to new designs, it should be considered a last resort. Existing application layer protocols in source form can be completely reused to satisfy a particular purpose, or tailored for the special requirements of an application. Small-scale code/design reuse can also be utilized to speed the development process. Finally, open source licenses were then discussed to identify code that can be reused and the consequences of doing so.

RESOURCES

The Open Source Initiative Approved Licenses List, http://www.opensource.org/licenses/

13 Protocol Survey

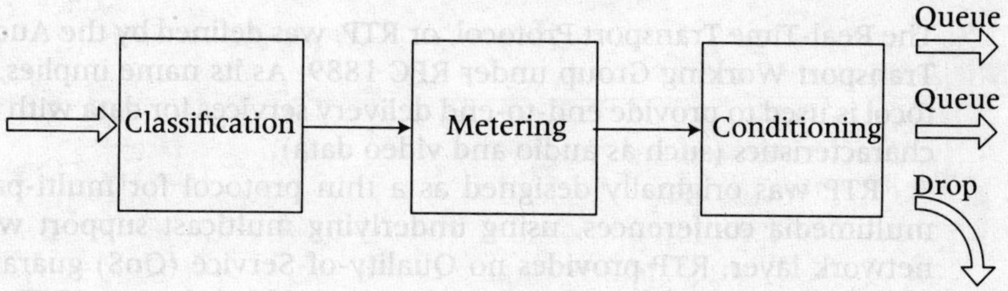

In this chapter, we'll look at new and uncommon network, transport, and application layer protocols not previously discussed in this text. While this text is about the development of application layer protocols, these protocols require the use of underlying transport and network layer protocols. For this reason, lower layer protocols will be discussed as they permit the construction of more complex and useful application layer protocols.

First, we'll review some of the new transport layer and network layer protocols that provide new capabilities to the application layer protocol developer. Next, we'll look at the state of the art for application layer protocols. Finally, we'll look into the future at distributed applications using Web services and migratory software.

INTRODUCTION

The original designers of the Internet protocols never could have imagined the role they were playing in changing the ways we work, perform research, and relax. The TCP/IP suite of protocols was the groundwork for many innovations in the last quarter century. The innovation continues, which is the topic of this chapter.

TRANSPORT AND NETWORK LAYER PROTOCOLS

In this section, we'll look at some of the new and not so common protocols in the transport and network layers.

Real-Time Transport Protocol

The Real-Time Transport Protocol, or RTP, was defined by the Audio-Video Transport Working Group under RFC 1889. As its name implies, the protocol is used to provide end-to-end delivery services for data with real-time characteristics (such as audio and video data).

RTP was originally designed as a thin protocol for multi-participant multimedia conferences, using underlying multicast support within the network layer. RTP provides no Quality-of-Service (QoS) guarantee, nor does it provide in-order delivery of packets. This is because RTP uses UDP as its transport. RTP does provide sequence numbers to permit the reconstruction of the data stream.

To support multiple participants and relay control information among them, RTP utilizes another control protocol called the RTP Control Protocol (RTCP). RTCP provides QoS feedback from receivers within group communication scenarios.

While RTP provides no QoS services internally, it utilizes protocols such as the Reservation Protocol (RSVP) to provide these facilities.

Stream Control Transport Protocol

The Stream Control Transport Protocol (SCTP) is a reliable transport protocol that operates over IP. It was designed for message-oriented applications and operates as a stream of messages instead of a stream of bytes (such as in TCP).

While SCTP can be configured to operate as UDP or TCP, it offers some very interesting features to the application layer. The more important features are discussed next.

SCTP supports multiple delivery modes. SCTP can support strict order-of-transmission behavior as exhibited by TCP (including retransmission) or it can support unordered delivery as exhibited by UDP.

SCTP can also preserve message boundaries in the messages transmitted. Using *chunks* (SCTP data structures), messages can be transferred and then retrieved in the order and size in which they were originally sent. This can be very beneficial to applications that desire reliable communication with message framing. Applications then need not read data from the socket and then accumulate and test to check that an entire message has been received (as is done today in many TCP applications).

One of the most interesting features of SCTP is multihoming. Multihoming offers resilience to failed network interfaces (NICs) and efficient recovery during network failures. SCTP provides this by supporting end-to-end communication with a single destination (socket peer), and upon failure, rerouting messages to an alternate IP address (on the same host) without breaking the connection. Therefore, when a route through a network breaks, automatic rerouting ensures that the communication continues unabated.

Connections with multiple destinations are known as *associations*. While SCTP is now an official standard (since October 2000), its adoption has been unsurprisingly slow. To enable developers to quickly port applications on top of SCTP, the BSD sockets interface is used. The socket API function is used to differentiate between SCTP and the different delivery modes, as shown in Listing 13.1.

LISTING 13.1 Using the socket API function for SCTP.

```
udpStyleSocket = socket( AF_INET, SOCK_SEQPACKET, IPPROTO_SCTP );
tcpStyleSocket = socket( AF_INET, SOCK_STREAM, IPPROTO_SCTP );
```

In order to create associations (a socket with multiple destinations), a new API function is introduced called `sctp_bindx` to bind to multiple peers.

One final feature provided by SCTP is a heartbeat keep-alive mechanism. SCTP sends heartbeat control packets to idle destinations (since more than one destination can be associated with the SCTP socket). The socket application is then notified when a specified number of heartbeats go unacknowledged.

IP Next Generation

In this section, we'll look at two options for the Network layer.

Simple Internet Protocol Plus

The Simple Internet Protocol Plus (SIPP), is a network layer protocol that is interoperable with IPv4. It solves the immediate addressing problem that exists with IPv4 (running out of addresses) using hierarchical addresses (with 64-bit addresses instead of IPv4's 32-bit scheme). SIPP also provides local-use addresses that provide "plug-and-play" capabilities.

SIPP was designed with headers that are easier to process and are smaller than those used in IPv4. This makes SIPP more efficient and maximizes the available bandwidth. This is especially important in low-bandwidth links such as those provided in wireless devices, but is equally important in high-bandwidth links.

SIPP also includes Quality of Service (QoS) features such as traffic flows with special handling constraints through packet labeling. Other useful features include authentication and privacy with support for data integrity and confidentiality.

IPv6

IPv6 has long been touted as the next generation IP. It solves many of the problems identified with IPv4 such as a larger address space and mobility.

IPv6 also includes IPsec that provides authentication, encryption, and compression of traffic. IPv6 also includes a replacement for ARP called the Neighbor Discovery Protocol (NDP). NDP provides the basic ARP functions (lookup service for IP to MAC addresses) but also a similar service for routers. Router lookups provide for autoconfiguration so that a host automatically knows the gateways available on the local subnet and the routes which they serve.

IPv6 also provides for duplicate address detection. In IPv4 networks, this is a common problem and can be very difficult to resolve in larger intranetworks.

While the problem of running out of IP addresses has been resolved through the of network address translation (sharing one public IP address among multiple private IP addresses), this solution may be short lived. Considering the spread of Internet-enabled devices in vehicles, consumer devices, and ubiquitous wireless devices, many of which provide access through the Internet, the need for public IP addresses may be growing. When the available public address space again runs thin, IPv6 or its successor will be ready.

QUALITY OF SERVICE

The original Internet was designed simply to route packets from a source to a destination without the help of either. At each hop, the proper routing is performed in order to get the packet to its destination. The behavior of the Internet is described as "best effort" since no guarantees are provided that a packet will arrive within a certain amount of time. There is also no guarantee that the packet will not be dropped along the way by one of the many routers that it will encounter.

Without any guarantees, the Internet is perfect for elastic protocols that have no performance requirements. For protocols that have real-time constraints (such as Internet Telephony), some guarantee is needed. With our current architecture, the complexity of the network is confined to the ends. In the middle of the network, routers are relatively simple devices that forward packets based upon their IP destination address. Advancing to an Internet architecture that provides QoS capabilities, the middle of the network becomes much more complicated. This is because hosts at the edge of networks must establish "circuits" through the Internet, reserving bandwidth at each of the hops along the way. The Internet is then more cognizant of the connections passing through it and therein lies the complexity.

IPv4 actually does support QoS in some form (consider the `Type-of-Service` field in the IP header), but implementing it across the public network is difficult due to political and organizational constraints. Therefore, while technically feasible, other factors are at play for QoS on the Internet.

QoS provides the Internet with an architecture to apply priorities to packets flowing through it. Therefore, users (through their applications) can identify whether their data should take the lowest-cost route or the highest-bandwidth route (due to real-time constraints). Other constraints are covered in the following section.

QoS Characteristics

Thus far, we've discussed QoS as providing guarantees, but what does this imply? The purpose of QoS is to effectively manage the available bandwidth using a number of related constraints. These constraints are as follows:

- Minimizing inter-packet delay (throughput)
- Minimizing packet inter-arrival variations (jitter)
- Minimizing dropped packets (loss)
- Minimizing per-packet charges (cost)
- Minimizing packet tampering or eavesdropping (security)

Simply stated, QoS means providing consistent and predictable data delivery in an end-to-end fashion while giving preferential treatment to certain flows. Research continues to advance QoS by investigating non-performance-related constraints such as security.

QoS Protocols and Architectures

Let's now look at some of the available QoS protocols and architectures. This is an incomplete list of the available technologies, but it provides a broad perspective on the different ways that QoS can be achieved.

Reservation Protocol (RSVP)

The Reservation Protocol (RSVP), is a signaling protocol that works with TCP or UDP Transport layer protocols to establish circuits through a network. The RSVP protocol works with RSVP-enabled routers to install paths for the defined session.

RSVP uses a number of messages to establish its circuits through the network. The sender uses the PATH message that contains the traffic specification (or the upper and lower bounds of bandwidth, delay, and jitter). The basic flow is shown in Figure 13.1. The PATH message flows through the network to install the PATH state at each of the intermediary routers. In some cases, a router may not support RSVP and will therefore transparently pass it through to the next hop. When the PATH message reaches the receiver, the downstream route is complete and the upstream route must be reserved.

Reserving the upstream route (from the receiver back to the sender) is performed using the RESV RSVP message. The RESV message contains the

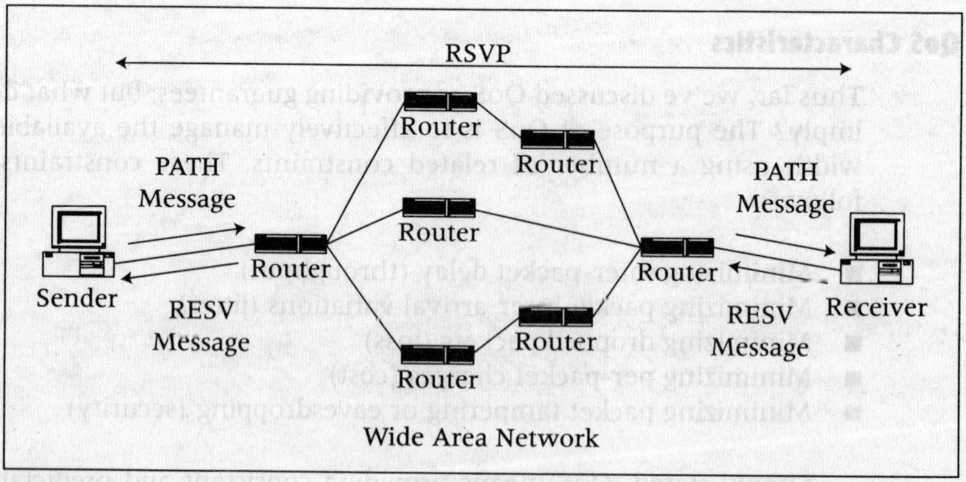

FIGURE 13.1 End-to-end QoS reservation made by RSVP.

reservation specification and follows the same path back to the sender. This message closes the loop and identifies a reserved session through the network. Upon receiving the RESV message, what looks like a virtual circuit is provided with QoS constraints as requested in the PATH message and confirmed in the RESV message.

Differentiated Services (`DiffServ`)

Differentiated Services (DiffServ), provides a simpler method for attaining QoS. While DiffServ does not provide the QoS control possible with RSVP, it does provides a more coarse-grained service with much less complexity and overhead. DiffServ was introduced by RFC 2475 with information on classifying packets in RFC 2474.

DiffServ constrains the QoS decisions of network flows at the edge of the network instead of throughout the interior. Since the edges can be managed, as they're most likely under our control, this method is significantly more realistic than RSVP and eminently more deployable.

The DiffServ model must manage traffic going out on the network as well as managing incoming traffic. To do this, we must first classify packets as belonging to a particular flow. A flow has an associated set of QoS constraints that are negotiated by the application based upon its needs.

Packet classification is performed by reviewing the Differentiated Services Code Point element of the IP header, otherwise known as `DSCP`. The `DSCP` replaces the IP `Type-of-Service` field and contains what is called the PHB or "Per Hop Behavior." Two standard PHBs exist which are *Expedited Forwarding* (EF) and *Assured Forwarding* (AF). EF is the highest level of QoS in DiffServ. Bandwidth allocated to an EF PHB will be guaranteed, while AF PHBs are given high priority but are not guaranteed. The lowest levels of service are termed *Best-Effort*.

So having classified a packet as part of a flow and via the DSCP knowing the packet's QoS constraints, what do we do next (see Figure 13.2)? The next step is called metering. This is the process by which statistics of a particular flow are gathered. In this step, we calculate how much bandwidth the particular flow is taking from our overall available bandwidth. The final step is conditioning (or traffic shaping). In this step we queue the packet to either be emitted as soon as is possible, place it in a queue that has a reduced priority (which adds delay to the outgoing packet), or drop the packet entirely.

The very simple diagram presented in Figure 13.2 illustrates the basic flow for Differentiated Services. In cases where no DSCP is applied to the packet (it's not part of a flow), then a *marker* process is performed which

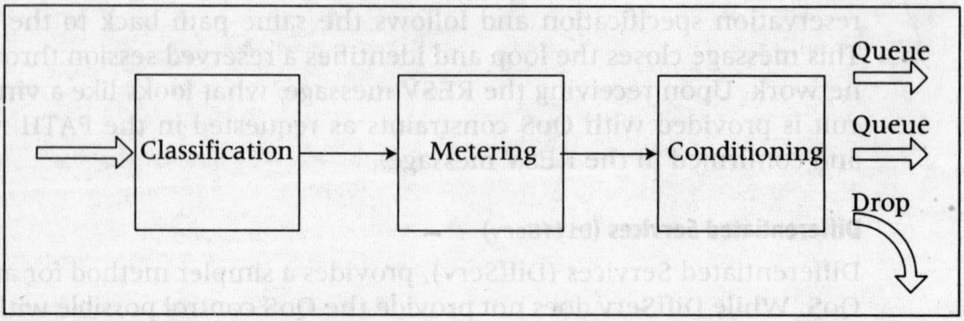

FIGURE 13.2 DiffServ architecture.

assigns a default DSCP to the packet so that it will be provided best-effort conditioning.

Multi-Protocol Label Switching (MPLS)

Multi-Protocol Label Switching is a very simple router-based protocol. MPLS is protocol independent (thus the moniker "Multi-Protocol") as it exists as a small header prefixed to WAN-bound packets. MPLS is not specifically a QoS mechanism, but instead increases performance by simplifying the routing process (by simplifying the forwarding decisions within interior routers).

MPLS begins at the first hop router of the network. Routers in MPLS are called Label Switching Routers (LSRs). The LSR looks at the header information and makes the determination of an appropriate label as specified by a local policy. The packet is then forwarded to the next LSR in the network.

The route taken by an MPLS-labeled packet is called the Label Switched Path (LSP). The LSP provides greater control over the route than simply what would be provided by the destination address. This gives network managers greater control over packet routing.

Queuing and Scheduling Algorithms

Queuing and scheduling algorithms are very important constructs within QoS architectures. These can be found not only within the interior network but also at the edges within the sending and receiving hosts.

Priority FIFO

Priority FIFO, as the name implies, consists of a number of First-In-First-Out queues with unique priorities. The queue with the highest priority gets first use of the link while lower-priority queues get use of the link only when no packets exist in higher-priority queues.

Stochastic Fairness Queuing (SFQ)

Stochastic Fairness Queuing (SFQ) uses a number of queues less than the number of managed flows. Packets are queued not based upon any label or priority, but instead by a hashing function of the packet. This means that a particular queue may contain one or more flows that are treated equally. Each of the queues is serviced in a round-robin fashion, but due to the probability of multiple flows per queue, fairness guarantees are probabilistic.

One of the greatest strengths of SFQ is that is requires little CPU time or memory and is therefore very efficient with available resources.

Weighted Fair Queuing (WFQ)

Weighted Fair Queuing (WFQ) is a packet scheduling mechanism that provides guaranteed bandwidth services. Sessions (users of a single link) have a unique FIFO for their packets, and each are serviced at a proportional rate. The queues are weighted along with this rate to specify how many bits can be transmitted from that queue during each round. This prevents flows containing large numbers of packets from crowding out those with fewer packets.

Token Bucket Filter (TBF)

The Token Bucket Filter (TBF) is a shaping construct that regulates the flow of packets. A bucket is defined that is fed by the packet classifier. The bucket is then given a token that provides the capability to send a number of bits onto the network. The number of tokens provided to the bucket is predefined (the configured rate). When enough tokens are collected for a packet, the packet can be sent. If the bucket becomes full, incoming packets are simply dropped.

Tokens cannot be accumulated by the bucket; if no packets are present in the bucket then the tokens are immediately relinquished to the TBF.

The TBF is a very simple construct for regulating flow. It is commonly used as an intermediate part of a QoS architecture, between packet classification and another queuing method.

Random Early Detect (RED)

Random Early Detect (RED) is a very interesting congestion avoidance algorithm using active queue management. RED consists of two elements, an average queue size estimator and the packet drop process. The size of the packet queue is actively computed using a simple exponentially weighted moving average. This is important since the size of the queue determines how many packets can be scheduled for the link. The next element is when to drop packets. Most queue management functions drop packets only when the queue is full. RED drops packets probabilistically proportional to the increasing size of the queue.

One might ask why a queue management algorithm would drop packets when space exists on the queue to buffer them. The answer is that RED simulates the congestion of the external network (based upon its queue size estimation and number of packets buffered). Therefore, the congestion can be limited to the edge of the network (or router) leaving the physical network uncongested.

Data Link Layer Technologies

QoS strategies also exist at the lowest layer of the stack. A number of data link layer QoS technologies exist to effectively provide QoS at the MAC sublayer.

Two popular data link layer QoS technologies are 802.1P and 802.1Q. 802.1P provides for eight priority levels of *traffic class expediting*. Traffic at higher priorities is given first access to the link while lower-priority traffic is effectively dropped.

The 802.1Q standard specifies the tagging of Ethernet packets with Virtual-LAN id (VLAN). This permits the operation of multiple logical Ethernets over a single physical Ethernet. Among other things, 802.1Q reduces broadcasts and improves security.

INTERNET SECURITY

In this section, we'll provide a quick introduction to two solutions to Internet security. The first is network-layer security (provided by IPSec) and the second is transport layer security (provided by Secure Sockets Layer). These methods are by no means the only available, but are the most common (see Figure 13.3).

IPSec Protocol

IPSec is a framework of open standards for network security consisting of a network layer protocol that provides interoperable cryptographically-based security for the Internet Protocol. IPSec provides access control, data

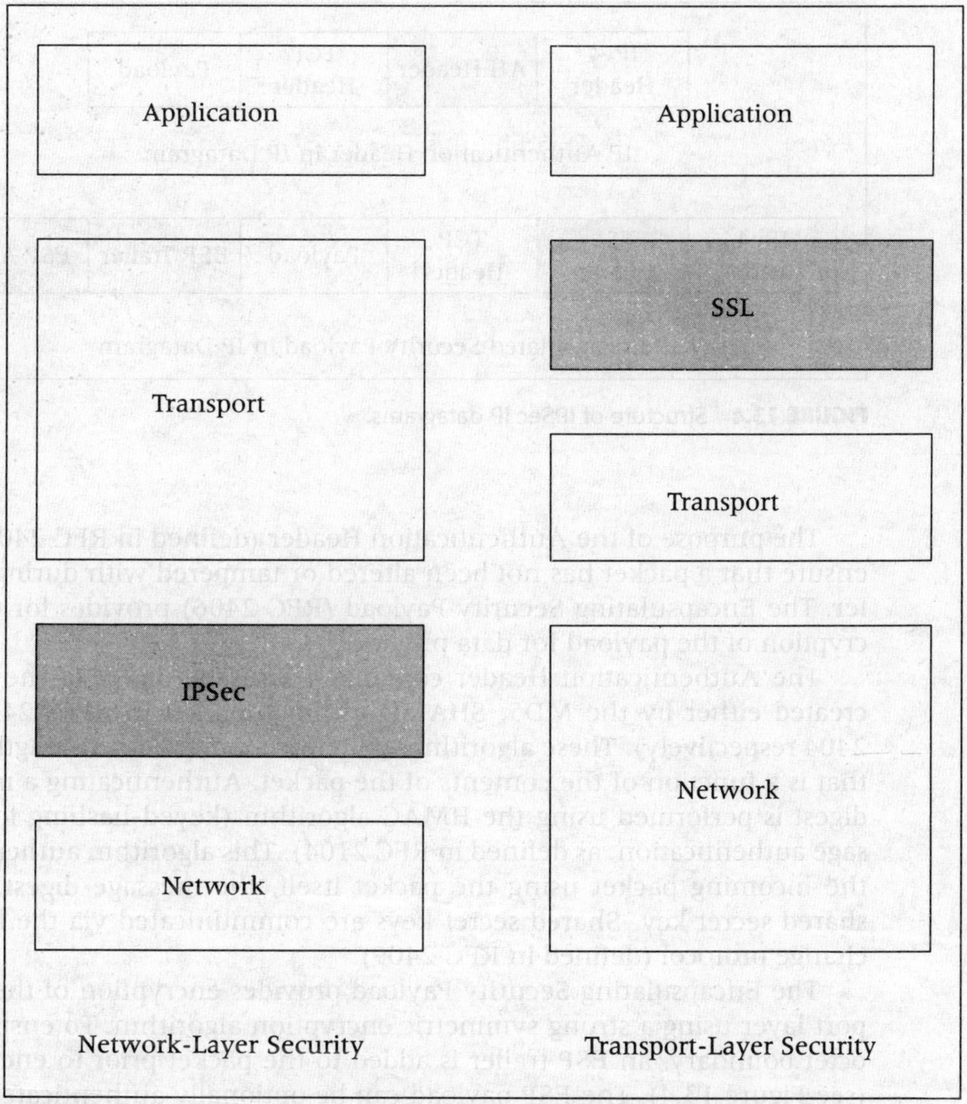

FIGURE 13.3 Relative layers of network and transport layer security.

origin authentication, and encryption of the IP payload thereby protecting upper layer protocols.

IPSec provides security using two specific mechanisms, the Authentication Header (AH) and the Encapsulating Security Payload (ESP). Both the AH and ESP are contained within the IP datagram, as shown in Figure 13.4.

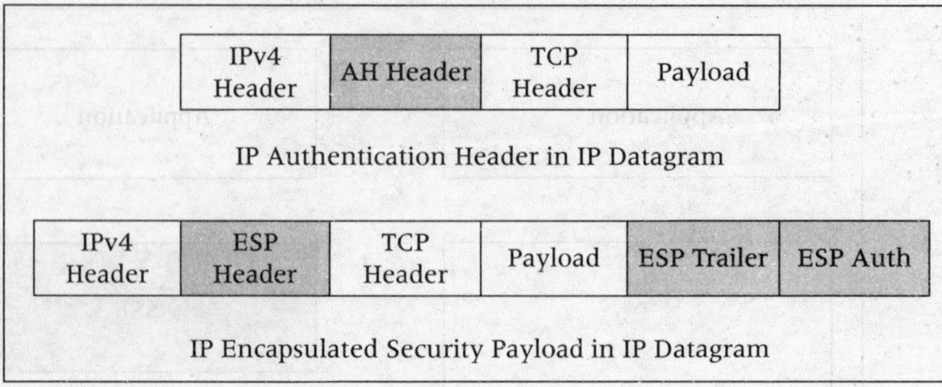

FIGURE 13.4 Structure of IPSec IP datagrams.

The purpose of the Authentication Header (defined in RFC 2402) is to ensure that a packet has not been altered or tampered with during transfer. The Encapsulating Security Payload (RFC 2406) provides for the encryption of the payload for data privacy.

The Authentication Header contains a message digest of the packet created either by the MD5, SHA algorithm (defined in RFCs 2403 and 2404 respectively). These algorithms generate a unique fixed-length string that is a function of the contents of the packet. Authenticating a message digest is performed using the HMAC algorithm (keyed-hashing for message authentication, as defined in RFC 2104). This algorithm authenticates the incoming packet using the packet itself, the message digest, and a shared secret key. Shared secret keys are communicated via the key exchange protocol (defined in RFC 2409).

The Encapsulating Security Payload provides encryption of the transport layer using a strong symmetric encryption algorithm. To ensure a 4-octet boundary, an ESP trailer is added to the packet prior to encryption (see Figure 13.4). The ESP payload can be optionally authenticated using a message-digest (ESP Auth).

Both the AH and ESP can be combined to provide encryption and authentication. The IP payload is first encrypted using ESP and then the entire packet is used to compute the AH fingerprint.

The primary advantage of the IPSec protocol is that the user application need not be modified since the changes are made in the network layer. Application layer protocols continue to use the standard BSD Sockets API. The disadvantage of IPSec is that the TCP/IP stack must be modified in order to use IPSec (since it fits within the stack at layer 3+).

Secure Sockets Layer (SSL)

The Secure Sockets Layer (SSL) is a new sockets interface that exists between the transport protocol and the application layer protocol. SSL is a layer 4+ protocol that sits on top of the TCP layer.

SSL provides for compression of data, authentication, and encryption. SSL was initially developed by Netscape for e-commerce applications.

An SSL-based session begins with the SSL handshake protocol. When a client first connects to an SSL server, the client and server communicate basic information to establish the basis for the connection. This information includes the version of the SSL protocol to be used, a cryptographic algorithm, and a public key encryption technique for initial socket setup. The client and server may also optionally authenticate each other. This entire process takes place during the `ClientHello/ServerHello` dialog.

The server and client can then send each other certificates to identify themselves. Within the certificate is what's known as a public key. The public key can be distributed between applications in order to encrypt a message. The only way to decrypt the message is to use the private key. This process is called *asymmetric cryptography* (see Figure 13.5). Therefore, if the client encrypts a message using the public key, the client knows that only the server holding the private key can decrypt it. As well as providing encryption, this process also provides a form of authentication.

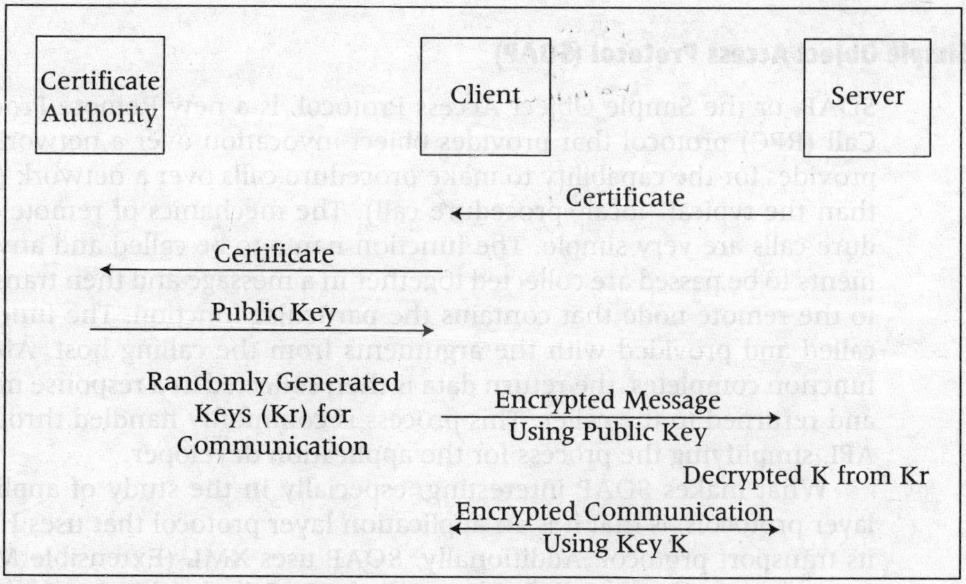

FIGURE 13.5 Secure Sockets Layer (SSL) handshake process.

Once the client receives the server's certificate, it contacts a Certificate Authority (CA) to validate the identity of the server (from Figure 13.5). The result is the public key of the server, which can be used to encrypt a set of random keys generated by the client. These random keys are sent to the server which are then decrypted at the server using the server's private key. Both the client and server now have the set of random keys and these are used for the duration of the connection to encrypt and decrypt the messages transferred between them. When the client receives a message encrypted with the random keys, the client knows that the server was able to decrypt the original message using the private key. Therefore, the client has also authenticated the server.

The advantage of SSL is that it is very simple and provides robust encryption and authentication. The disadvantage of SSL is that the application must be SSL-aware. A new set of socket calls must be used for secure sockets communication.

NEW APPLICATION LAYER PROTOCOLS

A number of interesting application layer protocols are now available to help build powerful Internet-based applications. In this section, we'll look at a few of these in preparation for a discussion of Web services that follows.

Simple Object Access Protocol (SOAP)

SOAP, or the Simple Object Access Protocol, is a new Remote Procedure Call (RPC) protocol that provides object invocation over a network. RPC provides for the capability to make procedure calls over a network (rather than the typical "local" procedure call). The mechanics of remote procedure calls are very simple. The function name to be called and any arguments to be passed are collected together in a message and then transferred to the remote node that contains the particular function. The function is called and provided with the arguments from the calling host. After the function completes, the return data is then collected in a response message and returned to the caller. This process is commonly handled through an API, simplifying the process for the application developer.

What makes SOAP interesting, especially in the study of application layer protocols, is that it is an application layer protocol that uses HTTP as its transport protocol. Additionally, SOAP uses XML (Extensible Markup Language) for its encoding. The goal of SOAP is the development of an open standard for a protocol that supports decentralized distributed system development.

To better understand SOAP and its capabilities, let's look at an example dialog between a client and server using SOAP (see Listings 13.2 and 13.3). In this example, a server provides battery temperatures given a battery name (client portion of dialog is shown with C:, where the server is shown with S:).

LISTING 13.2 SOAP message request.

```
C:  POST /Temperatures HTTP/1.1
C:  Host: 192.168.1.1
C:  Content-Type: text/xml; charset="utf-8"
C:  Content-Length: xxx
C:  SOAPAction : "URI"
C:
C:  <SOAP-ENV:Envelope
C:  xmlns:SOAP-
ENV="http://schemas.xmlsoap.org/soap/envelope/"
C:    SOAP-ENV:encodingStyle="http://schemas.xmlsoap.org/ \\
soap/encoding/">
C:    <SOAP-ENV:Body>
C:      <m:GetBatteryTemperature xmlns:m="URI">
C:        <string>NorthPanelA1</string>
C:      </m:GetBatteryTemperature>
C:    <SOAP-ENV:Body>
C:  </SOAP-ENV:Envelope>
```

LISTING 13.3 SOAP message response.

```
S:  HTTP/1.1 200 OK
S:  Content-Type: text/xml; charset="utf-8"
S:  Content-Length: yyy
S:
S:  <SOAP-ENV:Envelope
S:    xmlns:SOAP-
ENV="http://schemas.xmlsoap.org/soap/envelope/"
S:    SOAP-ENV:encodingStyle="http://schemas.xmlsoap.org/ \\
soap/encoding/">
S:    <SOAP-ENV:Body>
S:      <m:GetBatteryTemperature xmlns:m="URI">
S:        <int>62</int>
S:      </m:GetBatteryTemperature>
S:    <SOAP-ENV:Body>
S:  </SOAP-ENV:Envelope>
```

Before we discuss the SOAP request and response, let's first have a look at the SOAP messages to better understand their structure. First, SOAP messages are XML documents that consist of a SOAP envelope, an optional SOAP header and a SOAP body. The envelope defines two things, the envelope namespace and the encoding. The namespace validates that the XML message is in fact a SOAP message. The encoding defines the SOAP attributes such as `int` and `string`. The body, in the request/response shown in Listings 13.2 and 13.3, is used to marshall the RPC call and response.

Since SOAP uses HTTP to transport messages, the first thing we'll see in our request (from Listing 13.2) is an HTTP `POST` request. Recall that an HTTP `POST` request is the opposite of the `GET` request; `POST` pushes data to the server instead of getting it. The `POST` request is followed by a number of standard HTTP headers and concludes with a SOAP header. The `SOAPAction` header is defined as a number of things, but most commonly as the intent of the of the SOAP HTTP request. `SOAPAction` takes the form of a URI, although the SOAP specification makes no restrictions on the URI, not even that it be resolvable.

The SOAP envelope, which is used to encapsulate the entire SOAP message, follows. The SOAP body contains our marshalled request, in this case the request of a battery temperature, namely the "NorthPanelA1" battery.

The request and response function are performed over the network. If the call were to be performed locally, it would resemble Listing 13.4.

LISTING 13.4 Local function mirroring Listings 13.2 and 13.3.

```
temp = getBatteryTemperature( "NorthPanelA1" );

...


int GetBatteryTemperature( char *string )
{
  /* processing */

  /* Hard-coded response... */
  return 62;
}
```

Of course, developers need not concern themselves with the actual SOAP encoding (as shown in Listings 13.2 and 13.3). APIs for many languages exist (including C, Java, Perl, Python, and others). A developer need only understand the API bindings for dealing with SOAP invocations or providing functions through SOAP bindings.

XML-RPC (XML Remote Procedure Call)

SOAP is one of the available Internet RPC mechanisms that exist. A pure XML RPC protocol exists called XML-RPC. XML-RPC, which preceded the development of SOAP, uses the HTTP protocol to transport the XML messages. XML-RPC is much simpler than SOAP and provides very similar features. Consider the XML-RPC examples shown in Listings 13.5 and 13.6. These examples mirror SOAP examples from Listings 13.1 and 13.2.

LISTING 13.5 XML-RPC message request.

```
C:  POST /Temperatures HTTP/1.1
C:  Host: 192.168.1.1
C:  Content-Type: text/xml
C:  Content-Length: nnn
C:
C:  <?xml version="1.0"?>
C:  <methodCall>
C:    <methodName>GetBatteryTemperature</methodName>
C:    <params>
C:      <param>
C:        <value><string>NorthPanelA1</string></value>
C:      </param>
C:    </params>
C:  </methodcall>
```

LISTING 13.6 XML-RPC message response.

```
S:  HTTP/1.1 200 OK
S:  Connection: close
S:  Content-Type: text/xml
S:  Content-Length: yyy
S:
S:  <?xml version="1.0?>
S:  <methodResponse>
S:    <params>
S:      <param>
S:        <value><int>62</int></value>
S:      </param>
S:    </params>
S:  </methodResponse>
```

The basic formats of the SOAP and XML-RPC messages are obviously similar. Both are based upon XML, but only XML-RPC is pure XML. The request (see Listing 13.5) uses the `<methodCall>` to denote a remote procedure call and the `<methodname>` tag to define the remote function that is to be called. The parameter passed to the method is a string embedded with the `<params>` tag. The response is identified by the `<methodResponse>` tag (see Listing 13.6). The `<params>` tag is used to set one or more parameters; in this case we have one that is embedded within the `<param>` tag. The `<value>` tag defines a scalar value of type `<int>`. In this example, we're passing back the integer value of `62`.

XML-RPC also supports composite types for structures and arrays. Additionally, the `<base64>` tag permits the transport of Base64-encoded binary data.

While XML-RPC is both simple and elegant, SOAP is currently the predominant RPC standard.

Session Initiation Protocol (SIP)

The Session Initiation Protocol (SIP), is a signaling protocol that exists at the application layer. SIP is used to establish, modify, and terminate communications sessions among multiple users. A session can be anything from an Internet Telephony call (video and/or audio) to real-time games with users distributed around the Internet.

Another interesting application of SIP is for control of networked appliances. The draft specification, "Framework Draft for Networked Appliances using the Session Initiation Protocol," offers some very interesting ideas about SIP in control scenarios.

HTTPR

HTTPR (Hypertext Transfer Protocol Reliable) is a new protocol that provides reliable message transport between applications on the Internet. HTTPR provides this through HTTP by embedding the HTTPR protocol within the body of HTTP messages. One of the interesting features of HTTPR is that it provides exact delivery of a message exactly once, or reports the message as undeliverable.

At the extremes of the HTTPR protocol are messaging agents. These agents manage the messages that are received from the Internet, as well as provide transport for outgoing messages. Since HTTPR provides a transaction-like service (exactly-once delivery or error response), messaging agents must provide some storage of the incoming messages. In this way, if a communication error occurs, a client may inquire as to the status of a sent message and understand its status. All messages within HTTPR include a transaction identifier so those messages can be identified.

Another interesting aspect of HTTPR is that since it's based upon HTTP, it can be used through firewalls that would otherwise restrict their access.

HTTPR is an interesting advance to HTTP, especially considering the future of Web services, which we'll discuss in the next section.

HTTPS

HTTPS is HTTP over SSL (or Secure Sockets Layer). HTTPS allows client and server-side authentication via certificates (through a certification authority). The HTTPS protocol uses port 443 instead of the default port 80. When a client connects to a server through HTTPS, the peers negotiate the SSL protocol to use and then each side can present a certificate of authentication. The client and server then use a common key to cryptographically communicate with each other, making the connection secure.

WEB SERVICES

Let's now look at a certain class of new application layer protocols that show promise for component-based, dynamically-configured services on the Web.

Web services are not what most consider them to be. Instead of search engines and news sites that present personalized Web pages (as a service), Web services are of a new type of application that is more about application-to-application connectivity than typical user-interface connectivity.

What makes Web services different from our current expectations is that they do not extend an interface directly to the user. Web services in this regard are components that can be used by a variety of applications over the Web.

As an example, let's consider an embedded system within a vehicle that provides directions. Within our embedded system is a GPS (Global Positioning System) device that provides our coordinates. Given these coordinates, we can identify where we are in the world and more importantly, directions to the closest Starbucks. In this application, our embedded system would connect to the network and search for a service that provides Starbucks directions. Once found, we'd take our current position and heading and provide it to the service. The Web Service would then provide us with the information necessary to navigate us to the destination.

This may seem like a simplistic operation, but consider now that the Web Service that provides our directions is a service for which we're charged. Additionally, instead of a single Web Service to provide this information, there are several of them available on the Internet. How we choose may be based upon having a subscription to the service, the cost of the service, capabilities provided, and protocols and/or API supported, etc.

What Web services ultimately offer is the ability to construct complex distributed applications using predefined, modular, self-describing Web components. These components can be advertised and then invoked remotely from a variety of other remote applications.

The Web Services Stack

Web services builds upon other protocols to reduce complexity and workload of upper layer protocols. By using lower layer protocols for encoding, security, authentication, and transport, the upper layer protocols become more refined and more specific to the ultimate application.

As can be seen from Figure 13.6, two new elements are defined as part of the Web services stack. These new elements provide very specific capabilities, as discussed next.

Web Services Description Language (WSDL)

Web Services Description Language (WSDL) is an XML format for defining network services as a set of endpoints that operate on messages that contain either document-oriented or procedure-oriented information. The goal of WSDL is to provide service definitions that permit the automation of communication between applications.

A service is defined as a collection of networked endpoints (ports from the network perspective). Each endpoint provides a collection of operations that can be performed using SOAP messages.

WSDL is used to describe abstractly what a Web service provides, where it resides, and the variety of ways that it can be invoked. WSDL provides a template to describe services that can be dynamically bound by clients at run-time.

Let's now look at a concrete example of WSDL. Recall our SOAP request and response from Listings 13.2 and 13.3. The following WSDL specification, shown in Listing 13.7, defines the service for that dialog.

LISTING 13.7 Sample WSDL service definition for the temperature service.

```
<?xml version="1.0"?>
<definitions name="Temperatures"
    targetNamespace="http://example.mtjones.com/temperatures.wsdl"
    xmlns:tns="http://example.mtjones.com/temperatures.wsdl"
```

```
      xmlns:xsdl="http://example.mtjones.com/temperatures.xsd"
      xmlns:soap="http://schemas.xmlsoap.org/wsdl/soap/"
      xmlns="http://schemas.xmlsoap.org/wsdl/">

  <types>
    <schema targetNamespace="http://example.mtjones.com/
     temperatures.xsd"
       xmlns="http://www.w3.org/2000/10/XMLSchema">
     <element name="TemperatureRequest">
       <complexType>
         <all>
           <element name="batteryName" type="string"/>
         </all>
       </complexType>
     </element>
     <element name="CelciusTemperature">
       <complexType>
         <all>
           <element name="temperatureValue" type="int"/>
         </all>
       </complexType>
     </element>
    </schema>
  </types>

  <message name="GetBatteryTemperatureInput">
    <part name="body" element="xsdl:TemperatureRequest"/>
  </message>
  <message name="GetBatteryTemperatureOutput">
    <part name="body" element="xsdl:CelciusTemperature"/>
  </message>

  <portType name="TemperaturePortType">
    <operation name="GetBatteryTemperature">
      <input message="tns:GetBatteryTemperatureInput"/>
      <output message="tns:GetBatteryTemperatureOutput"/>
    </operation>
  </portType>

  <binding name="TemperatureBinding"
        type="tns:TemperaturePortType">
  <soap:binding style="document"
   transport="http://schemas.xmlsoap.org/soap/http"/>
    <operation name="GetBatteryTemperature">
```

```
    <soap:operation
      soapAction="http://example.mtjones.com/GetLastTradePrice"/>
        <input>
          <soap:body use="literal"
            namespace="http://example.mtjones.com/temperatures.xsd"
            encodingStyle=
              "http://schemas.xmlsoap.org/soap/encoding/"/>
        </input>
        <output>
          <soap:body use="literal"
            namespace="http://example.mtjones.com/temperatures.xsd"
            encodingStyle=
              "http://schemas.xmlsoap.org/soap/encoding/"/>
        </output>
    </operation>
  </binding>

  <service name="TemperatureService">
    <documentation>Embedded Device Temperature Service
    </documentation>
    <port name="TemperaturePort" binding="tns:TemperatureBinding">
      <soap:address
       location="http://example.mtjones.com/Temperatures"/>
    </port>
  </service>

  </definitions>
```

From our sample service definition, a flow should become apparent. After the name of the service is specified through the `definitions` tag, we specify the types that are used in the service (`batteryName` string as the passed parameter, and `temperatureValue` as the integer return value). The message is then defined for input and output (binding our prior input and output types). We then set the port for the service, and associate our input and output messages to the port. Then we associate the message format and protocol details for the operations and messages set by the port type. Finally, we complete the binding through the `service` tag.

Although this has been a very quick introduction to WSDL, it should be obvious that WSDL provides a unique mechanism to abstractly define Web services in a very specific way. What has not been covered here is the actual binding to our source code that performs the particular service. These services could be written in any language (C, Java, Perl, etc.) without any knowledge of the implementation to the service user. Through

XML, the client of the service is also unknown from an implementation perspective to the server. This allows a Perl client to connect to Java services, or any other language combination, given proper API bindings for the particular language. Developers can then implement their services (and clients) in any language they choose allowing XML and WSDL to take care of the binding.

Universal Description, Discovery and Integration (UDDI)

In the section on WSDL, we illustrated how to define the service to gather temperatures from a remote device. This application was intended to be a private application, but what if this application were public and we wanted to offer it to users on the Internet? The issue then becomes, how do we let developers know that our service exists and how to interface to it? The answer is Universal Description, Discovery and Integration (UDDI).

UDDI provides the capability to register services and their interfaces to a distributed and globally available registry and to allow searches of this registry to connect peer applications with their needed services. This can be important for mobile embedded systems that either extend a service or require the use of services.

UDDI is provided as an API that is split between two functions, `inquiry` and `publication`. The inquiry API permits an application to search and locate candidate business, Web services, and specifications. The publication API allows an application to register services, specifications, and other information in a global registry.

UDDI provides these capabilities through SOAP/XML encoding. Listing 13.8 illustrates the inquiry API function, `find_business`.

LISTING 13.8 UDDI example for `find_business`.

```
<?xml version="1.0" encoding="utf-8"?>
<s:Envelope
  xmlns:s"http://schemas.xmlsoap.org/soap/envelope/">
  <s:Body>
    <find_business generic="1.0" xmlns="urn:uddi-org:api">
      <name>Cogito LLC</name>
    </find_business>
  </s:Body>
</s:Envelope>
```

The result of Listing 13.8 might produce the SOAP/XML response shown in Listing 13.9.

LISTING 13.9 UDDI response for `find_business`.

```
<?xml version="1.0" encoding="utf-8"?>
<businessList generic="1.0" truncated="false"
  operator="Cogito LLC"
  xmlns="urn:uddi-org:api">
  <businessInfos>
    <businessInfo
    businessKey="0076A469-AB28-3138-BC09-AA311234l234">
      <name>Cogito LLC</name>
      <description xml:lang="en">Software through Innovation
      </description>
    </businessInfo>
    <serviceInfos>
      <serviceInfo>
        ...
      </serviceInfo>
    </serviceInfos>
  </businessInfos>
</businessList>
```

UDDI provides a number of other capabilities with its API. For example, as well as finding a business and then finding Web services available within that business, WSDL information can be gathered to bind an application to the advertised service. A rich API for publishing services is also available including the capability to publish services and the XML maps that define them.

Available Web Services Architectures

Building Web services can be performed using a number of different Web services architectures. The goal of these is to permit portability among the architectures so that Web services can be used and provided by anyone.

DotGNU

The DotGNU platform is a project being developed by FreeDevelopers.Net, Inc. This project is open sourced under the GNU Public License (GPL). Among other things, DotGNU consists of two major components. The first is the Secure Execution Environment (SEE). This component provides the capability to download the bytecode for a particular Web service in a secure fashion. The second component is called the Distributed Execution Environment (DEE). This component is described as an "operating system" for a distributed computer that consists of several instances of the DotGNU

SEE running on multiple computers. This component provides data replication to the SEE instances to mimic operation on a single platform.

DotGNU also includes free software tools to build and execute .NET applications. This includes a C# compiler and runtime engine (which currently runs on GNU/Linux).

DotGNU differs from the .NET strategy (discussed next) in that instead of the Web service running on a remote system where an application performs RPC calls to communicate, DotGNU downloads the Web service to the local computer and executes it there.

MONO

The MONO project is another initiative to develop an open source, Linux-based version of the .NET platform by Ximian. MONO provides the development environment for .NET (the Common Language Infrastructure, or CLI), a class library for the Common Language Runtime and a C# compiler.

Microsoft .NET

Microsoft .NET is the Microsoft platform for XML Web services. Microsoft's .NET platform consists of four elements: clients, servers, services, and tools. Client and server elements make it possible for systems to communicate in the .NET platform. The services element consists of the small reusable component applications that are used as building blocks to connect and build .NET distributed applications. Tools are primarily the Visual Studio (R) .NET and Microsoft .NET framework to build, run, and deploy Web services.

Other Prospective Web Services Architectures

In this section, we'll discuss two final alternatives for Web Services architectures. Just like languages, there is no single "right" answer and the solution depends upon the needs of the particular problem. Therefore, the plethora of architectures gives us great flexibility to solve Web Services problems.

Open Services Gateway Initiative

The Open Services Gateway Initiative (OSGi) is an independent forum working to define open specifications for the delivery of managed services to network endpoints such as homes, cars and other environments.

The OSGi framework permits service providers to install and manage services on an open services gateway (otherwise known as a residential gateway). OSGi provides an API for applications operating within the OSGi environment. These APIs cover service management, security, inter-service dependencies, and device and resource management.

OSGi's strength is the ability to operate over a variety of broadband networks and interface to a number of local networks at the edge device (such as Jini, UPnP, HAVi, Bluetooth, and others).

Mobile Agents

Mobile agents are an interesting class of software framework that is not dissimilar to Web Services. A mobile agent is nothing more than an independent piece of software that has the ability to migrate between physical hosts on a network. For example, a mobile agent can be started on a host, and then migrate to a new host to perform some processing there. It can then continue to migrate to other hosts, or return to the host that initially dispatched it. In addition to the application migrating between hosts, variables used by the agent are also included when the agent migrates. This allows the mobile agent to perform some work, move to another host, and then continue its work with it's data intact.

The idea of mobile agents began with operating system research in the 1980s. The problem was that in a network of available computers, how to identify where to run a particular computing job? The task of process migration was used to achieve this load balancing to ensure that no computer was tasked beyond its capacity.

Mobile agents are a new breed of migratory software that provides for load balancing, but also integrates new features that make it an interesting alternative to current Web Services architectures.

OTHER PROTOCOLS

In this section, we'll cover some of the other interesting protocol offerings that did not fit into any of the prior categories.

Active Networks

Active networks are a very simple but very powerful idea. An active network permits the execution of special packets that flow through the nodes of a network. Therefore, instead of packets simply flowing through a router en-route to their destination, the packet contains special instructions that alter the state of the router. This allows routers to be extensively programmed via a very simple interface (operating on the elements that they were initially defined to operate on). This permits computation within routers that were previously only possible at the endpoints.

Active networks enable optimizations within routers as well as the development of extensions to protocols and the construction of new protocols that satisfy existing and future requirements. For example, consider the Reservation Protocol (RSVP) covered in the previous QoS section. Active networks permit this type of functionality in a generic way. By embedded special instructions within the packet, the development of RSVP-like protocols is possible as well as a variety of others.

Knowledge Query and Manipulation Language (KQML)

An early information transport protocol was KQML, or the Knowledge Query and Manipulation Language. KQML is a language and a protocol for exchanging information and knowledge, as part of the larger ARPA Knowledge Sharing Effort. The goal of KQML is the development of large-scale knowledge bases that can be shared among a number of applications.

KQML provided a protocol that was very similar to what is now provided by XML. KQML uses tags in a LISP-like fashion, and allows an application to interact with an intelligent system or for two or more systems to share knowledge.

Going back to our temperature server example, the KQML message in Listing 13.10 illustrates the temperature request, and Listing 13.11 provides the subsequent response.

LISTING 13.10 KQML message request for temperature.

```
(ask-one
  :sender app1
  :content (TEMPERATURE NorthPanelA1 ?temperature)
  :receiver temperature-server
  :reply-with app1-temp-request
  :language LPROLOG
  :ontology CELSIUS-TEMP)
```

LISTING 13.11 KQML message response for temperature.

```
(tell
  :sender temperature-server
  :content (TEMPERATURE NorthPanelA1 62)
  :receiver app1
  :in-reply-to app1-temp-request
  :language LPROLOG
  :ontology CELSIUS-TEMP)
```

The first thing to note about the KQML messages are that the first element is the type. In KQML parlance, this is called a "performative." In our example, the KQML request was sent by `app1` to the `temperature-server`. We identify a `reply-with` key/value pair in order to correlate the response with our request.

The `ask-one` performative is a single request for the NorthPanelA1 temperature. The server responds with the `tell` message that is a response for the given `ask-one` request. The query is written in the language specified (LPROLOG). Finally, the ontology specifies the domain of knowledge for the particular information being communicated. The ontology is important in KQML because it defines how any application can interpret the data that results from the request in an unambiguous way. Since the goal of KQML is to share knowledge, a base of understanding is necessary so that both elements "understand" what they're communicating.

SUMMARY

In this chapter, we looked at a wide range of new protocols and architectures that exist to solve a variety of problems. We investigated a number of transport layer protocols (such as RTP and SCTP) including upcoming network layer protocols to replace IPv4. We then investigated Quality of Service and the protocols and architectures that are used to provide this feature. Next, we looked at two common Security methods and new and uncommon application layer protocols that provide a remote procedure control mechanism (such as SOAP and XML-RPC). We also looked at some new application layer protocols such as SIP and variations on HTTP (HTTPR and HTTPS). We then looked at Web Services and the varying protocols and architectures that compete in this space. Finally, we looked at a few alternative architectures that support Web Services, such as OSGi and Mobile Agents.

RESOURCES

Audio-Video Transport Working Group, "RTP: A Transport Protocol for Real-Time Applications," RFC 1889, January 1996. http://www.landfield.com/rfcs/rfc1889.html

Nichols, et al., "Definition of the Differentiated Services Field (DS Field) in the IPv4 and IPv6 Headers," RFC 2474, December 1998. http://www.landfield.org/rfcs/rfc2474.html

Blake, et al., "An Architecture for Differentiated Services," RFC 2475, December 1998. http://www.landfield.org/rfcs/rfc2475.html

Kilkki, Kalevi, *Differentiated Services for the Interne"*, Macmillan Technical Publishing, 1999.

Stewart, et al., "Stream Control Transmission Protocol," RFC 2960, October 2000. http://www.landfield.org/rfcs/rfc2960.html

Stewart and Metz, "SCTP: A New Transport Protocol for TCP/IP," Nov/Dec 2001. http://www.computer.org/internet/v5n6/w6wire.htm

"Recommendations on Queue Management and Congestion Avoidance in the Internet," RFC 2309, April 1998. http://www.landfield.org/rfcs/rfc2309.html

Simple Object Access Protocol (SOAP) 1.1, W3C Note 08 May 2000. http://www.w3.org/TR/SOAP/

Moyer, et al., "Framework Draft for Networked Appliances using the Session Initiation Protocol," , June 2001. http://www.argreenhouse.com/iapp/draft-moyer-sip-appliances-framework-02.pdf

Todd, et al., "Web Services: A Primer for HTTPR," IBM. http://www-106.ibm.com/developerworks/webservices/library/ws-phtt/?dwzone=webservices

"Web Services Description Language (WSDL) 1.1," W3C Note 15 March 2001. http://www.w3.org/TR/wsdl

"UDDI Technical White Paper," Ariba, IBM, Microsoft, September 2000. http://www.uddi.org/pubs/lru_UDDI_Technical_White_Paper.pdf

The DotGNU Project. http://www.gnu.org/projects/dotgnu

The MONO Project. http://www.go-mono.com/

Microsoft .NET. http://www.microsoft.com/net/

Open Services Gateway Initiative. http://www.osgi.org/

Jones, "Java Mobile Agents and the Aglets SDK." *Dr. Dobbs Journal*, January 2002. http://www.ddj.com/articles/2002/0201/

Active Networks. http://www.sds.lcs.mit.edu/darpa-activenet/

UMBC KQML Web. http://www.cs.umbc.edu/kqml/

APPENDIX

A BSD Sockets API Primer

This appendix introduces the BSD Sockets Application Programmers Interface. The BSD API is a common element of all modern operating systems. Although some implementations choose to change its name (such as Winsock), the API provides the means to communicate with any other device on the Internet that utilizes the TCP/IP protocol suite.

INTRODUCTION

As the name implies, the basic building block of the Sockets API is the socket. A *socket* is an endpoint for communication onto which a name (port number) is bound. There are different types of sockets. The socket type defines its communication properties. Socket types can be *stream* (reliable), *datagram* (message oriented) or *raw* (raw access to the underlying protocol).

The following sections provide an overview of the BSD API as well as notes on the use of the API in the embedded environment.

Embedded Notes

Most embedded protocol stack implementations include an API that resembles the BSD Sockets API. The word "resembles" is used here because the BSD Sockets API can require certain functionality from the target Real Time Operating System (RTOS) (blocking capability on the API, etc.). Therefore, some of the functions listed here may differ from your particular stack's implementation. When discrepancies occur, check your documentation.

Endianness

The problem of endianness is not a problem created by networking, but instead by a fundamental issue in the way computer architectures look at memory. Figure A.1 provides a graphical description of endianness. In little-endian architectures, the least significant byte is found first in linear memory. In big-endian architectures, it's the most significant byte that is found first. Architectures that use the little-endian representation include the Intel x86 variants and the DEC Alpha. Big-endian architectures include the MIPS, PowerPC, and Sun Sparc. The IBM and Motorola PowerPC processors support the ability to use either representation.

Because architectures differ on their representation, communication between machines that support different endian representations can create problems. To solve this problem, two representations were created to abstract away the details of this problem. These representations are called Network Byte Order (NBO) and Host Byte Order (HBO). Network byte order happens also to be big endian. This means that big-endian hosts have the same byte order as the network. A disadvantage of little-endian devices is that they must perform byte swapping to move from and to network byte order.

Four functions exist to perform byte ordering. These are `ntohs` (network to host short), `htons` (host to network short), `ntohl` (network to host long), and `htonl` (host to network long). These functions, as you can probably see, perform the necessary byte mapping from the particular architecture to network byte order. On big-endian architectures (such as PowerPC), these functions perform no function since the byte order is already network byte order. On little-endian architectures (such as the Pentium series), these functions perform the necessary byte swapping to provide the mapping to network byte order. Two different function sets exist to map shorts (16 bits or two octets) and longs (32 bits or four octets).

For portability reasons, one should always use these functions as they are commonly macros and yield no performance decrease on architectures that already represent network byte order.

Converting from host byte order to network byte order:

```
unsigned short htons ( unsigned short );
        unsigned long htonl ( unsigned long );
```

Converting from network byte order to host byte order:

```
unsigned short ntohs ( unsigned short );
        unsigned long ntohl ( unsigned long );
```

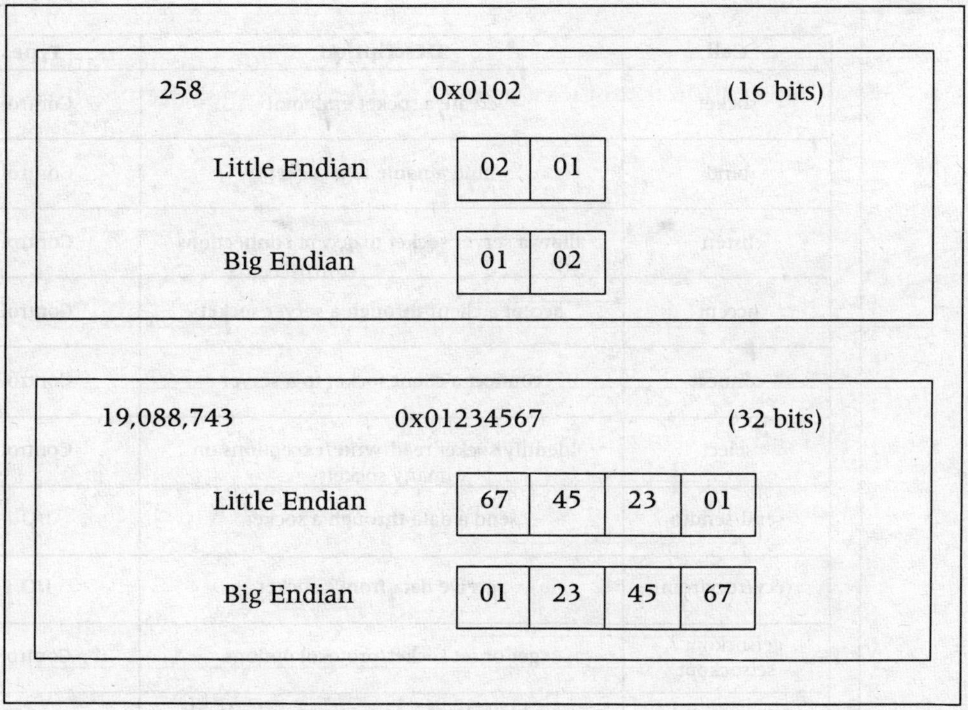

FIGURE A.1 Memory representations of endianness.

If an application layer protocol is to pass data that is architecture dependent, it should convert the data to network byte order before passing it unless the byte ordering is negotiated between endpoints prior to communication. Byte ordering is also important to some of the structures used by the BSD API calls, and will be identified where relevant.

SOCKETS API CALLS

This section provides a summary of the most used BSD API calls. Each call is shown in prototype form and includes a short description and example usage.

socket

```
#include <sys/types.h>
#include <sys/socket.h>

int socket ( int domain, int type, int protocol );
```

Call	Description	Type
socket	create a socket endpoint	Control
bind	bind a name to a socket	Control
listen	allow a server socket to accept connections	Control
accept	accept a client through a server socket	Control
connect	connect a client socket to a server	Control
select	Identify socket read/write/exceptions on many sockets	Control
send/sendto	send a data through a socket	I/O
recv/recvfrom	receive data from a socket	I/O
getsockopt / setsockopt	get or set socket/protocol options	Control
getpeername / getsockname	get address/port information on the local and remote ends of a socket	Control
close	close a socket	Control
shutdown	close a socket with control	Control
gethostbyname / gethostbyaddr	resolve a name or address using a domain name server	Conversion
inet_addr / inet_aton	convert a character string IP address to a binary network-byte order address	Conversion
inet_ntoa	convert a binary network-byte order address to a character string	Conversion

FIGURE A.2 Sockets API call summary.

Summary

The `socket` call is the most basic of the API primitives because it is required to create a socket to be used for communication. The call returns a socket descriptor (or '–1' if an error occurred).

The domain specifies the protocol family. Options include AF_UNIX for UNIX domain or local protocols, AF_INET for IPv4 protocols and AF_ROUTE for routing protocols. The type field may be SOCK_STREAM (for TCP), SOCK_DGRAM (for UDP), or SOCK_RAW (for raw or IPv4). SOCK_RAW sockets permit datagrams to bypass the transport layer altogether. These types are valid only for the AF_INET domain.

The protocol field is always '0', unless the type field is defined as SOCK_RAW. Details on raw socket protocols are not covered in this text.

Example Usage

TCP socket creation:

```
int sockFd;

sockFd = socket ( AF_INET, SOCK_STREAM, 0 );
```

UDP socket creation:

```
int sockFd;
sockFd = socket ( AF_INET, SOCK_DGRAM, 0 );
```

Routing socket creation (used to obtain and change routing table information):

```
int sockFd;
sockFd = socket ( AF_ROUTE, SOCK_RAW, 0 );
```

Special Notes

While protocol stack implementations provide the socket call, many don't provide the more advanced features supported by the socket call (such as support for routing sockets or less traditional combinations of domains and types). When in doubt, consultation with source/documentation or reviewing return status from the socket call can help determine what options are supported.

bind

```
#include <sys/types.h>
#include <sys/socket.h>

int bind ( int sockFd, const struct sockaddr *sockAddr,
           int addrLen );
```

Summary

The bind call gives the socket a name and local port address by which others may reference it. Its most common usage is for servers to bind a port number that clients will use to connect.

The sockFd argument is a socket descriptor previously created using the socket call. The sockaddr structure contains socket address information for a number of different kinds of sockets. For AF_UNIX (local domain), the structure used is:

```
struct sockaddr {
        unsigned short sa_family;      // Address Family (domain)
        char           sa_data[14]];   // Protocol Address
    };
```

Since we'll use AF_INET in the development of application layer protocols, we'll use the following structure that is easier to initialize:

```
    struct sockaddr_in {
        short          sin_family;     // Address Family
        unsigned short sin_port;       // Port Number
        struct in_addr sin_addr;       // Internet Address
        unsigned char  sin_zero[8];    // Pad structure
    };
```

Finally, socklen_t must be initialized with the size of the sockaddr structure.

The most common application of bind is to tie a port number to a server socket. But as you can see from the sockaddr_in structure, an Internet address may also be specified. Binding an IP address to a server socket has the effect of restricting incoming connections through only the interface specified (where the interface is identified by its IP address). This is useful for devices with multiple interfaces in which only one network, such as the internal network, has authority to access the server. A typical server will use the INADDR_ANY to allow any client to access.

Example Usage

Typical TCP Server Usage:

```
int sockfd;
struct sockaddr_in servaddr;

sockfd = socket( AF_INET, SOCK_STREAM, 0 );
```

```
bzero( &servaddr, sizeof(servaddr) );

servaddr.sin_family = AF_INET;
servaddr.sin_addr.s_addr = htonl( INADDR_ANY );
servaddr.sin_port = htons( MY_PORT_NUMBER );

bind( sockfd, (struct sockaddr *)&servaddr, sizeof(servaddr) );
```

Typical UDP server usage (change the following line):

```
sockfd = socket ( AF_INET, SOCK_DGRAM, 0 );
```

To allow the system to assign the port number (common client configuration), change the following line:

```
servaddr.sin_port = htons( 0 );
```

Special Notes

Although `bind` is used to bind a unique name to a socket, multiple sockets may be bound to a single name for use in multicast sockets. When this is required, the sockets must be modified using the `SO_REUSEADDR` socket option. Appendix A provides a sample multicast client application that illustrates this functionality.

listen

```
#include <sys/socket.h>
int listen ( int sockFd, int backlog );
```

Summary

The `listen` call is used by TCP servers and instructs the protocol stack that the socket argument passed is available for client connection through the accept call. Any application that expects clients to make contact with it (such as a server) will need to listen for connection requests.

The `sockFd` argument is the server socket that was previously created via the `socket` call and bound to a name through the `bind` call. The backlog argument is the number of allowable clients that may be queued on this server socket awaiting connection by the server through the `accept` call.

Example Usage

```
int sockFd;
```

```
sockFd = socket( AF_INET, SOCK_STREAM, 0 );

/* … */

listen ( sockFd, 5 );
```

Special Notes

The backlog value is commonly defined as 5 in most sample applications. In embedded implementations, single-threaded servers are common (such as is the case for the daytime server example in Chapter 1). Therefore, if supported by the protocol stack implementation, the backlog value should be increased in these situations to allow more client connections to be buffered until the server can accept them.

accept

```
#include <sys/types.h>
#include <sys/socket.h>

int accept ( int sockFd, struct sockaddr *clientAddr, int *addrLen );
```

Summary

The accept call is used by server applications in conjunction with listen to accept a pending connection from a client. It is assumed that the server has already created the socket, bound a name to it, and called listen to make the new server available.

The sockFd argument is a previously created socket. The clientAddr structure argument is used to collect information about the client that has connected to this server. When a connection has been made, this structure can be used to identify the IP address and port number of the client endpoint of the socket. The addrLen argument is pre-initialized with the size of the clientAddr structure. This tells the protocol stack how much space is available for sockaddr information. If the stack uses less space than was initially passed, the addrLen argument is modified and returned through the addrLen pointer

Example Usage

Typical server usage:

```
cliLen = sizeof( (struct sockaddr_in) );
connFd = accept(serverFd, (struct sockaddr *)&cliAddr, &cliLen);
```

```
printf( "Client endpoint is at %s, port %d\n",
    inet_ntoa(cliAddr.sin_addr), ntohs(cliAddr.sin_port) );
```

Server usage when information on the client endpoint is not needed:

```
connFd = accept( serverFd, (struct sockaddr *)NULL, NULL );
```

Special Notes

Some embedded systems lack support for blocking semantics and therefore the accept call cannot block. In these situations, polling or time-based execution of the server code should be used. The accept routine will return EWOULDBLOCK or a similar error code to identify that no connections are pending on the listening socket. Although it's officially an error return, the error is specific to the mode of the socket and therefore not a true error.

connect

```
#include <sys/types.h>
#include <sys/socket.h>

int connect ( int sockFd, struct sockaddr *servAddr, int addrLen );
```

Summary

The connect call is used by TCP (SOCK_STREAM) client applications to connect to a TCP server and by UDP (SOCK_DGRAM) clients to specify the peer to which this socket is to be associated. The connect call may be used only after a local socket address and port number have been assigned (within the sockaddr_in structure). A UDP socket in the connected state means that it will exchange datagrams with only one other host identified by the IP address in servAddr.

From the TCP perspective, the connect call arguments define the server address for which this socket should connect. For UDP, the connect call arguments define the peer from which datagrams may be received and to whom datagrams will be transmitted. While a TCP connection is persistent (connection exists for two endpoints), the UDP connect can be performed more than once. This means that the UDP socket can define a peer and then redefine it as necessary during operation.

The sockFd argument is the previously created socket. The servaddr argument specifies the peer to which we will connect. The addrLen argument is the previously computed size of the servaddr structure (in the case of the examples shown sockaddr_in).

Example Usage

Typical TCP client usage:

```
struct sockaddr_in servaddr;
int     connFd;

connFd = socket(AF_INET, SOCK_STREAM, 0);

memset(&servaddr, 0, sizeof(servaddr));
servaddr.sin_family = AF_INET;
servaddr.sin_port = htons(DAYTIME_SERVER_PORT);
servaddr.sin_addr.s_addr = inet_addr(DAYTIME_SERVER_IP_ADRS);

connect(connFd, (struct sockaddr *)&servaddr, sizeof(servaddr));
```

Typical UDP (connected) client usage:

```
struct sockaddr_in servaddr;
int     connFd;

connFd = socket(AF_INET, SOCK_DGRAM, 0);

memset(&servaddr, 0, sizeof(servaddr));
servaddr.sin_family = AF_INET;
servaddr.sin_port = htons(DAYTIME_SERVER_PORT);
servaddr.sin_addr.s_addr = inet_addr(DAYTIME_SERVER_IP_ADRS);

connect(connFd, (struct sockaddr *)&servaddr, sizeof(servaddr));
```

Special Notes

None.

SELECT

```
#include <sys/types.h>
#include <sys/time.h>
#include <unistd.h>

int select( int n, fd_set *read_fds, fd_set *write_fds,
            fd_set *exceptfds, struct timeval *timeout );
```

Summary

The `select` call allows an application to block a `select` call until something of interest occurs on the set of sockets or the specified timeout value expires. The application can specify four types of events of interest. These are sockets that have data available (read event), sockets that have buffer space available (write), sockets that have some kind of error (exception), and a condition in which too much time has expired (timeout).

The `n` argument refers to one more than the largest socket descriptor that is set in any of the `fd_set` structures. Any of the `fd_set` structures may be defined as null if the application has no interest that event.

The application identifies a set of socket descriptors that should be monitored for a particular event (read/write/exception). The socket descriptors are stored within a bitmap as defined by the `fd_set` structure. Socket layers provide a set of macros used to set, reset or check the presence of a socket event within the `fd_set` structure.

When the select call returns, the value defines the number of descriptors that have been set within the `fd_set` structures. If the return value is '`-1`,' then an error has occurred. Finally, if a '`0`' is returned, the time limit has expired.

Example Usage

In the following example, sockets for two servers (srvr1 and srvr2) have been created that we want to monitor for incoming requests. If five seconds pass, we'll do something else.

```
fd_set      readfds;
int         srvr1, srvr2;
int         maxfds, ret;
struct timeval timeout;

...


FDZERO(&readfds);

while (1) {

    timeout.tv_sec = 5;
    timeout.tv_usec = 0;

    FD_SET( srvr1, &readfds );
    FD_SET( srvr2, &readfds );
```

```
        maxfds = max( srvr1, srvr2 ) + 1;

        ret = select( maxfds, &readfds, NULL, NULL, &timeout );

        if (ret == 0) {

            /* Timeout processing... */

        } else if (ret == -1) {

            /* Error processing... */

        } else {

            if (FD_ISSET(srvr1, &readfds)) {

                /* Socket srvr1 is readable */

            }

            if (FD_ISSET(srvr2, &readfds)) {

                /* Socket srvr2 is readable */

            }

        }

    }
```

Sample Notes

While many embedded TCP/IP stacks provide this functionality, some embedded systems have no blocking capability (as is provided by the operating system/kernel). In these cases, the TCP/IP stack will often provide a callback mechanism to allow an application to be called when a registered event has been noted to the kernel. In most cases, this method is very efficient and can often lead to better performance than is available through the `select` primitive.

send/sendto

```
#include <sys/types.h>
#include <sys/socket.h>
```

```
int send ( int sockFd, const void *msg, int msgLen,
           unsigned int flags);
int sendto ( int sockFd, const void *msg, int msgLen,
             unsigned int flags,
             const struct sockaddr *to, int toLen);
```

Summary

The send and sendto calls are used to transfer data through a socket. The send call is used on connected sockets while the sendto is used on a socket that is in an unconnected state.

The send call arguments include the socket descriptor (sockFd), the actual data to be sent through the socket (msg), the length of that data (msgLen), and a set of binary flags to alter the operation of the call.

The sendto call is used for unconnected sockets, which means that there is no statically defined destination for the data. To provide this information, the sendto call includes the sockaddr structure to define the destination endpoint (to), and the length of this structure (toLen).

Both send and sendto return the number of bytes actually sent from the msg buffer. If the return value is not equal to the length of the message to send (msgLen), the user must call send or sendto again until all of the data is sent (while properly adjusting the msg pointer to offset for already sent data).

Example Usage

Typical TCP client usage:

```
struct sockaddr_in servaddr;
char   msg[48];
int    connFd;

strcpy( msg, "Test String" );

connFd = socket(AF_INET, SOCK_STREAM, 0);

memset(&servaddr, 0, sizeof(servaddr));
servaddr.sin_family = AF_INET;
servaddr.sin_port = htons(TEST_SERVER_PORT);
servaddr.sin_addr.s_addr = inet_addr(TEST_SERVER_IP_ADRS);

connect(connFd, (struct sockaddr_in *)&servaddr,
        sizeof(servaddr));
```

```
send( connFd, msg, strlen(msg), 0);
```

Typical unconnected UDP usage:

```
struct sockaddr_in servaddr;
char   msg[48];
int    connFd;

strcpy( msg, "Test String" );

connFd = socket(AF_INET, SOCK_DGRAM, 0);

memset(&servaddr, 0, sizeof(servaddr));
servaddr.sin_family = AF_INET;
servaddr.sin_port = htons(TEST_SERVER_PORT);
servaddr.sin_addr.s_addr = inet_addr(TEST_SERVER_IP_ADRS);

sendto( connFd, msg, strlen(msg), 0,
 (sockaddr_in *)servaddr, sizeof(servaddr) );
```

Special Notes

None.

recv/recvfrom

```
#include <sys/types.h>
#include <sys/socket.h>

int recv ( int sockFd, const void *msg, int msgLen,
           unsigned int flags);
int recvfrom ( int sockFd, const void *msg, int msgLen,
               unsigned int flags,
              const struct sockaddr *from, int *fromLen);
```

Summary

The `recv` and `recvfrom` calls are used to receive data through a socket. The `recv` call is used on connected sockets while `recvfrom` is used on a socket that can be in an unconnected state.

The `recv` call arguments include the socket descriptor (`sockFd`), a buffer to store the data received through the socket (`msg`), the maximum size of the buffer (`msgLen`), and a set of binary `flags` to alter the operation of the call.

The `recvfrom` call can be used for unconnected sockets, which means that there is no single peer connected to the alternate end of the socket. In this case, the `from` and `fromLen` arguments are set to null. If non-null arguments are passed for `from` and `fromLen`, these fields are filled to identify the source of the datagram.

Both functions return the number of bytes received through the socket, or, `-1` if an error occurred. When operating in blocking or non blocking-mode, a '`0`' return represents closure by the peer of the connection-oriented socket.

Example Usage

Typical TCP server usage:

```
struct sockaddr_in servaddr;
char   msg[48];
int    sockFd, connFd, msgLen;

sockFd = socket(AF_INET, SOCK_STREAM, 0);

memset(&servaddr, 0, sizeof(servaddr));
servaddr.sin_family = AF_INET;
servaddr.sin_port = htons(TEST_SERVER_PORT);
servaddr.sin_addr.s_addr = inet_addr(INADDR_ANY);

bind(sockFd, (struct sockaddr *)&servaddr, sizeof(servaddr));

listen(sockFd, 5);

connFd = accept(sockFd, (struct sockaddr *)NULL, NULL);

msgLen = recv( connFd, &msg, sizeof(msg), 0);
```

Typical unconnected UDP usage:

```
struct sockaddr_in servaddr;
char   msg[48];
int    connFd, msgLen, fromLen;

connFd = socket(AF_INET, SOCK_DGRAM, 0);

fromLen = sizeof(servaddr);

msgLen = recvfrom( connFd, &msg, sizeof(msg), 0,
       (sockaddr_in *)&servaddr, &fromLen );
```

```
printf("Received datagram from %s, port %d\n",
   inet_ntoa(((struct sockaddr_in *)&from)->sin_addr),
   ntohs(((struct sockaddr_in *)&from)->sin_port) );
```

Special Notes

None.

getsockopt/setsockopt

```
#include <sys/types.h>
#include <sys/socket.h>

int setsockopt ( int sd, int level, int optname,
                 const void *optval, socklen_t optlen);
int getsockopt ( int sd, int level, int optname,
                 void *optval, socklen_t *optlen );
```

Summary

The setsockopt is used to change the behavior of particular socket. The behavior is altered through modifying options that are available for the socket type. The getsockopt call is used to identify the value of a socket option.

Socket options are used only on open sockets (as specified by the sd argument). The level argument identifies which portion of the protocol stack should interpret the option (such as IP, TCP, or the socket layer). The option to be modified (or interrogated) is identified by the optname argument. The value of the option is contained within optval. This is a void pointer since the actual option may be a variety of different types or structures. In most cases, the option is represented by an integer value (32 bit value). The size of the passed or returned optval argument is defined by optlen.

A return value of 0 represents a successful setsockopt or getsockopt operation.

Example Usage

Getting the current time-to-live value set in IP packets:

```
int ttl, ttlLen;
getsockopt(sd, SOL_IP, SO_TTL, (void *)&ttl, &ttlLen);
printf("IP Packet TTL: %d\n", ttl);
```

To set the socket linger option (await transmission of outgoing data for some time before closing the socket):

```
struct linger sol;
sol.l_onoff = 1;
sol.l_linger = 10; /* seconds */
setsockopt(sd, SOL_SOCKET, SO_LINGER, (void *)&sol, sizeof(sol));
```

Special Notes

A variety of options exist although their availability is dependent upon the particular protocol stack implementation. Some of the options relevant in the embedded domain are covered in more detail in Appendix B.

getsockname/getpeername

```
#include <sys/socket.h>

int getsockname ( int sd, struct sockaddr *addr, int *addrLen );
int getpeername ( int sd, struct sockaddr *addr, int *addrLen );
```

Summary

The `getsockname` function provides the means to gather the local address information about a connected socket through the `sockaddr` structure while `getpeername` permits gathering remote (peer) address information. The remote information can also be gathered by a TCP server at the `accept` call or by an unconnected UDP socket through the `recvfrom` call. These calls operate only on sockets in the `AF_INET` domain.

Example Usage

Typical usage given an open and connected socket:

```
struct sockaddr_in laddr, raddr;

/* ... */

getsockname(sockFd, (struct sockaddr *)&laddr,
            sizeof(struct sockaddr_in));

getpeername(sockFd, (struct sockaddr *)&raddr,
            sizeof(struct sockaddr_in));

printf("Local Address %s, port %d\n",
       inet_ntoa(laddr.sin_addr), ntohs(laddr.sin_port) );
printf("Remote Address %s, port %d\n",
       inet_ntoa(raddr.sin_addr), ntohs(raddr.sin_port) );
```

Special Notes

None.

close

```
#include <sys/socket.h>

int close ( int sd );
```

Summary

The `close` function closes the socket for further communication (discards unsent data and rejects incoming data).

Example Usage

```
Int sockFd;
/* ... */
close(sockFd);
```

Special Notes

While the `close` call shuts down the socket for further reads and discards the remaining data for transmission, the `shutdown` call may be used for greater control of the socket shutdown process.

shutdown

```
#include <sys/socket.h>

int shutdown ( int sockFd, int how );
```

Summary

The `shutdown` function provides greater control of the socket shutdown process than the `close` call. The argument `how` is represented by one of the following values:

0 Stop receiving data for this socket and reject any further data received.

1 Stop transmitting data from this socket and discard any data waiting to be sent.

2 Stop both reception and transmission (options 0 and 1).

Example Usage

To permit all data to be sent but ignore incoming data:

```
int sockFd;
/* ... */
shutdown(sockFd, 0);
```

Special Notes

None.

gethostbyname/gethostbyaddr

```
#include <sys/netdb.h>
#include <sys/socket.h>

struct hostent *gethostbyname(const char *name);
struct hostent *gethostbyaddr(const char *addr, int len, int type);
```

Summary

The `gethostbyname` and `gethostbyaddr` functions provide the means to map domain names to addresses (`gethostbyname`) and from addresses to domain names (`gethostbyaddr`).

For `gethostbyname`, the name argument represents the domain name to be resolved to an IP address.

For `gethostbyaddr`, `addr` is the IP address in network byte order, `len` is the length of the address (4 in the case of IPv4) and `type` is `AF_INET` for the Internet address family.

Each function uses the hostent structure to provide the mapping information.

```
struct hostent {
char    *h_name;        /* official name of host */
char    **h_aliases;    /* alias list */
int     h_addrtype;     /* host address type */
int     hlength;        /* length of address */
char    **h_addr_list;  /* list of addresses */
}
#define h_addr  h_addr_list[0]  /* for backward compatibility */
```

Example Usage

Typical usage for resolving a fully qualified domain name to an IP address:

```
struct hostent server;

server = gethostbyname("sampledomain.org");
```

```
printf("The IP Address is : %s\n",
      inet_ntoa( *((struct in_addr *)server->h_addr)) );
```

Typical usage for resolving an IPv4 address to a fully qualified domain name:

```
struct hostent server;
char   ipadrs[4]={192, 168, 1, 1};

server = gethostbyaddr(ipadrs, 4, AF_INET);

printf("The host is : %s\n", server->h_name);
```

Special Notes

Resolving names with these functions implies the existence of a DNS resolver on the device. Despite the importance of these functions, some embedded implementations provide no such functionality and therefore your stack and sockets API implementation should be consulted.

MANAGING IP ADDRESSES

The following functions are used to simplify the manipulation of IP addresses and their translation from strings (common initial state) to a network byte order address format. Another function provides the means to convert from a binary network byte order address back to a string.

inet_addr / inet_aton

Convert an IP address in character string format to a network byte order integer format.

```
unsigned int inet_addr( char *adrs );
unsigned int inet_aton( const char *adrs, struct in_addr *in );
```

This function is most commonly used when filling in the `sockaddr_in` structure for `bind` or `connect`, as:

```
sockaddr_in servaddr;

servaddr.sin_addr.s_addr = inet_addr( "192.168.1.1" );
```

```
/* or */

inet_aton( "192.168.1.1", &servaddr.sin_addr.s_addr );
```

`inet_aton` returns `0` if the address converted was valid and is therefore preferable due to its error checking.

inet_ntoa

Convert an IP address in network byte order integer format to a character string:

```
char *inet_ntoa( unsigned int );
```

This function is used to convert a raw IP address into a string for display:

```
sockaddr_in servaddr;

/* ... */

printf("Address is : %s\n", inet_ntoa( servaddr.sin_addr.s_addr ) );
```

SAMPLE APPLICATIONS

The following section contains a number of example programs that utilize the API discussed in this appendix. We'll look again at the daytime server and client, but now we'll implement them using stream sockets (TCP), connected and unconnected datagram sockets (UDP), multicast sockets (UDP), and finally a broadcast implementation.

Stream Server and Client

The stream socket implementation is the most common because of the reliability of the transport protocol. TCP provides reliable service between the networked elements as well as guaranteeing proper packet delivery order and retransmission when necessary.

LISTING A.1 Daytime server using stream sockets.

```
#include <sys/socket.h>
#include <arpa/inet.h>
```

```
#include <stdio.h>
#include <time.h>
#include <unistd.h>

#define MAX_BUFFER              128
#define DAYTIME_SERVER_PORT         13

int main ( void )
{
  int serverFd, connectionFd;
  struct sockaddr_in servaddr;
  char timebuffer[MAX_BUFFER+1];
  time_t currentTime;

  serverFd = socket(AF_INET, SOCK_STREAM, 0);

  memset(&servaddr, 0, sizeof(servaddr));
  servaddr.sin_family = AF_INET;
  servaddr.sin_addr.s_addr = htonl(INADDR_ANY);
  servaddr.sin_port = htons(DAYTIME_SERVER_PORT);

  bind(serverFd, (struct sockaddr *)&servaddr, sizeof(servaddr));

  listen(serverFd, 5);

  while ( 1 ) {

    connectionFd = accept(serverFd, (struct sockaddr *)NULL, NULL);

    if (connectionFd >= 0) {

      currentTime = time(NULL);
      snprintf(timebuffer, MAX_BUFFER, "%s\n", ctime(&currentTime));

      write(connectionFd, timebuffer, strlen(timebuffer));
      close(connectionFd);
    }

  }

}
```

The notable characteristics of the TCP server (see Listing A.1) are that initially, the socket is created with the SOCK_STREAM type (defining this socket as a stream socket). Next, the bind call binds the port number and the wildcard address (INADDR_ANY) to our end of the socket. The bind call is not so much of a TCP characteristic as it is a server characteristic (UDP socket servers will perform the same functionality). The listen call enables our server socket to receive client connections. Finally, the accept call creates a new client socket for the server to handle workload of the server application. Note that we ignore the remote client data (which would be collected from arguments 2 and 3 of the accept call). Since this is a stream socket, there is only one other endpoint to which we may communicate. Therefore, we treat this anonymously since it is unimportant in this application.

The TCP daytime client is shown in Listing A.2. Again, a socket is created of type SOCK_STREAM, declaring this a stream socket. The sockaddr_in structure is loaded with the information to point to the stream server (through an IP address, via servaddr.sin_addr and a port number through servaddr.sin_port).

LISTING A.2 Daytime client using stream sockets.

```
#include <sys/socket.h>
#include <arpa/inet.h>
#include <stdio.h>
#include <unistd.h>
#include <time.h>

#define MAX_BUFFER          128
#define DAYTIME_SERVER_PORT  13

int main ( int argc, char *argv[] )
{
  int connectionFd, in;
  struct sockaddr_in servaddr;
  char timebuffer[MAX_BUFFER+1];

  if (argc != 2) {
    return(0);
  }

  connectionFd = socket(AF_INET, SOCK_STREAM, 0);

  memset(&servaddr, 0, sizeof(servaddr));
  servaddr.sin_family = AF_INET;
```

```
    servaddr.sin_port = htons(DAYTIME_SERVER_PORT);

    inet_pton(AF_INET, argv[1], &servaddr.sin_addr);

    connect(connectionFd,
            (struct sockaddr_in *)&servaddr, sizeof(servaddr));

    while ( (in = read(connectionFd, timebuffer, MAX_BUFFER)) > 0) {
      timebuffer[in] = 0;
      printf("\n%s", timebuffer);
    }

    close(connectionFd);

    return(0);
}
```

The `connect` call creates a connection between the client and the remote server. The socket (`connectionFd`) is now tied to the remote server and is the only entity to which we may communicate through this socket. This is another key characteristic of a stream client.

Unconnected Datagram Server and Client

The unconnected data socket implementation has some advantages over the stream socket version. First, in some respects it is simpler (fewer BSD API calls are required). Second, more flexibility is allowed due to the unconnected nature of communication. The client may contact multiple servers through a single socket. To do this, the `servaddr` structure (or another instance) that identifies the endpoint to which we communicate is changed for a different destination prior to the `sendto` call. Finally, it takes less time to communicate through a datagram connection than through a stream connection. This is because a stream connection must be built, which entails communication at the transport layer to synchronize both ends of the socket. Datagram sockets have no such requirement and therefore the available bandwidth can be better utilized. See Listing A.3 for the unconnected datagram server source listing.

The disadvantages, as we've outlined, are that there is no guarantee that datagrams will arrive in the order in which they were sent, or that they will arrive at all. This puts more responsibility on the individual applications to provide this guarantee (if applicable). Note that in this application, we would wait some amount of time for a response and if not received we'd simply send another request.

LISTING A.3 Daytime server using datagram sockets.

```
#include <sys/socket.h>
#include <arpa/inet.h>
#include <stdio.h>
#include <time.h>
#include <unistd.h>

#define MAX_BUFFER          128
#define DAYTIME_SERVER_PORT        45000

int main ( void )
{
  int serverFd, fromlen, msglen;
  struct sockaddr_in servaddr, from;
  char timebuffer[MAX_BUFFER+1];
  time_t currentTime;

  serverFd = socket(AF_INET, SOCK_DGRAM, 0);

  memset(&servaddr, 0, sizeof(servaddr));
  servaddr.sin_family = AF_INET;
  servaddr.sin_addr.s_addr = htonl(INADDR_ANY);
  servaddr.sin_port = htons(DAYTIME_SERVER_PORT);

  bind(serverFd, (struct sockaddr *)&servaddr, sizeof(servaddr));

  while ( 1 ) {

    fromlen = sizeof(from);
    msglen = recvfrom(serverFd, &timebuffer,
                      MAX_BUFFER, 0, &from, &fromlen);

    if (msglen >= 0) {

      currentTime = time(NULL);
      snprintf(timebuffer, MAX_BUFFER, "%s\n", ctime(&currentTime));

      sendto(serverFd, timebuffer, strlen(timebuffer), 0,
             (struct sockaddr *)&from, fromlen);

    }
```

```
    }

}
```

The notable characteristics of the datagram server are first that the socket is created with type `SOCK_DGRAM` (a datagram socket). We bind the address and port as we did with the stream server which in effect advertises the socket as available for connection at this host. Key differences from the stream server are the lack of a listen and accept call. These calls are specific to setting up a connection-oriented socket, in which the datagram connection is not statically tied to the two endpoints (may be changed without closing the socket).. For this reason, the datagram server must know from whom a datagram came in order to reply to it. This information is collected through the `recvfrom` call within the `from` argument.

LISTING A.4 Daytime client using datagram sockets.

```
#include <sys/socket.h>
#include <arpa/inet.h>
#include <stdio.h>
#include <unistd.h>
#include <time.h>

#define MAX_BUFFER          128
#define DAYTIME_SERVER_PORT     45000

int main ( int argc, char *argv[] )
{
  int connectionFd, in;
  struct sockaddr_in servaddr;
  char timebuffer[MAX_BUFFER+1];

  if (argc != 2) {
    return(0);
  }

  connectionFd = socket(AF_INET, SOCK_DGRAM, 0);

  memset(&servaddr, 0, sizeof(servaddr));
  servaddr.sin_family = AF_INET;
  servaddr.sin_port = htons(DAYTIME_SERVER_PORT);

  inet_pton(AF_INET, argv[1], &servaddr.sin_addr);
```

```
    sendto( connectionFd, timebuffer, 1, 0,
            (struct sockaddr_in *)&servaddr, sizeof(servaddr) );

    in = recv(connectionFd, timebuffer, MAX_BUFFER, 0 );
    timebuffer[in] = 0;

    printf("\n%s", timebuffer);

    close(connectionFd);

    return(0);
}
```

The datagram client is shown in Listing A.4. The key difference is again due to the unconnected nature of this method (i.e., no `connect` exists). Once the datagram client creates the `sockaddr_in` structure to identify the peer (to whom it will speak), datagrams are sent using the `sendto` call. Note that the `recv` call includes no naming information. This is because our socket is bound with an ephemeral (dynamic) port. Although we can't see this (but we could using the `getsockname` call on our socket), the information is used as the source of the datagram by the `sendto` call. When the server receives the datagram, it uses the source information provided by the `recvfrom` call for the reply. When the datagram arrives back at our host, the protocol stack takes care of identifying on which socket the datagram should be delivered. This mapping is performed using the local address/port number and remote address/port number.

It should be clear from this discussion that datagram sockets (particularly unconnected datagram sockets) are very similar to simple message passing. In fact, some message-passing systems utilize the UDP layer as their transport system.

Connected Datagram Server and Client

The connected datagram implementation has similarities to the stream version and the unconnected version of our daytime example. The similarities to the stream implementation are that the client utilizes the `send` call instead of the `sendto`. This is because the client has performed a `connect` call (as the stream server would) which causes the socket layer to associate this socket with the peer defined by `connect`. The connected datagram implementation shares the disadvantages with the unconnected datagram implementation (packet loss, out of order, etc.). Therefore, the similarities of the connected datagram client with the stream client are cosmetic and superficial. See Listing A.5 for the connected datagram client source listing.

The connected datagram client can re-associate its peer at any time by calling `connect` again. It can also use the `sendto` call to specify a different peer than the one provided through `connect`.

LISTING A.5 Daytime client using datagram sockets.

```
#include <sys/socket.h>
#include <arpa/inet.h>
#include <stdio.h>
#include <unistd.h>
#include <time.h>

#define MAX_BUFFER          128
#define DAYTIME_SERVER_PORT      45000

int main ( int argc, char *argv[] )
{
  int connectionFd, in;
  struct sockaddr_in servaddr;
  char timebuffer[MAX_BUFFER+1];

  if (argc != 2) {
    return(0);
  }

  connectionFd = socket(AF_INET, SOCK_DGRAM, 0);

  memset(&servaddr, 0, sizeof(servaddr));
  servaddr.sin_family = AF_INET;
  servaddr.sin_port = htons(DAYTIME_SERVER_PORT);

  inet_pton(AF_INET, argv[1], &servaddr.sin_addr);

  connect( connectionFd,
           (struct sockaddr_in *)&servaddr, sizeof(servaddr) );

  send( connectionFd, timebuffer, 1, 0 );

  in = recv(connectionFd, timebuffer, MAX_BUFFER, 0 );
  timebuffer[in] = 0;
```

```
    printf("\n%s", timebuffer);

    close(connectionFd);

    return(0);
}
```

The connected datagram server is identical to the unconnected version and can be seen in Listing A.3.

Multicast Server and Client

The multicast server and client are implemented differently from server/clients that we've seen in prior sections. Multicast allows applications to join a group or channel in which communication is distributed to all members of the group. Multicast is an efficient way for applications to receive notifications or events from more than one other application simultaneously. Writing this type of application using either TCP or UDP sockets would require that each client that desired events from the server would register that desire. In this way, the server could distribute events to all those clients that registered. This commonly is a function of the registration of a notification server. Multicast takes care of this for you and is very efficient since a single packet is multicast onto the network and hosts determine if a user desires receipt of the multicast packets. For TCP or UDP, the server would need to send a message to every peer that had registered. Multicast sockets are datagram since there is no connection establishment between the server and clients. Multicast datagrams are also emitted once from the source, and received by all hosts that belong to the multicast group.

In implementing our daytime server and client for multicast, a few changes are made. Instead of the client requesting the time from the server, the server simply emits the time at 10 second intervals to the multicast group. Multicast clients simply join the group and receive the updates as the server emits them.

The server, shown in Listing A.6, appears very similar to the unconnected datagram server. The server directs all packets to the multicast group and port that are preconfigured for this particular application. Within the infinite loop, the multicast server emits the time message to the group to whomever is currently listening.

LISTING A.6 Daytime server using multicast sockets.

```
#include <stdio.h>
#include <sys/socket.h>
```

```
#include <arpa/inet.h>
#include <unistd.h>
#include <time.h>

#define MCAST_GROUP       "239.0.0.2"
#define MCAST_PORT 45002

int main ()
{
  int    sock, cnt, addrLen;
  struct sockaddr_in addr;
  char   buffer[512];

  sock = socket(AF_INET, SOCK_DGRAM, 0);

  memset(&addr, 0, sizeof(addr));
  addr.sin_family = AF_INET;
  addr.sin_port = htons(MCAST_PORT);
  addr.sin_addr.s_addr = inet_addr(MCAST_GROUP);
  addrLen = sizeof(addr);

  while (1) {

    time_t t = time(0);

    sprintf(buffer, "%s\n", ctime(&t));

    printf("sending %s", buffer);

    cnt = sendto(sock, buffer, strlen(buffer), 0,
                 (struct sockaddr *)&addr, addrLen);

    printf("cnt = %d\n", cnt);

    sleep(10);

  }

}
```

The multicast client differs in a number of ways. The server is identified as multicast only because it directs its packets to a multicast group. The client must join the multicast group in order to receive the packets. The `bind` call is used to bind us to our multicast group port number. Next, we join the multicast group with the socket option IP_ADD_MEMBERSHIP. This option takes our socket descriptor (sock) and adds this to the multicast group identified by our ip_mreq structure. This structure has been initialized with our multicast group address that identifies which particular group we wish to join. From this point on, our code looks very much like a datagram client. We use recvfrom to enable us to display the actual IP address of the server generating the time messages.

LISTING A.7 Daytime client using multicast sockets.

```
#include <stdio.h>
#include <sys/socket.h>
#include <arpa/inet.h>
#include <unistd.h>

#define MCAST_GROUP        "239.0.0.2"
#define MCAST_PORT 45002

int main ()
{
  int     sock, cnt, addrlen;
  int     on=1;
  struct sockaddr_in addr;
  struct ip_mreq mreq;
  char    buffer[512];

  sock = socket(AF_INET, SOCK_DGRAM, 0);

  setsockopt(sock, SOL_SOCKET, SO_REUSEADDR, (char *)&on,
              sizeof(on));

  memset(&addr, 0, sizeof(addr));
  addr.sin_family = AF_INET;
  addr.sin_port = htons(MCAST_PORT);
  addr.sin_addr.s_addr = htonl(INADDR_ANY);

  bind(sock, (struct sockaddr *)&addr, sizeof(addr));

  mreq.imr_multiaddr.s_addr = inet_addr(MCAST_GROUP);
  mreq.imr_interface.s_addr = htonl(INADDR_ANY);
  setsockopt(sock, IPPROTO_IP, IP_ADD_MEMBERSHIP, &mreq,
              sizeof(mreq));

  while (1) {
```

```
    addrlen = sizeof(addr);

    cnt = recvfrom(sock, buffer, sizeof(buffer), 0,
                   (struct sockaddr *)&addr, &addrlen);

    buffer[cnt] = 0;

    printf("%s : %s\n", inet_ntoa(addr.sin_addr), buffer);

  }

}
```

One other difference worth noting is the first setsockopt call. The SO_REUSEADDR socket option allows more than one application to bind to a particular port number (in this case our multicast group port number). In normal cases, only one application may bind to a particular port number. In this special case, a host may have more than one application that desires access to the multicast group and therefore the socket option is used. Had this option not been used, subsequent bind calls after the first would have resulted in an error (commonly "address in use").

Broadcast Server and Client

Broadcast, as the name suggests, means sending a packet on the network for which all hosts comprise the destination. Broadcast isn't a very effective use of network bandwidth, but it is a good tool when either the device is unconfigured (i.e., has no IP address) or for communicating with unknown devices on the network. Recall from Chapter 1 that DHCP (Dynamic Host Configuration Protocol), which is used to dynamically obtain an IP address, uses broadcast datagrams to communicate with a DHCP server. Since the client device does not have an IP address, and doesn't know the IP address of the DHCP server, broadcast packets make the communication possible.

The daytime server follows our multicast server in that the server simply cmits the time on a regular basis (every 10 seconds). The client creates a broadcast socket and listens for the packets. When a packet is received, the time encoded within the packet is displayed.

One key differentiator to the server is enabling broadcast for the socket which is performed through the setsockopt call (see Listing A.8). Another is the choice of broadcast address. In this example we use the "limited" broadcast address (255.255.255.255). There are actually four types, but this particular type of broadcast address is sometimes the only one understood, especially by older systems.

LISTING A.8 Daytime server using broadcast sockets.

```
#include <stdio.h>
#include <sys/socket.h>
#include <arpa/inet.h>
#include <unistd.h>
#include <time.h>

#define BCAST_PORT 45003

int main ()
{
  int    sock, cnt, addrLen, on=1;
  struct sockaddr_in addr;
  char   buffer[512];

  sock = socket(AF_INET, SOCK_DGRAM, 0);

  setsockopt(sock, SOL_SOCKET, SO_BROADCAST, &on, sizeof(on));

  memset(&addr, 0, sizeof(addr));
  addr.sin_family = AF_INET;
  addr.sin_port = htons(BCAST_PORT);
  addr.sin_addr.s_addr = inet_addr("255.255.255.255");
  addrLen = sizeof(addr);

  while (1) {
    time_t t = time(0);

    sprintf(buffer, "%s\n", ctime(&t));

    printf("sending %s", buffer);

    cnt = sendto(sock, buffer, strlen(buffer), 0,
                 (struct sockaddr *)&addr, addrLen);

    printf("cnt = %d\n", cnt);

    sleep(10);
```

```
    }

}
```

The broadcast client must set its socket to broadcast (using `setsockopt`) but also specify that the port may be used by multiple applications (via `SO_REUSEADDR`). We bind the client's socket to our previously agreed upon broadcast port (`BCAST_PORT`) and then use `recvfrom` to capture the packets for display. See Listing A.9 for the broadcast client.

LISTING A.9 Daytime client using broadcast sockets.

```
#include <stdio.h>
#include <sys/socket.h>
#include <arpa/inet.h>
#include <unistd.h>

#define BCAST_PORT 45003

int main ()
{
  int    sock, cnt, addrlen, on=1;
  struct sockaddr_in addr;
  char   buffer[512];

  sock = socket(AF_INET, SOCK_DGRAM, 0);

  setsockopt(sock, SOL_SOCKET, SO_REUSEADDR, (char *)&on,
             sizeof(on));

  setsockopt(sock, SOL_SOCKET, SO_BROADCAST, (char *)&on,
             sizeof(on));

  memset(&addr, 0, sizeof(addr));
  addr.sin_family = AF_INET;
  addr.sin_port = htons(BCAST_PORT);
  addr.sin_addr.s_addr = htonl(INADDR_ANY);

  bind(sock, (struct sockaddr *)&addr, sizeof(addr));

  while (1) {

    addrlen = sizeof(addr);
```

```
    cnt = recvfrom(sock, buffer, sizeof(buffer), 0,
                   (struct sockaddr *)&addr, &addrlen);
    buffer[cnt] = 0;

    printf("%s : %s\n", inet_ntoa(addr.sin_addr), buffer);

  }

}
```

APPENDIX

B BSD Sockets API Options

INTRODUCTION

This appendix discusses some of the more interesting socket options that are available in the BSD sockets API. These options can be set using the `setsockopt` call and retrieved using the `getsockopt` call. Some others are available via different APIs (such as setting the blocking behavior of a socket, which is commonly available through the `fcntl` API function).

The API elements for dealing with socket options are defined in Listing B.1.

LISTING B.1 Socket options API functions.

```
#include <sys/types.h>
#include <sys/socket.h>

int setsockopt( int          sock,
                int          level,
                int          optname,
                const void *optvalue,
                socklen_t   optlen );

int getsockopt( int         sock,
                int         level,
                int         optname,
                void        *optvalue,
                socklen_t *optlen );
```

sock is the socket that is being manipulated (value created from the call to the socket function). The level parameter is the stack layer that the option is to address. The available level options are listed in Table B.1. The optname parameter is the option name and is dependent upon the level parameter provided (the option name must be valid for the particular level specified). The optvalue parameter is used as the value to set the parameter in the stack, or to retrieve it. This may be a variety of different types (dependent upon the particular parameter in question). Therefore, the type used to specify it is a void *. Finally, optlen is used to specify the size of the option value. In the set call, the application defines the size of the option value, in the get case, the application receives the size.

TABLE B.1 Available Options for the level parameter.

Level Option	*Stack Layer*
SOL_SOCKET	Sockets layer
IPPROTO_TCP	TCP
IPPROTO_IP	IP

Some implementations may choose different names for these standard elements (such as Winsock), therefore where details differ, refer to the particular API reference. The following discussion will be precise for target APIs that follow the BSD standard.

The functions to be discussed are listed in Table B.2.

TABLE B.2 Sample socket options.

Socket Option	*Layer*	*Description*
IP_TOS	Network	Manipulate the Type-Of-Service field
IP_TTL	Network	Manipulate the Time-To-Live field
IP_HDRINCL	Network	Permit IP header construction
TCP_NODELAY	Transport	Enable/Disable the Nagle Algorithm
TCP_MAXRT	Transport	Manipulate the TCP maximum retransmit time
TCP_MAXSEG	Transport	Manipulate the TCP Maximum Segment Size

(Continues)

TABLE B.2 Sample socket options (*continued*).

Socket Option	*Layer*	*Description*
SO_RCVBUF	Socket	Change the size of the receive socket buffer
SO_SNDBUF	Socket	Change the size of the transmit socket buffer
SO_RCVLOWAT	Socket	Change the low-water mark for socket buffer receipt
SO_SNDLOWAT	Socket	Change the low-water mark for socket buffer send
SO_BROADCAST	Socket	Change the socket to allow broadcast datagram
SO_LINGER	Socket	Change socket shutdown behavior
SO_REUSEADDR	Socket	Change address reuse behavior for a given address/port
SO_DONTROUTE	Socket	Ignore routing table for datagram transmission
SO_KEEPALIVE	Socket	Change the behavior for socket connection testing

NETWORK LAYER OPTIONS

The following options address the network layer:

IP_TOS (IPPROTO_IP)

```
#include <sys/socket.h>
#include <netinet/ip.h>
```

Summary

The `IP_TOS` option is used to manipulate the `Type-Of-Service` field that appears in the IP header. This is also called the `precedence` field and its original intention was to use this field as a quality-of-service designator. A user application could request a minimization of delay, maximization of throughput, maximization of reliability or minimization of cost.

This operation is performed either on a TCP or on UDP socket.

Example Usage

In this example, using Linux, we'll specify that our quality constraint is minimal cost.

```
int tosData, ret;

tosData = IPTOS_MINCOST;
```

```
ret = setsockopt( sock, IPPROTO_IP, IP_TOS,
                  (void *)&tosData, sizeof(tosData) );
```

The default `IP_TOS` field can also be retrieved from the stack using the `getsockopt` call.

Special Notes

It's important to note that this field is ignored within routers and on the Internet (WAN). For LAN connections, where one can actually control quality-of-service constraints, this field can be used.

IP_TTL (IPPROTO_IP)

```
#include <sys/socket.h>
#include <netinet/in.h>
```

Summary

The `IP_TTL` option is used to manipulate the `Time-To-Live` field that appears within the IP header. This field is a counter that is decremented each time the datagram flows through a router. If the field reaches zero, it is dropped. A user application may define the TTL for a given socket up to 255, although most stacks use default of 64 (reference RFC 1340).

Example Usage

In this example, we'll set our TTL to two. This represents a datagram that can pass through only one router before it is dropped (a TTL of one means that it won't leave our subnet).

```
int myTTL, ret;

myTTL = 2;

ret = setsockopt( sock, IPPROTO_IP, IP_TTL,
                  (void *)&myTTL, sizeof(myTTL) );
```

Special Notes

Another option called `IP_MULTICAST_TTL` is used to set the TTL value for outgoing multicast sockets. The only difference between this option and the `IP_TTL` option is that `IP_TTL` takes in an integer argument (as illustrated above with `myTTL`) and `IP_MULTICAST_TTL` uses an unsigned character argument.

IP_HDRINCL (IPPROTO_IP)

```
#include <sys/socket.h>
#include <netinet/in.h>
```

Summary

The IP_HDRINCL option is used to inform the stack that the user will provide the IP header for datagrams emitted on the socket for which the option was defined. This means that instead of simply emitting data to be transported through the socket, the user must precede the data with the IP header information.

Example Usage

The following example assumes the creation of a SOCK_RAW socket.

```
int sock, option=1;

sock = socket( AF_INET, SOCK_RAW, IPPROTO_IP );

...

ret= setsockopt( sock, IPPROTO_IP, IP_HDRINCL,
                 (void *)&option, sizeof(option) );
```

Special Notes

This option can be useful in the construction of raw IP packets. Structures are provided by the stack for IP headers that can be used to simplify the construction of the included header.

Some fields in the IP header are set by the stack and will therefore be overwritten by values provided by the user. For example, the IP header checksum is automatically computed and loaded by the stack. Others may exist and the stack vendor's documentation should be consulted.

TRANSPORT LAYER OPTIONS

The following options address the transport layer:

TCP_NODELAY (IPPROTO_TCP)

```
#include <sys/socket.h>
#include <netinet/in.h>
```

Summary

The TCP_NODELAY option is used to control the function of the Nagle algorithm (see RFC 896). The Nagle algorithm attempts to reduce the number of small packets (so called "tinygrams") that are emitted onto the network. What is at stake is pure performance.

Example Usage

In this example, we'll disable the Nagle algorithm (commonly it's enabled by default).

```
int option=0;

...

ret = setsockopt( sock, IPPROTO_TCP, TCP_NODELAY,
                  (void *)&option, sizeof(option) );
```

Special Notes

The Nagle algorithm provides a useful service within the stack and should therefore not be disabled without some careful consideration. Applications that commonly disable Nagle are those that have some user interaction (such as telnet clients).

TCP_MAXSEG (IPPROTO_TCP)

```
#include <sys/socket.h>
#include <netinet/in.h>
```

Summary

The TCP_MAXSEG option is used to manipulate the Maximum Segment Size, or MSS. This is the maximum amount of data that TCP will send to the peer in a single datagram. Typically, this is the MTU minus 40 bytes.

The user application may retrieve the current MSS value using the getsockopt function.

Example Usage

The following code example illustrates how to retrieve the current MSS value. This value can change over time and therefore it should never be assumed static.

```
int mss;
```

```
    ...

    ret = getsockopt( sock, IPPROTO_TCP, TCP_MAXSEG,
                      (void *)&mss, sizeof(mss) );
```

Special Notes

Since increasing the MSS has the effect of forcing IP fragmentation (since the provided data may no longer fit into a single MTU sized datagram), increasing the MSS is typically not permitted. The user may decrease the MSS for performance reasons if the network prefers smaller packets. Most TCP/IP stacks will automatically determine the MSS from the peer's SYN packet and MTU path discovery clamps this value. Therefore, user attempts to manipulate this value may be superceded by stack discovery mechanisms.

SOCKET LAYER OPTIONS

The following options address the BSD Sockets API layer:

SO_RCVBUF, SO_SNDBUF (SOL_SOCKET)

```
#include <sys/socket.h>
#include <netinet/in.h>
```

Summary

These options refer to the size of the socket receive buffer and send buffer. The receive buffer is used to hold incoming data from a particular socket and the send buffer is used to hold data that is to be transmitted.

These values are used by the underlying transport layer in its flow-control mechanism. The receive buffer size is used as the advertised windows (how much data the peer can accept for the socket before transmission must stop and await clearance to proceed).

Most stack implementations default the sizes of the socket buffers to 8192 bytes. Depending upon the link used, these can be altered to improve performance or resource management on the embedded device. We can identify the optimal sizes of the buffers using the bandwidth-delay product. We first find the RTT (round trip time) of the link, which can be determined with the ping command or estimated, based upon prior measurements. We multiply this value by the available bandwidth of the link and then divide by 8 to get back to bytes. Our receive buffer should be at least this size and the send buffer at least twice this size (for retransmits).

Let's take an example of a slow wireless network in which the ping times average 95 ms. The bandwidth of the link is a slow 19.2 Kbps.

$$((60 / 1000) * 19200) / 8$$

We find that our bandwidth delay product is 228 bytes. This value is far less than the default 8192 bytes that are allocated for each of the buffers. The buffer should be a multiple of the MSS with a minimum of 3 times that value.

As an example of a faster link, let's assume our embedded device sits on an Ethernet network where the full bandwidth of the link is available to it. The ping times on this network are 25 ms (which includes not only network communication time, but the time it takes the stacks to process the packets). The bandwidth of the Ethernet network is 10 Mbps. This yields:

$$((25 / 1000) * 10000000) / 8$$

which is a bandwidth delay product of 31,250 bytes. This is greater than the default buffer sizes so performance can be increased by updating the buffer sizes accordingly.

The user application may also view the default buffer sizes using the `getsockopt` function.

Example Usage

The following code illustrates setting the socket buffer sizes per our last example.

```
int bufsize;

...

bufsize = 32 * 1024;
ret = setsockopt( sock, SOL_SOCKET, SO_RCVBUF,
                  (void *)&bufsize, sizeof(bufsize) );

bufsize = 64 * 1024;
ret = setsockopt( sock, SOL_SOCKET, SO_SNDBUF,
                  (void *)&bufsize, sizeof(bufsize) );
```

Special Notes

Manipulation of the socket buffer sizes is one of the easiest ways to improve performance of a socket. Sizing the buffers too small can also have disastrous effects on system operation. For example, if the socket buffer is set to a value smaller than an incoming UDP datagram, the datagram is simply dropped. In this case the socket will never be able to receive the data. Therefore, as with any other option, great care and consideration should applied to its use.

SO_RCVLOWAT, SO_SNDLOWAT (SOL_SOCKET)

```
#include <sys/socket.h>
#include <netinet/in.h>
```

Summary

These options change the behavior of the `select` API function. Low-water marks are thresholds to specify when an event should occur. The `SO_RCVLOWAT` option specifies the low-water mark for the receive buffer. This is the minimum number of octets that must be present in the receive buffer before `select` will notify the user application that receive data is available. The `SO_SNDLOWAT` option specifies the low-water mark for the send buffer. This is the minimum amount of space that must be available in the send buffer before `select` will notify the user application that room is available for writing data. These options change the behavior when applications receive notification that data has arrived.

The `SO_RCVLOWAT` option defaults to `1`, thus forcing notification of the user application when a single octet is available. If the user is awaiting a block of data, notifying the user application on every byte can be very wasteful. Therefore, the application can specify the minimum size to optimize for performance.

`SO_SNDLOWAT` typically defaults to 2048, which is a reasonable value depending upon the size of the send buffer itself. If the user has a maximum buffer size that is emitted, this can be set as the `SO_SNDLOWAT` water mark to ensure that when space is available for an output packet, the packet is written to the transport layer.

The default low-water marks can also be retrieved using the `getsockopt` function.

Example Usage

In the following example, we'll specify our receive low-water mark (the minimum size packet that we'll receive) as 20 bytes and a send low-water mark of 1024 bytes:

```
int watermark;
...

watermark = 20;
ret = setsockopt( sock, SOL_SOCKET, SO_RCVLOWAT,
                  (void *)&watermark, sizeof(watermark) );

watermark = 1024;
ret = setsockopt( sock, SOL_SOCKET, SO_SNDLOWAT,
                  (void *)&watermark, sizeof(watermark) );
```

Special Notes

For applications that use the `select` API function, configuration of these low-water marks can have a significant impact on overall performance. In systems in which the switching time between kernel and user-level applications is high, these options can minimize this thrashing and work on buffer sizes that are relevant to the application instead of system-defined defaults.

SO_BROADCAST (SOL_SOCKET)

```
#include <sys/socket.h>
#include <netinet/in.h>
```

Summary

The `SO_BROADCAST` option allows a datagram socket to send broadcast packets. This option does not work on TCP sockets because TCP is connection based and provides no means to specify destinations on a datagram-by-datagram basis.

This option defaults to off and the current state of `SO_BROADCAST` can be retrieved via `getsockopt`.

Example Usage

In this example, a socket is configured to support broadcast output packets:

```
int state;

...

state = 1;
ret = setsockopt( sock, SOL_SOCKET, SO_BROADCAST,
                  (void *)&state, sizeof(state) );
```

Special Notes

This option is useful only on network interfaces that support broadcast packets. This includes Ethernet networks and excludes point-to-point networks such those provided by wireless networks (via PPP or SLIP).

SO_LINGER (SOL_SOCKET)

```
#include <sys/socket.h>
#include <netinet/in.h>
```

Summary

The SO_LINGER option specifies how a socket is closed for a connection-based socket. Without SO_LINGER, when a socket is closed, the stack will continue to try to deliver any unsent data (in the socket send buffer) to the peer. The SO_LINGER option allows us to change this behavior in a number of ways.

The following structure is used to communicate the SO_LINGERoptions to the stack:

```
struct linger {
  int  l_onoff;
  int  l_linger;
};
```

The l_onoff field is used to enable or disable the SO_LINGER option (1 is enable, 0 is disable).

The l_linger field is used to define the new SO_LINGER behavior. If l_linger is set to 0, the socket is closed immediately, discarding any data in the send and receiver buffers. If l_linger is non-zero, the value is used as a timeout (in seconds) and the socket will remain alive for the timeout period trying to send any remaining data. If the remaining data is sent within the timeout period, the socket is then closed. If the timeout expires, the data is discarded and the socket closed.

The application may identify the default (or whatever value it has defined for SO_LINGER) via the getsockopt function.

Example Usage

In this example, the socket in question is defined to SO_LINGER on close for 60 seconds.

```
struct linger lingvar;

...

lingvar.l_onoff = 1;
lingvar.l_linger = 60;

ret = setsockopt( sock, SOL_SOCKET, SO_LINGER,
                  (void *)&lingvar, sizeof(struct linger) );
```

Special Notes

The SO_LINGER option can interfere with the TCP state machine's natural socket expiration mechanism and should therefore be used with care. Instead of flowing through the TCP state machine for a normal socket close, the SO_LINGER option forces the close by sending an RST packet to the peer. A normal close involves four packet transactions and therefore the prior method leaves a peer in an odd state.

SO_REUSEADDR (SOL_SOCKET)

```
#include <sys/socket.h>
#include <netinet/in.h>
```

Summary

The SO_REUSEADDR option allows us to bind to a port that may have existing connections on it. A classic example of this option is starting a server socket application on a host. If the server crashes or exits and then tries to restart within two minutes, when binding is attempted, an error will be returned indicating "address already in use." By using the SO_REUSEADDR option, a server can bind to the address regardless of the state of the port.

Stevens (*Unix Network Programming, Volume 1*) provides another interesting example. In some cases, devices with multiple interfaces desire multiple servers that attach to each interface separately. For example, an HTTP server is available for the outside world on the WAN interface, and another on the internal interface for the LAN. When an HTTP server is started, it uses the SO_REUSEADDR option on the socket and then binds to one of the interfaces with port 80. The next server then uses SO_REUSEADDR and then binds to the other interface with port 80. This is legal because of the use of SO_REUSEADDR; without it the second server attempting to bind with the port would cause an error.

All servers must use the SO_REUSEADDR option. If one fails to use it, then subsequent binds will fail.

The option can also be used with getsockopt to identify the option state for a given socket.

Example Usage

In this example, we enable the option on our socket:

```
int state;

...

state = 1;
ret = setsockopt( sock, SOL_SOCKET, SO_REUSEADDR,
                  (void *)&state, sizeof(state) );
```

Special Notes

This option is also useful for multicast sockets that must bind to a given port to receive multicast datagrams.

SO_KEEPALIVE (SOL_SOCKET)

```
#include <sys/socket.h>
#include <netinet/in.h>
```

Summary

The SO_KEEPALIVE option is used to try to keep a socket connection (connection-based socket) up over long periods of time. Normally, when there is no data transmission on a TCP socket, there is no packet dialog either. This means that during periods of no data transmission, the peer could disappear and the socket would be declared dead only after data is attempted to be sent.

The solution to this problem is to enable SO_KEEPALIVE on the socket to routinely probe the peer to ensure it's still there. A probe will either result in an ACK being returned from the peer (it's alive), no response (host is gone?) or an RST packet indicating that the peer has closed its end of the socket.

Example Usage

In this example, we'll enable so_keepalive for our socket:

```
int state;

...

state = 1;
ret = setsockopt( sock, SOL_SOCKET, SO_KEEPALIVE,
                  (void *)&state, sizeof(state) );
```

Special Notes

so_keepalive performs the probe every two hours. Since this is a long period, some stack implementations provide another option called tcp_keepalive that permits the specification of the probe time.

SO_ERROR (SOL_SOCKET)

```
#include <sys/socket.h>
#include <netinet/in.h>
```

Summary

The SO_ERROR option is used to retrieve an error condition from the stack for a particular socket. An error is indicated when any of the socket API functions return an error (commonly a -1 value). In Unix systems, the errno variable can be used to retrieve any error condition. But since socket errors must be available regardless of the operating system in use (if any), some other means is necessary.

Example Usage

The following example illustrates the capturing of the current error value:

```
int errval;

...

ret = getsockopt( sock, SOL_SOCKET, SO_ERROR,
                  (void *)&errval, sizeof(errval) );

/* errval now contains any error value */
```

Special Notes

Since capturing error values is important to any application, all TCP/IP stacks provide some mechanism by which this is possible. Refer to your TCP/IP stack's documentation for the proper method.

IP_ADD_MEMBERSHIP / IP_DROP_MEMBERSHIP (IP_PROTOIP)

```
#include <sys/socket.h>
#include <netinet/in.h>
```

Summary

The IP_ADD_MEMBERSHIP and IP_DROP_MEMBERSHIP options are used to join and leave a multicast group as specified by the arguments in the ip_mreq structure. The IP_ADD_MEMBERSHIP option allows an application to join a particular multicast group for the purposes of receiving traffic that is being multicast to that group. Note that this option is not necessary to send traffic to the multicast group, only to receive it. The IP_DROP_MEMBERSHIP option is used to remove an application from receiving multicast traffic.

Each of the options uses the ip_mreq structure to specify the interface to be used to receive and transmit multicast datagrams and the multicast group to join/drop. The ip_mreq structure is shown here:

```
struct ip_mreq {
        struct in_addr imr_multiaddr;
        struct in_addr imr_interface;
};
```

The element imr_multiaddr specifies the class D multicast address and the imr_interface specifies the particular interface on the node that is to be used when communicating with this group. The symbol inaddr_any may be specified to encompass any available interface.

Example Usage

The following example illustrates joining and then dropping the RIP2 Routers multicast group:

```
struct ip_mreq mreq;

...

bzero( (void *)&mreq, sizeof(mreq) );
```

```
mreq.imr_multiaddr.s_addr = inet_addr( "224.0.0.9" );
mreq.imr_interface.s_addr = htonl( INADDR_ANY );

ret = setsockopt( sock, IP_PROTOIP, IP_ADD_MEMBERSHIP,
                  (char *)&mreq, sizeof(mreq) );

...

ret = setsockopt( sock, IP_PROTOIP, IP_DROP_MEMBERSHIP,
                  (char *)&mreq, sizeof(mreq) );
```

Special Notes

An application may join multiple multicast groups on a single socket as long as the multicast address differs from the prior addition. In some cases, the `IP_DROP_MEMBERSHIP` is rarely used. When the socket is closed, the membership is dropped automatically by the stack. Since stack implementations may differ, `IP_DROP_MEMBERSHIP` should always be performed.

RESOURCES

Reynolds and Postel, "Assigned Numbers," RFC 1340, July 1992. http://www.landfield.org/rfcs/rfc1340.html

Nagle, "Congestion Control in IP/TCP Internetworks," RFC 896, January 1984. http://www.landfield.org/rfcs/rfc896.html

Stevens, W. Richard, *Unix Network Programming: Volume 1*, Prentice Hall, 1998.

"Internet Multicast Addresses," IANA, February 2002. http://www.iana.org/assignments/multicast-addresses

APPENDIX

C TCP/IP Protocol Stacks

In this appendix, we'll look at a number of TCP/IP Stack implementations that target integration into embedded devices. We'll look at commercial implementations as well as those available in the open source domain and academic designs.

COMMERCIAL IMPLEMENTATIONS

The implementations discussed in this section are those that are not tied to any particular Real Time Operating System (RTOS). For example, Wind River and QNX Software Systems Limited (QSSL) include TCP/IP stacks which are efficient, but tied to their parent RTOS. The following stacks are portable to numerous computer architectures and may be integrated into a variety of operating system/kernels.

Many embedded devices need access only to the UDP transport protocol. This provides support for SNMP, name resolution through DNS, and other non-TCP related protocols. UDP/IP stacks are also much simpler and therefore require fewer resources and computational expense of the host processor.

EmStack—GlobespanVirata

EmStack is a small footprint TCP/IP stack designed for embedded devices. It scales down to 30 KB of ROM but includes more advanced features such as Slow Start, Congestion Avoidance, Fast Retransmit, and Fast Recovery algorithms. EmStack requires no target operating system and provides zero-copy mechanisms for high throughput.

Licensing

See the GlobespanVirata Web site for licensing details.
URL http://www.agranat.com/emweb/solutions/options.html#Stack

FlatStack

FlatStack is a specialized hardware/software device that was designed specifically for deeply embedded devices that typically include no network connectivity. The FlatStack integrates with the embedded system to provide Ethernet or Serial-based connectivity to the Internet.

Licensing

See the FlatStack Web site for licensing details.

URL

http://www.flatstack.com/whatisfs.htm

Fusion–Netsilicon

The Fusion TCP/IP stack is designed for embedded systems (both microprocessors and DSPs). It includes the standard suite of protocols as well as a BSD sockets API. The stack can run without an RTOS and includes runtime configuration to dynamically alter the behavior of the stack. Netsilicon also offers a variety of other protocols for routing, management, and other application layer protocols.

Licensing

The Fusion TCP/IP stack is sold with a royalty-free license.

URL

http://www.netsilicon.com/SftwrksWeb/InternetProtocol/fusion_tcp_ip.asp

KwikNet TCP/IP Stack–Kadak Products Ltd

KwikNet is a small TCP/IP stack focused on embedded Internet-enabled devices. It's compact (code footprint and RAM), reentrant, and can be ROMed. KwikNet includes a configuration builder (for Windows) that can be used to configure the stack for your particular application.

Licensing

Kwiknet protocols include a royalty-free license for source code.

URL

http://www.kadak.com/html/kdkp1030.htm

Mentat TCP—Mentat Inc.

The Mentat TCP stack, although appropriate for embedded systems, requires Mentat Streams or another SVR4-compatible STREAMS infrastructure. Mentat TCP is a fully functional TCP/IP stack and includes other necessary protocols such as ICMP and IGMP.

Licensing

Mentat TCP source code can be purchased. See the Mentat TCP Web site for more details.

URL

http://www.mentat.com/tcp/tcpdata.html

MicroNet—CMX Micro

The MicroNet TCP/IP stack was designed for embedded systems over a wide range of processor architectures (8 and 16 bit). It includes the standard TCP/IP protocol suite along with SLIP, DHCP, FTP and other application layer protocols. MicroNet is written in pure C for portability.

Licensing

Full source code can be purchased for a one-time fee with no royalties.

URL

http://www.cmx.com/micronet.htm

NexGenIP—NexGen Software

NexGenIP is an operating-system independent TCP/IP stack implementation designed for embedded devices (no CPU/OS dependencies). It's written in ANSI C and optimized for minimal footprint (< 40KB). NexGenIP provides a BSD4.4 socket-like interface and provides other useful protocols such as ICMP, IGMP, ARP, and multicast.

Licensing

NexGenIP includes a royalty-free license and can be purchased in source code or library form.

URL

http://www.nexgen-software.com/Modules/Products/NexGenIP.html

NicheStack—Interniche Technologies Inc.

The NicheStack is a tiny footprint TCP/IP stack that includes a variety of application layer protocols. A full-featured TCP/IP stack including DHCP compiles in under 43KB. It is designed to be portable to a variety of architectures and operating systems and includes a BSD 4.4 sockets interface. Interniche also provides a minimal version of their NicheStack called NicheLite. NicheLite includes a smaller version of the BSD sockets API with support for one interface.

Licensing

See the Interniche Technologies Web site for licensing information.

URL

http://www.iniche.com/products/commp.htm

ROM-DOS—Datalight Inc.

ROM-DOS includes a compact TCP/IP stack designed for the embedded device market. As a separate product, ROM-DOS can be accompanied by Sockets, the ROM-DOS Sockets API.

Licensing

See the DataLight Web site for licensing details.

URL

http://www.datalight.com/

RTIP—EBSnet Inc.

RTIP is a portable TCP/IP stack designed for embedded applications. It includes support for a number of operating systems/kernels and is written in 100% ANSI-C. RTIP can operate with a kernel or with no kernel in a polled mode. A BSD-like socket API is included with proprietary extensions. RTIP provides a simple porting layer where all modification occurs in one set of files (C and H).

Licensing

RTIP is sold with full source code in a royalty license.

URL

http://www.etcbin.com/

Socket Library SDK—Async Systems

The Socket Library SDK is an API for DOS environments (MS-DOS, DR-DOS). It provides a BSD 4.3-compliant sockets interface and includes a TCP/IP stack supporting ODI, Packet, and NDIS drivers. It requires minimal RAM and supports Ethernet, PPP/SLIP, and Token Ringer interfaces.

Licensing

Socket Library SDK with TCP can be purchased as a source code license, or through separate run-time licenses.

URL

http://www.asyncsystems.com/tcpip.htm

TargetTCP—Blunk Microsystems

The TargetTCP TCP/IP stack is a small reentrant stack designed for embedded systems. It is architecture and operating system-independent and includes optimization for RISC processors (at the data link layer). TargetTCP includes a BSD sockets layer with modifications for embedded systems (including time-outs and stack event callbacks).

Licensing

TargetTCP is sold with a royalty-free license and includes all source code.

URL

http://www.blunkmicro.com/tcp.htm

USNet Embedded Protocol Suite—U.S. Software (Lantronix)

USNet is a TCP/IP stack designed for real-time embedded applications. It is architecture- and operating system-independent and can be configured for minimal footprint. On most processors, the footprint is approximately 25KB. USNet is reentrant and can be ROMed.

Licensing

U.S. Software offers a royalty-free license including source code.

URL

http://www.ussw.com/products/usnet/index.html

OPEN-SOURCE IMPLEMENTATIONS

The following TCP/IP Stack implementations are available in the open source domain (which means that the source is available under some kind of licensing agreement). Prior to using any of these, it is wise to read and fully understand the licensing agreement from which it is released. Some limit commercial use of the code while others encourage it.

4.4 BSD TCP/IP Stack

The BSD stacks have historically been the starting points for other commercial stacks. Most proprietary TCP/IP stacks (such as what is found with the Wind-River VxWorks kernel) are derivatives of the BSD stack. This is because BSD offers their stack under the BSD licensing agreement. Their license gives you the ability to incorporate their code, in modified or unmodified form, without having to pay royalties to the creator. Compare this to the GPL license that requires you to open your source up in the GPL if you incorporate GPL sources.

BSD has also been the starting point for many innovations in the TCP/IP protocols (such as congestion control and avoidance in wide area networks).

Licensing

BSD license.

URL

ftp://ftp.FreeBSD.org/pub/FreeBSD/FreeBSD-stable/src/sys/netinet/

eCos TCP/IP Stack

The eCos TCP/IP stack is designed to run with the eCos operating system/kernel. eCos (and the TCP/IP stack) is supported by a number of processor architectures. The eCos TCP/IP stack is currently released as a beta as a separate module.

Licensing

Red Hat eCos public license.

URL

http://sources.redhat.com/ecos/getstart.html

lwIP

The lwIP (Lightweight) TCP/IP stack is a small implementation of the TCP/IP protocol suite (related to uIP). It includes the TCP and UDP transport layers with IP and ICMP. An optional BSD socket API is also provided. For performance, a zero-copy API is included.

The lwIP protocol stack is designed for embedded systems and can fit in under 40KB of ROM and a few hundred bytes of RAM. It is written in C for portability.

Licensing

BSD license.

URL

http://www.sics.se/~adam/lwip/

TinyTcp

The TinyTcp stack is a very small and simple implementation of TCP/IP which includes an FTP client. TinyTcp was designed for burning into ROM and at present appears to be useful initially for big-endian architectures (initial target was the 68000 chip). TinyTcp also includes a simple Ethernet driver for the 3Com multibus card.

Licensing

Public domain.

URL

ftp://ftp.ecs.soton.ac.uk/pub/elks/utils/tiny-tcp.txt

uc/ip

uC/IP (mew-kip) is a TCP/IP protocol stack designed for microcontrollers. The code is based upon the BSD (much like all other stacks) but with feature reduction for very small footprint. It currently builds for Linux and DOS targets.

Licensing

BSD license.

URL

http://ucip.sourceforge.net

uIP

uIP is a very small TCP/IP stack designed specifically for 8- and 16-bit microcontrollers. uIP is written entirely in C and is therefore portable to a wide variety of architectures and operating systems. A compiled stack can run within a few KB, or ROM and a few hundred bytes of RAM. uIP also includes an HTTP server for serving content.

Licensing

BSD license.

URL

http://dunkels.com/adam/uip/

WATTCP

WATTCP is a small TCP/IP stack designed for embedding into DOS-based systems. It includes a version for Real Mode DOS and another for the 32-bit extended environment.

Licensing

Free for non-commercial use.

URL

http://www.wattcp.com/

Xinu

The Xinu TCP/IP stack is an older port within the Xinu operating system distribution. Despite its age, it's a full featured TCP/IP stack with a variety of application layer protocols. The Xinu operating system has been ported to a variety of processing architectures including 68K, Pentium, and Sparc. Xinu also runs on VAX and the PDP-11 (which really shows its age).

Licensing

See source code for licensing details.

URL

ftp://ftp.cs.purdue.edu/pub/Xinu/

SPECIALIZED IMPLEMENTATIONS

The following TCP/IP stack implementations are specialized in terms of language of implementation or target constraints.

GeckOS TCP/IP Stack

The GeckOS TCP/IP Stack was designed for the 6502 microprocessor and runs within the GeckOS operating system. This TCP/IP stack includes TCP, IP, and SLIP layers (for communicating over serial links) as well as ICMP and simple TCP server protocols (echo, discard, and chargen). A telnet server is also provided.

Licensing

GNU public license.

URL

http://www.6502.org/users/andre/osa/index.html

iChip—ConnectOne

The iChip is a fully integrated hardware/software solution to provide Internet connectivity to devices. The iChip is a standalone TCP/IP module that provides connectivity via serial links to the host computer and to the Internet. The iChip also provides a variety of application layer protocols such as SMTP, HTTP, and POP3.

Licensing

See the ConnectOne Web site for licensing details.

URL

http://www.connectone.com/

ipStack–UBICOM

The ipStack is a TCP/IP stack module that runs on the Ubicom IP2022 Internet Processor. Although ipStack was designed to be deeply embedded, it includes a variety of advanced features found only in full-featured stacks (such as routing, multi-homing, round-trip estimation using Karn's algorithm, and zero-copy for performance). Ubicom also provides a variety of other protocols such as SNMP and HTTP.

Licensing

See the Ubicom Web site for further licensing details.

URL

http://www.ubicom.com/software/ipstack.html

KA9Q NOS–Phil Karn

The KA9Q NOS is a network operating system with a TCP/IP stack that operates over Packet Radio. It has a full set of application layer protocols (such as SMTP and FTP) and runs on standard PC hardware using SLIP over a serial link.

Licensing

See the source code for licensing details.

URL

http://people.qualcomm.com/karn/code/ka9qnos/

PowerNet TCP/IP–MicroProcessor Engineering Limited

The PowerNet TCP/IP stack is written in the Forth language for embedded systems. PowerNet is architecture-independent and provides a small memory footprint with good performance using near copy less packet transfers. PowerNet provides a simple high-level API with a choice of transport layers.

Licensing

PowerNet is royalty free and includes full source code.

URL

http://www.mpeltd.demon.co.uk/powernet.htm

SmartStack—eDevice Technology

The SmartStack is a TCP/IP stack designed to add Internet connectivity to non-connected devices. The stack runs on a single DSP and connects via Ethernet. A variety of application layer protocols, such as SMTP and HTTP can also be included.

Licensing

See the eDevice Web site for licensing details.

URL

http://www.edevice.com/content/solution/ethernet.htm

APPENDIX

D Packet Headers

In this appendix, we'll look at the packet formats for some of the major TCP/IP suite member protocols including both network and transport layer protocols. Packet headers to be discussed include IP, ICMP, UDP, and TCP.

INTERNET PROTOCOL (IP)

The Internet Protocol is described in RFC 791. IP is the network layer protocol that is responsible for communicating packets between hosts on the Internet (see Figure D.1).

The `Version` field identifies the version of IP that was used to construct the IP header. IPv4 is the current standard, so this field will be `4`. The `IHL` is the Internet Header Length which defines the size of the IP header in 32-bit words. When parsing IP datagrams, multiplying the `IHL` by four yields the octet offset of the next encapsulated protocol header (TCP or UDP header).

In most cases, the `Type-of-Service (TOS)` field is unused. The intended use of the `TOS` field is to define quality-of-service constraints for the transmission of the datagram through the network. One use of the `TOS` field exists within Differentiated Services where the field is renamed Differentiated Service Code Point (DSCP) and defines the per hop behavior of the datagram. `Total length` is the length of the entire datagram, which includes both the header and the payload.

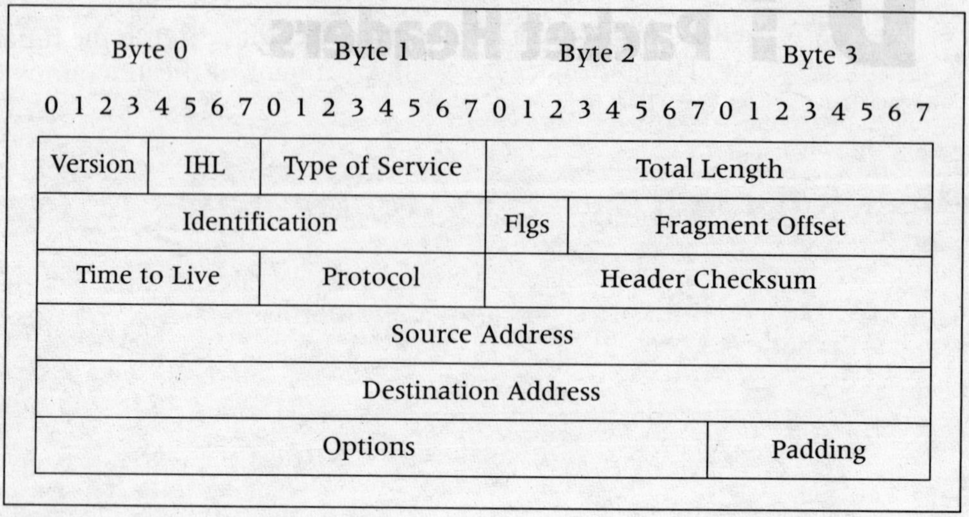

FIGURE D.1 Internet Protocol header.

The `Identification` field is used to uniquely identify each datagram emitted by a host. It is used primarily for datagram fragmentation and reassembly.

The `Flags` field is used for fragmentation. The `Fragment Offset` defines the offset (in 8 octet granularity) where this fragment belongs in the original datagram.

The `Time-To-Live` field indicates the maximum number of hops that the datagram is permitted to live in the Internet. Each time the packet is passed through a router, the TTL field is decremented. If the field reaches zero, the packet is dropped.

The `Protocol` field defines the protocol that is encapsulated within this IP datagram. From a layered stack approach, the field defines which protocol provided the datagram to the IP layer for transmission.

The `Header Checksum` is a simple checksum of the IP datagram header. The checksum is calculated as the 1s complement sum of the 1s complement sumof all 16-bit words in the IP datagram header (given that the initial header checksum is zero).

The `Source Address` is the IP address of the datagram source. The `Destination Address` is the IP address of the datagram destination. These values are 32-bits (four octets) and are in network byte order (big endian). All objects within the IP datagram header greater than 16 bits are in network byte order.

The `Options` field is a variable length object that extends the functionality of the IP datagram header. A full treatment of the IP options can be found in RFC 791.

INTERNET CONTROL MESSAGE PROTOCOL (ICMP)

The Internet Control Message Protocol is described in RFC 792. ICMP is used to communicate errors and other information between hosts on the Internet (see Figure D.2).

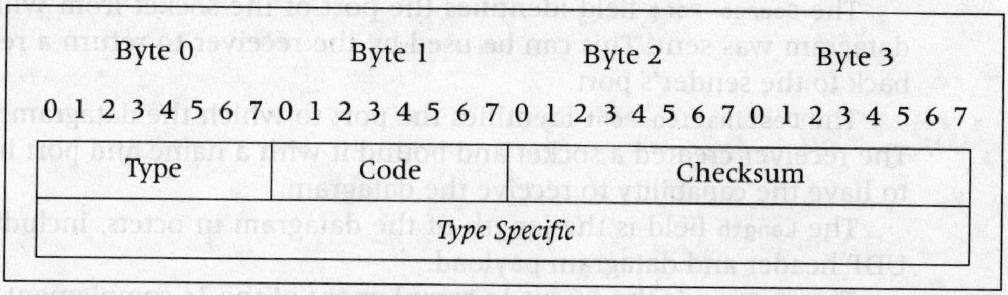

FIGURE D.2 Internet Control Message Protocol header.

The `Type` field identifies the type of the ICMP message. Numerous types exist (referenced in RFC 792). Some of the more commonly used types are `8` for echo request (ping) and `0` for echo reply (ping response). The `Type` field defines the format of the remaining data in the message.

The `Code` field is a further refinement of the message type and permits variations on the defined message type.

The `Checksum` field is the 16-bit 1s complement of the 1s complement sum of the ICMP message.

The remaining data within the ICMP message is dependent upon the initial type field.

USER DATAGRAM PROTOCOL (UDP)

The User Datagram Protocol is described in RFC 768. UDP provides a datagram mode of communication (connectionless packet-based communication) between hosts on the Internet (see Figure D.3).

Byte 0	Byte 1	Byte 2	Byte 3
0 1 2 3 4 5 6 7	0 1 2 3 4 5 6 7	0 1 2 3 4 5 6 7	0 1 2 3 4 5 6 7
Source Port		Destination Port	
Length		Checksum	

FIGURE D.3 User Datagram Protocol header.

The `Source Port` field identifies the port of the socket from which the datagram was sent. This can be used by the receiver to return a response back to the sender's port.

The `Destination Port` identifies the port to which the datagram is sent. The receiver created a socket and bound it with a name and port in order to have the capability to receive the datagram.

The `Length` field is the length of the datagram in octets, including the UDP header and datagram payload.

The `Checksum` is the 16-bit 1s complement of the 1s complement sum of the UDP header and data payload.

TRANSMISSION CONTROL PROTOCOL (TCP)

The Transmission Control Protocol is described in RFC 761. TCP provides a reliable host-to-host protocol for communication on the Internet (connection-oriented). See Figure D.4.

The `Source Port` field identifies the port of the socket from which the datagram was sent. As TCP is a connection-oriented protocol, the socket construct automatically handles where data is sent. A socket is the combination of the IP address and port number on the host.

The `Destination Port` identifies the port to which the datagram is sent.

The `Sequence Number` identifies the sequence of the byte contained within the data. Each byte transmitted has a representative sequence number, but only the first contained in the packet is identified in the `Sequence Number` field. When the TCP connection is first being started, the sequence number contains the Initial Sequence Number (ISN) that is defined as the first byte to be sent (the offset).

The `Acknowledgment Number` is sent from a receiver to a sender indicating which byte it is expecting next (as defined by the sent sequence number).

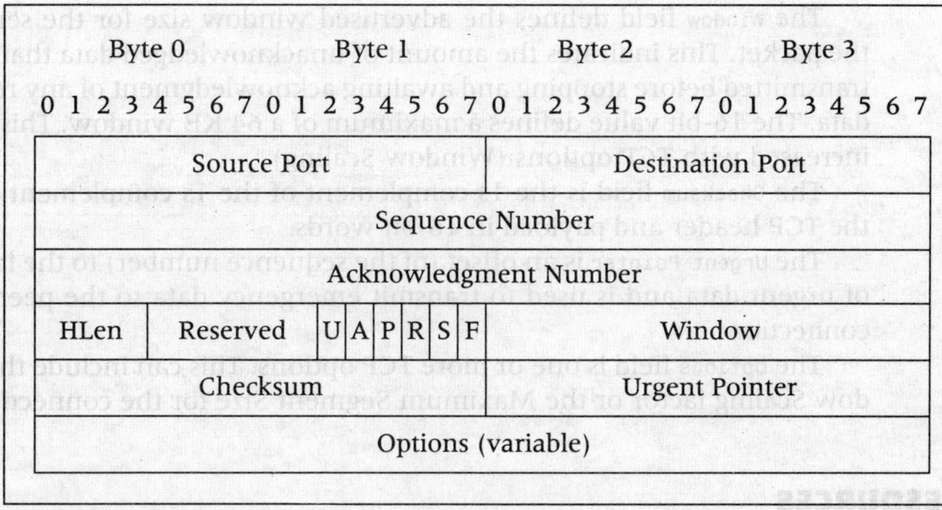

FIGURE D.4 Transmission Control Protocol header.

When a packet is received, the `acknowledgment number` is set to 1 plus the `sequence number`. If packets are lost, the `acknowledgment number` indicates to the sender that it should resend a particular sequence of bytes.

The `Header Length (Hlen)` is the length of the TCP header in 32-bit words. Multiplying the header length by four yields the octet offset of the TCP datagram payload.

The `Flags` field is a collection of flags that are used to relay specific information between peers on the particular connection. The flags are defined in Table D.1.

TABLE D.1 TCP flag fields.

Flag	*Description*
`(U)RG`	`Urgent`—The `Urgent` pointer is valid.
`(A)CK`	`AAcknowledge`—The `Acknowledgment` number is valid.
`(P)SH`	`Push`—The receiver should pass the payload data contained in this packet to the application as soon as possible.
`(R)ST`	`Reset`—Reset the connection.
`(S)YN`	`Synchronize`—Sequence Number contains the Initial Sequence Number (ISN) to be used for the first byte to send.
`(F)IN`	`Finish`—The sender desires to close the connection.

The `Window` field defines the advertised window size for the sender of the packet. This indicates the amount of unacknowledged data that can be transmitted before stopping and awaiting acknowledgment of any received data. The 16-bit value defines a maximum of a 64 KB window. This can be increased with TCP options (Window Scaling).

The `Checksum` field is the 1s complement of the 1s complement sum of the TCP header and payload in 16-bit words.

The `Urgent Pointer` is an offset (of the sequence number) to the last byte of urgent data and is used to transmit emergency data to the peer of the connection.

The `Options` field is one or more TCP options. This can include the Window Scaling factor or the Maximum Segment Size for the connection.

RESOURCES

Postel, Jon, "Internet Protocol Specification," RFC 791, September 1981. http://www.landfield.org/rfcs/rfc791.html

Postel, Jon, "Internet Control Message Protocol," RFC 792, September 1981. http://www.landfield.org/rfcs/rfc792.html

Postel, Jon, "User Datagram Protocol," RFC 768, August 1980. http://www.landfield.org/rfcs/rfc768.html

Postel, Jon, Editor, "Transmission Control Protocol," RFC 761, January 1980. http://www.landfield.org/rfcs/rfc761.html

APPENDIX E About the CD-ROM

This CD-ROM contains all software referenced in this book as well as the RFCs that are referenced in each of the chapters.

The CD-ROM contains two directories, `RFCS` and `software`.

The software subdirectory contains all of the software developed within this book. Each application is contained within the chapter under which it was discussed.

./software/ch1/daytime
Sample daytime client from Chapter 1

./software/ch4/emsmtpc
Embedded SMTP Client

./software/ch5/emsmtpd
Embedded SMTP Server

./software/ch6/empop3c
Embedded POP3 Client

./software/ch7/shttps
Simple HTTP Server

./software/ch7/emhttp
Embedded HTTP Server

./software/ch8/emsnmp
Embedded SNMP Server

./software/ch9/emcli
Embedded Command Line Interface

./software/ch10/emslp
Embedded Service Location Protocol Server and Client API

./software/ch11/emnntp
Embedded NNTP Client

./software/apdxA/bcast
Sample Broadcast Client and Server Reference Implementations

./software/apdxA/mcast
Sample Multicast Client and Server Reference Implementations

./software/apdxA/stream
Sample Stream Client and Server Reference Implementations

./software/apdxA/u_dgram
Sample Unconnected Datagram Client and Server Reference Implementations

./software/apdxA/c_dgram
Sample Connected Datagram Client and Server Reference Implementations

All software on this CD-ROM, with the exception of the SMTP server, is covered under a BSD-style License, as shown here:

The Embedded SMTP Server is covered under the GNU Public License, as shown here:

You must make sure that they, too, receive or can get the source code. And you must show them these terms so they know their rights.

We protect your rights with two steps: (1) copyright the software, and (2) offer you this license which gives you legal permission to copy, distribute and/or modify the software.

Also, for each author's protection and ours, we want to make certain that everyone understands that there is no warranty for this free software. If the software is modified by someone else and passed on, we want its recipients to know that what they have is not the original, so that any problems introduced by others will not reflect on the original authors' reputations.

Finally, any free program is threatened constantly by software patents. We wish to avoid the danger that redistributors of a free program will individually obtain patent licenses, in effect making the program proprietary. To prevent this, we have made it clear that any patent must be licensed for everyone's free use or not licensed at all.

The precise terms and conditions for copying, distribution and modification follow.

GNU GENERAL PUBLIC LICENSE

TERMS AND CONDITIONS FOR COPYING, DISTRIBUTION AND MODIFICATION

0. This License applies to any program or other work which contains a notice placed by the copyright holder saying it may be distributed under the terms of this General Public License. The "Program", below, refers to any such program or work, and a "work based on the Program" means either the Program or any derivative work under copyright law: that is to say, a work containing the Program or a portion of it, either verbatim or with modifications and/or translated into another language. (Hereinafter, translation is included without limitation in the term "modification".) Each licensee is addressed as "you".

Activities other than copying, distribution and modification are not covered by this License; they are outside its scope. The act of running the Program is not restricted, and the output from the Program is covered only if its contents constitute a work based on the Program (independent of having been made by running the Program).

Whether that is true depends on what the Program does.

1. You may copy and distribute verbatim copies of the Program's source code as you receive it, in any medium, provided that you conspicuously and

appropriately publish on each copy an appropriate copyright notice and disclaimer of warranty; keep intact all the notices that refer to this License and to the absence of any warranty; and give any other recipients of the Program a copy of this License along with the Program.

You may charge a fee for the physical act of transferring a copy, and you may at your option offer warranty protection in exchange for a fee.

2. You may modify your copy or copies of the Program or any portion of it, thus forming a work based on the Program, and copy and distribute such modifications or work under the terms of Section 1 above, provided that you also meet all of these conditions:

a) You must cause the modified files to carry prominent notices stating that you changed the files and the date of any change.

b) You must cause any work that you distribute or publish, that in whole or in part contains or is derived from the Program or any part thereof, to be licensed as a whole at no charge to all third parties under the terms of this License.

c) If the modified program normally reads commands interactively when run, you must cause it, when started running for such interactive use in the most ordinary way, to print or display an announcement including an appropriate copyright notice and a notice that there is no warranty (or else, saying that you provide a warranty) and that users may redistribute the program under these conditions, and telling the user how to view a copy of this License. (Exception: if the Program itself is interactive but does not normally print such an announcement, your work based on the Program is not required to print an announcement.)

These requirements apply to the modified work as a whole. If identifiable sections of that work are not derived from the Program, and can be reasonably considered independent and separate works in themselves, then this License, and its terms, do not apply to those sections when you distribute them as separate works. But when you distribute the same sections as part of a whole which is a work based on the Program, the distribution of the whole must be on the terms of this License, whose permissions for other licensees extend to the entire whole, and thus to each and every part regardless of who wrote it.

Thus, it is not the intent of this section to claim rights or contest your rights to work written entirely by you; rather, the intent is to exercise the right to control the distribution of derivative or collective works based on the Program.

In addition, mere aggregation of another work not based on the Program with the Program (or with a work based on the Program) on a volume of a storage or distribution medium does not bring the other work under the scope of this License.

3. You may copy and distribute the Program (or a work based on it, under Section 2) in object code or executable form under the terms of Sections 1 and 2 above provided that you also do one of the following:

   a) Accompany it with the complete corresponding machine-readable source code, which must be distributed under the terms of Sections 1 and 2 above on a medium customarily used for software interchange; or,

   b) Accompany it with a written offer, valid for at least three years, to give any third party, for a charge no more than your cost of physically performing source distribution, a complete machine-readable copy of the corresponding source code, to be distributed under the terms of Sections 1 and 2 above on a medium customarily used for software interchange; or,

   c) Accompany it with the information you received as to the offer to distribute corresponding source code. (This alternative is allowed only for noncommercial distribution and only if you received the program in object code or executable form with such an offer, in accord with Subsection b above.)

   The source code for a work means the preferred form of the work for making modifications to it. For an executable work, complete source code means all the source code for all modules it contains, plus any associated interface definition files, plus the scripts used to control compilation and installation of the executable. However, as a special exception, the source code distributed need not include anything that is normally distributed (in either source or binary form) with the major components (compiler, kernel, and so on) of the operating system on which the executable runs, unless that component itself accompanies the executable.

   If distribution of executable or object code is made by offering access to copy from a designated place, then offering equivalent access to copy the source code from the same place counts as distribution of the source code, even though third parties are not compelled to copy the source along with the object code.

4. You may not copy, modify, sublicense, or distribute the Program except as expressly provided under this License. Any attempt otherwise to copy, modify, sublicense or distribute the Program is void, and will automatically terminate your rights under this License.

However, parties who have received copies, or rights, from you under this License will not have their licenses terminated so long as such parties remain in full compliance.

5. You are not required to accept this License, since you have not signed it. However, nothing else grants you permission to modify or distribute the Program or its derivative works. These actions are prohibited by law if you do not accept this License. Therefore, by modifying or distributing the Program (or any work based on the Program), you indicate your acceptance of this License to do so, and all its terms and conditions for copying, distributing or modifying the Program or works based on it.

6. Each time you redistribute the Program (or any work based on the Program), the recipient automatically receives a license from the original licensor to copy, distribute or modify the Program subject to these terms and conditions. You may not impose any further restrictions on the recipients' exercise of the rights granted herein.

   You are not responsible for enforcing compliance by third parties to this License.

7. If, as a consequence of a court judgment or allegation of patent infringement or for any other reason (not limited to patent issues), conditions are imposed on you (whether by court order, agreement or otherwise) that contradict the conditions of this License, they do not excuse you from the conditions of this License. If you cannot distribute so as to satisfy simultaneously your obligations under this License and any other pertinent obligations, then as a consequence you may not distribute the Program at all. For example, if a patent license would not permit royalty-free redistribution of the Program by all those who receive copies directly or indirectly through you, then the only way you could satisfy both it and this License would be to refrain entirely from distribution of the Program.

   If any portion of this section is held invalid or unenforceable under any particular circumstance, the balance of the section is intended to apply and the section as a whole is intended to apply in other circumstances.

   It is not the purpose of this section to induce you to infringe any patents or other property right claims or to contest validity of any such claims; this section has the sole purpose of protecting the integrity of the free software distribution system, which is implemented by public license practices. Many people have made generous contributions to the wide range of software distributed through that system in reliance on consistent application of that system; it is up to the author/donor to decide if he or she is willing to distribute software through any other system and a licensee cannot impose that choice.

This section is intended to make thoroughly clear what is believed to be a consequence of the rest of this License.

8. If the distribution and/or use of the Program is restricted in certain countries either by patents or by copyrighted interfaces, the original copyright holder who places the Program under this License may add an explicit geographical distribution limitation excluding those countries, so that distribution is permitted only in or among countries not thus excluded. In such case, this License incorporates the limitation as if written in the body of this License.
9. The Free Software Foundation may publish revised and/or new versions of the General Public License from time to time. Such new versions will be similar in spirit to the present version, but may differ in detail to address new problems or concerns.

   Each version is given a distinguishing version number. If the Program specifies a version number of this License which applies to it and "any later version", you have the option of following the terms and conditions either of that version or of any later version published by the Free Software Foundation. If the Program does not specify a version number of this License, you may choose any version ever published by the Free Software Foundation.
10. If you wish to incorporate parts of the Program into other free programs whose distribution conditions are different, write to the author to ask for permission. For software which is copyrighted by the Free Software Foundation, write to the Free Software Foundation; we sometimes make exceptions for this. Our decision will be guided by the two goals of preserving the free status of all derivatives of our free software and of promoting the sharing and reuse of software generally.

NO WARRANTY

11. BECAUSE THE PROGRAM IS LICENSED FREE OF CHARGE, THERE IS NO WARRANTY FOR THE PROGRAM, TO THE EXTENT PERMITTED BY APPLICABLE LAW. EXCEPT WHEN OTHERWISE STATED IN WRITING THE COPYRIGHT HOLDERS AND/OR OTHER PARTIES PRO-

VIDE THE PROGRAM "AS IS" WITHOUT WARRANTY OF ANY KIND, EITHER EXPRESSED OR IMPLIED, INCLUDING, BUT NOT LIMITED TO, THE IMPLIED WARRANTIES OF

MERCHANTABILITY AND FITNESS FOR A PARTICULAR PURPOSE. THE ENTIRE RISK AS TO THE QUALITY AND PERFORMANCE OF THE PROGRAM IS WITH YOU. SHOULD THE PROGRAM PROVE DEFECTIVE, YOU ASSUME THE COST OF ALL NECESSARY SERVICING, REPAIR OR CORRECTION.

12. IN NO EVENT UNLESS REQUIRED BY APPLICABLE LAW OR AGREED TO IN WRITING WILL ANY COPYRIGHT HOLDER, OR ANY OTHER PARTY WHO MAY MODIFY AND/OR REDISTRIBUTE THE PROGRAM AS PERMITTED ABOVE, BE LIABLE TO YOU FOR DAMAGES, INCLUDING ANY GENERAL, SPECIAL, INCIDENTAL OR CONSEQUENTIAL DAMAGES ARISING OUT OF THE USE OR INABILITY TO USE THE PROGRAM (INCLUDING BUT NOT LIMITED TO LOSS OF DATA OR DATA BEING RENDERED INACCURATE OR LOSSES SUSTAINED BY

YOU OR THIRD PARTIES OR A FAILURE OF THE PROGRAM TO OPERATE WITH ANY OTHER PROGRAMS), EVEN IF SUCH HOLDER OR OTHER PARTY HAS BEEN ADVISED OF THE POSSIBILITY OF SUCH DAMAGES.

The RFCS directory contains the relevant RFCs used in this book. The RFCs included are listed here:

./RFCS/rfc-copyrights
Describes the copyrights under which RFCs are released.

./RFCS/rfc761.txt
DOD Standard Transmission Control Protocol
Information Sciences Institute, January 1980.

./RFCS/rfc768.txt
User Datagram Protocol
Jon Postel, ISI, August 1980.

./RFCS/rfc791.txt
Internet Protocol
ISI, September 1981.

./RFCS/rfc792.txt
Internet Control Message Protocol
Jon Postel, ISI, September 1981.

./RFCS/rfc821.txt
Simple Mail Transfer Protocol
Jon Postel, August 1982.

./RFCS/rfc822.txt
Standard for the Format of ARPA Internet Text Messages
David Crocker, University of Delaware, August 1982.

./RFCS/rfc896.txt
Congestion Control in IP/TCP Internetworks
John Nagle, Ford Aerospace and Communications Corp., January 1984.

./RFCS/rfc918.txt
Post Office Protocol
J. K. Reynolds, ISI, October 1984.

./RFCS/rfc977.txt
Network News Transfer Protocol
Kantor & Lapsley, February 1986.

./RFCS/rfc1036.txt
Standard for Interchange of USENET Messages
Horton & Adams, December 1987.

./RFCS/rfc1065.txt
Structure and Identification of Management Information for TCP/IP-based internets
Rose & McCloghrie, TWG, August 1988.

./RFCS/rfc1081.txt
Post Office Protocol – Version 3
Rose, TWG, November 1988.

./RFCS/rfc1123.txt
Requirements for Internet Hosts – Application and Support
IETF, R. Braden, Editor, October 1989.

./RFCS/rfc1144.txt
Compressing TCP/IP Headers for Low-Speed Serial Links
V. Jacobson, LBL, February 1990.

./RFCS/rfc1153.txt
Digest Message Format
Wancho, WSMR, April 1990.

./RFCS/rfc1157.txt
A Simple Network Management Protocol (SNMP)
Case, et al, May 1990.

./RFCS/rfc1191.txt
Path MTU Discovery
Mogul, et al, November 1990.

./RFCS/rfc1340.txt
Assigned Numbers
Reynolds & Postel, ISI, July 1992.

./RFCS/rfc1521.txt
MIME (Multipurpose Internet Mail Extensions) Part One: Mechanisms for Specifying and Describing the Format of Internet Message Bodies
Borenstein & Freed, Innosoft, September 1993..

./RFCS/rfc1522.txt
MIME (Multipurpose Internet Mail Extensions) Part Two: Message Header Extensions for Non-ASCII Text.
Moore, University of Tennessee, September 1993.

./RFCS/rfc1730.txt
Internet Message Access Protocol – Version 4
Crispin, University of Washington, December 1994.

./RFCS/rfc1766.txt
Tags for the Identification of Languages
Alvestrand, UNINETT, March 1995.

./RFCS/rfc1889.txt
RTP: A Transport Protocol for Real-Time Applications
Audio-Video Transport Working Group, January 1996.

./RFCS/rfc1931.txt
Dynamic RARP Extensions for Automatic Network Address Acquisition
Brownell, Sun Microsystems, Inc., April 1996.

./RFCS/rfc2001.txt
TCP Slow Start, Congestion Avoidance, Fast Retransmit, and Fast Recovery Algorithms
Stevens, NOAO, January 1997.

./RFCS/rfc2046.txt
Multipurpose Internet Mail Extensions (MIME) Part Two: Media Types
Freed & Borenstein, November 1996.

./RFCS/rfc2068.txt
Hypertext Transfer Protocol – HTTP/1.1
Fielding, et al, January 1997.

./RFCS/rfc2104.txt
HMAC: Keyed-Hashing for Message Authentication
Krawczyk, Bellare and Canetti. February 1997.

./RFCS/rfc2309.txt
Recommendations on Queue Management and Congestion Avoidance in the Internet
Braden, et al, April 1998.

./RFCS/rfc2401.txt
Security Architecture for the Internet Protocol
Kent and Atkinson, November 1998.

./RFCS/rfc2402.txt
IP Authentication Header
Kent and Atkinson, November 1998.

./RFCS/rfc2403.txt
The Use of HMAC-MD5-96 within ESP and AH
Madson and Glenn, November 1998.

./RFCS/rfc2404.txt
The Use of HMAC-SHA-1-96 within ESP and AH
Madson and Glenn, November 1998.

./RFCS/rfc2406.txt
IP Encapsulating Security Payload (ESP)
Kent and Atkinson, November 1998.

./RFCS/rfc2409.txt
The Internet Key Exchange (IKE)
Harkins and Carrel, November 1998.

./RFCS/rfc2474.txt
Definition of the Differentiated Services Field (DS Field) in the IPv4 and IPv6 Headers
Nichols, et al, December 1998.

./RFCS/rfc2475.txt
An Architecture for Differentiated Services
Blake, et al, December 1998.

./RFCS/rfc2608.txt
Service Location Protocol, Version 2
Guttman, et al, June 1999.

./RFCS/rfc2614.txt
An API for Service Location
Kempf & Guttman, Sun Microsystems, June 1999.

./RFCS/rfc2910.txt
Internet Printing Protocol/1.1: Encoding and Transport
Herriot, et al, September 2000.

./RFCS/rfc2960.txt
Stream Control Transmission Protocol
Stewart, et al, October 2000.

RFCs contained on this CD-ROM are covered under the following copyright.

Index

D

S

U

ISBN	TITLE	AUTHOR	PRICE	PAGES
	CALL CENTERS			
8170082196	**Call Centers Made Easy**	Stephen Medcroft	Rs. 195.00	310
	CISCO			
8170087481	**Enabling IP Routing with Cisco Routers**	R. Das, K. Chakrabarty	Rs. 295.00	486
817008749X	**Designing Networks with Cisco**	H. Pasricha, D. Jagu	Rs. 195.00	316
8170087503	**Cisco IP Routing Protocols: Troubleshooting Techniques**	V. Anand, K. Chakrabarty	Rs. 295.00	409
	DATABASES			
8170089530	**DBMS—Complete Practical Approach**	Sharad Maheshwari, Ruchin Jain	Rs. 350.00	656
8170082404	**Learn to Program Visual Basic-Examples**	John Smiley	Rs. 295.00	482
8170082412	**Learn to Program Visual Basic-Databases**	John Smiley	Rs. 325.00	653
8170082420	**Learn to Program Visual Basic-Objects**	John Smiley	Rs. 325.00	670
817008475X	**IT Resources-Access 2002 VBA Programming Access**	Michele Amelot	Rs. 195.00	424
8170084512	**The Power of Oracle 9i**	Rajiv Parida, Vinod Sharma	Rs. 475.00	1035
8170088518	**Principles and Implementation of Data Warehousing**	Rajiv A. Parida	Rs. 295.00	487
817008864X	**DBA Study Guide OCP Prep Guide**	Nazar Abdul	Rs. 295.00	474
8170088658	**Oracle 11i—The Complete Reference**	Rashmi Anandi	Rs. 495.00	975
8131800067	**Toxonomy of Database Management System**	Aditya Kumar Gupta	Rs. 75.00	146
8131800385	**Introduction to SQL and PL/SQL**	Sharad Maheshwari, Ruchin Jain	Rs. 200.00	389
	DOEACC 'O' LEVEL			
8170088089	**DOEACC 'O' Level Model Test Papers**	Ramesh Bangia	Rs. 175.00	296
8170089115	**DOEACC 'O' & 'A' Level Programming & Problem Solving Through 'C' Language (Model Test Paper with Solutions)**	Mukesh Sharma	Rs. 95.00	213
8170089069	**DOEACC 'O' & 'A' Level Business Systems (Model Test Paper with Solutions)**	Mukesh Sharma	Rs. 100.00	252
8170085640	**Programming and Problem Solving Through "C" Language**	Harsha Priya, R. Ranjeet	Rs. 95.00	306

Please write for a free color Firewall Media Catalog for details on the above books.

ISBN	TITLE	AUTHOR	PRICE	PAGES
8170084474	**IT Tools and Applications**	Ramesh Bangia	Rs. 145.00	370
8170085594	**Business Systems**	Ramesh Bangia	Rs. 175.00	452
8170089514	**Internet & Web Design**	Ramesh Bangia	Rs. 150.00	300

ELECTRONIC COMMERCE

ISBN	TITLE	AUTHOR	PRICE	PAGES
8170085497	**Electronic Commerce**	Pete Loshin, John Vacca	Rs. 295.00	472
817008119X	**E-Commerce**	Mamta Bhusry	Rs. 95.00	215
8170083524	**Marketing in the Cyber Age**	Kurt Rohner	Rs. 295.00	223

HARDWARE/EMBEDDED SYSTEMS

ISBN	TITLE	AUTHOR	PRICE	PAGES
8170087473	**Essential Electronics for PC Technicians**	John W. Farber	Rs. 295.00	546
8170086264	**Grid Computing: A Practical Guide to Technology and Applications**	Ahmar Abbas	Rs. 295.00	408
8170088186	**CD Cracking Uncovered Protection Against Unsanctioned CD Copy**	Kris Kaspersky	Rs. 295.00	422
8170083435	**Practical Linux Programming: Device Drivers, Embedded Systems and the Internet**	Ashfaq A. Khan	Rs. 295.00	420
8170083575	**TCP/IP Application Layer Protocols for Embedded Systems**	M. Tim Jones	Rs. 295.00	460
8131800520	**PC Repair and Maintenance : A Practical Guide**	Joel Rosenthal, Kevin Irwin	Rs. 195.00	362
8131800768	**The A+ Certification and PC Repair Handbook**	Christopher A Crayton, Joel Z. Rosenthal	Rs. 495.00	888

INTERNET & WEB TECHNOLOGY

ISBN	TITLE	AUTHOR	PRICE	PAGES
8170083206	**The Internet Handbook for Writers, Students and Teachers**	Mary McGuire, Linda Stilborne	Rs. 195.00	276
8170084776	**Way in-Internet Getting Started**	Elizabeth Bramire	Rs. 95.00	165
8170088976	**Web Technology**	Ramesh Bangia	Rs. 250.00	560
8170087163	**Web Design with Macromedia Studio MX 2004**	Eric Hunley	Rs. 295.00	558
8170083400	**Professional Web Design (Techniques and Templates)**	Clint Eccher	Rs. 295.00	425
8170088046	**HTML, XHTML, CSS and XML**	Teodoru Gugoiu	Rs. 195.00	355
8170083583	**FrontPage 2000 for Visual Learners**	Chris Charuhas	Rs. 95.00	200
8170083591	**HTML & Java Script for Visual Learners**	Chris Charuhas	Rs. 95.00	200

ISBN	TITLE	AUTHOR	PRICE	PAGES
8170083605	**The Visual Learners Guide to Managing Web Projects**	Chris Charuhas	Rs. 95.00	130
8170083613	**Dreamweaver 4 for Visual Learners**	Chris Charuhas	Rs. 95.00	200
8170084768	**IT Resource-Implementing XML: Managing and Formatting Data**	Johhny Brochard	Rs. 125.00	279
8170089476	**Design Your Web World**	Sunil Jalota	Rs. 75.00	146

KEEPING AHEAD SERIES

ISBN	TITLE	AUTHOR	PRICE	PAGES
8170084652	**Keeping Ahead-Exchange 2000 Server**	Philippe Levesque	Rs. 145.00	285
8170084660	**Keeping Ahead-Windows 2000 Professional**	Jose Dardoigne	Rs. 175.00	388
8170084679	**Keeping Ahead-Windows 2000 Server**	Philippe Mathon	Rs. 175.00	360
8170084687	**Keeping Ahead-Linux Administration Kernel Version 2.0 to 2.2**	Bruno Guèrin	Rs. 125.00	240
8170084695	**Keeping Ahead-Using Linux Kernel Version 2.0 to 2.2**	Bruno Guèrin	Rs. 125.00	258
8170084709	**Keeping Ahead-Java 2**	Benjamin Aumaille	Rs. 145.00	284
8170084717	**Keeping Ahead-SQL Server 7**	Joelle Mosset	Rs. 145.00	329
8170084725	**Keeping Ahead-JavaScript and VBScript**	Benjamin Aumaille	Rs. 145.00	313
8170084733	**Keeping Ahead-C++ Programming Language**	Bruno Dubois	Rs. 125.00	234
8170084741	**Keeping Ahead-TCP/IP in the NT Environment**	Bruno Ferec	Rs. 125.00	230

MCSE

ISBN	TITLE	AUTHOR	PRICE	PAGES
817008489X	**MCSE-Administering SQL Server 7.0**	Jerome Gabillaud	Rs. 295.00	580
8170084903	**MCSE-Networking Essentials**	Jose Dordoigne	Rs. 245.00	453
8170084911	**MCSE-Windows 2000 Professional**	Jose Dordoigne	Rs. 325.00	665
817008492X	**MCSE-Windows 2000 Server**	Philippe Mathon	Rs. 345.00	712

MULTIMEDIA AND ANIMATION

ISBN	TITLE	AUTHOR	PRICE	PAGES
8170088208	**3DS Max 6 Animation with Character Studio 4 and Plug-Ins**	Boris Kulagin, Dmitry Morozov	Rs. 175.00	216

ISBN	TITLE	AUTHOR	PRICE	PAGES
8170088216	**Adobe Audition: Soundtracks for Digital Video**	Roman Petelin, Yury Petelin	Rs. 195.00	278
8170086205	**Building A Digital Human**	Ken Brilliant	Rs. 295.00	380
8170086213	**Making Digital Videos**	Ben Long	Rs. 295.00	284
8170087171	**Illustrating with Macromedia Flash ™ MX2004**	Robert Firbaugh	Rs. 245.00	366
8170082439	**Multimedia Basics-Technology (Vol. I)**	Andreas Holzinger	Rs. 195.00	312
8170082447	**Multimedia Basics-Learning (Vol. II)**	Andreas Holzinger	Rs. 195.00	326
8170082455	**Multimedia Basics-Design (Vol. III)**	Andreas Holzinger	Rs. 195.00	280
8170083532	**Maya Feature Creature Creations**	Todd Palamar	Rs. 295.00	376
8170083540	**Sound Forge Power**	Scott R. Garrigus	Rs. 195.00	344
8131800288	**Multimedia and Web Technology**	Ramesh Bangia	Rs. 395.00	878
813180044X	**Photoshop CS**	Shruti Lal	Rs. 195.00	434

NETWORKING

ISBN	TITLE	AUTHOR	PRICE	PAGES
817008721X	**Networking Essentials**	Jose Dordoigne	Rs. 195.00	453
8170089328	**TCP/IP Distributed System**	Vivek Acharya	Rs. 250.00	474
8170087023	**Computer Networks**	Ajit Kumar Singh	Rs. 95.00	181
8131800148	**The Real—world Network Troubleshooting Manual**	Alan Sugano	Rs. 295.00	396
817008203X	**Telecom & Networking Glossary**	Robert Mastin	Rs. 300.00	250
8170082048	**Data Networking Made Easy**	Karen Patten	Rs. 360.00	350
8170082056	**Digital Convergence**	Andy Covell	Rs. 300.00	234

OFFICE AUTOMATION

ISBN	TITLE	AUTHOR	PRICE	PAGES
8170089891	**Desk Top Publishing**	Dinesh Maidasani	Rs. 150.00	311
8170087805	**Learning Computer Fundamentals, MS Office and Internet & Web Technology**	Dinesh Maidasani	Rs. 95.00	301
8170087686	**MS-Word 2000 Thumb-Rules and Details**	Snigdha Banerjee	Rs. 175.00	390
8170089239	**Computer Accounting with Tally 7.2**	Firewall Media	Rs. 195.00	330

ON YOUR SIDE SERIES

ISBN	TITLE	AUTHOR	PRICE	PAGES
8170084830	**On your Side-Powerpoint 2002**	Andrew Blackburn	Rs. 145.00	282
8170084849	**On your Side-Excel 2002**	Adrienne Tommy	Rs. 125.00	275

Please write for a free color Firewall Media Catalog for details on the above books.

ISBN	TITLE	AUTHOR	PRICE	PAGES
8170084857	**On your Side-Word 2002**	Adrienne Tommy	Rs. 125.00	289
8170084865	**On your Side-Access 2002**	Adrienne Tommy	Rs. 125.00	303
8170084873	**On your Side-Frontpage 2002**	Andrew Blackburn	Rs. 95.00	245
8170084881	**On your Side-Windows XP**	Adrienne Tommy	Rs. 125.00	310

OPERATING SYSTEMS

ISBN	TITLE	AUTHOR	PRICE	PAGES
8170087236	**Linux—A Practical Approach**	B. Mohamed Ibrahim	Rs. 95.00	187
8170088623	**Red Hat Linux Study Guide**	Vijay Shekhar	Rs. 350.00	635
8170088631	**Red Hat Linux-The Complete Bible**	Vijay Shekhar	Rs. 545.00	1176
8170089581	**Unix and Shell Programming**	Archana Verma	Rs. 80.00	137
8170089131	**Operating System Concepts**	P.S. Gill	Rs. 95.00	181
8170083427	**The MS-Windows XP Professional Handbook**	Louis Columbus	Rs. 295.00	330
8170084784	**Way in-Windows XP Home Edition**	Andrew Blackburn	Rs. 95.00	183
8170086221	**Cyber Rookies—Operating System Fundamentals**	D. Irtegov	Rs. 295.00	498

PROGRAMMING

ISBN	TITLE	AUTHOR	PRICE	PAGES
8170087791	**The Art of Programming Through Flowcharts & Algorithms**	Anil Bikas Chaudhuri	Rs. 95.00	160
8170086248	**Preventative Programming Techniques: Avoid and Correct Common Mistakes**	Brian Hawkins	Rs. 295.00	322
8170083443	**Learning Computer Programming : It's not about Languages**	Mary Farrell	Rs. 295.00	375
8170086256	**Object-Oriented Programming: From Problem Solving to Java**	José M. Garrido	Rs. 295.00	360
817008931X	**Object-Oriented Programming-Concept and Implementation**	A. Rajesh	Rs. 95.00	182
8170089107	**Java: J2SE-5 A Practical Approach**	B. Mohammad Ibrahim	Rs. 175.00	332
8170089409	**Advance Java**	Gajendra Gupta	Rs. 175.00	305
8170088038	**Assembly Language Programming for Intel Processors Family**	Vasile Lungu	Rs. 295.00	577
8170088178	**The Assembly Programming Master Book**	Vlad Pirogov	Rs. 395.00	726
813180075X	**Java Messaging**	Eric Bruno	Rs. 295.00	480

Please write for a free color Firewall Media Catalog for details on the above books.

ISBN	TITLE	AUTHOR	PRICE	PAGES
	PROGRAMMING - C#, C, C++			
8170083702	**The Power of C#**	Rajiv Parida	Rs. 295.00	576
8170085632	**Mastering Graphics Programming in 'C'**	Sudhir Dawra	Rs. 145.00	286
8170088879	**Programming in C and Numerical Analysis**	J.B. Dixit	Rs. 350.00	355
8170087074	**Mastering C Programs**	J.B. Dixit	Rs. 195.00	434
8170081262	**Programming in C**	J.B. Dixit	Rs. 295.00	506
8170087619	**Unix and C Programming**	Ashok Arora, Shefali Bansal	Rs. 295.00	606
817008878X	**C Interview Questions and Answers**	J. Rajaram	Rs. 75.00	139
8170089034	**Pragmatic C**	R.K. Jangda	Rs. 150.00	258
8170086140	**Data Structure for 'C' Programming**	Ajay Kumar	Rs. 145.00	290
8170081270	**Programming in C++**	J.B. Dixit	Rs. 260.00	602
8170088194	**Hackish C++ Pranks & Tricks**	Michael Flenov	Rs. 245.00	326
8170082889	**Basics of C++ Programming**	Nishant Kundalia	Rs. 95.00	168
8170083648	**Mastering C++ Programs**	J.B. Dixit	Rs. 295.00	598
817008623X	**Cyber Rookies—C++ Programming Fundamentals**	Chuck Easttom	Rs. 295.00	417
8131800202	**Data Structure using C++**	N. Jayalakshmi	Rs. 65.00	126
8170089123	**C++ Made Easy**	T.D. Malhotra	Rs. 250.00	449
8131800393	**C++ & Introduction to C#**	T.D. Malhotra, Rajeev A. Parida, A. Rajesh	Rs. 200.00	440
8131800350	**OOPS with C++**	M. Jaya Prasad	Rs. 150.00	317
	SECURITY			
8170083419	**Computer Forensics : Computer Crime Scene Investigation**	John Vacca	Rs. 445.00	731
8131800156	**Computer Evidence (Collection and Preservation)**	Christopher L.T. Brown	Rs. 295.00	394
8170083494	**Firewall Architecture for the Enterprise**	Norbert Pohlmann, Tim Crothers	Rs. 295.00	480
8170086272	**Net Spies**	Andrew Gauntlett	Rs. 195.00	210
3826607546	**Firewall Systems**	Norbert Pohlmann	Rs. 1630.00	544
8131800504	**Homeland Security Techniques and Technologies**	Jesus Mena	Rs. 295.00	346

ISBN	TITLE	AUTHOR	PRICE	PAGES

ENGINEERING AND TECHNOLOGY

ISBN	TITLE	AUTHOR	PRICE	PAGES
817008718X	**Human Aspects of Software Engineering**	James E. Tomayko, Orit Hazzan	Rs. 195.00	338
8131800032	**Management Information Systems**	Avdhesh Gupta, Anurag Malik	Rs. 195.00	400
8170087953	**Human Computer Interaction**	Rajendra Ranjan Kumar	Rs. 95.00	210
8170088097	**Structured System Analysis and Design**	Preeti Gupta	Rs. 125.00	192
817008802X	**Autocad 2005 for Engineers**	Ionel Simion	Rs. 175.00	271
8170088054	**Digital Signal Processing Fundamentals**	Ashfaq A. Khan	Rs. 295.00	391
8131800164	**Digital Communication System Using System VUE**	Dennis Silage	Rs. 295.00	365
8170089719	**Foundations of Computer Science**	Ashok Arora	Rs. 250.00	386
817008363X	**Practical Project Management**	Ivan Bayross	Rs. 195.00	342
8131800806	**Digital Signal Processing using MATLAB and Wavelets**	Michael Weeks	Rs. 350.00	452
8131800792	**Classical Electrodynamics**	Hans C. Dhanian	Rs. 395.00	620
8131800512	**The Software Vulnerability Guide**	Herbert H. Thompson, Scott G. Chase	Rs. 195.00	368
8131800776	**Robot Modelling and Kinematics**	Rachid Manseur	Rs. 295.00	380
8131800369	**System Software**	M. Joseph	Rs. 95.00	185

STRAIGHT TO THE POINT SERIES

ISBN	TITLE	AUTHOR	PRICE	PAGES
8170084601	**STTP : Word 2002**	Corinne Hervo	Rs. 45.00	154
817008461X	**STTP : Excel 2002**	Corinne Hervo	Rs. 45.00	153
8170084628	**STTP : Dreamweaver 4**	Corinne Hervo	Rs. 45.00	135
8170084636	**STTP : Flash 5**	Corinne Hervo	Rs. 45.00	183
8170084644	**STTP : Photoshop 6**	Corinne Hervo	Rs. 45.00	152
817008881X	**STTP : MS Office 2000**	Dinesh Maidasani	Rs. 125.00	290
8170086100	**STTP : MS Office 2003**	Dinesh Maidasani	Rs. 145.00	288
8170087651	**STTP : MS Word 2003**	Firewall Media	Rs. 60.00	150
8170088011	**STTP : Photoshop CS**	Firewall Media	Rs. 60.00	150
8170088143	**STTP : MS Excel 2003**	Firewall Media	Rs. 60.00	150
8170088151	**STTP : CorelDraw 12**	Firewall Media	Rs. 60.00	150
8131800105	**STTP : 3ds MAX 7**	Dinesh Maidasani	Rs. 95.00	182
8131800083	**STTP : Auto CAD 2006**	Dinesh Maidasani	Rs. 95.00	190
8131800245	**STTP : CorelDraw X3**	Dinesh Maidasani	Rs. 75.00	188

ISBN	TITLE	AUTHOR	PRICE	PAGES
8131800253	**STTP : Dreamweaver 8**	Dinesh Maidasani	Rs. 75.00	148
8131800237	**STTP : Photoshop CS2**	Dinesh Maidasani	Rs. 75.00	172
8170088380	**STTP : Tally 7.2**	Firewall Media	Rs. 175.00	322
8131800091	**STTP : Flash 8**	Dinesh Maidasani	Rs. 95.00	180
8131800407	**STTP : My SQL 5.0**	Dinesh Maidasani	Rs. 85.00	166
8131800458	**STTP : Microsoft Power Point 2003**	Dinesh Maidasani	Rs. 75.00	142

STUDIO FACTORY

ISBN	TITLE	AUTHOR	PRICE	PAGES
8170084792	**Studio Factory—Photoshop 6**	Christophe Aubry	Rs. 175.00	364
8170084806	**Studio Factory—Flash 5**	Sami Ben Yahiya	Rs. 145.00	314
8170084814	**Studio Factory—Dreamweaver Ultradev 4**	Phillippe Chatellier	Rs. 95.00	240
8170084822	**Studio Factory—Dreamweaver 4**	Christophe Aubry	Rs. 175.00	373
8170087643	**Studio Factory—Dreamweaver MX**	Christophe Aubry	Rs. 195.00	407
8170087627	**Studio Factory—Flash MX**	Arnaud Blanche	Rs. 145.00	337
817008766X	**Studio Factory—Photoshop 7**	Cyril Guerin	Rs. 195.00	420

LAXMI PUBLICATIONS (P) LTD

113, Golden House, Daryaganj, New Delhi-110002

Phone : **011 - 43 53 25 00**

Fax : **011 - 43 53 25 28**

EMAIL : info@laxmipublications.com

Website : www.laxmipublications.com

BRANCHES

- 129/1, IIIrd Main Road, IX Cross, Chamrajpet, **Bangalore** (*Phone* : 080-26 61 15 61)
- 26, Damodaran Street, T. Nagar, **Chennai** (*Phone* : 044-24 34 47 26)
- 43/1394D, St. Benedict's Road, Ernakulam North, **Cochin** (*Phone* : 0484-239 70 04)
- Pan Bazar, Rani Bari, **Guwahati** (*Phones* : 0361-254 36 69, 251 38 81)
- 4-2-453, Ist Floor, Ramkote, **Hyderabad** (*Phone* : 040-24 75 02 47)
- Adda Tanda Chowk, N.D. 365, **Jalandhar City** (*Phone* : 0181-222 12 72)
- 106/A, Ist Floor, S.N. Banerjee Road, **Kolkata** (*Phones* : 033-22 27 37 73, 22 27 52 47)
- 18, Madan Mohan Malviya Marg, **Lucknow** (*Phone* : 0522-220 95 78)
- 142-C, Victor House, Ground Floor, N.M. Joshi Marg, Lower Parel (W), **Mumbai** (*Phones* : 022-24 91 54 15, 24 92 78 69)
- Radha Govind Street, Tharpagna, **Ranchi** (*Phone* : 0651-230 77 64)